BARRON'S

CHILDREN'S
ENGLISH-CHINESE
CHINESE-ENGLISH
DICTIONARY

Editor-in-Chief
Zang Si-Ying

Editors
Zhou Yi Xing
Li Yun
Helen Forrest
Alison Macaulay

All inquiries should be addressed to:
Barron's Educational Series, Inc.
250 Wireless Boulevard
Hauppauge, NY 11788
www.barronseduc.com

ISBN-13: 978-0-7641-4106-5
ISBN-10: 0-7641-4106-6

Library of Congress Control Number 2008942587

Printed in China

9 8 7 6 5 4 3 2 1

CONTENTS

Appendices

International Phonetic Alphabet

Vowels

Phonetic Letter	Example	Phonetic Letter	Example
ɑː	calm /kɑːm/	ɒ	dog /dɒg/
æ	fat /fæt/	əʊ	coat /kəʊt/
aɪ	cry /kraɪ/	ɔː	fall /fɔː/
aɪə	fire /faɪə/	ɔɪ	boy /bɔɪ/
aʊ	out /aʊt/	ʊ	look /lʊk/
aʊə	hour /aʊə/	uː	blue /bluː/
e	pen /pen/	ʊə	poor /pʊə/
eɪ	say /seɪ/	ɜː	bird /bɜːd/
eə	care /keə/	ʌ	cup /kʌp/
ɪ	big /bɪg/	ə	about /əˈbaʊt/
iː	me /miː/	i	very /ˈveri/
ɪə	near /nɪə/		

Consonants

Phonetic Letter	Example	Phonetic Letter	Example
b	bed /bed/	s	snow /snəʊ/
d	red /red/	t	talk /tɔːk/
f	if /ɪf/	v	love /lʌv/
g	good /gʊd/	w	walk /wɔːk/
h	hat /hæt/	z	zoo /zuː/
j	you /juː/	ʃ	ship /ʃɪp/
k	king /kɪŋ/	ʒ	pleasure /ˈpleʒə/
l	long /lɒŋ/	ŋ	sing /sɪŋ/
m	mother /ˈmʌðə/	tʃ	teach /tiːtʃ/
n	nose /nəʊz/	θ	three /θriː/
p	paper /ˈpeɪpə/	ð	that /ðæt/
r	read /riːd/	dʒ	bridge /brɪdʒ/

The primary stress mark is designated by the /ˈ/ mark as in about /əˈbaʊt/.
The secondary stress is indicated by /ˌ/, as in afternoon /ˌɑːftəˈnuːn/.

PREFACE

Children's English-Chinese/Chinese-English Dictionary was conceived by the Chinese Department of Education for use in elementary education.

- This is a dual-purpose work, in that the Chinese-English section is to be used for looking up Chinese words, whereas the English-Chinese part is meant for consulting the corresponding English words and their expressions.

- The meanings of words are explained with precision and clarity. Most of the entries are only given their simplest, most appropriate definition. This lets the students understand the word's basic meaning, thus laying a foundation for learning more comprehensive definitions later on.

- Words are accompanied by examples of their usage, stressing their function in communication and often presented in common phrases and expressions. For example, **diàn huà (电话) telephone; dǎ diàn huà (打电话) make a phone call; jiē diàn huà (接电话) answer the phone; diàn huà hào mǎ (电话号码) phone number.**

- All examples stress common knowledge. The example, **The human body has two hundred and six bones (Ren ti you er bai ling liu kuai gu tou—人体有206块骨头。)** not only illustrates proper usage of the word *bone*, but also introduces information about the human skeleton, and **Birds of a feather flock together**, a common English proverb, is followed by the corresponding Chinese idiom **Wu yi lei ju, ren yi qun fen (物以类聚，人以群分)**. This highlights the cultural similarity of the Chinese and English languages.

- This dictionary is not only a two-way reference book, but it is also a bilingual window into Chinese and American lives, rich in details about the cultures of both countries. This is reflected in the functional word usage examples, as well as the myriad of endearing and humorous illustrations. Additionally, you will find many brief facts that broach different areas of study and aim to capture the interest of children.

- Often, this dictionary approaches vocabulary through simple compound words or pairs of words grouped with the main entry, which means that there is no need for readers to search and memorize new words separately. For example, if you consider the word *rain*, you will see the following compound words: *rainbow* (cǎi hóng—彩虹), *raincoat* (yǔ yī—雨衣), *raindrop* (yǔ dī—雨滴), *rain forest* (rè dài yǔ líng—热带雨林), and *rainwater* (yǔ shuǐ—雨水).

- In addition to the main text, five appendices appear at the end of the dictionary and provide useful information regarding Time, Dates, Numbers, whereas a sixth appendix adds hundreds of additional entries not covered in the main body of the book.

英汉词典

ENGLISH-CHINESE
DICTIONARY

A

A /eɪ/ （冠词）一个

–What a beautiful day! 多好的天气啊！

–Yes. Let's go to the park. 是啊，咱们去公园吧。

> **用法小贴士**
> a 用于读音以辅音音素开头的词前，如a banana，a car.

ABC /ˌeɪ biː ˈsiː/ （名词）字母表

–My little sister has learned to say her ABC's. 我的小妹妹已经学会英文字母了。

–That's wonderful! 真棒！

able /ˈeɪbəl/ （形容词）能够…的
The giant frog is able to jump three meters. 大青蛙能够跳3米远。

about¹ /əˈbaut/ （介词）关于

–What's the film about? 这部电影是关于什么的？

–It's about the earth. 是关于地球的。

about² /əˈbaut/ （副词）大约

–How many students are there in the class? 班里有多少学生？

–There are about fifty. 大约有50个。

above /əˈbʌv/ （介词）在…上面
The plane was flying above the clouds. 飞机在云上飞行。

> **反义词** below 在…下面

absent /ˈæbsənt/ （形容词）缺席的

–Why is Tom absent today? 汤姆今天为什么没来？

–He's ill. 他生病了。

accept /ækˈsept/ （动词）接受

–Did you accept his gift? 你接受他的礼物了吗？

–No, I didn't. 我没有。

accident /ˈæksɪdənt/ （名词）事故

–Why is the traffic so slow? 为什么车流这么慢？

–There's an accident. 出事故了。

ache¹ /eɪk/ （名词）疼痛

–Mom, I have a tummy ache. 妈妈，我肚子疼。

–This will make you feel better. 这会让你舒服些。

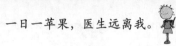
一日一苹果，医生远离我。

actor /'æktə/（名词）男演员,
演员

He's a famous actor. 他是一位名
演员。

用法小贴士

actor通常指男演员，但也有人用这个词来
泛指男演员或者女演员。女演员可以用
actress.

拓展词汇

toothache 牙疼　headache 头痛
stomach ache 胃疼

ache² /eɪk/（动词）疼

–My tooth aches. 我牙疼。
–You must see the dentist. 你得去
看牙医。

across /ə'krɒs/（介词）在…的
另一边

–Where do you live? 你住哪儿？
–I live just across the street. 我就住
在街对面。

act /ækt/（动词）扮演

Who acts the role of the Monkey
King? 是谁扮演孙悟空呀？

action /'ækʃn/（名词）行动

Actions speak louder than words.
行动胜于言辞。

active /'æktɪv/（形容词）活跃的

Tom is very active in football practice. 汤姆在足球训练中很活跃。

activity /æk'tɪvɪti/（名词）（复数
activities）活动

I take part in a lot of after-school
activities. 我参加很多课外活动。

actress /'æktrəs/（名词）女演员

–It's a great film! 电影太好看了！
–Yes, I like the actress very much.
是啊，我特别喜欢那个女演员。

ad /æd/（名词）广告

–Do you trust ads? 你相信广告吗？
–Not always. 不是总信。

add /æd/（动词）加

Add a little more sugar to the
coffee, please. 请再往咖啡里加点
儿糖。

反义词　minus 减

address /ə'dres/（名词）地址

My home address is 12 Nanjing
Road. 我的家庭住址是南京路12
号。

admit /æd'mɪt/ （动词）
（过去式、过去分词 **admitted**,
现在分词 **admitting**）承认
–You should admit that you made
a mistake. 你应该认错。
–But I did nothing wrong! 可我没
做错什么呀！

adult /'ædʌlt/ （名词）成年人
Adults don't always understand
children. 成年人不是总能理解孩
子。

adventure /æd'ventʃə/ （名词）
冒险活动
–Have you read *The Adventures of
Tintin*? 你看过《丁丁历险记》吗？
–Yes, I love it. 看过，我挺喜欢的。

advice /æd'vaɪs/ （名词）建议
–How can I learn English well? 我
怎样才能学好英语呢？
–The teacher can give you some
good advice. 老师能给你一些好
建议。

用法小贴士
advice是不可数名词，不可以说an
advice，一条建议可以说a piece of
advice。

afraid /ə'freɪd/ （形容词）害怕的
–Are you afraid of spiders? 你怕蜘
蛛吗？
–No, but I'm afraid of snakes. 不
怕，但我害怕蛇。

Africa /'æfrɪkə/ （名词）非洲
–Is Africa larger than Asia? 非洲比
亚洲大吗？
–No, it's smaller than Asia. 不，
比亚洲小。

拓展词汇
African 非洲的，非洲人
百科小贴士
非洲是世界第二大洲。非洲拥有世界上
最大的沙漠撒哈拉大沙漠，最长的河流
尼罗河。

after /'ɑːftə/ （介词）在…之后
She left the house after breakfast.
她吃完早饭就出门了。
反义词 before 在…之前

afternoon /ˌɑːftə'nuːn/ （名词）
下午
–Would you like to go swimming?
你想去游泳吗？
–Yes. Can we go this afternoon?
想。下午去行吗？

again /ə'gen/ （副词）再
Sorry, but could you say that
again? 抱歉，你能再说一遍吗？

一日一苹果，医生远离我。

against /ə'genst/ （介词）紧靠在
Mary pressed her nose against the window to look outside. 玛丽把鼻子紧贴在窗户上向外看。

age /eɪdʒ/ （名词）年龄
Children start school at the age of six. 孩子们6岁开始上学。

ago /ə'gəʊ/ （副词）以前
–Have you been to Beijing before? 你去过北京吗？
–Yes. I went there six years ago. 去过，6年前去的。

agree /ə'griː/ （动词）同意，赞同
Please raise your hand if you agree with me. 同意我意见的请举手。

ah /ɑː/ （叹词）啊
Ah, this coffee is good. 啊，这咖啡不错。

aha /ɑː'hɑː/ （叹词）啊哈
Aha! That's where you hid! 哈！原来你藏在这儿呀！

ahead /ə'hed/ （副词）在前面
The teacher walked ahead of the students to lead the way. 老师走在学生们前面带路。

aid /eɪd/ （名词）援助
–There has been a big flood in Guangdong. 广东发大水了。
–Other places have sent aid there. 其他地方送去了援助。

AIDS /eɪdz/ （名词）艾滋病
AIDS is a very serious sickness. 艾滋病是一种非常严重的疾病。

百科小贴士
艾滋病是一种致死性传染病。世界上第一名艾滋病患者于1981年发现于美国。每年的12月1日为"世界艾滋病日"，标志为红丝带。

air /eə/ （名词）
1. 空气
–We can't live without air. 没有空气我们就不能生存。
–Let's keep the air clean. 让我们保持空气清洁。
2. 空中，天空
The balloon floated up into the air. 气球飞到空中去了。

 An apple a day keeps the doctor away.

airplane /'eərəpleɪn/ （名词）飞机

–Who invented the airplane? 是谁发明了飞机？
–The Wright brothers, in 1903. 是莱特兄弟在1903年发明的。

airport /'eəpɔːt/ （名词）机场

–I'm coming to Shanghai by air. 我要乘飞机来上海。
–I'll meet you at the airport. 我会去机场接你。

alarm clock /ə'lɑːm klɒk/ （名词）闹钟

The alarm clock went off at seven and woke Jenny up. 闹钟7点钟响了，把珍妮叫醒了。

all /ɔːl/ （形容词）所有的

–Who's eaten all the cake? 谁把蛋糕都吃了？
–It's me. 是我。

allow /ə'laʊ/ （动词）允许，准许
Dogs are not allowed on buses. 不允许把狗带上公共汽车。

all right /ɔːl 'raɪt/ 好，行，可以

–How about playing ping-pong? 打乒乓球怎么样？
–All right. 好啊。

almost /'ɔːlməʊst/ （副词）几乎，差不多

I've almost finished my homework. 我快完成家庭作业了。

a lot of /ə 'lɒt əv/ 很多，许多

–I have a lot of picture books. 我有很多图画书。
–Can I borrow one? 我可以借一本吗？

用法小贴士

a lot of 既可修饰可数名词，也可修饰不可数名词。例如：I have a lot of free time. （我有很多空闲时间。）

alphabet /'ælfəbet/ （名词）字母表

The English alphabet has 26 letters. 英语字母表有26个字母。

already /ɔːl'redi/ （副词）已经

–Is your dad at home, John? 约翰，你爸爸在家吗？
–No, he's already gone to work. 不在，他已经去上班了。

also /'ɔːlsəʊ/ （副词）也

–Alice is good at playing the piano. 艾丽斯钢琴弹得很好。
–She is also good at sports. 她的体育也很好。

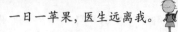

一日一苹果，医生远离我。

用法小贴士

also 和 too 在意思上很接近，但是，also 从不用在句末，too 常用于句末。

always /'ɔːlweɪz/（副词）总是

The teacher is always patient with her students. 老师对她的学生总是很耐心。

am¹ /æm/（动词）（**be** 的第一人称单数现在式）是

–What do you do? 你做什么工作？

–I'm (=I am) a teacher. 我是老师。

am² /æm/（助动词）（**be** 的第一人称单数现在式）

–What are you doing? 你在干什么？

–I'm watching a cartoon. 我在看动画片。

a.m. /ˌeɪ 'em/ 上午

–What are your school hours? 你上课的时间是几点到几点？

–From eight a.m. to three p.m. 从上午8点到下午3点。

用法小贴士

a.m.表示从半夜到中午的时间；p.m.表示从中午到半夜的时间。

America /ə'merɪkə/（名词）美国, 美洲

–What language do people speak in America? 美国人讲什么语言？

–They speak English. 讲英语。

拓展词汇

American 美国的，美国人

百科小贴士

美国的原住居民是美洲印第安人，现在的美国人大多是移民后裔。美国的首都是华盛顿。美国的全称是 United States of America，简写为 USA 或 U.S.

among /ə'mʌŋ/（介词）在…中间

The butterfly is flying among the flowers. 蝴蝶在花丛中飞舞。

an /æn/（冠词）一个

–Would you like an apple? 你想吃个苹果吗？

–No, thank you. 不，谢谢。

用法小贴士

an用于读音以元音音素开头的词前，如an egg, an orange.

ancient /'eɪnʃənt/（形容词）古代的

–The Great Wall was built in ancient China. 长城是在中国古代修建的。

–It's the longest wall in the world. 它是世界上最长的墙。

and /ænd/ （连词）和

Students sang and danced at the party. 学生们在派对上又唱又跳。

angel /'eɪndʒəl/ （名词）天使

–Can angels fly? 天使会飞吗？
–Yes, they have wings. 是的，他们长着翅膀。

百科小贴士

西方文学艺术中，天使的形象多为长着翅膀的少女或孩子。

angry /'æŋgri/ （形容词）

（比较级 **angrier**, 最高级 **angriest**）生气的

–Why was the teacher angry with you? 老师为什么对你生气？
–Because I was late for class. 因为我上课迟到了。

animal /'ænɪməl/ （名词）动物

–What animals do you like best? 你最喜欢什么动物？
–Cats and dogs. 我最喜欢猫和狗了。

another /ə'nʌðə/ （形容词）

另一的，再一个的

There is another answer to this question. 这个问题还有一个答案。

answer¹ /'ɑːnsə/ （名词）回答，答案

–How was your exam today? 今天你考得怎么样？
–It was easy. I knew all the answers! 太容易了，我知道所有答案！

answer² /'ɑːnsə/ （动词）回答

–How was your exam today? 你今天考试怎么样？
–I could answer all the questions. 所有问题我都会答。

ant /ænt/ （名词）蚂蚁

Sometimes millions of ants live in one nest. 有时候数百万只蚂蚁住在一个巢里。

拓展词汇

queen ant 蚁后　　worker ant 工蚁
soldier ant　兵蚁

any /'eni/ （形容词）一些（的）

–I'm so hungry! 我饿坏了！
–Oh dear! There isn't any food left! 天哪！什么吃的都没了！

anything /'eniθiŋ/ （代词）
任何事物

–Do you want anything to drink?
想喝点儿什么吗？

–May I have some apple juice, please? 来点儿苹果汁吧。

apartment /ə'pɑ:tmənt/
（名词）公寓

Our family has moved into a new apartment. 我们家搬进了新公寓。

用法小贴士

apartment是美国英语，英国英语用flat。

ape /eip/ （名词）（类人）猿

Apes have long arms and don't have tails. 猿长着长长的双臂，没有尾巴。

百科小贴士

类人猿又称无尾猿，包括黑猩猩、大猩猩、长臂猿和猩猩。

apologize /ə'pɒlədʒaɪz/
（动词）道歉

Tom apologized to the teacher for being late. 汤姆因迟到向老师道歉。

用法小贴士

表示道歉时，一般用I'm sorry，强调歉意时用I apologize。

apple /'æpəl/ （名词）苹果

An apple a day keeps the doctor away. 一日一苹果，医生远离我。

拓展词汇

apple juice 苹果汁 apple pie 苹果馅饼

百科小贴士

在10种对健康最有利的水果中苹果排名第一，因为苹果含有丰富的纤维物质，可以降低心脏病发病率，还可以减肥。苹果还富含锌，而锌与人的记忆力关系密切，因此苹果有"益智果"与"记忆果"的美称。在英语谚语中还有"An apple a day keeps the doctor away."的说法。

April /'eiprɪl/ （名词）四月

The sports meet is on the sixth of April. 运动会将在4月6号举行。

百科小贴士

April来源于拉丁文中的Aprilis，原意是大地回春、万象更新的意思。

April Fool's Day /ˌeiprɪl 'fu:lz deɪ/ （名词）愚人节

People tell funny lies on April Fool's Day. 四月份的愚人节，人们会说一些滑稽有趣的谎话。

百科小贴士

4月1日是西方的愚人节，人们互相开各种各样的玩笑，搞恶作剧。谁要是上当就被称为April Fool（愚人节傻瓜）。

are[1] /ɑ:/ （动词）（be 的复数及第二人称单数现在式）是
Animals are our friends. 动物是我们的朋友。

are[2] /ɑ:/ （助动词）（be 的复数及第二人称单数现在式）

An apple a day keeps the doctor away.

The students are taking an exam.
学生们正在考试。

arm /ɑːm/（名词）手臂，胳膊
I fell and broke my arm. 我摔了一跤把胳膊摔断了。

armchair /'ɑːmtʃeə/（名词）扶手椅
Grandpa has fallen asleep in his armchair. 爷爷在扶手椅上睡着了。

army /'ɑːmi/（名词）（复数 **armies**）军队
I want to join the army when I grow up. 我长大后想参军。

around /ə'raʊnd/（介词）围绕，在…周围
The students sit around the teacher. 学生们坐在老师周围。

arrive /ə'raɪv/（动词）到达
The plane arrived in Beijing at ten a.m. 飞机上午10点到了北京。

用法小贴士
一般说来，arrive 后面的介词按到达地点的大小来决定：at 用于较小的场所，如车站、港口等；in 用于较大的地方，如国家、城市等。

arrow /'ærəʊ/（名词）箭
The head of an arrow is sharp. 箭的头儿是尖的。

art /ɑːt/（名词）美术
I'm not good at art. 我不擅长美术。
拓展词汇
art class 美术课　art museum 美术馆

article /'ɑːtɪkəl/（名词）文章
The teacher read an interesting article to the class. 老师给学生念了一篇有趣的文章。

artist /'ɑːtɪst/（名词）艺术家
–A painter is an artist. 画家是艺术家。
–But artists aren't all painters. 但艺术家不一定都是画家。

as /æz/（连词）在…的时候
Lily listened to music as she did her homework. 莉莉一边听音乐，一边做作业。

Asia /'eɪʃə/（名词）亚洲
–Where's China on the map? 中国在地图的哪个位置？
–It's in Asia. 中国在亚洲。
拓展词汇
Asian 亚洲的，亚洲人

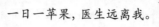一日一苹果，医生远离我。

百科小贴士
亚洲是世界第一大洲。亚洲拥有世界上最高的山峰珠穆朗玛峰，最高的高原青藏高原，最深的湖泊贝加尔湖，最大的咸水湖里海，和最大的半岛阿拉伯半岛。

ask /ɑːsk/ （动词）
1. 问，询问
–May I ask a question, sir? 老师，我可以问一个问题吗？
–Sure, go ahead. 当然可以了。
2. 邀请
–Mom, can I ask my classmates to my birthday party? 妈妈，我可以邀请同学参加我的生日派对吗？
–Of course you can. 当然可以啦。

asleep /əˈsliːp/ （形容词）睡着的
–Is the baby asleep? 小宝宝睡着了吗？
–She's awake. 她醒着呢。

反义词 awake 醒着的

aspirin /ˈæspɪrɪn/ （名词）阿司匹林
–I have a bad headache. 我的头很疼。
–You can take some aspirin. 你可以吃点儿阿司匹林。

百科小贴士
阿司匹林具有镇痛、退烧的功用，可以治疗感冒、发热、头痛、牙痛等。阿司匹林一般不会引起不良反应，但长期大量用药则较易产生副作用。

astronaut /ˈæstrənɔːt/ （名词）宇航员
–Do you know Yang Liwei? 你知道杨利伟吗？
–Yes. He was the first Chinese astronaut to travel in space. 知道，他是中国第一个邀游太空的宇航员。

at /ət/ （介词）
1. （表示时间）在…时候
School starts at eight o'clock. 学校8点钟开始上课。
2. （表示地点或位置）在…地方
–Is the teacher at school or at home now? 老师这会儿在学校还是在家？
–She's at school. 她在学校。

athlete /ˈæθliːt/ （名词）运动员
Many athletes take part in the Olympic Games. 许多运动员参加奥运会。

ATM /ˌeɪ tiː ˈem/ （名词）自动取款机
All American and Chinese cities have ATMs. 所有美国和中国的城市里都有自动取款机。

attend /ə'tend/ （动词）参加，出席
Students must attend classes every day. 学生必须每天上课。

attention /ə'tenʃən/ （名词）注意
–What did I say just now? 我刚刚说什么来着?
–Sorry, but I wasn't paying attention. 对不起，我没注意。

August /'ɔːgəst/ （名词）八月
–Is August the hottest season in Beijing? 8月是北京最热的季节吗?
–No, July is. 不，7月最热。

百科小贴士
August来源于古罗马皇帝屋大维。他登基后，罗马元老院在8月授予他 Augustus（奥古斯都）的尊号，August便由这位皇帝的拉丁语尊号演变而来。

aunt /ɑːnt/ （名词）婶娘，姑妈，伯母，舅妈，姨妈
–Aunt Susan is my mother's younger sister. 苏珊姨妈是我妈妈的妹妹。
–Aunt Jennifer is my father's older sister. 珍妮弗姑妈是我爸爸的姐姐。

用法小贴士
auntie是 aunt的口语表达方式。

Australia /ɒ'streɪlɪə/ （名词）澳大利亚
Kangaroos come from Australia. 袋鼠产自澳大利亚。

拓展词汇
Australian 澳大利亚的，澳大利亚人

author /'ɔːθə/ （名词）作者，作家
Lu Xun is a great author. 鲁迅是一位伟大的作家。

autumn /'ɔːtəm/ （名词）秋天
Spring is warm. Autumn is cool. 春天暖和，秋天凉爽。
用法小贴士
autumn是英国英语，美国英语用fall。

awake /ə'weɪk/ （形）醒着的
Tom is awake, but he doesn't want to get up. 汤姆醒着，但他不想起床。
反义词 asleep 睡着的

away /ə'weɪ/ （副词）
1. 离开
Don't go away. 不要走开。
2. 离…有某段距离
–Where is the nearest hospital? 最近的医院在哪里?
–It's three kilometers away. 3公里以外。

ax /æks/ （名词）斧头
The farmer cut down the tree with an ax. 农夫用斧头把树砍倒了。

Better late than never.

B

baby /'beɪbi/ （名词）（复数
babies）婴儿
The mother is holding her baby in
her arms. 妈妈把婴儿抱在怀里。

拓展词汇

baby boy 男婴　　baby girl 女婴
baby food 婴儿食品　　baby tooth 乳牙

back /bæk/ （名词）背部
–Something is crawling up my
back. 有什么东西在我背上爬。
–Oh no! It's a spider! 哎呀，是只
蜘蛛！

backpack /'bækpæk/ （名词）
双肩背包
–Your backpack is cool. 你的双肩
包真酷。
–Thank you. 谢谢。

百科小贴士

在中国传统文化中，得到别人夸奖时，要
表示自谦，在西方文化中则应表示感谢。

bad /bæd/ （形容词）（比较级
worse /wɜːs/, 最高级 **worst** /wɜːst/）
不好的，坏的

–How are you today? 今天感觉
怎样？
–Not bad. 还不错。

反义词　good 好的

badminton /'bædmɪntən/
（名词）羽毛球
–Do you want to play badminton?
你想打羽毛球吗？
–I'd love to. But I'm busy at the
moment. 我想打，但我现在太忙了。

bag /bæg/ （名词）包，袋子
–Guess what's in the bag? 猜猜袋
子里是什么？
–Wow! It's a cat! 哇，是只猫！

拓展词汇

trash bag 垃圾袋　　schoolbag 书包
shopping bag 购物袋

baggage /'bægɪdʒ/ （名词）
行李
–Can you help me with my
baggage? 你能帮我拿一下行李吗？
–Sure, no problem. 当然，没问题。

迟做总比不做好。

用法小贴士

baggage是不可数名词，表示一件行李要说a piece of baggage。行李在英国英语中常用luggage，美国英语常用baggage。

bake /beɪk/ （动词）烘，烤

–Mom's baking a cake. 妈妈正在烤蛋糕。
–It smells good. 真好闻。

拓展词汇

baker 面包师   bakery 面包店

用法小贴士

以元音字母e结尾的动词，且e之前又是辅音字母的，其现在分词的构成是，去e后加ing，如bake的现在分词是baking。

ball /bɔ:l/ （名词）球

–Mom, can I go out and play with my new ball? 妈妈，我能出去玩我的新球吗？
–No, it's going to rain. 不行，快要下雨了。

拓展词汇

basketball 篮球   football 足球
ping-pong ball 乒乓球
tennis ball 网球   volleyball 排球

ballet /'bæleɪ/ （名词）芭蕾舞

I take a ballet class every week. 我每周上一次芭蕾课。

balloon /bə'lu:n/ （名词）气球

–Why is the baby crying? 宝宝干吗哭呀？
–Because his balloon is flying away! 因为他的气球飞走啦！

拓展词汇

hot-air balloon 热气球

bamboo /bæm'bu:/ （名词）竹子

–What do pandas eat? 大熊猫吃什么？
–They eat bamboo. 它们吃竹子。

拓展词汇

bamboo chair 竹椅   bamboo forest 竹林

banana /bə'nɑ:nə/ （名词）香蕉

Bananas grow in hot areas. 香蕉生长在炎热的地区。

band /bænd/ （名词）乐队

–What do you play in the school band? 你在校乐队里演奏什么乐器？
–The violin. 小提琴。

bank /bæŋk/ （名词）银行

My dad's got $10,000 in the bank.
我爸爸在银行里存有1万英镑。

用法小贴士

bank还有"河岸"的意思。有个脑筋急转弯说，为什么河非常富有？答案是：因为河有两个河岸（Because a river has two banks.）。你猜对了吗？

bar /bɑ:/ （名词）酒吧

–What does your uncle do? 你叔叔在哪里上班呀？

–He works in a bar. 他在酒吧上班。

百科小贴士

酒吧是英国人社交聚会的重要场所。据说，伦敦地区酒吧达两万家之多，一般花4—5个英镑就可以在酒吧呆上一个晚上。

barber /'bɑ:bə/ （名词）理发师

My father is a barber. 我爸爸是理发师。

拓展词汇

barber's 理发店

用法小贴士

在英语里，barber特指为男士服务的理发师，为女士服务的理发师叫hairdresser。

bark /bɑ:k/ （动词）（狗）吠叫

Mom, that dog's barking at us! 妈妈，那条狗在朝咱们叫！

baseball /'beɪsbɔ:l/ （名词）棒球

–Come and play baseball with us, Tom. 汤姆，过来和我们玩棒球吧。

–I can't. I haven't done my homework yet! 不行，我还没做功课呢！

basin /'beɪsən/ （名词）脸盆

I poured some hot water in the basin and washed my face. 我往脸盆里倒了点儿热水洗了脸。

basket /'bɑ:skɪt/ （名词）篮子，筐

Don't put all your eggs in one basket. 不要把所有鸡蛋放在一个篮子里。

拓展词汇

wastepaper basket 废纸篓
shopping basket 购物篮

basketball /'bɑ:skɪtbɔ:l/ （名词）篮球

Yao Ming is a basketball star. 姚明是一位篮球明星。

bat /bæt/ （名词）蝙蝠

–Is a bat a bird? 蝙蝠是鸟吗？

–No. It's a mammal. 不是，蝙蝠是哺乳动物。

百科小贴士

蝙蝠是唯一没有羽毛但却能飞的哺乳动物。大多数蝙蝠吃害虫，也有一些蝙蝠吸血，吸食花蜜、花粉，甚至抓小鱼呢！

bath /bɑ:θ/ （名词）洗澡

–Tom! Look at your dirty hands and face! 汤姆，瞧瞧你的脏手和脏脸！

–I know, Mom. I'll take a bath at once. 知道啦，妈妈。我马上就洗个澡。

拓展词汇

bathroom 浴室　bath towel 浴巾
bath water 洗澡水

battle /ˈbætəl/（名词）战斗

The hero was killed in battle. 英雄是在战斗中牺牲的。

拓展词汇

gun battle 枪战　battlefield 战场
battleship 战舰

be¹ /biː/（动词）（过去式 was /wɒz/、were /wɜː/，过去分词 been /biːn/）是

When we were students we were good friends. 我们当学生时就是好朋友了。

be² /biː/（助动词）（过去式 was /wɒz/、were /wɜː/，过去分词 been /biːn/）

At the library we were both reading. 我们曾在图书馆一起读书。

用法小贴士

动词be根据其主语和时态不同有不同形式。

beach /biːtʃ/（名词）（复数 beaches）沙滩

I like collecting shells on the beach. 我喜欢在沙滩上拾贝壳。

拓展词汇

beach ball 沙滩球　beach volleyball 沙滩排球　beach chair 沙滩椅

bean /biːn/（名词）豆子

We make tofu with beans. 我们用豆子做豆腐。

bear /beə/（名词）熊

Some bears sleep all winter without eating. 有些熊冬天睡觉不吃东西。

beard /bɪəd/（名词）胡子

The old man has a long white beard. 老人长着长长的白胡子。

beautiful /ˈbjuːtɪfʊl/（形容词）

1.（形容人或物）美丽的
What a beautiful little girl! 多美的小姑娘呀！
2.（形容天气）美好的
It's a beautiful day today. 今天天气很好。

because /bɪ'kʌz/ （连词）因为
–Why were you late for class? 你为什么上课迟到了？
–Because I got up late. 因为起晚了。

become /bɪ'kʌm/ （动词）（过去式 **became** /bɪ'keɪm/, 过去分词 **become**）变成
–What happened to the frog when the princess kissed it? 公主吻了青蛙后青蛙怎样了？
–It became a handsome prince. 变成了一个英俊的王子。

bed /bed/ （名词）床
–Mom, what time is it? 妈妈，几点啦？
–It's already nine. It's time for bed. 都9点啦，该睡觉了。

拓展词汇

bedroom 卧室　　bedtime 睡觉时间

bee /biː/ （名词）蜜蜂
–Why are the bees flying from flower to flower? 小蜜蜂们为什么在花丛里飞来飞去呀？
–They're working. 它们在劳动。

beef /biːf/ （名词）牛肉
–Which would you prefer, beef or pork? 你想吃什么，牛肉还是猪肉？
–Neither. Chicken, please. 都不要。请来点鸡肉。

beer /bɪə/ （名词）啤酒
–Can I have a glass of beer? 我能喝杯啤酒吗？
–No, it's not for kids. 不行，小孩不能喝。

百科小贴士

啤酒有健脾开胃等功效，有人把它当作日常饮料，但过量饮用有害健康。

before[1] /bɪ'fɔː/ （介词）在…前面
In the alphabet, A is before all the other letters. 在字母表中，A排在所有其他字母前面。

before[2] /bɪ'fɔː/ （副词）以前
–Have you been to Shanghai before? 你以前来过上海吗？
–No, this is my first time. 没有，这是第一次。

begin /bɪ'gɪn/ （动词）（过去式 **began** /bɪ'gæn/, 过去分词 **begun** /bɪ'gʌn/, 现在分词 **beginning**）开始
Be quiet! The film is beginning. 安静！电影开演了。

beginner /bɪ'gɪnə/（名词）
初学者
–You speak good English. 你的英语说得挺好。
–Really? Thank you. I'm only a beginner! 真的？谢谢。我还只是个初学者呢！

behind /bɪ'haɪnd/（介词）在…后面
I can see you behind the door, Jack. 杰克，我能看见你躲在门后。

believe /bɪ'liːv/（动词）相信
–Did Mr. Dongguo believe the wolf? 东郭先生相信了狼的话吗？
–Yes, he did. 是的，他信了。

bell /bel/（名词）铃
–Listen! There goes the bell! 听，铃响了！
–Let's hurry up! 咱们快点儿吧！
拓展词汇
doorbell 门铃　bluebell 风铃草

below /bɪ'ləʊ/（介词）在…下面
–Can you see the fish? 你能看见那些鱼吗？

–Yes, they're swimming below the water plants. 看见了，它们在水草下游来游去。
反义词　above 在…上面

bench /bentʃ/（名词）（复数 benches）长椅
–I'm tired after all this walking. 走了这么久我累啦！
–Look, there's a bench over there. 看，那边有条长椅。

beside /bɪ'saɪd/（介词）在…旁边
–Can I sit beside you? 我可以坐你旁边吗？
–Sorry, the seat is already taken. 对不起，这个座位已经有人坐啦！

best¹ /best/（形容词）最好的
East, west, home is best. 东好西好，不如自家好。

best² /best/（副词）最
–What subject do you like best? 你最喜欢哪门功课？
–English, of course. 当然是英语了。

better¹ /'betə/（形容词）更好的
–How do you feel today? 你今天感觉怎么样？
–Much better, thank you. 好多了，谢谢你。

better² /'betə/ （副词）更好地
He sings better than I. 他唱歌比我好。

between /bɪ'twiːn/ （介词）在…之间
We take a break between every class. 我们每节课之间都要休息。

bicycle /'baɪsɪkəl/ （名词）（口语形式 **bike**）自行车
I go to school by bicycle. 我骑自行车上学。

big /bɪg/ （形容词）（比较级 **bigger**，最高级 **biggest**）大的
This dress is too big. That one is too small. 这条连衣裙太大了，那条又太小了。
反义词 small 小的

bike /baɪk/ （名词）（口语）自行车
I want to learn to ride a bike. 我想学骑自行车。

bill /bɪl/ （名词）账单
–Waiter, can I have the bill, please? 服务员，结账。
–Sure. It's thirty yuan, sir. 好的。一共是30元，先生。

billion /'bɪljən/ （数词）十亿
There are about six billion people in the world. 全世界大约有60亿人口。

bird /bɜːd/ （名词）鸟
–Can all birds fly? 所有的鸟都能飞吗?
–No. For example, penguins can't fly. 不是。例如，企鹅就不会飞。

拓展词汇
seabird 海鸟　waterbird 水鸟

birthday /'bɜːθdeɪ/ （名词）生日
Happy birthday to you, Emma! 祝你生日快乐，埃玛!

迟做总比不做好。

B

拓展词汇

birthday cake 生日蛋糕　birthday card 生日贺卡　birthday present 生日礼物　birthday party 生日派对

biscuit /'bɪskɪt/ （名词）饼干
Would you like biscuits or bread? 你想要饼干还是蛋糕？

bitter /'bɪtə/ （形容词）苦的
This medicine tastes bitter. 这药很苦。

反义词 sweet 甜的

black¹ /blæk/ （形容词）黑色的
She has long black hair. 她留着黑色的长发。

反义词 white 白色的

拓展词汇

black coffee 黑咖啡（不加牛奶）
black-and-white TV 黑白电视
black box 黑匣子
black sheep 害群之马

black² /blæk/ （名词）黑色
–Do I look good in black? 我穿黑色好看吗？
–No, black isn't your color. 不好看，黑色不适合你。

blackboard /'blækbɔːd/ （名词）黑板
Look at the blackboard, please. 请看黑板。

反义词 whiteboard 白板

blanket /'blæŋkɪt/ （名词）毯子，地毯
–Mom, can I have a blanket? I feel cold. 妈妈，我能盖个毛毯吗？我觉得冷。
–You don't look very well. You must be ill. 你的脸色不好，一定是病了。

blind /blaɪnd/ （形容词）瞎的
He went blind after a car accident. 一次车祸后他失明了。

拓展词汇

color blind 色盲

用法小贴士

在有些形容词前加定冠词 the 就指某类人，如 the rich and the poor 指富人与穷人。

blow /bləʊ/ （动词）（过去式 blew /bluː/，过去分词 blown /bləʊn/）吹
This wind's blowing so hard that I can't open my umbrella. 风太大了，我打不开伞。

blue¹ /bluː/ （形容词）蓝色的
–What color is the sea? 大海是什么颜色？
–It's blue. 蓝色。

blue² /bluː/ （名词）蓝色

She was dressed in blue and white. 她穿着蓝白相间的衣服。

boat /bəut/ （名词）船

–How are you going to the island? 你们怎么去岛上？

–We're going by boat. 我们坐船去。

拓展词汇

fishing boat 渔船　　boatman 船夫

body /ˈbɒdi/ （名词）（复数 **bodies**） 身体

We need food and exercise to keep our bodies healthy. 我们需要食物和锻炼来保持身体健康。

拓展词汇

body language 身体语言
body shape 体形

bomb /bɒm/ （名词）炸弹

A bomb went off and killed three people. 一颗炸弹爆炸了，炸死了3个人。

拓展词汇

time bomb 定时炸弹

bone /bəun/ （名词）骨头

The human body has two hundred and six bones. 人体有206块骨头。

bonfire /ˈbɒnfaɪə/ （名词）篝火

We built a bonfire and started singing and dancing. 我们搭起了篝火，开始唱歌跳舞。

book /buk/ （名词）书

Open your books and turn to page ten, please. 请打开书，翻到第10页。

拓展词汇

bookcase 书架　　bookshop 书店
bookworm 书虫

boot /buːt/ （名词）靴子

–Your boots look nice. 你的靴子很漂亮。

–They're warm, too. 它们也很暖和。

boring /ˈbɔːrɪŋ/ （形容词） 乏味的，枯燥的

–The storybook was very boring. 这本故事书太没意思了。

–Really? I think it's interesting. 是吗？我觉得挺有意思的。

反义词　interesting 有趣的

borrow /'bɒrəʊ/ （动词）

（向别人）借

–Can I borrow your pencil, please? 我可以借你的铅笔吗？
–Yes, here you are. 可以，给你。

反义词 lend 借出

用法小贴士

borrow指从别人那里借东西，lend指把东西借给别人。

boss /bɒs/ （名词）老板

My father is the boss of a company. 我爸爸是一家公司的老板。

both¹ /bəʊθ/ （形容词）两个都

–The match was exciting. 这场比赛很刺激。
–Yes, both teams played well. 是的，两个队表现都很好。

both² /bəʊθ/ （代词）两者

I want to buy both of the books. 这两本书我都想买。

bottle /'bɒtəl/ （名词）瓶子

I bought two bottles of juice. 我买了两瓶果汁。

拓展词汇

glass bottle 玻璃瓶   milk bottle 奶瓶
water bottle 水瓶   wine bottle 酒瓶

bow /bəʊ/ （名词）

1. 蝴蝶结
Mary wore a pretty bow in her hair. 玛丽的头发上别了个漂亮的蝴蝶结。
2. 弓
In ancient times, people hunted with bows and arrows. 在古代，人们用弓和箭打猎。

bowl /bəʊl/ （名词）碗

–One more bowl of rice? 再来碗米饭吧？
–No, thank you. I'm full! 不了，谢谢，我已经饱了！

box /bɒks/ （名词）（复数 boxes）

盒子

The kitten's hiding inside the box. 小猫藏在盒子里。

拓展词汇

pencil box 铅笔盒   music box 八音盒
toolbox 工具箱

boy /bɔɪ/ （名词）男孩

The boy liked to dance. The girls thought he was cool. 这个男孩喜欢跳舞，女孩们认为他很酷。

Better late than never.

brain /breɪn/ （名词）大脑
The more we use our brains, the cleverer we become. 我们的大脑越用越聪明。

brand /brænd/ （名词）品牌，牌子
What brand of toothpaste do you use? 你用什么牌子的牙膏？

brave /breɪv/ （形容词）勇敢的
–Mom, my foot hurts. 妈妈，我的脚疼。
–Be a brave boy and don't cry, Tommy. 做个勇敢的孩子，别哭了，汤米。

bread /bred/ （名词）面包
I have a piece of bread and a glass of milk for breakfast. 我早餐吃一片面包，喝一杯牛奶。

break¹ /breɪk/ （动词）（过去式）broke /brəʊk/，过去分词 broken /'brəʊkən/）打碎，损坏
–Who broke the window? 是谁打碎了窗玻璃？
–Sorry, I did it. 对不起，是我干的。

break² /breɪk/ （名词）课间休息
–Class is over. 下课了。
–Let's take a break. 我们休息一下吧。

breakfast /'brekfəst/ （名词）早餐
–Have you had breakfast? 你吃早饭了吗？
–Not yet. I just got up. 还没呢，我刚起床。

bridge /brɪdʒ/ （名词）桥
–How can we cross the river? 咱们怎么过河呀？
–There's a bridge over there. 那边有座桥。

迟做总比不做好。

bright /braɪt/ （形容词）

1. 明亮的，灿烂的
There's a bright moon in the sky. 一轮明月挂在天上。
2. 聪明的，伶俐的
Mark isn't very bright, but he's hardworking. 马克不是很聪明，但很努力。

bring /brɪŋ/ （动词）（过去式、过去分词 **brought** /brɔːt/）带来，拿来
Please bring your new textbooks to school tomorrow. 明天请带新课本到学校。

反义词 take 带走

broccoli /ˈbrɒkəli/ （名词）花椰菜
–I don't like broccoli. 我不爱吃花椰菜。
–But it's good for you. 但它对健康有利。

brother /ˈbrʌðə/ （名词）兄，弟
The twin brothers look the same, but the elder brother is a little taller. 这对双胞胎兄弟长得一模一样，只是哥哥高一点儿。

brown¹ /braʊn/ （形容词）褐色的，棕色的
–What's your favorite color? 你最喜欢什么颜色？
–Brown, because I have brown hair and brown eyes. 褐色，因为我有褐色的头发和褐色的眼睛。

brown² /braʊn/ （名词）褐色，棕色
The wall is painted brown. 这面墙被刷成棕色。

brush¹ /brʌʃ/ （名词）（复数 **brushes**）刷子
–Where is my hair brush? 我的发刷呢？
–It's under the desk. 在桌子底下。

拓展词汇
toothbrush 牙刷　　shoe brush 鞋刷
paintbrush 画笔

brush² /brʌʃ/ （动词）刷

–Would you like an ice cream? 吃个冰激凌吧。

–No, thanks. I've already brushed my teeth. 不，谢谢。我已经刷过牙了。

bubble /ˈbʌbəl/ （名词）泡泡，泡沫

I like blowing bubbles. 我喜欢吹泡泡。

拓展词汇

bubblegum 泡泡糖
soap bubble 肥皂泡

build /bɪld/ （动词）（过去式、过去分词 **built** /bɪlt/）建造

–What's the mother bird doing? 鸟妈妈在干吗呀？

–She's building a nest for her babies. 她在为小鸟们搭窝呢。

building /ˈbɪldɪŋ/ （名词）建筑物

–This is our new school building. 这是我们的新教学楼。

–It's beautiful! 真漂亮！

bull /bʊl/ （名词）公牛

–A bull has two horns. A cow has horns, too, doesn't it? 公牛有两只角，母牛也长角，对吗？

–Don't be silly! 别犯傻了！

拓展词汇

bullfrog 牛蛙　　bullfight 斗牛

bullet /ˈbʊlɪt/ （名词）子弹

–I need some bullets for my toy gun. 我的玩具枪没子弹了。

–Dad's going to the toy shop this afternoon. 爸爸下午会去玩具店。

bumper car /ˈbʌmpə kɑː/ （名词）碰碰车

It's fun to ride in a bumper car. 开碰碰车很好玩儿。

burn /bɜːn/ （动词）（过去式、过去分词 **burned**）燃烧，烧坏

Don't stay in the hot sun. It'll burn your skin. 别呆在烈日下，会晒伤你的皮肤。

迟做总比不做好。

bus /bʌs/ （名词）（复数 **buses** ）
公共汽车
–Why's Joe running? 乔干吗跑呀？
–He's trying to catch the bus.
哦，赶公共汽车。

拓展词汇

bus driver 公交司机　bus stop 公共汽车站　school bus 校车

busy /ˈbɪzi/ （形容词）（比较级 **busier**，最高级 **busiest** ）忙的，忙碌的
–It's exam time. 要考试了。
–No wonder everybody's so busy.
难怪人人都这么忙。

but /bʌt/ （连词）但是
–Are you hungry? 你饿吗？
–No, but I'm thirsty. 不饿，但我渴了。

butter /ˈbʌtə/ （名词）黄油
–Do you want some butter on your bread? 你的面包上要抹点儿黄油吗？
–No, thanks. 不，谢谢。

拓展词汇

butter and bread 黄油面包片

butterfly /ˈbʌtəflaɪ/ （名词）
（复数 **butterflies** ）蝴蝶

–How long can a butterfly live? 蝴蝶能活多久？
–Many butterflies can live about one month. The smallest butterflies may live only a week. 许多蝴蝶能活一个月左右，但最小的蝴蝶只能活一个星期。

button /ˈbʌtən/ （名词）
1. 纽扣
–Your shirt looks funny. 你的衬衫看起来怪怪的。
–Oh, I got the buttons wrong! 啊，我把扣子系错啦！
2. 开关

–What's the matter with the radio? It doesn't work. 收音机怎么了，没有声音。
–You forgot to press the power button. 你忘按电源开关了。

buy /baɪ/ （动词）（过去式、过去分词 **bought** /bɔːt/ ）买，购买
–Where did you buy your schoolbag? 你的书包在哪儿买的？
–I bought it on the Internet. 从网上买的。

反义词　sell 卖

25

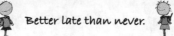

B

by /baɪ/（介词）

1. 在…旁边
There's a castle by the sea. 海边有一座城堡。

2. 乘坐（交通工具）
–Did you come by bus? 你坐公交车来的吗？
–No, I came by bike. 不，我骑自行车来的。

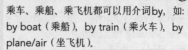

用法小贴士
乘车、乘船、乘飞机都可以用介词by，如：by boat（乘船）、by train（乘火车）、by plane/air（坐飞机）。

bye /baɪ/（叹词）再见

–Bye! 再见！
–See you tomorrow. 明天见。

cabbage /'kæbɪdʒ/ （名词）卷
心菜
Cabbage is a common vegetable.
卷心菜是一种常见的蔬菜。

百科小贴士
各种研究表明，卷心菜具有提高免疫力、
预防感冒和增进人体健康的功效。

café /'kæfeɪ/ （名词）咖啡店，
咖啡馆
–What does the café sell? 这家咖
啡店卖什么？
–Coffee, tea, and snacks. 咖啡、茶、
零食。

cage /keɪdʒ/ （名词）笼子
–Why does the little bird look so
unhappy? 为什么小鸟很不开心？
–Because it doesn't want to live in
a cage. 因为它不喜欢生活在笼中。

cake /keɪk/ （名词）蛋糕
–What did you have for your birthday? 你过生日时吃什么了？
–A birthday cake, of course. 当然是
生日蛋糕啦。

拓展词汇
fruitcake 水果蛋糕   chocolate cake
巧克力蛋糕   cheesecake 奶酪蛋糕

call¹ /kɔ:l/ （动词）
1. 称呼
–What do you call your doggie? 你
的小狗叫什么名字呀？
–I call him Tommy. 叫汤米。
2. 打电话
When I can't get home on time, I
always call Mom to let her know.
当我不能按时回家时，总会给妈妈
打个电话。

call² /kɔ:l/ （名词）电话
–Give me a call if you need any help.
如果你需要帮助就给我来电话。
–Thank you very much! 非常感谢！

camel /'kæməl/ （名词）骆驼
Camels are called "ships of the
desert." 骆驼被称作"沙漠之舟"。
百科小贴士
骆驼之所以适应在沙漠中的生活，有3个原
因：1. 骆驼鼻孔中的瓣膜、眼睛外面长而
密的睫毛以及双重的眼睑让骆驼不怕风
沙；2. 驼峰里蓄满脂肪，在饥饿和营养缺
乏时逐渐转化为身体所需的水分和营养，
能够适应沙漠中缺少食物的状况；3. 骆驼
的脚趾宽厚，适合在沙漠上行走。

camera /'kæmrə/ （名词）照相机

–My camera isn't working. 我的照相机没法用。
–Maybe you've forgotten to put in film. 也许你忘了装胶卷了。

百科小贴士

传统相机需要胶卷，数码照相机（digital camera，简称DC）将照片存在储存器中，可立即显示，我们还可以在电脑上对照片进行修改。

camp /kæmp/ （名词）营地

–What are you going to do this summer? 今年夏天你准备干什么？
–I'm going to a summer camp to learn English. 我要去参加一个英语夏令营。

can¹ /kæn/ （名词）罐头

Tom opened a can of Coke and began to drink from it. 汤姆打开一听可乐，然后喝起来。

用法小贴士

美国人习惯用can来表示罐头，而英国人则用tin。"一听罐头"的"听"就是从英语的 tin 音译过来的。

can² /kæn/ （情态动词）能够，会

–Can you sing English songs? 你会唱英文歌吗？

–Yes, I can sing a few. 是的，会唱几首。

Canada /'kænədə/ （名词）

加拿大

Canada is in North America. 加拿大在北美洲。

拓展词汇

Canadian 加拿大的，加拿大人

百科小贴士

加拿大位于北美洲，是世界第二大国，首都为渥太华，官方语言为英语和法语。加拿大境内多枫树，有"枫叶之国"的美誉。

candle /'kændəl/ （名词）蜡烛

–The power is off. 停电了。
–Let's light a candle. 点支蜡烛吧。

candy /'kændi/ （名词）糖果

–I love candy. 我喜欢吃糖。
–Me too. But too much candy is bad for your teeth. 我也喜欢。但是吃太多糖对牙齿不好。

拓展词汇

candy bar 糖果柜台   cotton candy （美）棉花糖

用法小贴士

candy既可作可数名词又可作不可数名词，candy是美国英语，英国英语用sweet，为可数名词，复数形式是sweets。

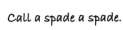

cap /kæp/ （名词）帽子

–That's a nice cap. 你的帽子很好看。
–Thank you. 谢谢！

拓展词汇

swimming cap 泳帽　shower cap 浴帽
baseball cap 棒球帽　flat cap 鸭舌帽

用法小贴士

汉语中我们都说"帽子"，英文中却有 cap 和 hat 两个词，cap 通常是指没有帽沿，或者只是在前面有帽沿的帽子；hat 指有一圈帽沿的帽子。具体差别见下图。

capital /ˈkæpɪtəl/ （名词）首都，省会

Beijing is the capital of China. 北京是中国的首都。
Hangzhou is the capital of Zhejiang. 杭州是浙江的省会。

captain /ˈkæptɪn/ （名词）

1. 船长
Captain James Cook discovered Australia in 1770. 詹姆斯·库克船长于1770年发现了澳大利亚。
2. 队长
Jack is the captain of our football team. 杰克是我们足球队的队长。

car /kɑː/ （名词）轿车

More and more Chinese families have their own cars. 越来越多的中国家庭拥有了自己的汽车。

拓展词汇

police car 警车　racing car 赛车
sports car 跑车

card /kɑːd/ （名词）卡片

–Thank you for your New Year card! 谢谢你的新年卡！
–I made it myself. 是我自己动手做的。

拓展词汇

bank card 银行卡　greetings card 贺卡
postcard 明信片　phone card 电话卡

care¹ /keə/ （名词）照顾

I'm old enough to take care of myself. 我已经长大了，能照顾自己了。

care² /keə/ （动词）关心

–Germany won the match last night! 德国队昨晚赢了！
–I don't care. 我可不关心。

careful /ˈkeəfʊl/ （形容词）小心的

She's always careful with her homework. 她做作业总是一丝不苟。

carpet /ˈkɑːpɪt/ （名词）地毯

When you walk on a carpet, you don't make a noise. 走在地毯上不会出声。

carriage /ˈkærɪdʒ/ （名词）马车

The fairy turned the pumpkin into a beautiful carriage. 仙女把南瓜变成了一辆漂亮的马车。

carrot /ˈkærət/ （名词）胡萝卜

–What do rabbits eat? 兔子吃什么？
–They like carrots. 它们喜欢吃胡萝卜。

百科小贴士

胡萝卜含有较高的维生素B和C，以及丰富的胡萝卜素。胡萝卜素在人体内可转化为维生素A。不过，生吃胡萝卜就不利于胡萝卜素的吸收了。

carry /ˈkæri/ （动词）（第三人称单数 **carries**，过去式、过去分词 **carried**，现在分词 **carrying**）

1. 搬运
–I can't carry the bag. It's too heavy. 我提不动这个包，太沉了。
–Let me help you. 我来帮你吧。
2. 抱，背
The mother monkey carried her baby on her back. 猴妈妈把猴宝宝背在背上。

cartoon /kɑːˈtuːn/ （名词）

1. 漫画
Cartoons are usually very funny. 漫画一般都很逗。
2. 卡通片，动画片
Almost all children like cartoons. 几乎所有的孩子都喜欢看卡通片。

case /keɪs/ （名词）箱子，盒子
–Do you know the story of "Buy the Case but Return the Pearl"? 你知道"买椟还珠"的故事吗？
–Yes. It's about a silly man in ancient times. 知道，它讲的是古代一个蠢人的故事。

拓展词汇

pencil case 铅笔盒 bookcase 书柜

castle /ˈkɑːsəl/ （名词）城堡

–Where do princes and princesses live in fairy tales? 童话故事中的王子和公主住在哪里？
–They usually live in beautiful castles. 他们通常住在漂亮的城堡里。

cat /kæt/ （名词）（**kitty** /ˈkɪti/, **kitten** /ˈkɪtən/ 指小猫）猫

When the cat's away, the mice will play. 猫儿不在，老鼠玩得自在。

catch /kætʃ/ （动词）（过去式、过去分词 **caught** /kɔːt/）

1. 抓住，捕捉
–How many fish did you catch? 你抓到几条鱼？
–Five. 5条。
2. 赶上
–Did you catch the last bus? 你赶上末班车了吗？
–No, I missed it. 没有，我错过了。

cause /kɔ:z/ （动词）导致，引起

Smoking can cause lung cancer. 吸烟可导致肺癌。

cave /keɪv/ （名词）洞穴，山洞

–Where do bats live? 蝙蝠住在哪里？
–They live in mountain caves. 住在山洞里。

CD /ˌsi: 'di:/ （名词）激光唱片
–Can I borrow your new CD? 能把你的新唱片借给我吗？
–Yes, but please give it back to me before Saturday. 可以，不过请在周六前还我。

拓展词汇
CD player　激光唱机

cent /sent/ （名词）分
–Here's your change: fifty-five cents. 找零5角5分。
–Just keep it, please. 不用找了。

center /'sentə/ （名词）中心

Tian'anmen Square is in the center of Beijing. 天安门广场位于北京的中心。

拓展词汇
shopping center　购物中心
city center　市中心

century /'sentʃəri/ （名词）
（复数 **centuries**）世纪
–How many years are there in a century? 一个世纪是多少年？
–One hundred. 100年。

百科小贴士
人们把公元元年到公元 99 年称为第 1 个世纪，因此 1900 年到 1999 年是 20 世纪，2000 年到 2099 年是 21 世纪。

certainly /'sɜːtənli/ （副词）

1. 确实，一定
–I'll certainly help you when you need me. 你需要时我一定会帮助你。
–That's very kind of you. 你真好。
2. 当然
–Dad, can I go to the park alone? 爸爸，我能一个人去公园吗？
–Certainly not. 当然不行。

chair /tʃeə/ （名词）椅子
–This chair is too high for the table. 这把椅子配这张桌子太高了。
–Take a lower one, then. 那就换一把矮点儿的。

拓展词汇

armchair 扶手椅　high chair 高脚椅
wheelchair 轮椅

chalk /tʃɔ:k/ （名词）粉笔
–That's a nice drawing. 这幅画画得真不错。
–It's done in chalk. 是用粉笔画的。

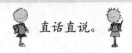

用法小贴士

chalk是不可数名词，一根粉笔要说a piece of chalk，两根粉笔说 two pieces of chalk，依此类推。

champion /'tʃæmpiən/ （名词）冠军

–Who were the women's volleyball champions in the 2004 Olympics? 谁是2004年奥运会女排冠军？
–The Chinese team. 中国队。

chat¹ /tʃæt/ （名词）闲聊

–What did you do in the café last night? 昨晚你们在咖啡馆做什么了？
–We had a chat about our summer vacation. 我们聊了聊暑假的事儿。

chat² /tʃæt/ （动词）（过去式、过去分词 **chatted**，现在分词 **chatting**）闲聊

–Your line was busy for a long time. 你的电话好长时间都占线。
–Sorry, I was chatting with friends on the Internet. 对不起，我正在网上和朋友聊天。

拓展词汇
chat room 聊天室

cheap /tʃiːp/ （形容词）便宜的

–This pen is too expensive. 这支笔太贵了。
–This one is cheaper, but it's also quite good. 这支便宜些，但也很好用。

反义词 expensive 贵的

cheese /tʃiːz/ （名词）奶酪

Cheese, bread, egg, and milk make a good breakfast. 奶酪、面包、鸡蛋加牛奶，就是一顿丰盛的早餐。

百科小贴士
奶酪富含蛋白质、钙、磷等矿物质和维生素。奶酪的营养成分特别容易被人体消化和吸收，其中蛋白质的消化率达到 96%—98%。

chemistry /'kemɪstri/ （名词）化学

–Chemistry is an interesting subject. 化学课很有意思。
–Yes, it's fun to change one thing into another. 是的，把一样东西变成另一样东西很好玩儿。

cherry /'tʃeri/ （名词）（复数 **cherries**）樱桃

–How do these cherries taste? 这些樱桃味道怎样？
–They're very sweet. 很甜。

拓展词汇
cherry tomato 圣女果（小西红柿）

百科小贴士
樱桃中铁含量很高，是特别适合女性吃的水果，有养血排毒的功效。美国研究人员还发现吃樱桃能明显减轻疼痛感以及预防龋齿。

chess /tʃes/ （名词）国际象棋

–Can you play chess? 你会下国际象棋吗？

–No, but I can play Chinese chess. 不会，但我会下中国象棋。

百科小贴士

国际象棋起源于印度或中国的古棋。通常为两人对弈，棋盘为黑白相间的64个方格，每方各16枚棋子。每枚棋子按照自己固有的法则移动。如果将对方的王棋将死，即获胜。20世纪90年代以来，中国的国际象棋迅速崛起，尤其是女棋手，获得了多次世界个人和团体冠军。著名棋手有谢军、诸宸等。

chicken /'tʃɪkɪn/ （名词）

1. 鸡（**chick** /tʃɪk/ 指小鸡）
Chickens are raised on farms. 鸡在农场饲养。
2. 鸡肉
I had some chicken soup for supper. 我晚餐喝了点儿鸡汤。

child /tʃaɪld/ （名词）（复数 children /'tʃɪldrən/）儿童，孩子

This book is for children. 这本书是给孩子看的。

拓展词汇

only child 独生子   schoolchild 学童
Children's Day 儿童节

百科小贴士

世界上许多国家都将6月1日定为儿童节，包括中国。但有的国家就不同，例如，韩国儿童节：5月5日；印尼儿童节：7月23日；新加坡儿童节：10月1日。

childhood /'tʃaɪldhʊd/ （名词）童年

I had a happy childhood. 我的童年很快乐。

China /'tʃaɪnə/ （名词）中国

China is our motherland. 中国是我们的祖国。

拓展词汇

Chinese 中国的，汉语的，中国人，汉语

用法小贴士

China 写成 china 的形式，意思就变成"瓷器"了。

百科小贴士

中国是世界文明古国之一，汉语是世界上少有的仍在使用的古老语言之一，中国有56个民族，其中汉族人数最多。

Chinatown /'tʃaɪnətaʊn/ （名词）中国城，唐人街

chip /tʃɪp/ （名词）

1. 炸薯条
Potato chips can be salty. 土豆片有咸味的。

用法小贴士

美国英语中炸薯条是 French fry。

2. 芯片
Chips are important parts of a computer. 芯片是电脑的重要元件。

chocolate /'tʃɒklɪt/ （名词）巧克力

–Is all chocolate brown? 巧克力都是棕色的吗？

—No. There's white chocolate, too.
不是，也有白巧克力。

chopstick /'tʃɒpstɪk/ （名词）

Small children can't use chopsticks
well. 小孩子用不好筷子。

百科小贴士

在中国、日本、朝鲜和韩国，筷子是最常
用的餐具。西方人进餐时用刀叉。在有的
国家，人们吃饭直接用手，而不用任何餐具。

Christmas /'krɪsməs/ （名词）

圣诞节

Christmas is the most important
holiday in the West. 圣诞节是西方
最重要的节日。

拓展词汇

Christmas Day 圣诞日　Christmas Eve
平安夜　Christmas card　圣诞贺卡
Christmas tree　圣诞树

百科小贴士

圣诞节在每年的12月25日，圣诞节前夕称
为"平安夜"，小孩子们会在睡前把袜子挂在
床头或壁炉旁，等待圣诞老人把礼物放在里
面。当然，真正放礼物的是他们的爸爸妈妈。

church /tʃɜːtʃ/ （名词）（复数

churches）教堂

There is a church near our school.
我们学校附近有座教堂。

cigarette /ˌsɪɡəˈret/ （名词）

香烟

Cigarettes are bad for our health.
香烟有害健康。

百科小贴士

科学试验发现，一支烟所含的尼古丁可毒
死一只小白鼠。吸烟不仅损害吸烟者本人
的健康，还会危及身边的人。

cinema /'sɪnɪmɑː/ （名词）电

影院

—What do you want to do on
Sunday? 你周日想做什么？
—I want to go to the cinema. 我想
去看电影。

用法小贴士

cinema是英国英语，美国英语用movie
house 或 movie theater.

circle /'sɜːkəl/ （名词）圆圈

Draw a circle in your exercise
book, please. 请在你的练习本上画
个圆圈。

circus /'sɜːkəs/ （名词）（复数

circuses）马戏团

—What did you see at the circus?
在马戏团你看了什么？
—I saw animals doing tricks. 我看了
动物表演特技。

city /'sɪti/ （名词）（复数 **cities**）
城市
Hong Kong is a beautiful city. 香港是一座美丽的城市。

class /klɑːs/ （名词）（复数 **classes**）

1. 班级
–What class and grade are you in? 你在几年级几班？
–I'm in Class Two, Grade Five. 我在五年级二班。
2. （几节或几堂）课
–How many classes do you have on Friday? 星期五你有几节课？
–Four. 4节。
3. 科目
We'll take a computer class next year. 我们明年要上计算机课。

classmate /'klɑːsmeɪt/ （名词）
同学
–What do you do with your classmates after school? 你和同学们放学后做什么？
–We sometimes play ping-pong together. 我们有时一起打乒乓球。

classroom /'klɑːsruːm/（名词）
教室

–Where is your classroom? 你的教室在哪儿？
–It's on the third floor. 在4楼。

clean¹ /kliːn/ （形容词）干净的，清洁的
Cats are clean animals. 猫是爱清洁的动物。

反义词　dirty　脏的

clean² /kliːn/ （动词）打扫，弄干净
We clean our classroom every day. 我们每天都打扫教室。

clever /'klevə/ （形容词）聪明的
–Robert's a clever boy. 罗伯特是个聪明的男孩。
–But he doesn't study hard. 但他学习不努力。

climb /klaɪm/ （动词）爬，攀登
–What's the boy doing? 那男孩在干什么？
–He is trying to climb over the fence. 他想爬过围栏。

–No, it's close to the school. 不远, 我家离学校很近。

反义词 far 远的

clock /klɒk/ （名词）钟
–What time is it now? 现在几点了?
–Three o'clock. But the clock is ten minutes fast. 3点，不过这个钟快10分钟。

拓展词汇

alarm clock 闹钟　　body clock　生物钟

clothes /kləʊðz/ （名词）衣服
–It's cold outside. 外面挺冷的。
–Let's put on warm clothes before we go out. 咱们出门前穿暖和点儿吧。

用法小贴士

clothes泛指"衣物"，具体的衣服有专门的词汇，如shirt（衬衫）、trousers（长裤）、skirt（裙子）等。

Clothes

Shirt

trousers

clone /kləʊn/ （动词）克隆
Dolly was the first cloned sheep in the world. 多莉是世界上第一只克隆羊。

百科小贴士

克隆技术是一种无性繁殖技术，它通过使用父亲或者母亲的体细胞获取DNA（脱氧核糖核酸）来进行细胞或整个生物体的复制。它打破了千古不变的自然规律。

cloud /klaʊd/ （名词）云
–The clouds are getting dark. 云在变暗。
–It's going to rain, I'm afraid. 恐怕要下雨了。

close¹ /kləʊz/ （动词）
1. 关闭，合上
Close the door, please. 请把门关上。
2. （商店等）关门，下班
The shop is closed today. 这家商店今天不营业。

反义词 open 打开，营业

cloudy /ˈklaʊdi/ （形容词）（比较级 **cloudier**，最高级 **cloudiest**）
多云的，阴天的
–It's cloudy today. 今天阴天。
–Maybe it's going to rain. 可能会下雨。

close² /kləʊs/ （形容词）近的，接近的
–Is your house far from the school? 你家离学校远吗?

clown /klaʊn/ （名词）小丑
–Who is the funniest man in the circus? 马戏团最滑稽的人是谁?

–It's the clown. He makes people laugh. 是小丑。他让人们发笑。

coach /kəʊtʃ/（名词）（复数 coaches）

1. 四轮马车
The king had a beautiful big coach. 国王有一驾又大又漂亮的马车。
2. 长途汽车
A motor coach passes here every hour. 每小时都有一辆长途汽车经过这里。
3. 教练
–Our school basketball team often wins. 我们的校篮球队经常赢球。
–You must have a good coach. 你们一定有个好教练。

coast /kəʊst/（名词）海岸，海滨
People on the coast make a living from fishing. 沿海地区的人们靠打鱼为生。

coat /kəʊt/（名词）外套，大衣
She wears a heavy coat in winter. 冬天她穿一件厚大衣。

coffee /ˈkɒfi/（名词）咖啡
–Would you like a cup of coffee? 想喝杯咖啡吗?
–No, thank you. 不了，谢谢。

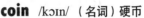
百科小贴士
咖啡含咖啡因等刺激性物质，具有提神醒脑的作用。但是儿童应该少饮用咖啡，因为咖啡因对生长发育期的大脑有负面作用。

coin /kɔɪn/（名词）硬币
–What's your hobby? 你的爱好是什么?
–I like to collect coins. 我喜欢收藏硬币。

Coke® /kəʊk/（名词）（也作 Coca-Cola®）可口可乐
Coke is a soft drink. 可口可乐是一种软饮料。

百科小贴士
软饮料指不含酒精的饮料。

cola /ˈkəʊlə/（名词）可乐
–I'm thirsty. 我渴了。
–Have a glass of cola. 来杯可乐吧。

cold¹ /kəʊld/（形容词）冷的，凉的
Let's go home. It's cold outside. 我们回家吧，外面很冷。

cold² /kəʊld/（名词）感冒
–You look ill. 你看上去好像病了。
–Yes, I've got a bad cold. 是的，我得了重感冒。

college /ˈkɒlɪdʒ/ （名词）学院，大学
–What do you want to do after secondary school? 中学毕业后你想干什么？
–I want to go to college. 我想上大学。

color /ˈkʌlə/ （名词）颜色
–What's the color of your new pen? 你的新钢笔是什么颜色的？
–It's blue. 蓝色的。

come /kʌm/ （动词）(过去式 **came** /keɪm/，过去分词 **come**，现在分词 **coming**)
1. 来，过来
–Come here please, John. 约翰，请到这儿来。
–Coming. 来啦。
2. 到达
My dad was very tired when he came home yesterday. 我爸爸昨天回家时非常累。

comedy /ˈkʌmedi/ （喜剧）
–We went to the theater and saw a comedy. 我们去了剧院并观看了一场喜剧。

comfortable /ˈkʌmftəbəl/ （形容词）舒服的，自在的
This is a very comfortable chair. 这把椅子很舒服。
–Do you feel comfortable in your new school? 你在新学校感觉自在吗？
–Yes, because everybody is friendly. 是的，因为每个人都很友好。

company /ˈkʌmpəni/ （名词）
1. （复数 **companies**）公司
Jenny's dad works for a large company. 珍妮的爸爸在一家大公司工作。
2. 同伴，伙伴
Only children are often very lonely, because they don't have any company at home. 独生子女通常很孤独，因为他们在家里没人作伴。

composition /ˌkɒmpəˈzɪʃən/ （名词）作文
The teacher asked us to write a composition. 老师要求我们写一篇作文。

computer /kəmˈpjuːtə/ （名词）计算机，电脑
–We're learning how to use computers at school. 我们正在学校里学习如何使用电脑。
–That's very good, because you can use computers to do many things. 太好了，因为用电脑能做很多事情。

拓展词汇
computer game 电脑游戏

百科小贴士
1946年2月14日，世界上第一台计算机ENIAC在美国宾夕法尼亚大学诞生。这部机器占地近380平方米，重达176吨。

congratulations /kənˌgrætʃuˈleɪʃənz/ （名词）恭喜
–Mike, I've won the race! 迈克，赛跑我赢了！

–Oh, really? Congratulations! 哦, 真的？祝贺你！

contest /'kɒntest/ （名词）比赛, 竞赛
–Did you take part in the speech contest? 你参加演讲比赛了吗？
–Yes, I did. 是的，我参加了。

cook¹ /kʊk/ （动词）烹调，做饭
–Where's Mom? 妈妈在哪儿？
–She's cooking in the kitchen. 她在厨房做饭。

cook² /kʊk/ （名词）厨师
–My father is a cook. 我爸爸是个厨师。
–You're very lucky. Nobody in my family cooks well. 你真幸运。我们家谁都做不好饭。

cookie /'kʊki/ （名词）甜饼干
–What can we have for dessert? 我们饭后甜点吃什么？
–We'll have some cookies. 吃点儿甜饼干吧。

用法小贴士
cookie是美国英语

cool /kuːl/ （形容词）

1. 凉快的
Autumn is coming. It's getting cooler and cooler. 秋天快到了，天气越来越凉。
反义词　warm　温暖的
2. 很棒的，酷的
–Look, Sam! My new bicycle! 萨姆，看！我的新自行车！
–Oh, it's really cool! 哦，真酷！

copy¹ /'kɒpi/ （动词）（第三人称单数 **copies**，过去式、过去分词 **copied**，现在分词 **copying**）抄写，复制
I copied the phone number into my address book. 我把那个电话号码抄到了我的地址簿上。

copy² /'kɒpi/ （名词）（复数 **copies**）拷贝，复制品
–I really like this photograph. 我真喜欢这张照片。
–I'll make a copy for you. 我给你洗一张吧。

corn /kɔːn/ （名词）玉米
–Where's the bear? 熊在哪里？
–It's in the corn field. 在玉米地里。

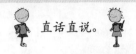

直话直说。

用法小贴士

corn是不可数名词，一粒玉米不能说a corn, 应该说 a grain of corn。

corner /ˈkɔːnə/ （名词）角落，拐角

–Where's my other shoe? 我的另一只鞋在哪儿？

–The dog has put it over in that corner. 在那个角落里。是狗给衔过去的。

correct /kəˈrekt/ （形容词）正确的

This question has more than one correct answer. 这个问题的正确答案不只一个。

反义词 wrong 错误的

cotton /ˈkɒtən/ （名词）棉花

Clothes made of cotton are very comfortable. 棉质衣服穿着很舒服。

拓展词汇

cotton candy （美）棉花糖
cotton cloth 棉布

cough[1] /kɒf/ （动词）咳嗽

The patient coughed all night. 那个病人一晚上都在咳嗽。

cough[2] /kɒf/ （名词）咳嗽

This medicine is good for coughs. 这种药治咳嗽很好。

country /ˈkʌntri/ （名词）

1. （复数 **countries**）国家
China and Japan are Asian countries. 中国和日本是亚洲国家。

百科小贴士

世界七大洲中，除南极洲外，都有国家分布，各大洲的国家分布是不均衡的，非洲的国家最多。面积最大的国家是俄罗斯，面积最小的国家是梵蒂冈，总面积只有0.44平方公里。

2. 乡下，农村
–Where did you go yesterday, Mary? 玛丽，你昨天去哪儿了？
–We went for a picnic in the country. 我们去乡下野餐了。

course /kɔːs/ （名词）课程
–How many courses are you taking this term? 你们这学期要上几门课?
–Seven: Chinese, math, English, fine art, music, geography, and history. 7门，有语文、数学、英语、美术、音乐、地理和历史。

拓展词汇

course book 课本　　course work 功课

cousin /ˈkʌzən/ （名词）堂（或表）兄弟，堂（或表）姐妹
Laura is my little cousin. Her mother is my mother's younger sister. 劳拉是我的表妹，她妈妈是我妈妈的妹妹。

cow /kaʊ/ （名词）奶牛，母牛
Cows eat grass and give us milk. 奶牛吃草，供给我们牛奶。

crayon /ˈkreɪɒn/ （名词）蜡笔
–I've bought a new box of crayons. 我买了一盒新蜡笔。
–Wow, there are forty-eight colors! 哇，有48种颜色!

cream /kriːm/ （名词）奶油
Cream comes from milk. 奶油是用牛奶做的。

拓展词汇

ice cream 冰激凌
cream cake 奶油蛋糕

cricket /ˈkrɪkɪt/ （名词）蟋蟀
Listen! A cricket is singing in the grass. 听！一只蟋蟀正在草丛里唱歌。

百科小贴士

蟋蟀属昆虫，它的叫声并不是发自嗓子，它的发声器官是翅膀。蟋蟀吃庄稼的嫩叶和花，是一种害虫。

crisp /krɪsp/ （形容词）脆的
–The apple is sweet and crisp. 这苹果又脆又甜。
–I'll have one then. 那我来一个。

crocodile /ˈkrɒkədaɪl/ （名词）鳄鱼
–Crocodiles have large sharp teeth. 鳄鱼有锋利的巨齿。
–If they lose any teeth, new ones will grow. 如果它们掉了牙，新牙又会长起来。

百科小贴士

人们常用"鳄鱼的眼泪"（crocodile tears）比喻假慈悲。鳄鱼流眼泪不是因为伤心，是因为在排泄体内多余的盐分。这些多余的盐分要靠一种特殊的盐腺排泄，鳄鱼的盐腺正好位于眼睛附近。

crop /krɒp/ （名词）庄稼
The main crop in China is rice.
中国的主要作物是水稻。

cross[1] /krɒs/ （动词）穿过
Don't cross. The light is red. 不要过
马路，现在是红灯。

cross[2] /krɒs/（名词）十字号，叉号
–You look unhappy. Why? 你好像
不高兴，怎么啦？
–There are more crosses than
checks on my homework. 我的作
业上叉号比对号还多。

crossroad /ˈkrɒsrəʊd/
（名词）十字路口
–Excuse me, how can I get to the
post office? 劳驾，去邮局怎么走？
–Turn left at the next crossroad.
在下个十字路口向左拐。

crow /krəʊ/ （名词）乌鸦
The crow opened its mouth to
sing and the meat dropped
down. 乌鸦张开嘴唱歌,那块肉就
掉了下来。

百科小贴士
尽管人类不太喜欢乌鸦，但在加拿大一名
科学家的"鸟类智慧排行榜"上，乌鸦却
名列榜首。

crown /kraʊn/ （名词）王冠
The queen wore a crown. 女王戴
着王冠。

cry /kraɪ/ （动词）（第三人称单
数 **cries**，过去式、过去分词 **cried**,
现在分词 **crying**）哭，哭泣
–Why are you crying, Mom? 妈妈，
你怎么哭了？
–Oh, it's the onion. The onion's made
me cry. 哦，是洋葱把我弄哭了。

cucumber /ˈkjuːkʌmbə/
（名词）黄瓜
Cucumber is a kind of vegetable.
黄瓜是一种蔬菜。

culture /ˈkʌltʃə/ （名词）文化
Chinese culture has a 5000-year
history. 中国文化有着5000年的历史。

cup /kʌp/ （名词）杯子
–Would you like a cup of tea? 来杯
茶好吗？
–No, thank you. I'd like a glass of
water. 不，谢谢。我想喝杯水。
拓展词汇
teacup 茶杯　　coffee cup 咖啡杯

42

Call a spade a spade.

用法小贴士

汉语中饮水的用具都叫 "杯子"，英文中喝茶和咖啡的杯子叫 cup，一般是瓷器，喝水、饮酒的杯子叫 glass，一般是玻璃的。

cupboard /ˈkʌbəd/ （名词）橱柜

–What's that noise in the cupboard? 橱柜里有什么声音？

–Maybe it's the kitten. 可能是小猫。

curry /ˈkʌri/ （名词）咖喱食品

–What would you like for lunch? 你午饭想吃什么？

–I'll have chicken curry. 我想吃咖喱鸡。

cut /kʌt/ （动词）（过去式、过去分词 **cut**，现在分词 **cutting**）切，割，剪，砍

She cut a picture out of the newspaper. 她从报纸上剪下一幅画。

D

dad /dæd/ （名词）（儿语
daddy /'dædi/）爸爸
–Dad, why are giraffes' necks so long? 爸爸，为什么长颈鹿的脖子那么长呢？
–So they can eat the leaves on the trees. 这样它们就可以吃到树上的叶子了。

dance /dɑ:ns/ （动词）跳舞
–You dance really well. 你跳舞跳得真好。
–Thank you. I started to learn dancing when I was a child. 谢谢。我从小就开始学习舞蹈。

dancer /'dɑ:nsə/ （名词）舞者，舞蹈演员
–Yang Liping is a great dancer. 杨丽萍是个了不起的舞蹈家。
–Yes, she taught herself how to dance. 是的，她是自学成才的。

dare /deə/ （动词）敢，胆敢
–Why didn't the little horse dare to cross the river? 小马为什么不敢过河？
–Because the squirrel said the water was too deep. 因为松鼠说水太深。

dark /dɑ:k/ （形容词）黑暗的
–It's dark in this room. 房间里很暗。
–Let me turn on the light. 我把灯打开吧。

date /deɪt/ （名词）日期
–What's the date today? 今天是几号？
–It's December 31. Tomorrow is New Year's Day. 今天是12月31号，明天就是新年啦。

daughter /'dɔ:tə/ （名词）女儿
The king loved his little daughter, but the new queen didn't like her. 国王很爱他的小女儿，可是新王后不喜欢她。

day /deɪ/ （名词）
1. 天
–How many days are there in a week? 一周有几天？
–Seven. 7天。

2. 白天

Owls sleep during the day and catch food at night. 猫头鹰白天睡觉，晚上捕食。

反义词 night 晚上

dead /ded/ （形容词）死的

Dead leaves fall off trees in autumn. 秋天，枯死的树叶从树上落下。

deaf /def/ （形容词）聋的

Our old dog is deaf, but we still love him. 我们家的老狗聋了，但我们仍然爱它。

百科小贴士

耳疾可能导致耳聋，用药不当也有可能导致耳聋。例如，过量或长期使用庆大霉素就可能致聋。因此，用药时一定要了解药物的性能及其副作用。

dear¹ /dɪə/ （形容词）亲爱的，心爱的

–Who's this baby in the picture, Mom? 妈妈，照片里的婴儿是谁啊？
–Oh, it's you, my dear son. 是你啊，我亲爱的儿子。

用法小贴士

英文书信开头一般用dear称呼对方，如Dear Katie，Dear Mr. Johnson。这里的dear多是客套用语，不一定表达任何感情。

dear² /dɪə/ （名词）亲爱的

–Mom, my doll fell on the floor and broke. 妈妈，我的洋娃娃掉在地上摔坏了。
–Don't cry, my dear. I'll buy you a new one. 别哭了，宝贝。我给你买个新的。

December /dɪ'sembə/ （名词）十二月

December is the last month of the year. 12月是一年中最后一个月。

decide /dɪ'saɪd/ （动词）决定

–Have you decided to go? 你决定去了吗？
–Yes, I have. 是的，我决定去。

deep /diːp/ （形容词）

–How deep is the water? 水有多深？
–Two meters. 两米深。

反义词 shallow 浅的

deer /dɪə/ （名词）（复数 deer）鹿

The deer is a shy animal. 鹿是害羞的动物。

百科小贴士

中国是世界上鹿的种类最丰富的国家。鹿喜清洁，爱安静，感觉敏锐，善于奔跑，多在晨昏活动，白天休息。

45

delicious /dɪˈlɪʃəs/ （形容词）
美味的，好吃的
–Did you enjoy the meal? 你觉得这顿饭怎么样？
–It was all delicious. 每道菜都很好吃。

dentist /ˈdentɪst/ （名词）牙科医生
–I have a toothache! 我牙疼！
–You should see a dentist. 你应该去看牙医。

department store /dɪˈpɑːt-mənt stɔː/ （名词）百货商店
–We need to buy lots of things for our holiday. 我们需要为过节买许多东西。
–Let's go to a department store, then. 那我们去百货商店吧。

desert /ˈdezət/ （名词）沙漠
There are few animals and plants in the desert. 沙漠里的动植物很少。

百科小贴士
世界上最大的沙漠是非洲的撒哈拉沙漠。新疆的塔克拉玛干沙漠是中国最大的沙漠。沙漠生物主要有骆驼、蜥蜴、蛇、仙人掌等。

desk /desk/ （名词）书桌
–Dad, my desk is too low for me. 爸爸，我的书桌太矮了。
–Oh, yes. You've grown so tall. 哦，是的。你已经长高了。

dessert /dɪˈzɜːt/ （名词）（饭后）甜点
–What are we having for dessert? 我们甜点吃什么？
–Ice cream. 冰激凌。

百科小贴士
西方人有在主餐后用甜点的习惯，冰激凌、蛋糕、各种点心都可以，同时喝点咖啡或茶。

detective /dɪˈtektɪv/ （名词）侦探
Mike wants to be a detective when he grows up. 迈克长大后想当侦探。

dew /djuː/ （名词）露水
In the ant's house the dew is a flood. 在蚁穴里，露水就是洪水。

dialogue /ˈdaɪəlɒg/ （名词）对话
–The teacher asked us to practice the English dialogue. 老师让我们练习英语对话。
–It was very interesting. 挺有意思的。

凡事不可半途而废。

diary /'daɪəri/ （名词）（复数 **diaries**）日记

–Do you keep a diary? 你记日记吗？
–Yes, but I don't write in it every day. 是的，但不是每天都写。

dictionary /'dɪkʃənri/ （名词）（复数 **dictionaries**）词典，字典

–I don't know the meaning of this word. 我不知道这个词的意思。
–You can look it up in a dictionary. 你可以查查词典。

die /daɪ/ （动词）（过去式、过去分词 **died**，现在分词 **dying**）死

–Fish will die without clean water. 没有清洁的水鱼就会死去。
–That's right. We must keep our rivers clean. 对，我们必须保持河流清洁。

difficult /'dɪfɪkəlt/ （形容词）困难的

–This jigsaw puzzle is too difficult. 这个拼图太难了。
–Let me have a try. 让我试试吧！

反义词 easy 容易的

dig /dɪg/ （动词）（过去式、过去分词 **dug** /dʌg/，现在分词 **digging**）挖

Henry dug a hole in the ground and planted a tree. 亨利在地上了挖了个坑，种了一棵树。

dining room /'daɪnɪŋ ruːm/ （名词）餐厅

–Where do you usually eat your dinner? In the kitchen? 你通常在哪里吃饭？在厨房吗？
–No, in the dining room. 不，在餐厅。

dinner /'dɪnə/ （名词）正餐

–Shall we have dinner out tonight? 我们今晚出去吃饭好吗？
–Good idea! 好主意！

用法小贴士
dinner指正餐，较丰富，一般是午餐或晚餐。meal意为（一顿）饭，是一日三餐的通称，包括 breakfast（早饭）、lunch（午饭）和supper（晚饭）。

dinosaur /'daɪnəsɔː/ （名词）恐龙

–Has anybody seen a real dinosaur? 有人见过真正的恐龙吗？
–No. They lived long before human history. 没有，它们生活的时代比人类历史早很多年。

百科小贴士
恐龙是陆生动物，属爬行纲，有剑龙、雷龙、原角龙等。最早的恐龙出现在距今约

47

2.2亿年前，由于至今尚不明确的原因，它们在 6500 万年前灭绝了。

–Yes. It's sweet and sour fish. 有，是糖醋鱼。

dirty /'dɜːti/ （形容词）（比较级 dirtier，最高级 dirtiest）脏的
–These clothes are dirty. 这些衣服是脏的。
–Put them in the washing machine. 把它们放进洗衣机里吧。
反义词 clean 干净的

discover /dɪs'kʌvə/ （动词）发现
Scientists work to discover new things. 科学家致力于发现新事物。

discuss /dɪs'kʌs/ （动词）讨论
–What are you talking about? 你们在谈论什么？
–We're discussing today's English exam. 我们在讨论今天的英语考试。
拓展词汇
discussion 讨论

dish /dɪʃ/ （名词）（复数 dishes）
1. 盘子，碟子
There's a large dish of fruit on the table. 桌子上有一大盘子水果。
2. 一道菜
–Do you have a special dish today? 今天有特色菜供应吗？

disk /dɪsk/ （名词）磁盘
–How does a computer store information? 电脑是怎样储存信息的？
–It saves information on a hard disk or on floppy disks. 存在硬盘或软盘上。

百科小贴士
磁盘包括硬盘（hard disk）和软盘（floppy disk），用来存储数据。硬盘存储量较大，不易丢失；软盘较便宜，容易携带，但易损坏。移动硬盘（movable hard disk）兼有两者的优点。

do¹ /duː/ （动词）（第三人称单数 does /dʌz/，过去式 did /dɪd/，过去分词 done /dʌn/）做
–What are you doing? 你在做什么？
–I'm doing my homework. 我在做作业。

do² /duː/ （助动词）
–Do you know the new teacher's name? 你知道新老师的名字吗？
–Yes. Her name is Miss Smith. 是的，她的名字是司密斯夫人。

doctor /'dɒktə/ （名词）医生
–I don't feel well. 我身体不舒服。
–You should see a doctor. 你应该去看医生。

用法小贴士
doctor泛指"医生"，英文中各科医生都有专名，如牙科医生叫dentist，外科医生叫surgeon。

dog /dɒg/ （名词）（儿语 **doggie** /'dɒgi/ ）狗

Dogs such as guide dogs and police dogs are clever animals. 狗如导盲犬和警犬都很聪明。

拓展词汇

hot dog 热狗　　sheepdog 牧羊犬

doll /dɒl/ （名词）洋娃娃

–Katie has lots of dolls. 凯蒂有许多洋娃娃。

–Some of them can talk. 有些还会说话呢。

dollar /'dɒlə/ （名词）元

–How much is the doll? 这个洋娃娃多少钱呀？

–Five dollars. 5元。

百科小贴士

dollar是美国、加拿大、澳大利亚、新加坡等国的货币单位，1元等于100分。

dolphin /'dɒlfin/ （名词）海豚

–Dolphins are friendly animals. 海豚是友善的动物。

–Yes, and they're beautiful, too. 是的，它们也很漂亮。

百科小贴士

海豚主要以小鱼、乌贼、虾、蟹为食。海豚是一种聪明伶俐的哺乳动物。经过训练，能打乒乓球、跳火圈等。海豚有高超的游泳和异乎寻常的潜水本领。据有人测验，海豚的潜水记录是300米深，而人不穿潜水衣，只能下潜20米。它的游泳速度可达每小时40公里，相当于鱼雷快艇的中等速度。

donkey /'dɒŋki/ （名词）驴

–Donkeys are smaller than horses. 驴比马小。

–They're slower, too. 它们也没有马跑得快。

door /dɔː/ （名词）门

–Someone's knocking at the door. 有人在敲门。

–I'll open it. 我去开门。

拓展词汇

doorman 看门人　　doorbell 门铃

用法小贴士

door指由建筑物内通往户外的门，或建筑物内部一室通向另一室的门。gate指院落四周围墙上的门，一般比较结实，带有门栓。

dormitory /'dɔːmɪtri/ （名词）
（口语形式 **dorm**）宿舍
–Where is your dormitory room?
你的宿舍在几层？
–It's on the sixth floor. 在7层。

dough /dəʊ/ （名词）（和好的）
面，面团
–The dough is too dry. 这面团太干了。
–Add a little water, then. 那就加点水吧。

dove /dʌv/ （名词）鸽子
The dove is often used as a symbol of peace. 鸽子常被当作和平的象征。

down /daʊn/ （副词）向下
–Come down, kitty! 小猫，下来！
–No, I don't dare! 不，我不敢！

反义词 up 向上

dragon /'drægən/ （名词）龙
–Were you born in the year of the snake? 你是属蛇的吗？
–No, the year of the dragon. 不是，我属龙。

拓展词汇
dragon boat 龙舟　dragonfly 蜻蜓

draw /drɔː/ （动词）（过去式
drew /druː/, 过去分词 **drawn**
/drɔːn/）画画
–What are you drawing? 你在画什么？
–A tiger. 画一只老虎。

drawing /'drɔːɪŋ/ （名词）画，
图画
–That's a pretty drawing. 这幅画很好看。
–Thank you. I did it myself. 谢谢，是我自己画的。

dream[1] /driːm/ （名词）梦
–Good night. Sweet dreams. 晚安，做个美梦。
–Good night, Mom. 晚安，妈妈。

拓展词汇
daydream 白日梦　bad dream 恶梦

dream[2] /driːm/ （动词）（过去式、过去分词 **dreamed**
–I heard you laugh in your sleep.
我听见你在睡梦中笑。
–Really? Maybe it's because I was dreaming about my best friend.
真的？可能是因为我梦见了我最好的朋友。

dress¹ /dres/ （名词）连衣裙
–You look pretty in your new dress. 你穿这件新连衣裙真漂亮。
–Thank you. My mom made it for me. 谢谢。是我妈妈给我做的。

dress² /dres/ （动词）穿衣
–Can Kelly dress herself? 凯莉会自己穿衣服吗？
–No. She's too little to do that. 不会，她还太小。

drink¹ /drɪŋk/ （名词）饮料
–Would you like a drink? 你想喝点什么吗？
–A glass of water, please. 来杯水吧。

drink² /drɪŋk/ （动词）（过去式 **drank** /dræŋk/，过去分词 **drunk** /drʌŋk/）喝
–I've caught a cold. 我感冒了。
–You should drink lots of water. 你应该多喝水。

drive /draɪv/ （动词）
（过去式 **drove** /drəʊv/，过去分词 **driven** /'drɪvən/）驾驶
Don't drink and drive. 不要酒后驾车。

driver /'draɪvə/ （名词）司机
Drivers must always put safety first.
司机必须随时把安全放在第一位。
拓展词汇
bus driver 公交司机 taxi driver 出租司机

drum /drʌm/ （名词）鼓
Beating the drum and passing the flower is an interesting game. 击鼓传花是个有趣的游戏。

dry /draɪ/ （形容词）（比较级 **drier**，最高级 **driest**）干燥的
–What's the weather like in the desert? 沙漠里的天气是怎样的？
–It's hot and dry. 又热又干。

duck /dʌk/ （名词）鸭子
Ducks are birds, but they can swim better than they can fly. 鸭子是鸟，但它们善于游水，不大会飞。

duckling /'dʌklɪŋ/ （名词）
小鸭
The Ugly Duckling is the most beautiful story I've ever read. 《丑小鸭》是我读过的最美的故事。

during /'djʊərɪŋ/ （介词）在…期间
–You've read so many books! 你读了这么多书啊！
–Yes, I read them during the holiday. 是啊，我在假期中读的。

dust /dʌst/ （名词）尘土
–Everything in this room is covered with dust. 这屋里所有东西都布满灰尘。
–We need to give it a good cleaning. 我们需要好好搞一下卫生。

duty /'djuːti/ （名词）责任
–Who's on duty today? 今天谁值日？
–I am. 是我。

East or west, home is best.

E

each¹ /iːtʃ/ （形容词）每

Each pupil received a gift from the teacher on Children's Day. 儿童节那天，每个学生都从老师那里得到了一份礼物。

each² /iːtʃ/ （代词）每个

–How do you play this game? 这个游戏怎么玩？

–Each of us should cover our eyes and draw a picture. 我们每个人都要蒙上眼睛画幅画。

each other /iːtʃ ˈʌðə/ 互相

Friends should help each other. 朋友应该互相帮助。

eager /ˈiːgə/ （形容词）渴望的

He was eager to see the film. 他极想看那部电影。

eagle /ˈiːgəl/ （名词）鹰

–Eagles have very good eyesight. 鹰的视力非常好。

–Sure. They can see very small animals far away. 是的，它们能看到远处很小的动物。

百科小贴士

鹰属于猛禽，一般不成群出没，喜栖高处，喜食肉类，常见的有苍鹰、雀鹰等。

ear /ɪə/ （名词）耳朵

Elephants have big ears. Rabbits have long ears.
大象的耳朵大，兔子的耳朵长。

拓展词汇

earphone 耳机　　earring 耳环

early¹ /ˈɜːli/ （副词）（比较级 **earlier**，最高级 **earliest**）早

–Do you get up early in the morning? 你早上起得早吗？

–Yes. I also go to bed early at night. 是的。我晚上睡得也早。

反义词 late 晚

early² /ˈɜːli/ （形容词）（比较级 **earlier**，最高级 **earliest**）早的

The early bird catches the worm. 早起的鸟儿有虫吃。

反义词 late 晚的

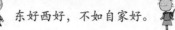
东好西好，不如自家好。

Earth /ɜ:θ/ （名词）地球

Earth moves around the sun. The moon moves around Earth. 地球绕着太阳转，月亮绕着地球转。

拓展词汇

earthquake 地震　earthworm 蚯蚓

百科小贴士

地球是太阳系八大行星之一。天文学家原来认为太阳系有九大行星，后来发现冥王星是个"小个头"，于是在2006年国际天文学联合会大会上将冥王星降为矮行星。

east /i:st/ （名词）东方

The sun rises in the east and sets in the west. 太阳东升西落。

反义词　west 西方

eastern /ˈi:stən/ （形容词）东部的，向东的

–The eastern part of China is lower than the western part. 中国的东部比西部低。
–Oh, that's why many rivers flow from west to east. 哦，那就是为什么许多河都从西往东流。

反义词　west 西部的，向西的

easy /ˈi:zi/ （形容词）（比较级

easier, 最高级 easiest）容易的
–Is English easy to learn? 英语容易学吗？
–Yes, but you need to practice a lot. 容易，但你得多练才行。

反义词　difficult 难的

eat /i:t/ （动词）（过去式 ate /et/, 过去分词 eaten /ˈi:tən/）吃

–I have a stomachache. 我肚子疼。
–Did you eat something bad? 你是不是吃什么不对劲的东西了？

education /ˌedʒʊˈkeɪʃən/ （名词）教育

Education is important for everyone. 教育对每个人都很重要。

egg /eg/ （名词）蛋

–Where do birds come from? 鸟是怎么生出来的？
–From eggs. 从蛋里生出来的。

拓展词汇

eggplant （美）茄子　eggshell 蛋壳

Egypt /ˈi:dʒɪpt/ （名词）埃及

–Egypt is one of the most ancient countries in the world. 埃及是世界上最古老的国家之一。
–Just like China, isn't it? 正如中国一样，是吧？

拓展词汇

Egyptian 埃及的，埃及人的，埃及人

54

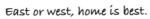 East or west, home is best.

百科小贴士
埃及是世界四大文明古国之一。埃及最有名的是金字塔了，被列为世界七大奇观之一。埃及的金字塔建于4500年以前，是古埃及国王为自己修建的陵墓。埃及人讲阿拉伯语。

用法小贴士
either和too都是"也"的意思。两者区别在于，too用于肯定句，either用于否定句。

eight /eɪt/ （数词）八
–How many legs does a spider have? 蜘蛛有几条腿？
–eight. 8条。

elder /'eldə/ （形容词）年龄较大的
–Do you have any brothers and sisters? 你有兄弟姐妹吗？
–I have an elder sister. 我有一个姐姐。
反义词 younger 年龄较小的

用法小贴士
elder是old的比较级，通常置于名词之前，不与than连用。

eighteen /ˌeɪ'tiːn/ （数词）十八
Most students are eighteen years old when they go to a university. 大多数学生上大学时都是18岁。

eighty /'eɪti/ （数词）八十
–The old man is eighty years old. 这位老人80岁了。
–But he looks much younger. 但他看上去年轻得多。

elephant /'elɪfənt/ （名词）大象
–What's the biggest animal on land? 陆地上最大的动物是什么？
–The elephant. 是大象。

百科小贴士
大象主要分布在非洲和亚洲。由于象牙可以制造珍贵的工艺品，象经常遭到偷猎者的袭击。大象的生育周期较长，因此非常容易灭绝。目前各国为保护象已经禁止象牙交易。

eleven /ɪ'levən/ （数词）十一
–How old are you, Julia? 朱莉娅，你几岁了？
–I'll be eleven in November. 我到11月份就11岁啦。

either /'aɪðə/ （副词）也
–I don't like this dish. 我不喜欢这道菜。
–I don't like it either. It's too hot. 我也不喜欢，太辣了。

e-mail /'iːmeɪl/ （名词）电子邮件
–What's the fastest way to send a letter? 最快的寄信方式是什么？

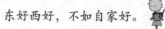
–By e-mail. 通过电子邮件。

拓展词汇

e-mail address 电子邮件地址

百科小贴士

电子邮件是通过联网计算机传递文字及图片信息的方式，几乎可以即刻传递到对方的计算机，并不受距离的影响。

emperor /'empərə/ （名词）皇帝

–Who was the first emperor in China? 中国第一位皇帝是谁？
–Qin Shihuang. 秦始皇。

百科小贴士

秦始皇是中国历史上第一位专制帝王。公元前221年秦统一全国后，秦王嬴政决定兼采三皇之"皇"与五帝之"帝"，号称"皇帝"。嬴政自称"始皇帝"，其后世依次称二世、三世以至万世。不过秦朝在二世统治时就灭亡了。

empty /'empti/ （形容词）（比较级 **emptier**，最高级 **emptiest**）空的
–Is the bottle empty? 这瓶子是空的吗？
–No, it's full of air. 不是，里面充满空气。

enemy /'enəmi/ （名词）（复数 **enemies**）敌人
–Cats are the natural enemies of mice. 猫是老鼠的天敌。
–I see. So birds are the natural enemies of insects. 我明白了，那么鸟就是虫子的天敌了。

England /'ɪŋglənd/ （名词）英格兰

England is famous for its beautiful villages. 英格兰以其美丽的乡村著称。

百科小贴士

英格兰是英国的一部分，不是一个国家，英国全称为大不列颠及北爱尔兰联合王国。

English¹ /'ɪŋglɪʃ/ （形容词）英格兰的，英国的
–Do you know what a typical English breakfast is? 你知道典型的英式早餐是什么样的吗？
–Yes. It includes eggs, bacon, and toast. 知道，英式早餐包括鸡蛋、熏肉，还有烤面包。

English² /'ɪŋglɪʃ/ （名词）英语，英格兰人
–Learning English is very useful. 学习英语很有用。
–Yes. It is used in many parts of the world. 是啊，世界上很多地方都说英语。

East or west, home is best.

enjoy /ɪn'dʒɔɪ/ （动词）喜欢

做…，从…得到乐趣

–What sport do you like? 你喜欢什
么运动？
–I enjoy playing basketball. 我喜欢
打篮球。

enough /ɪ'nʌf/ （形容词）足够的

–Is this bag big enough? 这包够大
吗？
–Oh, more than enough. I need a
smaller one. 啊，太大了。我需要
个小点儿的。

envelope /'envələʊp/ （名词）

信封

–How do I mail this letter? 我怎样
从邮局寄信？
–You need to put a stamp on the
envelope. 你需要在信封上贴张邮票。

environment /ɪn'vaɪərənmənt/

（名词）环境

A good home environment is
important for children. 良好的家庭
环境对孩子很重要。

Europe /'jʊərəp/ （名词）欧洲

Europe is the birthplace of Western
culture. 欧洲是西方文化的发源地。

拓展词汇

European 欧洲的，欧洲人

evening /'iːvnɪŋ/ （名词）傍晚

The sun rises in the morning and
sets in the evening. 太阳早晨升起，
傍晚落下。

every /'evri/ （形容词）每个

–Is English taught in your school?
你们学校教英语吗？
–Yes, it is taught in every school in
this area. 是的，我们这个地区每个
学校都教英语。

everybody /'evribɒdi/ （代词）

每人

Come on, everybody! Let's sing
and dance together! 来，大家一起
唱歌跳舞吧！

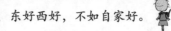 东好西好，不如自家好。

everyday /'evrideɪ/ （形容词）

日常的

The Internet has become a part of our everyday life. 因特网已经成了我们日常生活的一部分。

everyone /'evriwʌn/ （代词）

每人

–Is everyone here? 大家都到了吗？

–No, Bill hasn't come yet. 没有，比尔还没到。

everything /'evrɪθɪŋ/ （代词）

所有事物

–The flood washed away everything. 洪水冲走了一切。

–We'll have to rebuild our home. 我们得重建家园。

exam /ɪg'zæm/ （名词）考试

–Mom, I've passed all my exams! 妈妈，我所有的考试都通过了！

–Oh, really? Congratulations! 哦，是吗？祝贺你！

example /ɪg'zɑːmpəl/ （名词）

例子

–Can you give an example of an insect? 你能举一个昆虫的例子吗？

–Ants, for example. 例如蚂蚁。

exciting /ɪk'saɪtɪŋ/ （形容词）

令人兴奋的

–Our school football team has won the match. 我们的校足球队赢了比赛。

–What exciting news! 真是激动人心的消息！

excuse /ɪk'skjuːz/ （动词）

–Excuse me. What time is it? 劳驾，请问几点了？

–It's a quarter to seven. 6点45。

exercise /'eksəsaɪz/ （名词）

1. 运动

–Do you do any exercises? 你做什么运动吗？

–Yes, I run for twenty minutes every morning. 是的，我每天早上跑20分钟。

2. 练习

–What's today's math homework? 今天的数学作业是什么？

–Exercise 2 and exercise 3 on page 25. 第25页的练习2和练习3。

拓展词汇

exercise book 练习本

expensive /ɪk'spensɪv/ （形容词）昂贵的

–This pen is too expensive. 这支笔太贵了。

–The blue one is cheaper. Do you like it? 这个蓝色的便宜一些，你喜欢吗？

反义词　cheap　便宜的

explain /ɪk'spleɪn/ （动词）解释

–Can you explain the meaning of this word? 你能解释这个词的意思吗？

–No. Let's look it up in the dictionary. 不能，让我们查词典吧。

eye /aɪ/ （名词）眼睛

Katy has big eyes and Linda has small eyes. 凯蒂是大眼睛，琳达是小眼睛。

拓展词汇

eyeball 眼珠　eyeglasses 眼镜

百科小贴士

现在学生近视眼的比例越来越高，一定要从小注意用眼卫生。读写姿势要正确，如不要在走路或乘车时看书，不要躺着看书，不要在暗弱的光线或直射的阳光下看书，不要歪着头写字。读写一小时左右要让眼睛休息片刻。

A friend in need is a friend indeed.

F

fable /ˈfeɪbəl/ （名词）寓言
–I like *Aesop's Fables*. They're so
interesting. 我喜欢读《伊索寓言》，
可有趣了。
–They teach us many things, too.
那些故事也教给我们许多东西。

face /feɪs/ （名词）脸
–Human faces are different from
each other. 人类的脸各不相同。
–This means we can tell one
person from another. 这样我们就
能把一个人与另一个人区分开。

拓展词汇
make faces 做鬼脸
pull a long face 闷闷不乐

fact /fækt/ （名词）事实
Facts speak louder than words.
事实胜于雄辩。

factory /ˈfæktri/ （名词）（复数
factories）工厂
–There's a car factory near my
home. 我家附近有一个汽车厂。
–Can we go and see how cars are
made? 我们能去看看汽车是怎么造
出来的吗?

拓展词汇
factory worker 工厂工人

fail /feɪl/ （动词）
1. 失败
He failed to arrive on time. 他没能
按时赶到。
2. 不及格
–You look unhappy. What
happened? 你看起来闷闷不乐的，
怎么了?
–I failed the math exam. 我数学考
试没及格。

fair /feə/ （形容词）（比较级
fairer，最高级 **fairest**）（头发）
金色的，（皮肤）白皙的
Many white people have blue eyes
and fair hair. 大多数白种人都长着
蓝眼睛和金色头发。

fairy tale /ˈfeəri teɪl/ （名词）
童话
Most fairy tales have happy end-
ings. 大多数童话都有幸福的结尾。

fall /fɔ:l/（动词）（过去式 fell /fel/，过去分词 fallen /'fɔ:lən/）

1. 落下

The leaves of many trees fall in autumn. 许多树在秋天都会落叶。

2. 跌倒，摔倒

–What's happened? 你怎么了？

–I fell off my bike and broke my arm. 我从自行车上摔下来，把胳膊摔断了。

family /'fæmɪli/（名词）（复数 families）家，家庭

–How many people are there in your family? 你家有几口人？

–Three: Father, Mother, and me. 3口：爸爸、妈妈和我。

用法小贴士

family表示一个整体时视为单数，但用来表示家庭成员时则视为复数。例如：All my family love animals.（我们全家都爱动物。）

family name /'fæmɪli neɪm/（名词）姓

His name is Bill Gates. Bill is his first name. Gates is his family name. 他叫比尔·盖茨。比尔是名，盖茨是姓。

百科小贴士

英语人名顺序和汉语人名顺序相反。英语人名先是名（first name，given name 或 Christian name），然后是姓（family name 或 surname）。

famous /'feɪməs/（形容词）著名的

–Who is the most famous monkey in China? 中国最著名的猴子是哪个？

–It's Monkey King Sun Wukong! 是猴王孙悟空呀！

fan /fæn/（名词）

1. 扇子，风扇

–It's so hot. Why not turn the fan on? 太热了，为什么不把电扇打开呢？

–I've got a bad cold. 我得了重感冒。

拓展词汇

electric fan 电风扇　ceiling fan 吊扇

百科小贴士

扇子在我国已有三四千年的历史了。传说原始社会末期的舜，为了寻找贤人辅佐自己，曾亲自制扇作为赠品。最早的扇子有羽毛制和竹子制的两种。到了汉代，作为摇风用的扇子就较为普遍了。

2. 追星族，…迷

–Do you know Yao Ming? 你知道姚明吗？

–Of course. I'm a big fan of his. 当然知道啦，我是他的球迷。

拓展词汇

football fan 足球迷

A friend in need is a friend indeed.

fantastic /fæn'tæstɪk/ （形容词）棒极的，极好的

–Look! There's a roller coaster over there. 看！那边有过山车！
–Fantastic! Let's go and take a ride! 太棒了！咱们去坐吧。

far¹ /fɑː/ （形容词）（比较级 farther/'fɑːðə/或 further /fɜːðə/, 最高级 farthest /'fɑːðɪst/或 furthest /'fɜːðɪst/）远的

–Is the sun far from the earth? 太阳离地球很遥远吗？
–Very far indeed, or it would be much hotter on the earth. 的确很远，不然的话地球上会热多了。

反义词　near 近的

far² /fɑː/ （副词）（比较级 farther/'fɑːðə/或 further/'fɜːðə/, 最高级 farthest /'fɑːðɪst/或 furthest /'fɜːðɪst/）远，遥远地

–Can I go for a walk, Mom? 妈妈，我去散散步行吗？
–OK. Don't go too far. It's getting dark. 好的，但别走太远，天快黑了。

farm /fɑːm/ （名词）农场，养殖场

Farmers plant crops on the farm. 农民在农场种庄稼。

拓展词汇
chicken farm 养鸡场　　pig farm 养猪场
farm worker 农场工人

farmer /'fɑːmə/ （名词）农场主，农民

These days many farmers come to work in cities. 现在许多农民进城工作。

fast¹ /fɑːst/ （形容词）快的，快速的

–Mike is the fastest runner in his class. 迈克是他班上跑得最快的。
–I'm not surprised. Look at his long legs. 这不意外，看看他的长腿。

反义词　slow 慢的
拓展词汇
fast food 快餐

fast² /fɑːst/ （副词）快地，快速地

The hare ran faster, but the tortoise won the race. 兔子跑得更快，但是乌龟却赢得了比赛。

患难见真情。

fat /fæt/ （形容词）（比较级 fatter，最高级 fattest）肥胖的

–You'll get fat if you eat too much chocolate. 如果你吃过多的巧克力就会发胖。

–OK. This is the last piece. 好吧，这是最后一块。

反义词 thin 瘦的

用法小贴士

fat是最常用的指人肥胖的形容词，但含有贬义，因此用这个词不太礼貌。要想显得礼貌，可以用large。

father /ˈfɑːðə/ （名词）父亲，爸爸

–My father is a doctor. 我爸爸是个医生。

–Oh, he must be very clever. 哦，他一定很聪明。

用法小贴士

父亲一词在口语中常用dad，儿语常用daddy, papa等。

Father Christmas /ˌfɑːðə ˈkrɪsməs/ （名词）圣诞老人

Father Christmas has a long white beard and is dressed in a red suit. 圣诞老人留着长长的白胡子，穿着红外套。

百科小贴士

圣诞老人的故乡在芬兰，传说在圣诞节时会乘坐鹿拉的雪橇给孩子们送去礼物。圣诞节前，孩子们在睡觉前将长筒袜挂在床头或壁炉旁，以迎接圣诞老人的礼物。

Father's Day /ˈfɑːðəz deɪ/ （名词）父亲节

–It's Father's Day again. 又到父亲节了。

–I have a special gift for my father. 我给爸爸准备了一份特殊的礼物。

百科小贴士

1910年6月19日，华盛顿州斯波坎（Spokane）的人们庆祝了世界上第一个父亲节。当时，凡是父亲已故的人都佩戴一朵白玫瑰，父亲在世的人则佩戴红玫瑰。这种习俗一直流传至今。1924年，父亲节成为美国全国性的节日。1966年，美国总统签署总统令，宣布将每年6月的第3个星期天定为父亲节。全世界有二十多个国家通过教堂仪式、送卡和礼物来纪念父亲节。

fault /fɔːlt/ （名词）

1. 过错，过失

–Look! You've spoiled my painting! 看，你把我的画都弄坏了！

–I'm really sorry. It's all my fault. 真对不起，都是我的错。

2. 缺点，毛病

Everyone has faults. 每个人都有缺点。

favorite /ˈfeɪvərɪt/ （形容词）最喜爱的

–Red is my favorite color. What's yours? 我最喜欢红色，你呢？

–I like green best. 我最喜欢绿色。

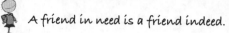

fear¹ /fɪə/ （名词）害怕，恐惧

There's a look of fear in Harry's eyes. 哈里眼里有一丝恐惧。

fear² /fɪə/ （动词）害怕，恐惧

It's quite safe; there is nothing to fear. 很安全，没什么好害怕的。

feather /ˈfeðə/ （名词）羽毛

Birds of a feather flock together. 物以类聚，人以群分。

February /ˈfebjuəri/ （名词）二月

–There are 28 or 29 days in February. 2月有28天或29天。

–Yes, it's the shortest month in a year. 对，2月是一年中最短的月份。

百科小贴士

February 是由拉丁文 Februarius（即净化节）演变而来。2月是古罗马年历的12月。岁末，罗马人要举行净化赎罪的宗教仪式，以赎一年之罪，净化自己的灵魂。

2月是比较特殊的一个月，2月有28天的那一年叫平年，有29天的那一年叫闰年。

feed /fiːd/ （动词）（过去式、过去分词 **fed** /fed/ ）喂养，饲养

–How often do you feed your puppy a day? 你的小狗一天喂几次？

–Four times a day. 一天4次。

feel /fiːl/ （动词）（过去式、过去分词 **felt** /felt/ ）

1. 感觉

–Are you feeling better? 你感觉好点儿了吗？

–Much better. Thank you. 好多了，谢谢你。

2. 摸，触摸

Mom, feel this stone. Isn't it smooth? 妈妈，你摸摸这块石头，很光滑吧？

female /ˈfiːmeɪl/ （形容词）女性的，雌性的

This school has more female students than male students. 这个学校女生比男生多。

fence /fens/ （名词）栅栏，篱笆

I was talking to my neighbor across the garden fence. 我和邻居在隔着花园篱笆谈话。

festival /ˈfestɪvəl/ （名词）节日

–The Spring Festival is a traditional Chinese festival. 春节是中国的传统节日。

–It's the most important holiday of the year. 它是一年中最重要的节日。

拓展词汇

Dragon Boat Festival 端午节
Mid-autumn Festival 中秋节

fetch /fetʃ/ （动词）取来，拿来

–Can you fetch my coat from the dry cleaner's? 你能把我的大衣从干洗店取回来吗？

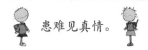

–Sure. I'll stop by on my way home. 当然，我回家路上去取。

用法小贴士

bring指把某物带来，fetch指去取某物并把它带回来，take指把某物拿走。

fever /ˈfiːvə/ （名词）发热，发烧

–Tom has a fever. 汤姆发烧了。
–Let's take him to the hospital. 咱们送他去医院吧。

few /fjuː/ （形容词）很少，几乎没有

–Are there many fish in the pond? 池塘里鱼多吗？
–Very few. 很少。

用法小贴士

few和little是"几乎没有"的意思，a few和a little是"有一些"的意思。few和a few用于修饰可数名词，如a few books（几本书）。little和a little用于修饰不可数名词，如a little milk（一点儿牛奶）。

field /fiːld/ （名词）田地，田野

–Where do farmers work? 农民在哪里工作？
–They plant crops in the fields. 他们在地里种庄稼。

拓展词汇

rice field 稻田   wheat field 麦田

fierce /fɪəs/ （形容词）凶猛的，凶恶的

The fierce dog chased away the thief. 凶猛的狗赶走了小偷。

fifteen /ˌfɪfˈtiːn/ （数词）十五

–There are all together fifteen monkeys in the tree. 树上共有15只猴子。
–Really? Let me count them one by one. 是吗？我一只只数数看吧。

fifty /ˈfɪfti/ （数词）五十

The classroom is too small for fifty students. 这教室太小，坐不下50位学生。

fight /faɪt/ （动词）（过去式、过去分词fought /fɔːt/）打架，争斗

Two dogs are fighting over a bone. 两条狗正在争抢一块骨头。

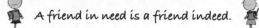

figure /ˈfɪgə/ （名词）数字

She's good with figures, so she did well on the math test. 她很擅长数字，因此她的数学考得很好。

拓展词汇

Arabic figures 阿拉伯数字
double figures 两位数
three figures 三位数

fill /fɪl/ （动词）装满，注满，填满

Please fill this glass for me. 请把这个杯子给我倒满。

film /fɪlm/ （名词）电影

–Do you like watching films? 你喜欢看电影吗？
–Yes, but I don't have time to go to the cinema often. 喜欢，但我没有时间经常去看。

拓展词汇

film director 电影导演 film industry 电影业 film star 电影明星

百科小贴士

电影诞生于1895年的法国。一百多年以来，电影的形态发生了很大的变化，从无声到有声，从黑白到彩色。中国第一部电影诞生于1905年，是一部默声片，名叫《定军山》。

final /ˈfaɪnəl/ （形容词）最后的，最终的

–When are we taking the final exams? 我们什么时候期末考试？
–Next week. We need to start reviewing our lessons now. 下周，我们现在就该开始复习功课了。

finally /ˈfaɪnəli/ （副词）最后

–Have you found your football? 你找到你的足球了吗？

–Yes. I finally found it under the bed. 找到了，我最终在床底下找到的。

find /faɪnd/ （动词）（过去式、过去分词found /faʊnd/）找到，发现

–Have you found your keys? 你找到钥匙了吗？
–Yes, I found them in my shopping bag. 找到了，在购物袋里。

用法小贴士

look for表示"寻找"，强调动作，而find则表示"找到"，强调结果。

fine /faɪn/ （形容词）

1. 晴朗的
If it's fine tomorrow, we can go for a picnic. 如果明天天气好，我们可以去野餐。

拓展词汇

fine day/weather 晴天

2. 健康的
I had a cold last week, but I'm fine now. 我上星期得了感冒，但现在好了。

finger /ˈfɪŋgə/ （名词）手指

–What's wrong with your finger? 你的手指怎么了？
–I cut it by accident. It really hurts. 我不小心把它割伤了，真疼啊。

患难见真情。

fingernail 手指甲　　forefinger 食指
little finger 小指　　middle finger 中指
ring finger 无名指

指尖的神经末梢非常密集，是人体触觉的中心，手指表面的指纹进一步增强了其敏感度。盲人可以用手指读盲文。

fire /faɪə/ （名词）火

There is no smoke without fire. 无火不起烟，无风不起浪。

fire alarm 火警警报　　fire exit 安全出口
fire station 消防站　　firefly 萤火虫

人类使用火的历史可追溯到几十万年以前。据考古记载，50万年前，北京猿人聚集的周口店龙骨山北坡的洞穴里留下了厚厚的灰烬积层、木炭和烧黑的兽骨。学会使用火既是人类的一个重大进步，也为人类社会文明创造了前提条件。

first /fɜːst/ （形容词）第一的

–Can you tell me the first month of the year in English? 你知道1月用英语怎么说吗？
–Sure! It's January. 当然！是January。

反义词　last 最后的

first lady 第一夫人

first floor /ˌfɜːst ˈflɔː/ （名词）

（英国）二楼，（美国）一楼，底楼
–"First floor" means the "ground floor" in American English. "first floor" 在美国英语中指"底楼"。
–It means the "floor above the ground floor" in British English. 在英国英语中它指"二楼"。

first name /ˈfɜːst neɪm/

（名词）名
–Bill, do you know what your first name means? 比尔，你知道你的名字是什么意思吗？
–Yes, my father told me Bill means someone who looks after you. 知道，爸爸告诉我Bill的含义是"保护你的人"。

fish¹ /fɪʃ/ （名词）（复数 fish）

鱼
–Fish cannot live without water. 鱼离了水就不能生存。
–Just as land animals cannot live without air. 就像陆地动物离了空气就不能生存一样。

fish² /fɪʃ/ （动词）钓鱼

My grandfather goes fishing every Sunday. 我爷爷每周日都去钓鱼。

A friend in need is a friend indeed.

five /faɪv/ （数词）五
We have two hands. Each hand has five fingers. 我们有两只手, 每只手有5根手指。

flag /flæg/ （名词）旗
–Can you see the top of the mountain? 你能看见山顶吗?
–Yes. A red flag is flying there. 能, 那儿有一面红旗在飘扬。

flat¹ /flæt/ （形容词）（比较级 **flatter**, 最高级 **flattest**）平（坦）的
City streets are usually flat and straight. 城市街道一般都是平坦、笔直的。

flat² /flæt/ （名词）公寓
–How many bedrooms does your flat have? 你的公寓有几个房间?
–Two bedrooms. 有两间卧室。

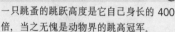

用法小贴士
在美国英语中用 apartment 表示公寓。

flea /fliː/ （名词）跳蚤
The flea is the champion of the high jump in the animal world. 跳蚤是动物界的跳高冠军。

拓展词汇
flea market 跳蚤市场, 旧货市场

百科小贴士
一只跳蚤的跳跃高度是它自己身长的 400 倍, 当之无愧是动物界的跳高冠军。

flood /flʌd/ （名词）洪水
–There's a big flood in the south. 南方发大洪水了。
–But it's very dry in the north. 而北方又这么干旱。

floor /flɔː/ （名词）
1. 地板
–The floor is made of wood. 这地板是木头做的。
–It feels cool in summer and warm in winter. 它让人在夏天感觉凉爽, 冬天感觉暖和。
2. （楼）层
–This building has 28 floors. 这座楼有28层。
–It's the highest building in our city. 这是我们市最高的建筑物。

flour /flaʊə/ （名词）面粉
–What is bread made from? 面包是用什么做的?
–It's usually made from wheat flour. 一般是用面粉做的。

用法小贴士
flour是不可数名词, 一般指面粉, 也可指米粉、玉米粉, 或其他粉状物。

flower /flaʊə/ （名词）花
–What is Grandma doing in the garden? 奶奶在花园里干什么?
–She's watering the flowers. 她在给花浇水。

68

follow /'fɒləu/ （动词）跟随
–Excuse me. Where is the library?
打扰一下，请问图书馆在哪儿？
–Follow me. I'll show you the way.
跟我来，我告诉你怎么走。

food /fuːd/ （名词）食物
–What's your favorite food? 你最喜
欢吃什么？
–I like seafood very much. 我非常
喜欢海鲜。

拓展词汇

flowerbed 花坛　　flower garden 花园
flowerpot 花盆

fly¹ /flaɪ/ （动词）（第三人称单数
flies，过去式 **flew** /fluː/，过去分
词 **flown** /fləʊn/，现在分词 **flying**）
飞（行）
–Birds can fly. 鸟会飞翔。
–People can fly, too. We fly by airplane. 人也会飞，我们乘飞机飞行。

fly² /flaɪ/ （名词）（复数 **flies**）苍蝇
Flies live in dirty places. 苍蝇生活
在肮脏的地方。

百科小贴士

苍蝇的6只脚上各有一个"爪"，在爪的基
部有被茸毛遮住的爪垫盘。当苍蝇爬动时，
脚部茸毛尖处分泌出一种具有黏附力的液
体，因而苍蝇能在光滑的表面爬行。苍蝇
带有大量各式各样的细菌，是一种对人有
害的昆虫。

fog /fɒg/ （名词）雾
The fog is very heavy here. Traffic
has come to a stop. 这里雾太大了，
交通都中断了。

百科小贴士

深秋初冬是大雾经常发生的季节，雾的形
成需要具备两个基本条件：一是近地面层
的水汽丰富；二是晚上晴空或云层较薄，
早晚温差大，风力小。

拓展词汇

Chinese food 中餐
Western food 西餐

fool /fuːl/ （名词）傻瓜
Don't be a fool! You'll get hurt if
you jump from the tree. 别做傻事，
你从树上跳下来会受伤的。

拓展词汇

make a fool of oneself 出洋相
make a fool of somebody 让某人出洋相

foolish /'fuːlɪʃ/ （形容词）
愚蠢的
Even clever people may do foolish
things sometimes. 即便是聪明人有
时也会做蠢事。

反义词　clever 聪明的

foot /fʊt/（名词）(复数 **feet** /fiːt/)
脚
–Do you go to school by bike or on foot? 你是骑车还是走路上学？
–On foot. I live near the school. 步行，我住得离学校很近。

拓展词汇

footbridge 人行桥

football /'fʊtbɔːl/（名词）足球
–Do you like football? 你喜欢足球吗？
–Of course! I'm a member of our school's football team. 当然啦！我是我们学校足球队的队员。

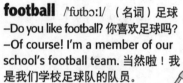

用法小贴士

football 在美国英语中指橄榄球，美国人用soccer表示足球，soccer在英国英语中也指足球。

for /fɔː/（介词）为了，给
–I've bought some flowers for my mom. 我给妈妈买了些花儿。
–Oh, it's Mother's Day today. 哦，今天是母亲节。

foreign /'fɒrɪn/（形容词）
外国的
–Can you speak any foreign languages? 你会讲外语吗？
–I can speak a little English. 我会讲一点儿英语。

foreigner /'fɒrɪnə/（名词）
外国人
–There are many foreigners in Beijing. 北京有很多外国人。
–Yes. I have a foreign friend. Her name's Jenny. 对，我有一个外国朋友，她叫珍妮。

forest /'fɒrɪst/（名词）森林
–Forests are home to many animals and plants. 森林是许多动植物的家园。
–We must take care of our forests. 因此我们必须爱护森林。

forever /fə'revə/（副词）永远
Nobody lives forever. 没有人能够长生不死。

forget /fə'get/（动词）(过去式 **forgot** /fə'gɒt/, 过去分词 **forgotten** /fə'gɒtən/, 现在分词 **forgetting**)
忘记
–I'm sorry I've forgotten your name. 很抱歉，我忘了你的名字。
–I'm John. We met on the first day of school. 我叫约翰，我们在开学第一天见过面。

反义词　remember 记住

fork /fɔːk/（名词）叉子
–Knives and forks are for Western food. 吃西餐用刀叉。
–Chopsticks are for Chinese food. 吃中餐用筷子。

患难见真情。

百科小贴士
中西方所用餐具不同与饮食习惯有关。西餐以肉食为主，惯用刀叉。中国人主食是米饭或馒头，副食以蔬菜为主，佐以少量鱼肉，主副食都可用筷子。

forty /ˈfɔːti/ （数词）四十
–Dad, how many hours do you work every day? 爸爸，你每天工作几小时？
–Eight hours. That's forty hours a week. 8小时，也就是每周40小时。

four /fɔː/ （数词）四
–How many seasons are there in a year? 一年有几个季节？
–Four seasons: spring, summer, autumn, and winter. 一年有四季：春夏秋冬。

fourteen /ˌfɔːˈtiːn/ （数词）十四
Fourteen divided by seven is two. 14除以7等于2。

fox /fɒks/ （名词）（复数 foxes）狐狸
–Foxes are clever animals. 狐狸是聪明的动物。
–I think they are beautiful, too. 我觉得它们也很漂亮。

France /frɑːns/ （名词）法国
–What's France famous for? 法国以什么著称？
–Wine. 葡萄酒。

百科小贴士
法国位于欧洲西部，其标志性建筑是埃菲尔铁塔。

拓展词汇
French 法国的，法国人的，法语，法国人 French fries （美）炸薯条

free /friː/ （形容词）
1. 自由的
Don't keep the birds in the cage. Set them free. 别把鸟关在笼子里，把它们放了吧。

2. 免费的
–When shall we go to the museum? 我们什么时候去参观博物馆？
–How about Sunday? It's free for students. 星期天怎么样？那天对学生免费。

fresh /freʃ/ （形容词）新鲜的
–These vegetables are really fresh. 这些蔬菜真新鲜。
–They'll be good for making salad. 用它们做色拉不错。

拓展词汇
fresh air 新鲜空气　freshwater 淡水

Friday /ˈfraɪdeɪ/ （名词）星期五
–When is the English test? 我们什么时候考英语？
–Next Friday. 下周五。

fridge /frɪdʒ/ （名词）冰箱
We can keep food longer in the fridge. 用冰箱保存食物时间长些。

71

A friend in need is a friend indeed.

friend /frend/ （名词）朋友
A friend in need is a friend indeed.
患难见真情。

friendly /'frendli/ （形容词）
（比较级 **friendlier**，最高级
friendliest）友好的
–What do you think of Mary?
你觉得玛丽怎么样？
–She is beautiful, honest,
and friendly. 她漂亮、诚实，
待人友好。

frog /frɒg/ （名词）青蛙
Frogs eat insects and protect the
crops. 青蛙吃害虫，保护庄稼。

百科小贴士
一只青蛙一年能够消灭各类害虫一万多只，
大约能够保护15万公斤庄稼免遭虫害。

from /frɒm/ （介词）从…
–How long does it take from your
home to school? 从你家到学校需
要多少时间？
–It takes ten minutes by bus and
fifteen minutes by bike. 坐公共汽
车要10分钟，骑自行车要15分钟。

front /frʌnt/ （名词）前面
–Shorter students sit at the front of
the classroom. 个子矮些的学生坐
在教室前面。

–Taller ones sit at the back. 高一些
的坐在后面。

fruit /fruːt/ （名词）水果
–Is a tomato a fruit or a vegetable?
西红柿是水果还是蔬菜？
–It's a fruit, but we eat it like a
vegetable. 西红柿是一种水果，
我们把它当蔬菜吃。

百科小贴士
水果含维生素较多，另外还富含胡萝卜素、
糖分、纤维素。

拓展词汇
fruitcake 水果蛋糕　　fruit juice 果汁
fruit salad 水果色拉

full /fʊl/ （形容词）
1. 满的
The pond is full of water after the
rain. 下过雨后，池塘里蓄满了水。
2. 饱的
–Would you like a little more rice?
你要不要再来点儿米饭？
–No, thanks. I'm full. 不用，谢谢。
我饱了。
反义词　hungry 饿的

fun /fʌn/ （名词）乐趣
–Studying can be fun. 学习可以充
满乐趣。
–I agree. But you've got to know
how to study. 我同意，但你得知道
怎样学习才行。

funny /'fʌni/ （形容词）（比较级
funnier，最高级 **funniest**）滑稽的，
好玩的

患难见真情。

–Tom, don't make funny faces in class. 汤姆，上课的时候别做滑稽的鬼脸。

future /ˈfjuːtʃə/ （名词）未来
–What do you think cars will be like in the future? 你觉得未来的汽车会是什么样？
–Maybe they will be driven by computers. 也许会靠电脑驾驶。

Great hopes make a great man.

G

game /geɪm/ （名词）

1. 游戏
–What kind of game do you like playing? 你喜欢玩什么样的游戏？
–I like to play hide-and-seek. 我喜欢玩捉迷藏。
2. 运动（项目），比赛
–Do you take part in any sports games? 你参加什么运动项目吗？
–No, but I like watching them. 不，但我喜欢观看体育比赛。

拓展词汇
Olympic Games 奥运会

garage /'gærɑːʒ/ （名词）车库
–Dad, can I put my bike in the garage, too? 爸爸，我能把自行车也放到车库里吗？
–Of course you can. 当然可以啦。

garbage /'gɑːbɪdʒ/ （名词）
垃圾，废物
–Where can I throw the garbage? 哪儿可以扔垃圾？
–There's a garbage can over there. 那边有个垃圾箱。

拓展词汇
garbage truck 垃圾车

用法小贴士
garbage 为美国英语，英国英语用rubbish。

百科小贴士
垃圾会污染大气、水和土壤，对人们的健康构成威胁。垃圾处理需要大量资金投入，而每个人举手之劳，都可减少垃圾，如垃圾分类、废物利用、尽量不用一次性商品等。

garden /'gɑːdən/ （名词）花园
–Have you ever been to Suzhou? 你去过苏州吗？
–Yes. It's a beautiful garden city. 去过，苏州是一个美丽的园林城市。

百科小贴士
中国园林在世界园林发展史上与法国园林和阿拉伯园林三足鼎立。中国园林在世界建筑史上是延续历史最长、分布地域最广的艺术体系之一。中国园艺模拟中国的山水画，艺术化地再现大自然的景色。

garlic /'gɑːlɪk/ （名词）大蒜
–Mom, why do you put garlic in these dishes? 妈妈，你为什么要在菜里放大蒜？
–To make them taste better. 这样味道更好啊。

百科小贴士
吃蒜能够杀菌解毒，有益健康，但不是吃得越多越好。大量食用大蒜对眼睛有刺激作用，而且不宜空腹食用。吃完大蒜后喝

一杯咖啡、牛奶或绿茶，可以消除口中的大蒜味儿。

gas /gæs/ （名词）（复数 gases 或 gasses）气体，煤气
–Do you have a gas stove in your house? 你家里有煤气炉吗？
–Yes. We also use gas to heat our water. 有，我们还用煤气烧水洗澡。

拓展词汇

gas mask 防毒面具　gas station（美）加油站　gas lamp 煤气灯

gate /geɪt/ （名词）大门，入口
–Where shall we meet tomorrow morning? 我们明天早晨在哪里集合？
–At the park gate. 在公园门口。

拓展词汇

gatekeeper 看门人

gather /'gæðə/ （动词）
1. 聚集
When tiny water drops in the air gather together, they form clouds. 空气中的微小水滴聚集起来就形成了云。
2. 采集
–What is Julia doing in the garden? 朱莉娅在花园里做什么？
–She's gathering strawberries. 她在采草莓。

general /'dʒenrəl/ （名词）将军
A general directs battles, while soldiers fight battles. 将军指挥战斗，士兵参加战斗。

gentleman /'dʒentəlmən/ （名词）（复数 gentlemen）绅士，先生
Good morning, ladies and gentlemen, welcome to our school. 早上好，女士们，先生们，欢迎来到我们学校。

geography /dʒi'ɒgrəfi/ （名词）地理
–We have learned to read maps in our geography class. 我们在地理课上学会看地图了。
–Then tell me the position of our city. 那你告诉我咱们城市的位置。

Germany /'dʒɜːməni/ （名词）德国
–Is Germany in the middle of Europe? 德国在欧洲中部吗？
–Yes, it's to the east of France. 是的，它在法国东边。

拓展词汇

German 德国的，德国人的，德国人，德语

百科小贴士

德国全称德意志联邦共和国，不少世界知名作家、诗人、哲学家、音乐大师都出自德国，如歌德、席勒、马克思、恩格斯、贝多芬、巴赫等。

get /get/ （动词）（过去式、过去分词 got /gɒt/，现在分词 getting）
得到

–You look very happy. 你看上去很高兴。
–Yes, got an A on the exam. 是的，我考试得了优。

拓展词汇

get onto 上（车）　get off 下（车）
get up 起床

ghost /gəʊst/ （名词）幽灵，鬼魂

–Are there really ghosts in the world? 世上真的有鬼魂吗？
–I don't think so. 我想没有。

giant /'dʒaɪənt/ （名词）巨人

Elephants are the giants of land animals. 大象是陆地动物中的巨人。

gift /gɪft/ （名词）礼物

–Did you get any gifts for your birthday? 你过生日收到礼物了吗？
–Oh, yes. I got quite a few. 啊，是的，收到不少呢。

ginger /'dʒɪndʒə/ （名词）姜

–I don't like the taste of ginger. 我不喜欢姜的味道。

–Neither do I. 我也不喜欢。

百科小贴士

姜是中餐常用的调料，原产于东南亚一带，开黄绿色花。姜经过泡制还可以作中药材。

giraffe /dʒɪ'rɑːf/ （名词）长颈鹿

–Giraffes are the tallest animals in the world. 长颈鹿是世界上最高的动物。
–They have very long necks. 它们的脖子特别长。

百科小贴士

长颈鹿是生活在非洲的反刍类哺乳动物，身高可达 5 米，以非洲草原上鲜嫩的树叶为食。

girl /gɜːl/ （名词）女孩

–Look at the girl next to Alice. They're very much alike. 看艾丽斯旁边的那个小女孩，她们长得真像。
–She's Alice's twin sister. 她是艾丽斯的孪生妹妹。

give /gɪv/ （动词）（过去式 gave /geɪv/, 过去分词 given /'gɪvən/）给，传递

–Tomorrow is Sam's birthday. 明天是萨姆的生日。
–I'll give him a basketball as a present. 我要送他一个篮球作礼物。

拓展词汇

give in 让步　give up 放弃

glad /glæd/ （形容词）高兴的

–Hi, Tom! This is Kate. 汤姆，你好。这是凯特。
–Glad to meet you, Kate. 很高兴认识你，凯特。

glass /glɑːs/ （名词）

1. 玻璃

–Glass is an important building material. 玻璃是重要的建筑材料。

–Yes, we use it in windows. 是的，我们用它来做窗户。

2.（复数 glasses）玻璃杯

–Would you like a glass of juice? 来杯果汁好吗？

–No, thank you. Please give me a glass of water. 不，谢谢。请给我一杯水。

glasses /ˈglɑːsɪz/ （名词）眼镜

–Where did I put my glasses? 我把眼镜放哪儿了？

–Oh, Grandpa. They're hanging around your neck. 哦，爷爷，就在你脖子上挂着呢。

拓展词汇

sunglasses 太阳镜，墨镜

用法小贴士

一副眼镜的说法为 a pair of glasses.

globe /gləʊb/ （名词）地球仪

–Can you find Egypt on the globe? 你能在地球仪上找到埃及吗？

–Here it is! In Africa. 在这儿呢！在非洲。

用法小贴士

globe 的本义是"星球"，the globe 特指"地球"。

glove /glʌv/ （名词）手套

–Let's go out and make a snowman. 咱们出去堆雪人吧。

–OK, but put on your gloves first. 好的，但得先戴上手套。

用法小贴士

glove 是五指分开的手套，没有分开的称为 mitten。

glue /gluː/ （名词）胶水

–I need some glue to make a paper plane. 我需要点儿胶水来做纸飞机。

–It's on the shelf. 就在书架上。

go /gəʊ/ （动词）（过去式 **went** /went/，过去分词 **gone** /gɒn/）

去，离开

–I go to school at seven o'clock every morning. 我每天早晨7点去上学。

goal /gəʊl/ （名词）目标

Our goal is to win the match. 我们的目标就是赢得这场比赛。

拓展词汇

goalkeeper 守门员

goat /gəʊt/ （名词）山羊
–What's the difference between a goat and a sheep? 山羊和绵羊有什么不同？
–A goat has longer legs and a thinner coat. 山羊的腿长些，皮毛薄些。

百科小贴士
山羊有向后弯的角，四肢强壮，善于跳跃。公羊有须。山羊的习性是将草根全部刨出来吃掉，过量饲养山羊会严重破坏植被。

God¹ /gɒd/ （名词）上帝

百科小贴士
上帝是基督教所信奉的神。

god² /gɒd/ （叹词）天啊！
–Oh, my god. The car has been stolen! 哦，天哪，汽车被偷了！
–Go and report it to the police at once. 马上去报警。

gold /gəʊld/ （名词）金，金子
Gold is more expensive than silver. 金比银昂贵。

golden /'gəʊldən/ （形容词）金色的
–Mary has golden hair and blue eyes. 玛丽长着金色头发和蓝眼睛。
–Just like her mother. 跟她妈妈一样。

goldfish /'gəʊldfɪʃ/ （名词）（复数goldfish）金鱼
–Look at my goldfish. Aren't they lovely? 看我养的金鱼，可爱吧？
–Yes. Did you buy them at the pet store? 是啊，你是在宠物店买的吗？

百科小贴士
中国是金鱼的原产国，杭州是金鱼的故乡。金鱼是鲫鱼的变种，因其色赤而鳞片闪烁若金，故名金鱼。唐朝时就开始将金黄色的野生鲫鱼进行"家化"养殖，距今已有一千七百多年的历史。

golf /gɒlf/ （名词）高尔夫球
Tiger Woods is an excellent golf player. 泰格·伍兹是一名杰出的高尔夫球运动员。

百科小贴士
苏格兰是高尔夫球的故乡，这里的高地和茵茵绿地为高尔夫运动提供了最好的运动场所。在苏格兰，打高尔夫球不是一项奢侈运动，而是一种大众化运动。

good /gʊd/ （形容词）（比较级better，最高级best）好的，优秀的
–She's good at math. 她数学很好。
–Not strange. Her father is a math teacher. 不奇怪呀，她爸爸是数学老师。

goodbye /ˌgʊd'baɪ/ （叹词）再见
–Class is over. See you tomorrow. 下课了，明天见。
–Goodbye! 再见！

goods /gʊdz/ （名词）商品

This shop sells all kinds of goods. 这个商店卖各种各样的商品。

goose /guːs/ （名词）（复数 **geese** /giːs/ ）鹅

–Look! The goose has laid a big egg. 快来看！那只鹅下了一个大蛋。
–It's so much bigger than a chicken egg. 比鸡蛋可大多了。

grade /greɪd/ （名词）年级，等级

–What grade are you in? 你上几年级？
–I'm in grade four. 我上四年级。

grain /greɪn/ （名词）谷物，谷粒

To a hen, a grain is better than a jewel. 对一只鸡来说，一粒谷子好过一颗宝石。

grammar /'græmə/ （名词）语法

–Do you find English grammar difficult? 你觉得英语语法难吗？
–Not too difficult. 不是太难。

grandchild /'græntʃaɪld/ （名词）（复数 **grandchildren** ）孙子，孙女，外孙，外孙女

Mrs. Smith has three grandchildren. 史密斯夫人有3个孙子和孙女。

granddaughter /'grændɔːtə/ （名词）孙女，外孙女

Mr. Jones has three sons and three granddaughters. 琼斯先生有3个儿子，3个孙女。

grandfather /'grænfɑːðə/ （名词）祖父，外祖父

–How old is your grandfather? 你爷爷多大岁数了？
–He's seventy-five and still in good health. 他75岁了，身体还很好。

grandma /'grænmɑː/ （名词）（口语）奶奶，外婆

–Who looked after you when you were small? 你小时候谁照顾你？
–My grandma. My mother was too busy then. 我外婆，那时我妈妈太忙了。

grandmother /'grænmʌðə/ （名词）祖母，外祖母

–Your grandmother looks very young. How old is she? 你的奶奶看起来真年轻。她今年多大年纪了？

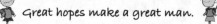
–Oh, that's a secret! 哦，那可是秘密！

grandpa /'grænpɑ:/ （名词）（口语）爷爷，外公

–What did your grandpa do when he was young? 你爷爷年轻的时候是干什么的？

–He was a sailor. 他是一名水手。

grandson /'grænsʌn/ （名词）孙子，外孙

His grandson is the apple of his eye. 他孙子是他的掌上明珠。

granny /'græni/ （名词）（口语）奶奶，外婆，老奶奶

–Are you all right, Granny? 奶奶，您还好吧？

–I'm fine. Thank you for coming. 我挺好，谢谢你来看我。

grape /greɪp/ （名词）葡萄

–What's wine made from? 葡萄酒是用什么做的？

–It's made from grapes. 用葡萄做的。

grass /grɑ:s/ （名词）草，草地

–Keep off the grass, please. 请勿践踏草地。

–I'm sorry. 对不起。

拓展词汇

grassland 草原，牧场　　wild grass 野草

grasshopper /'grɑ:shɒpə/ （名词）蝗虫，蚂蚱

–Grasshoppers are great singers. 蚂蚱唱歌很好听。

–Yes, but do you know they sing with their legs and wings? 是的，但你知道它们是用腿和翅膀唱歌的吗？

百科小贴士

蝗虫俗称蚂蚱，属昆虫，身体细长，呈绿色或黄褐色，雄虫用后足和前翅相互摩擦会发出清脆的叫声。蝗虫是一种农业害虫。

gray¹ /greɪ/ （形容词）灰色的

–Look! The sky is gray. 看！天是灰的。

–It's going to rain. 快下雨了。

gray² /greɪ/ （名词）灰色

great /greɪt/ （形容词）

1. 大的，伟大的

–Do you know Confucius? 你知道孔子吗？

–Of course. He was a great teacher in ancient China. 当然啦，他是中国古代伟大的教育家。

2. 极好的，很棒的

–Would you join us for dinner? 跟我们一起吃饭好吗？

–Great! 好啊！

Greece /griːs/ （名词）希腊

The Olympic Games first began in Greece. 奥运会起源于希腊。

拓展词汇

Greek 希腊的，希腊人的，希腊语，希腊人

百科小贴士

希腊是西方文明的发源地之一，其首都为雅典。希腊神话是西方文学的起源，其中最著名的神话人物有智慧女神雅典娜、太阳神阿波罗等。

greedy /'griːdi/ （形容词）（比较级 **greedier**，最高级 **greediest**）贪心的

Don't be greedy. Let the others have some cake, too. 别太贪心了，让其他人也吃点儿蛋糕。

green[1] /griːn/ （形容词）绿色的

–Can we cross the street now? 我们现在能过马路吗？

–No, wait for the green light. 不行，等绿灯亮了再过。

拓展词汇

green food 绿色食品　green tea 绿茶
greenhouse 温室

green[2] /griːn/ （名词）绿色

Green is the color of life. 绿色是生命之色。

ground /graʊnd/ （名词）地面

–Why is that deer lying on the ground? 你怎么躺在地上呀？

–She's hurt her leg! 我的腿受伤了。

group /gruːp/ （名词）一组，一群

Students came to school in groups of three or five. 学生们三五成群地来到学校。

grow /grəʊ/ （动词）（过去式 **grew** /gruː/，过去分词 **grown** /grəʊn/ ）

1. 成长，生长

–Plants grow fast in warm and rainy places. 植物在温暖多雨的地方生长得很快。

–They grow slowly in cold and dry places. 在寒冷干燥的地方就长得慢了。

Great hopes make a great man.

2. 栽种，种植
–Farmers grow grains and vegetables on the farm. 农民在农场种粮食和蔬菜。
–Some of them also grow flowers and fruit. 有些农民也种花卉和水果。

guard /gɑːd/ （名词）守卫，警卫
–Look, there are four guards at the gate. 看，这个大门口有4个警卫。
–This must be an important place. 这一定是个重要的地方。

guess[1] /ges/ （动词）猜，猜测
–I didn't know the answer. But I guessed it. 我并不知道答案，但我猜对了。
–Lucky you! 你真幸运！

guess[2] /ges/ （名词）猜测，猜想
–Do you really think John will come? 你真的认为约翰会来吗？
–Well, it's only a guess. 呃，这只是我的猜测而已。

guest /gest/ （名词）客人，宾客
–How many guests went to the party? 有多少客人参加了派对？
–More than a hundred. 有一百多人。

guide /gaɪd/ （名词）向导，导游
–We may get lost in the forest. We need a guide. 我们可能会在森林里迷路，我们需要一个向导。
–Let's find someone with experience. 咱们找个有经验的人吧。

guitar /gɪ'tɑː/ （名词）吉他
–Can you play the guitar? 你会弹吉他吗？
–Just a little. 会一点点。

gun /gʌn/ （名词）枪，炮
–Look out! The thief's got a gun! 小心！那小偷手里有枪！
–Don't run after him! Call the police! 别追他，快叫警察！

guy /gaɪ/ （名词）（口语）男人，家伙
–Allen's a funny guy! 艾伦是个有趣的家伙。
–Oh yes. He's got a good sense of humor. 哦，是的，他很幽默。

大希望造就大人物。

gym /dʒɪm/ （名词）（口语）体育馆
–Where do you play badminton?
你在哪儿打羽毛球?

–At the gym near school. 在学校附近的体育馆。

H

habit /'hæbɪt/ （名词）习惯

–It's a bad habit to talk with your mouth full. 满口食物讲话是一种坏习惯。

–You might choke. 你可能会哽咽的。

hair /heə/ （名词）

1. 头发

–I forgot to comb my hair this morning. 我今天早上忘梳头了。

–No wonder it's a mess! 难怪乱蓬蓬的。

拓展词汇

hairbrush 梳子　hairdresser 理发师

2. （动物的）毛

Most animals have hair to keep warm. 大多数动物都靠身上的毛保暖。

half /hɑːf/ （名词）（复数 halves /hɑːvz/)

1. 一半

–How can we share this cake? 我们怎么分这块蛋糕呢？

–I'll cut it in half. 我把它切成两半吧。

2. 半小时

–When shall we meet? 我们什么时候见面？

–Let's say half past two. 两点半怎么样？

hall /hɔːl/ （名词）大厅

–What's the biggest hall in China? 中国最大的厅是哪个？

–It's the Great Hall of the People in Beijing. 是北京的人民大会堂。

拓展词汇

concert hall 音乐厅　city hall 市政厅
dining hall 餐厅　lecture hall 讲堂

Halloween /ˌhæləʊ'iːn/

（名词）万圣节前夜

–What day is Halloween? 万圣节前夜是哪天？

–It's the last day of October. 是10月的最后一天。

百科小贴士

万圣节前夜是英美国家的传统节日，也叫"鬼节"。万圣节前夜的一项习俗是制作南瓜灯，即把南瓜挖空雕刻成鬼脸，在里边点上蜡烛。孩子们穿上鬼怪服装，挨家挨户讨糖吃，讨糖的时候要说"Trick or treat.（不请吃就捣乱。）"。

ham /hæm/ （名词）火腿

–What would you like for breakfast? 你早餐想吃什么？

–Ham and eggs, please. 请来点儿火腿蛋。

hamburger /'hæmbɜːgə/

（名词）汉堡包

–Hamburgers contain a lot of fat. 汉堡包的脂肪含量很高。

–It's not good to eat too many of them. 吃太多可不好。

百科小贴士

虽然我们熟悉的汉堡包都来自美国的快餐连锁店，但事实上汉堡包原为德国城市汉堡（Hamburg）的一般家庭食品，由德国移民传入美国而得名。

hammer /'hæmə/ （名词）锤子

–What do you need a hammer and nails for? 你需要锤子和钉子干什么呢？

–I want to build a house for my puppy. 我想给小狗建个房子。

hand¹ /hænd/ （名词）

1. 手

Shaking hands is a sign of welcome. 握手是表示欢迎的一种方式。

2. （时钟的）针

–Do you know how to tell the time from a clock? 你知道怎么认钟吗？

–Sure. The shortest hand is the hour hand, the second shortest tells the minute, and the longest tells the second. 当然啦。最短的是时针，第二短的是分针，最长的是秒针。

3. 帮忙

–Susan, could you give me a hand? 苏珊，你能帮我个忙吗？

–With pleasure. 我很乐意。

拓展词汇

handbag 手提包　　handbook 手册

hand² /hænd/ （动词）递给

–May, please hand me that dictionary. 梅，请把那本字典递给我。

–Here you are. 给你。

handle /'hændəl/ （名词）把手，柄

–The door handle is broken. 门把手坏了。

–I'll fix it. 我来修。

handsome /'hænsəm/ （形容词）（男子）英俊的

–Is that Sam? 那个人是萨姆吗？

–Yes. He's become a handsome young man. 是啊。他已经长成一个帅小伙了。

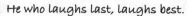

He who laughs last, laughs best.

用法小贴士

形容男性"英俊"时，常常用handsome，而形容女性"漂亮"时，通常用pretty，beautiful。

handwriting /ˈhændraɪtɪŋ/

（名词）笔迹，书法

Clear handwriting is important in exams. 考试时笔迹清楚很重要。

hang /hæŋ/ （动词）（过去式、过去分词 **hung** /hʌŋ/）悬挂

–Where did you put the alphabet chart? 你把字母表挂图放哪里了？
–I've hung it on the wall of my bedroom. 我把它挂到我卧室的墙上了。

happen /ˈhæpən/ （动词）发生

–What's happened to your computer? 你的电脑怎么了？
–I've no idea. I can't start it. 我也不知道。我无法开机。

happy /ˈhæpi/ （形容词）（比较级 **happier**，最高级 **happiest**）快乐的，幸福的

Exercise more and you will be healthy and happy. 多做运动，你会健康又快乐。

hard¹ /hɑːd/ （形容词）

1. 坚硬的
Crabs have hard shells to protect them. 螃蟹的壳很硬，能保护自己。

反义词 soft 柔软的

2. 困难的
–Did you finish your exam paper? 你答完了考卷了吗？
–No, I didn't. The questions were too hard. 没有，试题太难了。

反义词 easy 简单的

hard² /hɑːd/ （副词）努力地

–Chris always gets high marks on exams. 克里斯考试总是得高分。
–That's because he studies hard. 那是因为他学习努力呀。

拓展词汇
hardworking 勤奋的

hardly /ˈhɑːdli/ （副词）几乎不

–How do you feel after your long walk? 走了这么远的路，感觉怎么样？
–My legs hurt so much I can hardly stand. 我的腿很疼，我都要站不稳了。

谁笑到最后，谁笑得最好。

hare /heə/ （名词）野兔

–What's the difference between a hare and a rabbit? 野兔和家兔有什么区别？

–Hares are larger, have longer ears, and run faster than rabbits. 和家兔比起来，野兔个头更大，耳朵更长，跑得也更快。

harvest¹ /ˈhɑːvɪst/ （名词）收获

–What's the happiest time for farmers? 农民什么时候最幸福？

–Harvest time, of course. 当然是收获时节啦。

harvest² /ˈhɑːvɪst/ （动词）收获

Farmers plant crops in spring and harvest them in autumn. 农民春天播种，秋天收获。

hat /hæt/ （名词）帽子

–What a lovely hat! 多可爱的帽子呀！

–Thank you. My mother made it for me. 谢谢！是我妈妈给我做的。

拓展词汇

top hat 高顶礼帽　　sun hat 太阳帽
cowboy hat 牛仔帽　　hunting cap 猎帽

hate /heɪt/ （动词）仇恨，讨厌

–Sam, time to take your medicine. 萨姆，你该吃药了。

–But I hate medicine. 可我讨厌吃药。

have¹ /hæv/ （动词）（第三人称单数 has /hæz/，过去式、过去分词 had /hæd/）有

–Do you have an extra pen? 你有多余的钢笔吗？

–Sorry, I have only one. 对不起，我只有一支。

拓展词汇

have a look 看一看　　have a talk 聊一聊
have a taste 尝一尝

have² /hæv/ （助动词）（与过去分词一起表达完成时态）

–Have you done your homework? 你做家庭作业了吗？

–Yes, I have. 是的，已经做了。

hawk /hɔːk/ （名词）鹰

–Hawks are fierce birds. 鹰是凶猛的鸟。

–They can eat small animals. 它们会吃小动物呢。

he /hiː/ （代词）他

–Who's that boy? 那个男孩是谁？

–He's my best friend, Jimmy. 他是我最好的朋友，吉米。

head /hed/ （名词）

1. 头

Nod your head if you agree, and shake your head if you don't. 如果你同意就点头，如果不同意就摇头。

2. 头脑

Use your head and think it over. 动动你的脑子，再仔细想想。

headache /'hedeɪk/ （名词）头痛

–Are you all right? You look pale. 你身体不舒服吗？你脸色苍白。
–I have a bad headache. 我头疼得厉害。

headmaster /ˌhed'mɑːstə/ （名词）（中小学）校长

–Could I speak to the headmaster, please? 我能请校长接一下电话吗？
–Sorry, he's at a meeting right now. 对不起，校长在开会。

用法小贴士
headmaster在英国指中小学校长，在美国通常指私立学校的校长，英国英语中也用head teacher指校长。

health /helθ/ （名词）健康

–Which would you choose, health or wealth? 健康和财富，你选择哪一个？
–Health, if I have to choose one. 如果非得选一个的话，我选健康。

healthy /'helθi/ （形容词）（比较级 **healthier**, 最高级 **healthiest**）健康的

–How can we keep healthy? 怎样才能保持健康？

–Eat healthy food and exercise. 吃健康食品，做运动。

hear /hɪə/ （动词）（过去式、过去分词 **heard** /hɜːd/） 听见

–Can you all hear me? 你们都能听见我说话吗？
–Speak louder, please. 请说大声点儿。

用法小贴士
hear 和 listen to 都是 "听" 的意思，但 hear意为 "听到"，listen to 则强调听的动作。

heart /hɑːt/ （名词）心脏
Exercise can make our heart strong. 锻炼可以使我们的心脏强健。

heat¹ /hiːt/ （名词）热量

–The sun gives us heat and light. 太阳给我们光和热。
–We cannot live without the sun. 没有太阳我们就不能生存。

heat² /hiːt/ （动词）加热

–The milk is cold. 牛奶是凉的。
–I'll heat it for you if you want. 如果你需要我可以把它加热。

heaven /'hevən/ （名词）天堂

–Hangzhou is a beautiful place. 杭州是个美丽的地方。
–Oh, yes. We call it "heaven on earth." 哦，是的。我们称它为 "人间天堂"。

拓展词汇
Good heavens! 天哪！
Thank heavens! 谢天谢地！

heavy /'hevi/ （形容词）（比较级 **heavier**，最高级 **heaviest**）重的

–Can you lift the box, Alice? 艾丽斯，你能搬动这只箱子吗？
–No, it's too heavy for me. 不行，太重了。

反义词 light 轻的

height /haɪt/ （名词）高度

–Please tell me your height and weight. 请告诉我你的身高和体重。
–I'm five feet tall and weigh ninety pounds. 我身高五英尺，体重九十磅。

helicopter /'helikɒptə/ （名词）直升机

A helicopter can take off and land almost anywhere. 直升机几乎可以在任何地方起飞和降落。

百科小贴士
1907 年法国人科尔尼制造出第一架载人的直升机，能作简单的垂直飞行。美籍俄裔科学家西科尔斯基设计出世界上第一架实用的直升机，于 1939 年首次试飞成功。

hell /hel/ （名词）地狱

Her life has been hell since she became ill. 自从生病以后，她的生活就变得一团糟。

hello /he'ləʊ/ （叹词）你好

–Hello, Ann, this is my friend Paul. 你好，安。这是我的朋友保罗。
–Hello, Paul. Nice to meet you. 你好，保罗。很高兴认识你。

help¹ /help/ （动词）帮助

–Jenny, can you help me pick up the needles from the floor? 珍妮，你能帮我把地上的针捡起来吗？
–No problem, Grandma. 没问题，奶奶。

help² /help/ （名词）帮助

Thank you for your kind help. 谢谢你的热心帮忙。

help³ /help/ （叹词）救命

"Help! Help! I can't swim," Mary cried. "救命啊！我不会游泳。"玛丽大声喊道。

helpful /'helpfʊl/ （形容词）有用的

–Thank you. You've been very helpful. 谢谢你，你可帮了大忙了。
–You're welcome. 不客气。

hen /hen/ （名词）母鸡

The hen keeps her chicks under her wings to keep them warm.

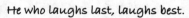
母鸡把小鸡拢在翅膀下帮它们保暖。

her¹ /hɜː/ （代词）她

–Did you see Anne? 你看见安妮了吗？

–I saw her five minutes ago. 我5分钟前见到她的。

her² /hɜː/ （形容词）她的

The old lady loves her dog dearly. 这位老太太十分宠爱她的狗。

here /hɪə/ （副词）这里

–Is everybody here? 每个人都在这里吗？

–Yes, we're all here. 是的，我们都在这儿。

hero /ˈhɪərəʊ/ （名词）（复数 **heroes**）英雄

–Do you know Yue Fei? 你知道岳飞吗？

–Of course. He was a hero in ancient China. 当然知道。他是中国古代的一位英雄。

拓展词汇

war hero 战争英雄
national hero 民族英雄

hers /hɜːz/ （代词）她的

–Is this Susan's schoolbag? 这是苏珊的书包吗？

–Yes, it's hers. 是的，是她的。

herself /həˈself/ （代词）她自己

–Did Jill tell you the news herself? 是吉尔亲口告诉你这消息的吗？

–That's right. She told me this morning. 对，她今天早晨告诉我的。

hi /haɪ/ （叹词）（口语）你好

–Hi, Helen. 你好，海伦。

–Hi, Linda. 你好，琳达。

用法小贴士

hi比 hello 更随意些。

hide /haɪd/ （动词）（过去式 **hid** /hɪd/，过去分词 **hidden** /ˈhɪdən/）隐藏

Butterflies use their colors to hide from their enemies. 蝴蝶利用身上的色彩躲避天敌。

拓展词汇

hide-and-seek 捉迷藏

high /haɪ/ （形容词）高的

It's usually cold on high mountains. 高山上一般都比较冷。

反义词 low 低的

谁笑到最后，谁笑得最好。

high jump 跳高

hill /hɪl/ （名词）小山

–Do you want to climb over the hill or go around it? 你想爬过这小山还是绕过它？
–Let's climb over it. 咱们爬过去吧。

him /hɪm/ （代词）他

–Did you see John? 你看见约翰了吗？
–I saw him playing football over there. 我看见他在那边踢足球。

himself /hɪm'self/ （代词）他自己

–Does he live with his parents? 他和父母一块儿住吗？
–No. He lives by himself. 不，他独自一人住。

his /hɪz/ （形容词）他的

–Richard is looking for his bike. Which one is his? 理查德在找他的自行车，哪个是他的？
–The red one. 那辆红色的。

history /'hɪstəri/ （名词）历史

China has a history of 5000 years. 中国有5000年的历史。

hit /hɪt/ （动词）（过去式、过去分词 hit，现在分词 hitting）打

An apple fell and hit Newton on the head. 一个苹果从树上掉下来，砸在牛顿头上。

hobby /'hɒbi/ （名词）（复数 hobbies）爱好

–What's your hobby? 你的爱好是什么？
–I like collecting stamps. 我喜欢集邮。

hold /həʊld/ （动词）（过去式、过去分词 held /held/）拿住，抓住

Julie held the cat in her arms. 朱莉把小猫搂在怀里。

hole /həʊl/ （名词）洞

–Why is there so much water in the house? 屋子里怎么有这么多水？
–Can't you see the hole in the roof? 你没看见屋顶上有个洞吗？

holiday /'hɒlɪdeɪ/ （名词）假期

–Where do you want to go for the holiday? 你假期想去哪儿？
–I want to go somewhere in the south. 我想去南方某个地方。

拓展词汇

summer holiday 暑假
winter holiday 寒假

home /həʊm/ （名词）家

East or west, home is best. 东好西好，不如自家好。

hometown /ˌhəʊm'taʊn/

（名词）家乡

–Where's your hometown? 你的老家在哪里？
–Beijing. I was born and grew up there. 北京。我在那里出生长大的。

homework /'həʊmwɜːk/

（名词）作业

–How much homework do you have? 你有多少家庭作业？
–A lot. Chinese, English, math, and something else. 好多呢！语文、英语、数学，还有点儿其他的。

honest /'ɒnɪst/ （形容词）诚实的

–Sorry, I broke the window. 对不起，我把窗玻璃打破了。
–It was very honest of you to tell me. 你能告诉我，很诚实。

honey /'hʌni/ （名词）蜂蜜

–Tommy, do you know where honey comes from? 汤米，你知道蜂蜜是从哪里来的吗？
–Sure, it's made by bees. 当然知道，是蜜蜂酿的。

拓展词汇

honeybee 蜜蜂

hope[1] /həʊp/ （动词）希望

–Do you think it will rain? 你觉得会下雨吗？
–I hope so. It's too hot. 我希望会下。天太热了。

hope[2] /həʊp/ （名词）希望

Where there's life, there's hope. 有生命的地方，就有希望。

horn /hɔːn/ （名词）角

–What animals have horns? 什么动物长角？
–Many, such as bulls and goats. 许多都长，如公牛和山羊。

horrible /'hɒrɪbəl/ （形容词）糟透的

–Horrible weather, isn't it? 天气糟透了，是不是？
–Yes. It's going to rain again. 是啊，又要下雨了！

谁笑到最后，谁笑得最好。

horse /hɔːs/ （名词）马

–That white horse looks so cool! Can I ride it? 那匹白马看起来太酷了。我可以骑它吗？
–Yes, but be careful. 可以，但要小心点。

拓展词汇

horseback riding 骑马　horseman 骑手
horseshoe 马掌

hospital /ˈhɒspɪtəl/ （名词）医院

–You look ill. 你看上去好像病了。
–Yes. I'm going to the hospital. 是的，我正要去医院。

host[1] /həʊst/ （名词）主人

–Where's the host? 主人在哪儿呢？
–He's at the door, greeting new guests. 他在门口迎接新来的客人。

用法小贴士

host 一般指男主人，女主人用hostess。

host[2] /həʊst/ （动词）主办

Beijing hosted the Olympic Games in 2008. 北京将主办2008年奥运会。

hot /hɒt/ （形容词）（比较级 hotter，最高级 hottest）热的

–It's so hot! Shall we have some ice cream? 真热啊！咱们来点儿冰激凌吧？
–Why not? 好啊。

反义词　cold 冷的

hot dog /ˌhɒt ˈdɒg/ （名词）热狗

–What did you have for lunch? 你中午吃的什么？
–A hot dog and a cup of hot chocolate. 一个热狗和一杯热巧克力。

百科小贴士

热狗是美国的一种快餐食品，就是在长形的面包里夹一根热香肠。

hotel /ˌhəʊˈtel/ （名词）宾馆，酒店

–This hotel looks beautiful. 这家宾馆看上去很漂亮。
–It's a five-star hotel. 这是家五星级宾馆。

hour /aʊə/ （名词）小时

–How many hours are there in a day? 一天有多少个小时？
–Twenty-four. 24小时。

house /haʊs/ （名词）房子，房屋

–What's the difference between a house and a flat? 房子和公寓有什么不同？
–A house is usually a building on its own. A flat is a small part of a large building. 房子通常是一个独立的建筑，公寓是一个大建筑的一小部分。

He who laughs last, laughs best.

housewife 家庭主妇　housework 家务活

how /haʊ/（副词）

1. 怎么，怎样
–How do you go to school every day? 你每天怎么去上学？
–I take the school bus. 我坐校车去。

2.（用以询问数量、年龄等）多少
How much is this T-shirt? 这件T恤衫多少钱？
How many apples did you buy? 你买了多少个苹果？
How old are you? 你多大了？

hug /hʌg/（动词）拥抱

In Europe, it's common for friends to hug each other. 在欧洲，朋友之间互相拥抱很平常。

huge /hjuːdʒ/（形容词）巨大的

–What a huge plane! 这架飞机真大呀！
–It can take 400 passengers. 它能载400名乘客呢。

反义词　tiny 微小的

human /hjuːmən/（名词）人类

Humans are the wisest animals in the world. 人类是世界上最聪明的动物。

拓展词汇
human rights 人权
human society 人类社会

humor /hjuːmə/（名词）幽默

–Have you seen any of Chaplin's films? 你看过卓别林的电影吗？

–Quite a few. He was a master of humor. 看过不少，他可是幽默大师。

用法小贴士
幽默是英语 humor 的音译词。

humorous /ˈhjuːmərəs/（形容词）幽默的

–What kind of stories do you like? 你喜欢什么样的故事？
–I like humorous ones. 我喜欢幽默故事。

hundred /ˈhʌndrəd/（数词）一百

Hundreds of people go to the museum every day. 每天都有成百上千的人去博物馆。

hungry /ˈhʌŋgri/（形容词）（比较级 hungrier，最高级 hungriest）饥饿的

–Tommy, are you hungry? 汤米，你饿了吗？

–Yes, I could eat a horse! 是的，我快饿死啦！

反义词 full 饱的

hunter /'hʌntə/ （名词）猎人

The hunter drove the wolf away. 猎人把狼赶跑了。

hurry /'hʌri/ （动词）（第三人称单数 hurries，过去式、过去分词 hurried，现在分词 hurrying）赶快

–Hurry up. We're already late. 快点儿，咱们已经晚了！
–Take a taxi, then. 那就打辆车吧。

hurt /hɜːt/ （动词）（过去式、过去分词 hurt）痛

–Where does it hurt? 你哪里疼？
–My back hurts. 我背疼。

husband /'hʌzbənd/ （名词）丈夫

When a man and a woman get married, they become husband and wife. 男人和女人结婚后就结为夫妻了。

hut /hʌt/ （名词）小屋

–Look! There's a hut higher up the mountain. 看，山上高高的地方有一栋小屋。
–We can take shelter there. 我们可以在那儿藏身。

I

I /aɪ/ （代词）我

–I'm in grade five. How about you?
我上五年级。你呢？
–I'm in grade six. 我上六年级了。

ice /aɪs/ （名词）冰

–Let's go skating on the lake. 我们去湖面滑冰吧！
–The ice isn't thick enough. 冰还不够厚呢。

拓展词汇

ice cold 极冷的   iceberg 冰山
ice water 冰水   ice lantern 冰灯

ice cream /ˌaɪs 'kriːm/ （名词）冰激凌

–Ice cream is my favorite snack. 冰激凌是我最喜欢吃的零食。
–I like it, too. 我也喜欢吃。

ice-skate /'aɪskeɪt/ （动词）溜冰

Ice-skating is a popular sport in the northeast of China. 滑冰是中国东北较普及的运动。

idea /aɪ'diːə/ （名词）主意

–Shall we go swimming this afternoon? 我们今天下午去游泳好吗？
–That's a good idea! 好主意！

if /ɪf/ （连词）如果

–What shall we do if it rains tomorrow? 如果明天下雨我们做什么？
–We can stay at home and do some reading. 我们可以呆在家里看书。

ill /ɪl/ （形容词）有病的

–What's wrong with you? 你怎么啦？
–I feel ill. 我感觉不舒服。

用法小贴士
ill 通常不用于名词前；英国英语用ill表示身体不健康，美国英语一般用sick。

illness /'ɪlnəs/ （名词）（疾）病

He died of a terrible illness. 他死于一场可怕的疾病。

一次不成功，努力再努力。

imagination /ɪˌmædʒɪˈneɪʃən/
（名词）想象（力）

–Artists must have a lot of imagination. 艺术家必须有丰富的想象力。
–Scientists, too. 科学家也一样。

imagine /ɪˈmædʒɪn/ （动词）
想象，设想

Close your eyes and imagine you are in a forest. 闭上眼睛想象一下你在森林里。

immediately /ɪˈmiːdiətli/
（副词）立刻，马上

–When do you want me to come? 你想让我什么时候来？
–Immediately. There's no time to lose. 马上来，没有时间了。

important /ɪmˈpɔːtənt/ （形容词）重要的

It's important to look both ways before you cross the street. 过马路前要左右两边看，这很重要。

impossible /ɪmˈpɒsɪbəl/ （形容词）不可能的

It's impossible for people to live on the moon. 人们不可能在月球上生活。

反义词 possible 可能的

in /ɪn/ （介词）在…里面

–Dad, can I go swimming in the sea? 爸爸，我能去海里游泳吗？
–No. It's safer to swim in the swimming pool. 不行，在游泳池里游泳要安全些。

include /ɪnˈkluːd/ （动词）包括

–How many people are there in your family? 你家里有几口人？
–I have a big family. It includes my grandparents, my parents, and me. 我有个大家庭，包括爷爷、奶奶、爸爸、妈妈和我。

increase /ɪnˈkriːs/ （动词）增长，增加

Reading can increase our knowledge. 阅读可以增长知识。

indeed /ɪnˈdiːd/ （副词）真正地，确实

A friend in need is a friend indeed. 患难见真情。

ink /ɪŋk/ （名词）墨水

–My pen has run out of ink. 我的钢笔没墨水了。

–I have a bottle here. 我这儿有一瓶。

拓展词汇

ink bottle 墨水瓶

insect /'ɪnsekt/ （名词）昆虫

–What does an insect look like? 昆虫长得什么样？
–An insect has three body parts and six legs, and some insects have wings. 嗯，昆虫的身体由3部分组成，有6条腿，有的昆虫还有翅膀。

百科小贴士

地球上最多的生物便是昆虫，目前已知约有100万种昆虫，占动物的80%以上。世界上仍有大量的昆虫未被发现，估计可能还有300—500万种有待于人们去发现。

inside¹ /ɪn'saɪd/ （介词）

在…里面

–What can you see inside this egg? 你能看到这个蛋里面是什么吗？
–Oh, it's a chick! 啊，是只小鸡！

inside² /ˌɪn'saɪd/ （副词）

在里面

–It's raining. We'd better go inside. 下雨了，我们进屋吧。
–I'd like to. But I left the key inside. 我也希望能进屋，但我把钥匙落在屋里了。

instead /ɪn'sted/ （副词）代替，而不是

–Why was your father angry with you? 你爸爸为什么生你的气了？
–He told me to do my homework, but I watched TV instead. 他叫我做家庭作业，我却看电视了。

interest /'ɪntrəst/ （名词）兴趣

She has a strong interest in music. 她对音乐很感兴趣。

interested /'ɪntrestɪd/ （形容词）

感兴趣的

–Are you interested in English? 你对英语感兴趣吗？
–Very interested. 很感兴趣。

interesting /'ɪntrestɪŋ/ （形容词）有趣的，有意思的

–What do you think of this book? 你觉得这本书怎么样？
–It's very interesting. 很有意思。

Internet /'ɪntənet/ （名词）

因特网

–The Internet has made the world smaller. 因特网使世界变小了。

–That's because it has made communication faster. 那是因为它使交流变快了。

拓展词汇

Internet café 网吧

interrupt /ˌɪntəˈrʌpt/ （动词）打断

–It's not polite to interrupt others when they are speaking. 打断别人的讲话是不礼貌的。
–I'm sorry to interrupt you, but I have something important to tell you. 抱歉打断你，但我有重要的事情告诉你。

into /ˈɪntuː/ （介词）到…里面

–I've finished my homework, Mom. 妈妈，我完成家庭作业了。
–Put all your books into your schoolbag, then. 把你所有的书都放进书包里吧。

introduce /ˌɪntrəˈdjuːs/ （动词）介绍

–Tom, let me introduce my friend Jim to you. 汤姆，向你介绍一下我的朋友吉姆。
–Nice to meet you, Jim. 认识你很高兴，吉姆。

invent /ɪnˈvent/ （动词）发明

–Who invented the telephone? 是谁发明了电话？
–Bell invented the telephone in 1876. 贝尔在1876年发明了电话。

invention /ɪnˈvenʃən/ （名词）发明

The lightbulb was a great invention by Edison. 电灯泡是爱迪生的一项伟大发明。

invite /ɪnˈvaɪt/ （动词）邀请

–Mom, can I invite my friends to my birthday dinner? 妈妈，过生日时我能邀请朋友来吃饭吗？
–OK. But you have to clear up afterward. 可以，但结束后你要打扫卫生。

is¹ /ɪz/ （动词）(**be** 的第三人称单数现在式）是

–Is that tall boy your cousin? 那个高个子是你的表兄吗？
–No, he's my new classmate. 不是，他是我的新同学。

is² /ɪz/ （助动词）(**be** 的第三人称单数现在式）

–What's happened? Why is Mom crying? 发生了什么事了？为什么妈妈在哭？
–Nothing. She was cutting onions just now. 没什么，刚才她在切洋葱。

island /ˈaɪlənd/ （名词）岛（屿）

–Which is the largest island in the world? 世界上最大的岛屿是哪个？
–Greenland. 格陵兰岛。

百科小贴士

全世界岛屿的面积约占陆地总面积的 1/15。世界上最大的岛屿是格陵兰岛，它位于北美洲的东北部，在北冰洋和大西洋之间。

it /ɪt/ （代词）它（指物、动植物等，或指时间、天气、日期等）
–Where is the key? 钥匙在哪里？
–It's on the table. 在桌子上。

its /ɪts/ （形容词）它的
Look, the peacock has opened its tail feathers! 看，那只孔雀开屏了！

用法小贴士
请勿将 its 和 it's 混淆。its 是 it 的物主形式，意为"它的"，而 it's 是 it is、it was 或 it has 的缩写形式。

itself /ɪt'self/ （代词）它自己
The puppy first looked at itself in the mirror and then went behind it. 小狗先看着镜中的自己，然后绕到镜子后面。

J

jacket /'dʒækɪt/ （名词）夹克衫
–It's a bit cool today. 今天有点儿凉。
–Put your jacket on when you go out. 出门时穿上夹克衫吧。

jam /dʒæm/ （名词）

1. 果酱
–Do you want some jam on your bread? 你想在面包上抹点儿果酱吗？
–Yes, strawberry jam please. 好，请来点儿草莓酱。
2. 阻塞
–Why are you late? 你为什么迟到了？
–My bus was caught in a traffic jam. 我坐的公共汽车碰上堵车了。

January /'dʒænjəri/ （名词）一月
–Is the Spring Festival in January or February? 春节在 1 月还是 2 月？
–It's usually in February, but sometimes in January. 一般在 2 月，有时也在 1 月。

百科小贴士
January 起源于拉丁文 Januarius，源自罗马人的守护神杰纳斯（Janus）。杰纳斯有两副面孔，前脸注视未来，后脸回顾过去，主管保卫门户和万物的始终。

Japan /dʒə'pæn/ （名词）日本
–Is Japan far from China? 日本离中国远吗？
–No, it's a close neighbor to the east of China. 不远，它是中国东面的近邻。

拓展词汇
Japanese 日本的，日本人的，日语，日本人

百科小贴士
日本是中国东面的一个岛国，主要由北海道、本州、四国、九州 4 个大岛组成，首都是东京。日本虽然面积不大，却是当今世界的第二大经济强国。

jar /dʒɑ:/ （名词）广口瓶，罐子
–Do you have cooled boiled water? 你有凉开水吗？
–Yes, it's in the jar on the table. 有的，在桌上的广口瓶里。

jaw /dʒɔ:/ （名词）下巴
–The elder brother has a square jaw. 哥哥长着方下巴。

–The younger brother has a pointed jaw. 弟弟长着尖下巴。

jealous /'dʒeləs/ （形容词）嫉妒的

–Why did the queen want to kill Snow White? 王后为什么想杀害白雪公主？
–Because she was jealous of Snow White's beauty. 因为她嫉妒白雪公主的美丽。

jeans /dʒiːnz/ （名词）牛仔裤

–Were cowboys the first to wear jeans? 最先穿牛仔裤的人是牛仔吗？
–No, they weren't. 不，不是。

百科小贴士
19世纪初，旧金山的淘金客向"牛仔裤之父"李维·史特劳斯抱怨，金沙老从口袋里漏出去，这激发了李维用帐篷布料缝制耐磨裤子的创意——牛仔裤于是诞生。

jelly /'dʒeli/ （名词）（复数 jellies）果冻

–Fruit jellies come in many pretty colors. 果冻的颜色又多又好看。
–They taste good, too, but are not very healthy. 它们味道也不错，但不是健康食品。

百科小贴士
果冻大多是用琼脂、明胶等增稠剂添加合成香精、着色剂等制成，不宜多吃。

jewel /'dʒuːəl/ （名词）宝石

–There's a big jewel on the queen's crown. 女王的王冠上有一颗大宝石。

–It's the most expensive jewel in the country. 它是该国最昂贵的宝石。

jigsaw puzzle /'dʒɪgsɔː ˌpʌzəl/ （名词）拼图玩具，拼图游戏

–Do you like doing jigsaw puzzles? 你喜欢玩拼图吗？
–Yes, let's start one now. 喜欢，我们现在就玩吧。

job /dʒɒb/ （名词）工作

–What's your father's job? 你爸爸是做什么工作的？
–He's an English teacher. 他是英语教师。

join /dʒɔɪn/ （动词）加入

–Do you want to join us in the game? 你想跟我们一起玩游戏吗？
–Of course, thank you! 当然啦，谢谢！

joke[1] /dʒəuk/ （名词）笑话

–Why are you all laughing? 你们为什么都在笑啊？
–Tom told a really good joke just now. 刚才汤姆讲了一个特别好的笑话。

百科小贴士

果汁并不等于水果。瓶装果汁中一般都含有各种人工制剂，即使是自己动手榨的果汁，也由于固体残渣被浪费掉，大大降低了其中的纤维素含量。

joke² /dʒəuk/ （动词）开玩笑

–I can run 100 meters in 13 seconds. 我能够在 13 秒内跑 100 米。
–You must be joking. 你肯定是在开玩笑吧！

joy /dʒɔɪ/ （名词）快乐

To Tom's joy, he won first prize in the tennis game. 让汤姆高兴的是，他获得了网球比赛的第一名。

judge /dʒʌdʒ/ （名词）法官

–What does your mother do? 你妈妈是做什么的？
–She's a judge, and I want to be a judge, too. 她是法官，我也想当一名法官。

juice /dʒuːs/ （名词）果汁

–I've made some fresh orange juice. 我榨了些鲜橙汁。
–May I have a glass? 我能喝一杯吗？

July /dʒʊˈlaɪ/ （名词）七月

–What are the summer months in Beijing? 北京的夏季是哪几个月？
–June, July, and August. 6 月、7 月和 8 月。

百科小贴士

July 来源于古罗马统治者恺撒大帝，他死后人们以他的名字 Julius 命名 7 月。

jump /dʒʌmp/ （动词）跳

–Can we jump across the stream? 我们能跳越这条小溪吗？
–We can try. 我们可以试一下。

June /dʒuːn/ （名词）六月

–What's the date for Children's Day in China? 中国的儿童节是哪天？
–It's the first of June. 是 6 月 1 日。

百科小贴士

June 源于古罗马神话中的天后朱诺（Juno），罗马人为了纪念她，就把 6 月称为朱诺月（Junius）。英文中 6 月就是从 Junius 演变而来的。

junk food /'dʒʌŋk fuːd/

（名词）垃圾食品

–Why do many people like junk food, like chips? 为什么许多人喜欢垃圾食品，如炸薯条？

–Maybe they don't know what junk food is. 也许他们不知道什么样的食品是垃圾食品。

百科小贴士

世界卫生组织公布的十大垃圾食品是：油炸类、腌制类、加工肉类、饼干类、汽水可乐类、方便类（主要指方便面和膨化食品）、罐头类、话梅蜜饯类、冷冻甜品类和烧烤类。

just /dʒʌst/ （副词）

1. 刚好

–Can you wear this shirt? 你能穿这件衬衫吗？

–It's just the right size for me. 尺寸正好适合我。

2. 仅仅

–Look at the picture, Julie. Is that you? 朱莉，看这张照片，这是你吗？

–Yes. I was just a child then. 是啊，我那时还是个孩子。

K

kangaroo /ˌkæŋgə'ruː/ （名词）
（复数 **kangaroos**）袋鼠

–How does a kangaroo move? 袋鼠是怎么走路的？

–It doesn't walk. It jumps. 袋鼠不能走，只能跳。

百科小贴士
袋鼠是大洋洲特有的动物，是澳大利亚的象征。袋鼠有很多品种，最有名的就是体形最大的红袋鼠。母袋鼠腹部有育儿袋，小袋鼠出生后需要在育儿袋里呆至少半年。

keep /kiːp/ （动词）（过去式、过去分词 **kept** /kept/）保留

–How long can I keep this book? 这本书我可以保留多久？

–You can keep it for one month. 你可以保留 1 个月。

ketchup /'ketʃʌp/ （名词）
番茄酱

–Is ketchup used with Chinese or Western food? 番茄酱用于中餐还是西餐？

–It's used in Western cooking. 用于西餐。

key /kiː/ （名词）钥匙

–I can't turn the key in the lock. 我的钥匙在锁里转不动。

–Maybe it's the wrong key. 也许拿错钥匙了。

keyboard /'kiːbɔːd/ （名词）
键盘

–My keyboard doesn't work well. 我的键盘不太好用。

–Maybe you should clean it. 可能你要把它清洁一下了。

kick /kɪk/ （动词）踢

Jim kicked the ball into the goal in the last minute. 吉姆在最后一分钟把球踢进了球门。

kid¹ /kɪd/ （口语）儿童，孩子

–How many kids are there in this kindergarten? 这个幼儿园有多少个孩子？

–There are one hundred and twenty. 有120个。

kid² /kɪd/ （动词）（过去式、过去分词 **kidded**, 现在分词 **kidding**）开玩笑

–You have won a million yuan! 你赢了100万元！
–You must be kidding. 你一定是在开玩笑。

kill /kɪl/ （动词）杀死

The forest fire killed many animals. 森林大火烧死了许多动物。

kilo /'kiːləu/ （名词）（复数 **kilos**）千克

–How much does this bag of rice weigh? 这袋米有多重？
–Twenty kilos. 20千克。

kilometer /'kɪləmiːtə/ （名词）千米

–What travels the fastest in the world? 世界上什么速度最快？
–Light. It can travel about 300,000 kilometers a second. 光, 光速约为每秒钟30万千米。

kind¹ /kaɪnd/ （形容词）好心的, 好意的

–It's very kind of you to lend me the dictionary! 感谢你把词典借给我！
–Not at all. 不客气。

kind² /kaɪnd/ （名词）种类

There are different kinds of food in a supermarket. 超市里有不同种类的食品。

kindergarten /'kɪndəɡɑːtən/ （名词）幼儿园

–What did you learn in kindergarten? 你在幼儿园学了些什么？
–I learned to sing and dance, and to speak a little English. 我学会了唱歌、跳舞, 还学会说一点儿英语。

king /kɪŋ/ （名词）国王

–Does France have a king? 法国有国王吗？
–No, it doesn't. It has a president. 没有, 有总统。

百科小贴士
当今世界仍有几十个国家有国王或者女王, 这些国家包括: 比利时、丹麦、荷兰、挪威、日本、瑞典、泰国、西班牙、英国等。

kiss /kɪs/ （动词）亲吻

–What do Russians do when they greet each other? 俄罗斯人见面如何打招呼？
–They kiss each other on the cheek. 他们互相亲吻对方的脸颊。

百科小贴士
西方人, 尤其是在欧洲南部国家, 亲吻是一种普通的礼仪, 表达对对方的喜爱、祝福、爱等感情。而在中国, 亲吻则含蓄得多, 在公共场合亲吻是不礼貌的。

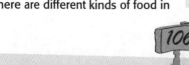

Knowledge is power.

kitchen /'kɪtʃɪn/ （名词）厨房

–Do you eat in the dining room?
你们在餐厅吃饭吗？
–No. We eat in the kitchen. 不，
我们在厨房吃饭。

kite /kaɪt/ （名词）风筝

–It's windy today. Let's fly our
kites. 今天有风，我们去放风筝吧！
–Good idea! 好主意！

kitten /'kɪtən/ （名词）小猫

–Where is the kitten? 猫咪在哪
里呀？
–It's playing with the puppy! 它在
和小狗玩呢！

knife /naɪf/ （名词）（复数 knives /naɪvz/ ）刀

–How should we use our knife
and fork? 应该怎样使用刀叉？
–Use the knife with your right
hand and the fork with your left
hand. 左手使叉，右手使刀。

百科小贴士
吃西餐一般使用刀叉，应尽量避免刀叉和
餐具碰撞发出声响，否则会被认为不礼貌。

knock /nɒk/ （动词）敲打，敲击

–Listen! Someone is knocking at
the door. 听！有人在敲门。
–Who can it be? 会是谁呢？

know /nəʊ/ （动词）（过去式 knew /njuː/，过去分词 known /nəʊn/ ）知道，认识

–Do you know his phone number?
你知道他的电话号码吗？
–Yes. It's 881120. 知道，881120。

knowledge /'nɒlɪdʒ/ （名词）知识

Knowledge is power. 知识就是力量。

koala /kəʊ'ɑːlə/ （名词）考拉

–Where does the koala come
from? 考拉产自哪里？
–Australia. 澳大利亚。

百科小贴士
考拉又称树袋熊、无尾熊，生活在澳大利
亚，以桉树叶为食。刚出生的小考拉宝宝
只有 2 厘米长，没有视力、没毛、没耳朵，
必须在妈妈的育儿袋里呆上 7 个月才能完
全发育好。

107

Like father, like son.

L

lab /læb/ （名词）实验室

–Does your school have a lab?
你们学校有实验室吗？
–Yes, we have a chemistry lab.
有，我们有一个化学实验室。

用法小贴士
lab 是 laboratory 的缩略形式。

labor /'leɪbə/ （名词）劳动

In the factory, workers are paid for
their labor. 工厂里工人按劳动获得
报酬。

拓展词汇
Labor Day 劳动节　laborer 劳动者

用法小贴士
labor主要指体力劳动。

lace /leɪs/ （名词）鞋带

–Your laces have come loose. 你的
鞋带开了。
–Oh. Thank you! 哦，谢谢！

ladder /'lædə/ （名词）梯子

–My cat has climbed up the tree
but is afraid to come down. 我的猫
爬到树上去却不敢下来。
–Let's find a ladder to get it down.
我们找架梯子把它接下来吧。

lady /'leɪdi/ （名词）(复数 ladies）
女士

–Who's the young lady in the
picture? 照片里的年轻女士是谁？
–It's my older sister. 是我姐姐。

ladybug /'leɪdibʌg/ （名词）
瓢虫

–If a ladybug lands on you, it's a
sign of luck. 如果一只瓢虫落在你
的身上，那预兆吉祥。
–Oh, that's just a myth. 喔，
那只是一种神话。

用法小贴士
美国英语用 ladybug，ladybird 为英国英
语。

百科小贴士
瓢虫有许多不同的种类，通常是红色或黄
色带有黑点，颜色鲜明。大多数瓢虫捕食
昆虫，如七星瓢虫就是捕食蚜虫的能手。
许多瓢虫的名字是以它们身上的星点数命
名的。

有其父必有其子。

lake /leɪk/ （名词）湖

–Let's have our picnic by the lake.
我们在湖边野餐吧。
–Good idea! Let's go! 好主意！走吧！

lamb /læm/ （名词）羊羔

There's a lovely lamb over there.
那边有一只很可爱的小羊。

用法小贴士

lamb 也可指羊羔肉。

lamp /læmp/ （名词）灯

–This room doesn't have much light. 房间里光线不足。
–You can turn on the table lamp if you want to read. 如果你想看书就把台灯打开吧。

拓展词汇

oil lamp 油灯　　street lamp 路灯

land /lænd/ （名词）土地

–What are the green parts on the globe? 地球仪上的绿色区域是什么？
–The green parts are land, and the blue parts are water. 绿色区域是陆地，蓝色区域是水。

language /ˈlæŋgwɪdʒ/ （名词）语言

–How many languages can you speak? 你会说几种语言？

–I speak Chinese and a little English.
我说中文，还会一点儿英文。

拓展词汇

body language 肢体语言　foreign language 外语　spoken language 口语　written language 书面语

百科小贴士

世界上的语言有五六千种，但在国际上经常使用的也就几十种。联合国通用语言有英语、法语、俄语、西班牙语、阿拉伯语和汉语 6 种。

lantern /ˈlæntən/ （名词）灯笼

–What a lovely lantern! 好可爱的灯笼！
–Thank you. I made it myself. 谢谢！是我自己做的。

拓展词汇

Lantern Festival 元宵节

large /lɑːdʒ/ （形容词）大的

–This coat is a bit small for me. Do you have a larger size? 这件大衣我穿有点儿小。有大一号的吗？
–Sorry. This is the largest size we have. 对不起，这是我们最大号的了。

反义词　small 小的　　little 小的

109

last /lɑːst/ （形容词）

1. 最后的
John was the first to come to the party and the last to leave. 约翰是第一个来到派对，最后一个离开的。
2. 刚过去的
last night 昨晚　　last week 上周
last month 上月　　last year 去年

last name /lɑːst 'neɪm/

（名词）姓

–You have the same last name. Are you from the same family? 你们的姓一样，是一家人吗？
–No, we just happen to have the same last name. 不是，我们只是碰巧姓一个姓。

百科小贴士

见 family name 百科小贴士。

late /leɪt/ （形容词）

1. 迟到的
–Hurry up, or we'll be late for school! 快点，不然上学要迟到了！
–Don't worry. There's still twenty minutes left. 不用着急，还有20分钟呢。
2. 晚的
–I have a lot of work and will be home late today. 今天有很多工作，我会晚点儿回家。
–OK, but don't be too late. 好的，但不要太晚。

反义词 early 早的

later /'leɪtə/ （副词）以后

–Someone's knocking at the door. I'll call you back later. 有人敲门，我过会儿给你打回去。

–Talk to you later, then. 那就一会儿再聊吧。

laugh /lɑːf/ （动词）（大）笑

–Why are you laughing so loudly? 你怎么笑得这么大声？
–I'm watching a funny cartoon film. 我正在看一部挺逗的卡通片。

反义词 cry 哭

law /lɔː/ （名词）法律

–A new law was passed to protect these rare wildflowers. 一条保护这些稀有野花的新法律已经通过。
–That's great! 那太好了！

拓展词汇

lawyer 律师

lay /leɪ/ （动词）（过去式、过去分词 laid /leɪd/）产（蛋）

–Do sea turtles lay their eggs in the sea? 海龟在海里下蛋吗？
–No, they lay their eggs in the sand. 不，它们在海滩上下蛋。

lazy /ˈleɪzi/（形容词）（比较级 **lazier**，最高级 **laziest**）懒惰的

My cat is very lazy. He sleeps most of the time. 我的猫很懒，大部分时间都在睡觉。

lead /liːd/（动词）（过去式、过去分词 **led** /led/）带领

–Look! The dog is leading the blind man across the street. 看！那条狗正领着那个盲人过马路。
–It's a guide dog. 那是条导盲犬。

拓展词汇
leader 领导人

leaf /liːf/（名词）（复数 **leaves** /liːvz/）叶子

The leaves on the tree turn into different colors in autumn. 树叶在秋天变成各种不同的颜色。

lean /liːn/（动词）（过去式、过去分词 **leaned**）倾斜

Jack leaned the ladder against the wall and climbed up it. 杰克把梯子靠在墙上，爬了上去。

leap /liːp/（动词）（过去式、过去分词 **leaped** /lept/）跳

–Did you see a dog just now? 你刚才有没有看到一条狗？
–Yes, I saw it leap over the fence. 看到了，我看见它跳到篱笆那边去了。

learn /lɜːn/（动词）（过去式、过去分词 **learned**）学，学习

–I learned a poem at school. 我在学校学了首诗。
–Can you read it to us? 你能读给我们听吗？

拓展词汇
learner 学习者

least /liːst/（形容词）最少的

Do the most important thing first and the least important thing last. 首先做最重要的事，最后做最不重要的事。

拓展词汇
at least 至少

leather /ˈleðə/（名词）皮革

These shoes are made of leather. 这些鞋子是皮革的。

leave /liːv/（动词）（过去式、过去分词 **left** /left/）

1. 离开
–Oh, you're still here! 哦，你还在这儿呢！
–Yes, I'm leaving tomorrow. 对，我明天离开。

2. 放下，留下
–Hello, may I speak to Susan please? 喂，我能跟苏珊讲话吗？
–She's out. Do you want to leave a message? 她出去了，你想留言吗？

left¹ /left/（形容词）左边的

–Do you write with your left hand or your right hand? 你用左手写字还是用右手写字？

Like father, like son.

−Right hand. 右手。

反义词 right 右边的

left² /left/ （名词）左边，左侧

Mary sits on my left and Peter on my right. 玛丽坐在我的左边，彼得坐在我的右边。

反义词 right 右边

leg /leg/ （名词）腿

−How many legs does an ant have? 蚂蚁有几条腿？
−Six. 6条。

lemon /'lemən/ （名词）柠檬

−Do you want some lemon juice in your drink? 你想在饮料里加点儿柠檬汁吗？
−Just a little, please. 请来一点点。

百科小贴士
柠檬是一种富含维生素 C 的营养水果。鲜柠檬汁是调制鸡尾酒的重要成分，也是西餐烹饪中常用的调味品。柠檬也有除臭功能，将柠檬切片放入冰箱，可清除冰箱异味。

lend /lend/ （动词）（过去式、过去分词 lent）借给，借出

−Can you lend me ten yuan? I don't have any money with me. 你能借我 10 块钱吗？我身上没钱。

−OK, here you are. 好的，给你。

反义词 borrow 借来

用法小贴士
注意 lend 和 borrow 意思相反。lend 指把东西借给别人，而 borrow 则指向别人借东西。

length /leŋθ/ （名词）长度

−What is the length and height of the wall? 这面墙的长度和高度是多少？
−It's 17 feet long and 10 feet high. 它有17英尺长，10 英尺高

less /les/ （形容词）更少的

There's less traffic on the weekend than on weekdays. 周末比平时车辆少。

反义词 more 更多的

用法小贴士
less 和 fewer 的意义相近，但 less 用在不可数名词前面，而 fewer 用在可数名词前面。如：I should eat less fat.（我应该少吃肥肉。）I should eat fewer sweets.（我应该少吃糖。）

lesson /'lesən/ （名词）

1. 课
−How many lessons does the textbook have? 这本教材有几课？
−It has 15 lessons. 有15课。
2. 教训
The accident taught me a good lesson. 这次事故给了我一个深刻的教训。

let /let/ （动词）（过去式、过去分词 let，现在分词 letting）让

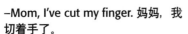

–Mom, I've cut my finger. 妈妈，我切着手了。
–Oh, dear. Let me have a look. 哦，天哪，让我看看。

letter /'letə/ （名词）

1. 信
–Could you send this letter for me? 你能帮我把这封信寄出去吗？
–No problem! 没问题！
2. 字母
–What letter is missing in this word? 这个单词中少了哪个字母？
–P. 字母p。

library /'laɪbrəri/ （名词）
（复数 **libraries**）图书馆

–Where did you get this book? 你从哪里弄到这本书的？
–I borrowed it from the school library. 我从学校图书馆借的。

拓展词汇

library card 借书卡

lie¹ /laɪ/ （动词）

1. 躺下（过去式 **lay** /leɪ/，过去分词 **lain** /leɪn/，现在分词 **lying** /laɪɪŋ/ ）
Please lie down and let the doctor check you. 请躺下让医生检查一下。
2. 说谎（过去式、过去分词 **lied** /laɪd/，现在分词 **lying** ）
–Don't lie to me. 不要对我说谎。
–I'm not lying. I'm telling the truth. 我没说谎，我说的是实话。

lie² /laɪ/ （名词）谎言

He's an honest person. He never tells a lie. 他是个诚实的人，从不撒谎。

拓展词汇

white lie 善意的谎言

life /laɪf/ （名词）

1. 生命
–Do you think there is life in space? 你觉得太空中有生命吗？
–Probably. 可能有吧。

拓展词汇

lifeboat 救生船　　life jacket 救生衣
life science 生命科学　　lifetime 终生

2. 生活
–School life is quite busy. 学校生活很忙碌。
–It's fun, too. Isn't it? 也很有乐趣，不是吗？

lift¹ /lɪft/ （动词）举起，提起

–Can you lift this bag of rice? 你能提起这袋米吗？
–Let me try. 让我试试。

lift² /lɪft/ （名词）电梯

–Can you lift the fingerprints off the glass? 你能不能把玻璃杯上的指纹除掉？
–Yes, they're very clear. 行，它们还挺明显哩。

用法小贴士
lift 是英国英语，美国英语用 elevator.

light¹ /laɪt/ （名词）光

–It's getting dark outside. 外边开始变黑了。
–There's more light near the window. 窗边光线亮一些。

拓展词汇
lightbulb 灯泡

light² /laɪt/ （形容词）轻的

–That bag is too heavy for me. 那个包我拿太重了。
–Carry this bag. It's the lightest. 拿这个包吧，这个最轻。

反义词 heavy 重的

lightning /ˈlaɪtnɪŋ/ （名词）闪电

–Do we see lightning or hear thunder first in a storm? 在暴风雨中，我们先看到闪电还是先听到雷鸣？

–We see lightning first, because light travels faster than sound. 先看到闪电，因为光的传播速度比声音快。

like¹ /laɪk/ （动词）喜欢

–I like the color of this dress. 我喜欢这条裙子的颜色。
–It suits you. 这颜色很适合你。

like² /laɪk/ （介词）像…一样

–Our teacher is like a friend to us. 我们的老师就像我们的朋友一样。
–You're very lucky. 你们真幸运。

line /laɪn/ （名词）

1. 线
–How many lines are there in a triangle? 三角形由几条线组成？
–Three. 3条。
2. 行
–On which line is the word "lucky"? lucky 这个词在哪一行？
–It's in line nine. 在第9行。

lion /ˈlaɪən/ （名词）狮子

–I've got two tickets for *The Lion King*. 我有两张《狮子王》的票。
–Can I go with you? 我能跟你一块儿去吗？

拓展词汇
sea lion 海狮

百科小贴士
狮子多生活于草原上，喜集群狩猎。雌狮是主要的猎手，但争夺地盘主要靠雄狮。

lip /lɪp/ （名词）嘴唇

–Can you tell Mary from Cathy?
你能区分出玛丽和凯茜吗？
–Sure. Mary has fuller lips. 当然能，
玛丽的嘴唇厚一些。

拓展词汇
lipstick 唇膏

liquid /'lɪkwɪd/ （名词）液体

–Can you give an example of a
liquid? 你能举出一种液体的例子
吗？
–Water is a liquid. 水是液体。

list /lɪst/ （名词）单子

–We have many things to buy. 我
们需要买许多东西。
–We'd better make a list. 我们最好
列一个清单。

拓展词汇
name list 名单   price list 价目单
shopping list 购物清单

listen /'lɪsən/ （动词）听

–Listen to me, please. 请听我说。
–I am listening. 我正听着呢。

little /'lɪtəl/ （形容词）小的

–Which do you want, the little one
or the big one?你要哪一个，小的
还是大的？
–The little one, please. 请给我小的。

反义词 big 大的
拓展词汇
little finger 小拇指

live /lɪv/ （动词）住

–Where do you live? 你住在哪儿？
–I live in the city center. 我住在市
中心。

拓展词汇
living room 起居室

lively /'laɪvli/ （形容词）（比较级 livelier，最高级 liveliest）活泼的

–The two sisters are very different.
这姐妹俩挺不一样。
–Yes. One is lively, while the other
is quiet. 是啊，一个活泼，另一个
安静。

lizard /'lɪzəd/ （名词）蜥蜴

–Have you seen a real lizard? 你见
过真的蜥蜴吗？
–No, I haven't. 没见过。

百科小贴士
蜥蜴为变温动物，适宜生活在温度为10至
30摄氏度的环境中。尾巴细长，容易断，
能再生，这也是蜥蜴逃生的一种本领。

Like father, like son.

lobster /ˈlɒbstə/ （名词）龙虾
Lobsters are expensive seafood. 龙虾是昂贵的海鲜。

lock¹ /lɒk/ （名词）锁
–What're you doing there? 你在那儿做什么呢？
–My key is stuck in the lock, and I can't open the door. 我的钥匙卡在锁里，开不开门了。

lock² /lɒk/ （动词）上锁，锁门
–You forgot to lock the door! 你忘记锁门了！
–Sorry, I was in a hurry. 对不起，我当时太着急了。

lollipop /ˈlɒlipɒp/ （名词）棒棒糖
–Do you have any fruit lollipops? 你这里有水果味的棒棒糖吗？
–Sure. How many do you want? 有，你要几个？

London /ˈlʌndən/ （名词）伦敦
–London is the capital of the United Kingdom. 伦敦是英国的首都。
–How many people live in London? 伦敦有多少人居住？
–About seven million. 大约700万。

百科小贴士
伦敦建都于11世纪，至今已有九百多年的历史。伦敦位于泰晤士河下游两岸。大英博物馆、伦敦塔、白金汉宫、大本钟均为著名的旅游景点。

lonely /ˈləʊnli/ （形容词）（比较级 **lonelier**，最高级 **loneliest**）孤独的，寂寞的
–Do you feel lonely when you're alone? 你一个人呆着的时候会寂寞吗？
–No. I like being alone. 不寂寞，我喜欢一个人呆着。

long /lɒŋ/ （形容词）长的
–Is the Yellow River the longest river in China? 黄河是中国最长的河流吗？
–No. The Yangtze River is the longest. 不是，长江是中国最长的河。

拓展词汇
long jump 跳远

look¹ /lʊk/ （动词）看
–Look! Here comes your mom. 看，你妈妈来了！
–I've seen her already. 我已经看见她了。

look² /lʊk/ （名词）看，瞧
–May I have a look at your new pen? 我能看一眼你的新钢笔吗？
–Sure. It writes very well. 当然，挺好用的。

用法小贴士
look 和 see 都是"看"的意思，前者指"看"的动作，后者指"看见"。此外，look 很少单独使用，往往与介词构成动词短语，如：look after（照看），look at（看），look for（寻找）。

loose¹ /luːs/ （形容词）松的

–Mom, one of my teeth has become loose. 妈妈，我的一颗牙松动了。
–Don't worry. A new one will grow in after it falls out. 别着急，它掉了以后会长出一颗新牙。

loose² /luːs/ （形容词）松的

–He has a loose tongue. 他咀巴毫无约束，随便乱讲。
–Yes, you can't tell him any secrets. 是的，你不能告诉他任何秘密。

lose /luːz/ （动词）（过去式、过去分词 lost /lɒst/ ）

1. 丢失
–I've lost my keys. 我把钥匙丢了。
–Did you search all your pockets? 你把所有口袋都找过了吗？

拓展词汇
lose face 丢脸　　lose one's way 迷路

2. 失败
–Did you win the football match? 你们赢了足球赛吗？
–No. We lost 2 to 3. 没有。我们2比3输了。

反义词　win 赢得

loud /laʊd/ （形容词）大声的，响亮的

–The music is too loud. Please turn it down. 音乐太闹了，把它调低点。
–All right. 好的。

拓展词汇
loudspeaker 扩音器，喇叭

love¹ /lʌv/ （名词）爱，爱情

–What's the film about? 这部电影是讲什么的？
–It's about love and friendship. 是关于爱情和友谊的。

拓展词汇
love song 情歌　　love letter 情书

love² /lʌv/ （动词）爱，喜欢

–I love you, Mom. 我爱你，妈妈。
–I love you, too. 我也爱你。

lovely /ˈlʌvli/ （形容词）（比较级 lovelier，最高级 loveliest ）可爱的

What a lovely baby! 多可爱的小宝宝啊！

low /ləʊ/ （形容词）低的，矮的

Rivers flow from high places to low places. 河流从高处流向低处。

反义词　high 高的

Like father, like son.

luck /lʌk/ （名词）运气
–Good luck on the exam! 考试好运哦！
–Thank you! 谢谢！

lucky /'lʌki/ （形容词）（比较级 **luckier**, 最高级 **luckiest**）幸运的
–It's raining now. 现在下雨啦。
–How lucky I am! I've just arrived home. 我真幸运！我刚好到家。

lunch /lʌntʃ/ （名词）午餐
–What shall we have for lunch? 我们中饭吃什么？
–Tofu, eggs, and rice. 豆腐、鸡蛋和米饭。

L

Many men, many minds.

M

machine /mə'ʃiːn/ （名词）机器

Machines do most of the work in modern factories. 在现代工厂里大部分工作都是由机器做的。

拓展词汇

machine gun 机关枪　sewing machine 缝纫机　washing machine 洗衣机

mad /mæd/ （形容词）（比较级 **madder**, 最高级 **maddest**）疯狂的

–The noise is driving me mad! What's going on upstairs? 这噪音快把我吵疯了！楼上干吗呢？
–I'll go and take a look. 我去看看。

madam /'mædəm/ （名词）女士，太太

–Can I help you, Madam? 女士，我能帮助您吗？
–Yes, I'd like to try on these shoes. 是的，我想试试这双鞋。

用法小贴士

madam 是对不知名女性的礼貌称呼。

magazine /ˌmægə'ziːn/ （名词）杂志

–You know so many stories! 你知道的故事真多！
–That's because I read a magazine every week. 那是因为我每周都看一本杂志。

mail¹ /meɪl/ （名词）邮件

–I want the letter to go quickly. 我想要这封信寄得快一点。
–OK, I'm sending it by express mail. 好吧，我用特快专递来寄。

拓展词汇

airmail 航空邮件　e-mail 电子邮件
mailbox 邮箱

mail² /meɪl/ （动词）邮寄

–I can't bring all these books with me. 我带不了这么多书。
–I'll mail them to you. 我给你邮寄过去吧。

用法小贴士

mail 在此处为美国英语的用法，英国英语表达此意时用 post。

main /meɪn/ （形容词）主要的

–What's the main problem? 主要问题是什么？
–The main problem is bad traffic. 主要问题是交通很糟糕。

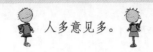

拓展词汇

main building 主楼   main course 主菜   main street 大街

make /meɪk/ （动词）（过去式、过去分词 made /meɪd/）

1. 制作，制造

–Did you buy the gift in New York? 这礼物是你在纽约买的吗？

–Yes, but it was made in China! 是的，但它是中国制造的！

2. 获得，赚（钱）

People must work to make money. 人们必须工作才能赚钱。

拓展词汇

make a living 谋生

male /meɪl/ （形容词）男性的，雄性的

Male birds are usually more beautiful than female birds. 雄鸟一般比雌鸟漂亮。

man /mæn/ （名词）

（复数 men /men/）男人

–Is that young man a teacher? 那个年轻人是老师吗？

–No, he's a lawyer. 不，他是律师。

manager /'mænɪdʒə/ （名词）

经理

–Can I speak to the manager? 我能和经理谈谈吗？

–Sorry. He's busy now. 抱歉，他现在很忙。

mango /'mæŋgəʊ/ （名词）

（或 mangoes 复数 mangos）芒果

Mangoes grow in hot, wet places. 芒果生长在炎热而潮湿的地方。

百科小贴士

芒果是著名的热带水果，风味独特，维生素含量高，但有些人食用后易过敏。

mankind /ˌmæn'kaɪnd/ （名词）

人类

Mankind must share this world with animals. 人类必须与动物共享这个世界。

manners /'mænəz/ （名词）

礼貌

It is bad manners to interrupt others when they are talking. 打断别人谈话是非常不礼貌的。

many[1] /'meni/ （形容词）（比较级 more，最高级 most）许多的

–Are there many boys in your class? 你们班有很多男生吗？

–Yes, more than half the class are boys. 有很多，一半以上都是男生。

many[2] /'meni/ （代词）许多

–Are you all from the same school? 你们都来自同一个学校吗？

–Many of us are. 我们中许多人是。

map /mæp/ （名词）地图

–Where is the zoo? 动物园在哪里？
–Let's check the map. 查一下地图吧。

March /mɑ:tʃ/ （名词）三月

International Women's Day is on March 8. 国际妇女节在3月8号。

百科小贴士

March 起源于拉丁文 Martius，源自古罗马宗教中的战神玛尔斯（Mars）。在战时，这个月因冬去春来，气候回暖，也是重新组织战役的时机。

mark /mɑ:k/ （名词）分数

–What mark did you get on your English exam? 你的英语考试得了什么分数（成绩）？
–I got a B. 我得了一个B。

拓展词汇

low marks 低分　　high marks 高分

market /'mɑ:kɪt/ （名词）市场

–Where do you buy fruits and vegetables? 你们在哪里买水果和蔬菜？
–From the market near our home. 从我们家附近的市场买。

marry /'mæri/ （动词）（第三人称单数**marries**，过去式、过去分词**married**，现在分词**marrying**）结婚，嫁，娶

The handsome prince married a beautiful princess. 英俊的王子娶了一位美丽的公主。

match /mætʃ/ （名词）（复数 **matches**）

1. 比赛

–Did you watch the tennis match? 你看过网球比赛了吗？
–Yes. It was exciting! 是的，太精彩了！

拓展词汇

match point 赛点

2. 火柴

–I'd like a box of matches. 我想要一盒火柴。
–Here you are. Fifty cents, please. 给你，50分。

拓展词汇

matchbox 火柴盒

mathematics /ˌmæθə'mætɪks/ （名词）（口语形式 **math** /mæθ/ ）数学

–What are the main subjects for primary students? 小学生的主要学科有什么？
–Chinese, mathematics, and English. 语文、数学和英语。

matter[1] /'mætə/ （名词）问题，麻烦

–What's the matter with you? 你怎么啦？
–I don't feel well. 我感觉不舒服。

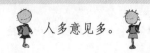

matter² /'mætə/ （动词）要紧，有关系

–I'm sorry to call you so late. 很抱歉这么晚给你打电话。

–It doesn't matter. 没关系。

用法小贴士

matter作为动词常用于疑问句或否定句中。

may /meɪ/ （情态动词）可以

–May I come in? 我可以进来吗？

–Come in, please. 请进来吧。

May /meɪ/ （名词）五月

International Labor Day falls on May 1. 国际劳动节在5月1号。

拓展词汇

May Day 五一国际劳动节

百科小贴士

May 起源于拉丁文 Maius，源自主管生长的自然女神迈亚（Maia），纪念她的庆祝节在5月举行，所以5月也叫做 May。

maybe /'meɪbi/ （副词）大概，可能，或许

–Are you playing soccer today? 你今天要去踢足球吗？

–Maybe. I'm not sure I'll have time. 可能会去，我不知道有没有时间。

me /mi/ （代词）我

–Please pass the book to me. 请把那本书递给我。

–Here you are. 给你。

meal /miːl/ （名词）饭，餐

–What time do you have your evening meal? 你们什么时候吃晚饭？

–Around six o'clock usually. 通常在6点钟左右。

用法小贴士

一天三顿饭的说法分别为：breakfast（早饭），lunch（午饭），supper（晚饭）。

mean /miːn/ （动词）（过去式、过去分词 **meant** /ment/） 意思是

The red light means "stop." The green light means "go." 红灯表示"停"，绿灯表示"行"。

meaning /'miːnɪŋ/ （名词）意思，意义

–What's the meaning of this word? 这个词是什么意思？

–It has several meanings. 它有几个意思呢。

meat /miːt/ （名词）肉

–Mom, I can help you cut up the meat. 妈妈，我可以帮你切肉。

–OK, but be careful. 好吧，但要小心。

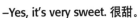
拓展词汇

meatball 肉丸　frozen meat 冻肉

raw meat 生肉

用法小贴士

肉的名称: beef 牛肉　chicken 鸡肉

lamb 羔羊肉　mutton 羊肉　pork 猪肉

百科小贴士

在一些西方国家里，鸡肉和猪肉等被称为白色肉类（white meat），牛肉、羊肉等被称为红色肉类（red meat），这主要是根据烹饪过后的不同颜色而分类的。

medicine /'medsən/ （名词）药, 药物

–Take this medicine three times a day. 这种药每天服用3次。

–Thank you, doctor. 谢谢你，医生。

meet /miːt/ （动词）（过去式、过去分词 met /met/）遇见，见面

–Have you two met before? 你俩以前见过吗？

–No. This is the first time we've met. 没有，这是我们第一次见面。

meeting /'miːtɪŋ/ （名词）会, 会议

We'll have a class meeting after school. 我们放学后要开个班会。

拓展词汇

meeting room 会议室

melon /'melən/ （名词）瓜，甜瓜

–Is the melon sweet? 这瓜甜吗？

–Yes, it's very sweet. 很甜。

拓展词汇

melon seed 瓜子　watermelon 西瓜

member /'membə/ （名词）成员，会员

–I'm a member of the school football team. 我是学校足球队的成员。

–Do you always train together? 你们经常在一起训练吗？

拓展词汇

family member 家庭成员

team member 队员

member country 成员国

mend /mend/ （动词）修理

–Mom, I fell down and ripped my shirt. 妈妈，我跌倒了，把衬衫也撕破了。

–Let's mend it together. 咱们一起修吧。

menu /'menjuː/ （名词）菜单

–Can we have the menu, please? 让我们看看菜单好吗？

–Sure, here you are. 好的，给您。

mermaid /'mɜːmeɪd/ （名词）美人鱼

The Little Mermaid lives in the sea. 小美人鱼生活在海里。

百科小贴士

《小美人鱼》是丹麦作家安徒生写的一个美丽的童话故事。在丹麦的哥本哈根海港有美人鱼的雕像。

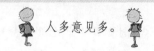
mess /mes/ （名词）脏乱

–What a mess your room is! 你的
房间可真乱！

–I'll clean it up in a minute. 我马上
就打扫。

message /'mesɪdʒ/ （名词）
消息，口信

–I'm going to visit Julie. 我要去看
朱莉。

–Will you take a message for me?
你给我带个口信好吗？

拓展词汇

text message （手机）短信

metal /'metəl/ （名词）金属

Gold, silver, and iron are all metals.
金、银和铁都是金属。

meter /'mi:tə/ （名词）米

–Yao Ming is more than two
meters tall. 姚明身高有两米多。

–Oh, he's almost twice as tall as
I am. 哦，他的身高几乎是我的两倍。

middle /'mɪdəl/ （名词）中间

–Here's a picture of my family. I'm
the one in the middle. 这是一张我
的全家照，中间那个是我。

–You were so little at that time.
那时候你真小。

拓展词汇

middle finger 中指　　middle school 中学

mile /maɪl/ （名词）英里

–Which is longer, a mile or a kilo-
meter? 1英里长还是1公里长？

–A mile is longer. 1英里长些。

百科小贴士

1英里约为 1609 米。

milk /mɪlk/ （名词）牛奶，奶

–I drink a glass of milk every
morning. 我每天早上喝一杯牛奶。

–It's a good habit. 这是个好习惯。

拓展词汇

milkman 送牛奶的人　　powdered milk 奶粉

milk white 乳白色的

the Milky Way 银河

百科小贴士

除膳食纤维外，牛奶含有人体所需要的各
种营养物质。牛奶经过巴氏杀菌后，可直
接饮用。若需加热，温热即可，过热会破
坏其营养成分。

million /'mɪliən/ （数词）一百万

The sun is about ninety-three
million miles away from us. 太阳距
离我们大约有9300万英里远。

拓展词汇

millionaire 百万富翁

mind[1] /maɪnd/ （动词）介意

–Do you mind if I open the
window? 你介意我打开窗户吗？

–Of course not. Go ahead. 当然不
会了，开吧。

mind² /maɪnd/ （名词）主意，想法

–You said you would go with me. 你说过你要和我一起去的。
–Sorry, but I've changed my mind. 对不起，我改变主意了。

拓展词汇

make up one's mind 下决心，打定主意

mine /maɪn/ （代词）我的

–Is this umbrella yours? 这把雨伞是你的吗？
–No, it's not mine. 不，不是我的。

minute /'mɪnɪt/ （名词）

1. 分，分钟
–What time is it now? 现在几点了？
–Ten minutes to seven. 差10分钟7点。
2. 片刻，一会儿
–Shall we go now? 我们现在走吗？
–Wait a minute. I'll turn off the TV. 稍等片刻，我要关掉电视。

拓展词汇

minute hand 分针

mirror /'mɪrə/ （名词）镜子

–Look in the mirror. What happened to your face? 照照镜子，你的脸怎么了？
–Oh, there's some ink on my face. 哦，我脸上沾了些墨水。

miss¹ /mɪs/ （名词）小姐

–Tony, this is Miss Black, our new neighbor. 托尼，这是布莱克小姐，我们的新邻居。
–Nice to meet you, Miss Black. 很高兴认识你，布莱克小姐。

用法小贴士

Miss 用来称呼未婚女子，放在姓氏或姓名之前，如可以说 Miss Black，也可以说 Miss Mary Black，但不可以说 Miss Mary。如果不知道对方是否已婚，可用 Ms（女士）称呼。

miss² /mɪs/ （动词）

1. 错过，未命中
–Did you get on the train? 你坐上火车了吗？
–No, I missed it. 没有，没赶上。

2. 想念，思念
–Goodbye! I'll miss you. 再见！我会想你的。
–I'll miss you, too. 我也会想你的。

mistake /mɪ'steɪk/ （名词）错误

–I am afraid you've made a mistake. My name is Jock, not Jack. 恐怕你弄错了。我叫乔克，不叫杰克。
–Oh, sorry, Jock. 噢，对不起，乔克。

人多意见多。

mix /mɪks/ （动词）混合，搀和
–Oil doesn't mix with water. 油不溶于水。
–Right. It'll stay on the surface of the water. 对，油会浮在水面上。

mobile phone /ˈməʊbaɪl ˈfəʊn/
（名词）手机，移动电话
Mobile phones have made communication so easy. 手机使通讯变得太容易了。

model /ˈmɒdəl/ （名词）模型
–What are you doing? 你在做什么？
–I'm building a model airplane. 我在做一架模型飞机。

拓展词汇
model ship 船模

modern /ˈmɒdən/ （形容词）现代化的，时髦的
Shanghai is a busy, modern city. 上海是一个繁忙的现代化都市。

mom /mʌm/ （名词）（儿语
mommy /ˈmʌmi/）妈妈
–Can I speak to your mom? 我能跟你妈妈讲话吗？

–She's not home yet. Please call in ten minutes. 她还没到家，请10分钟后来电话。

用法小贴士
mom是mother的口语化称谓，mommy是mom的儿语，都是英国英语，美国英语称为 mommy 或 mom。

moment /ˈməʊmənt/ （名词）
1. 时刻，时候
Just at that moment, the policemen arrived. 就在那时，警察赶到了。

2. 片刻，瞬间
–Can we begin now? 我们现在可以开始吗？
–Wait a moment, please. 请稍等片刻。

Monday /ˈmʌndeɪ/ （名词）
星期一
–It's Monday tomorrow. 明天是星期一。
–I wish the weekend were longer. 真希望周末能长一点。

money /ˈmʌni/ （名词）钱
–Do you have any money with you? 你身上带钱了吗？
–Yes, but not much. 是的，但不多。

126

拓展词汇

pocket money 零用钱

monitor /'mɒnɪtə/ （名词）

班长

–Who's the class monitor? 谁是这个班的班长啊？

–I am. 是我。

monkey /'mʌŋki/ （名词）猴子

Monkeys are good at climbing trees. 猴子善于爬树。

百科小贴士

猴子和人一样，属于灵长目。全世界猴子的种类约有 200 种。由于生态环境的破坏，猴子濒临灭种的危险。世界自然保护联盟呼吁人们保护自然，保护濒危动物。

month /mʌnθ/ （名词）月

–How many months are there in a year? 一年有几个月？

–Twelve months. 12个月。

moon /muːn/ （名词）月亮

–Does the moon give out light? 月亮本身发光吗？

–No, its light comes from the sun. 不发光，它的光来自太阳。

拓展词汇

moon cake 月饼　moonlight 月光
full moon 满月　half moon 半月

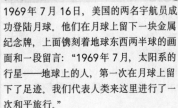

百科小贴士

1969 年 7 月 16 日，美国的两名宇航员成功登陆月球。他们在月球上留下一块金属纪念牌，上面镌刻着地球东西两半球的画面和一段留言："1969 年 7 月，太阳系的行星——地球上的人，第一次在月球上留下了足迹。我们代表人类来这里进行了一次和平旅行。"

mop¹ /mɒp/ （名词）拖把

–There's water on the floor. 地板上有水。

–I'll go and get a mop. 我去拿个拖把来。

mop² /mɒp/ （动词）（过去式、过去分词 **mopped**，现在分词 **mopping**）拖地

–There's such a mess. I'll have to mop the floor. 这儿真乱，我要拖一下地板。

–Let's sweep it before mopping it. 先扫一下再拖吧。

more¹ /mɔː/ （形容词）

（**many** 和 **much** 的比较级）更多的

–Can you give me a little more time? 你能再给我一点儿时间吗？

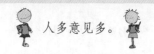

–I'm sorry. But time is already up. 很抱歉，时间已经到了。

more² /mɔː/ （副词）（**much** 的比较级）更

–This book is very interesting. 这本书很有趣。

–But I think that one is more interesting. 但我认为那一本更有趣。

morning /'mɔːnɪŋ/ （名词）早晨，上午

It's cooler in the morning than in the afternoon. 上午比下午凉快。

most¹ /məʊst/ （形容词）（**many** 和 **much** 的最高级）大多数的

–Most tree leaves turn yellow in autumn. 大多数树叶在秋天会变黄。

–Some turn red. 有的会变红。

most² /məʊst/ （副词）（**much** 的最高级）最

–Which season do you like most? 你最喜欢哪个季节？

–Spring. It's the most beautiful season of the year. 春天，因为这是一年中最美丽的季节。

most³ /məʊst/ （代词）大多数

Most of us are going. 我们中大多数人都要去。

mother /'mʌðə/ （名词）母亲

–Do you help your mother with housework? 你帮妈妈做家务吗？

–Yes. My father helps, too. 是的，我爸爸也帮着做。

拓展词汇

mother country 祖国　Mother Nature 大自然　mother tongue 母语

Mother's Day /'mʌðəz deɪ/ 母亲节

–What will you give your mother on Mother's Day? 母亲节那天你送什么给你妈妈？

–I'll make a card and buy some flowers for her. 我会做张卡，还会买些花送她。

百科小贴士

母亲节起源于美国，是每年5月的第2个星期日。第一个现代母亲节于1908年5月10日在西弗吉尼亚和宾夕法尼亚州举行，在这次节日里，康乃馨被选中为献给母亲的花，并流传下来。

motorbike /'məʊtəbaɪk/ （名词）摩托车

–Can you ride a motorbike? 你会骑摩托车吗？

–No, but I can drive a car. 不会，但我会开汽车。

mountain /'maʊntɪn/ （名词）
山

–Mountain climbing is an exciting sport. 登山是一项很刺激的运动。
–Yes, but you need special gear. 是啊，但是你需要有特殊的工具。

mouse /maʊs/ （名词）（复数 mice /maɪs/ ）

1. 老鼠
Mice can spread diseases. 老鼠能传播疾病。

百科小贴士
世界上最著名的老鼠当属沃尔特·迪斯尼公司的米老鼠（Mickey Mouse）。米老鼠诞生于1928年，是家喻户晓的动画形象。

2. 鼠标
Early computers did not have a mouse. 早期的电脑没有鼠标。

mouth /maʊθ/ （名词）嘴巴
–I have a toothache. 我牙疼。
–Open your mouth and let me check. 张开嘴，让我检查一下。

move /muːv/ （动词）

1. 移动，运动
Earth is moving all the time. 地球一刻不停地在运动。

2. 搬动
–Please move the table into the dining room. 请把桌子搬到餐厅里。
–I can't move it by myself. 我一个人搬不动。

3. 感动
Everyone was moved by her kindness. 每个人都被她的善良所感动。

Mr. /'mɪstə/ （名词）先生
–May I speak with Mr. Brown, please? 能请布朗先生接电话吗？
–He isn't in at the moment. 他这会儿不在。

用法小贴士
Mr 是 Mister 的缩略形式。

Mrs. /'mɪsɪz/ （名词）太太
–Can I help you, Mrs. Brown? 布朗太太，你想买点什么？
–Yes, I want to buy a carpet. 我想买一块地毯。

Ms. /mɪz/ （名词）女士
–This is Ms. Green. 这位是格林女士。
–Glad to meet you, Ms. Green. 很高兴认识你，格林女士。

用法小贴士
Miss 指女孩或未婚女士，Mrs 指已婚妇女，Ms 既可以用作对未婚女子的称呼，也可以用作对已婚女子的称呼。

人多意见多。

much¹ /mʌtʃ/ （形容词）（比较级 **more**，最高级 **most**）许多

–There's so much food here. 这儿有这么多吃的。

–Shall we invite some friends to share it? 咱们请几个朋友来一块吃怎么样？

much² /mʌtʃ/ （副词）（比较级 **more**，最高级 **most**）非常

–Sir, your wallet. You've left it on the table. 先生，你的钱包，你忘在桌上了。

–Oh, really? Thank you very much! 哦，真的，太谢谢你了！

much³ /mʌtʃ/ （名词）大量

–Have you finished your work? 你们工作做完了吗？

–No, there's still much to do. 没有，还有好多没做。

mud /mʌd/ （名词）泥，泥土

–You've got mud on your trousers. 你裤子上有泥。

–I was walking in the rain. 我刚才在雨中走来着。

mule /mjuːl/ （名词）骡子

Mules can carry heavy weight. 骡子能驮重物。

museum /mjuːˈziːəm/ （名词）博物馆

–Did you see anything interesting at the museum? 你在博物馆看到好玩的东西了吗？

–Yes. I saw the bones of a dinosaur. 是的，我看到了恐龙的骨骼。

mushroom /ˈmʌʃruːm/ （名词）蘑菇

Look, a lot of mushrooms have grown after the rain. 看，雨后长出了好多蘑菇。

M

music /'mjuːzɪk/ （名词）音乐

They danced to the music. 他们伴着音乐翩翩起舞。

拓展词汇

music box 八音盒

must /mʌst/ （情态动词）必须

–Do we have to finish this today? 我们非得今天把这个做完吗？
–Yes, we must. 是的，我们必须做完。

mutton /'mʌtən/ （名词）羊肉

–Do you want mutton or pork? 你想要羊肉还是猪肉？
–I'd like some mutton. 我想要点儿羊肉。

my /maɪ/ （代词）我的

–Where're my glasses? 我的眼镜哪儿去了？

–Oh, Granny. They're right on your nose. 哦，奶奶，眼镜就在您鼻子上。

myself /maɪ'self/ （代词）我自己

–Do you need any help? 你需要帮忙吗？
–No, thank you. I'll do it myself. 不用，谢谢。我要自己做。

N

nail /neɪl/ （名词）钉子

–What happened to your trousers? 你的裤子怎么啦？

–They got caught on a nail. 让钉子给挂了。

name /neɪm/ （名词）名字

–What's your name? 你叫什么名字？

–My name is Dan Smith. And yours? 我叫丹·史密斯。你呢？

百科小贴士

西方人的名字一般分为 first name（名）和 last name（姓），名在前，姓在后，与汉语的姓名顺序相反。

nap /næp/ （名词）小睡

–I want to take a nap after lunch. 我午饭后想睡个午觉。

–You'd better set your alarm clock first. 你最好先把闹钟设好。

narrow /ˈnærəʊ/ （形容词）

狭窄的

This part of the river is narrow, so the boats can only go through one by one. 这段河很窄，所以船只能一只接一只地过。

反义词 wide 宽阔的

拓展词汇

narrow-minded 心胸狭窄的

nation /ˈneɪʃən/ （名词）

1. 国家

The United Nations has nearly 200 member nations. 联合国有近200个成员国。

2. 民族

Different nations speak different languages. 不同的民族讲不同的语言。

national /ˈnæʃənəl/ （形容词）

国家的，全国的

–What day is our National Day? 我们的国庆节是哪一天？

–It's the first of October. 是 10 月 1 日。

nature /ˈneɪtʃə/ （名词）

1. 自然

Some flowers grow wild in nature. 有些花是大自然中野生的。

2. 天性

It's human nature to care about people. 关心别人是人的天性。

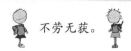
naughty /'nɔ:ti/（形容词）

（比较级 **naughtier**，最高级 **naughtiest**）淘气的

–Tom broke the window again. 汤姆又把窗户打碎了。
–What a naughty boy! 真是个淘气孩子！

near[1] /nɪə/（介词）靠近

–Is the hotel near the sea? 旅馆离海近吗？
–Yes, it's only a stone's throw from the beach. 近，离海滨非常近。

near[2] /nɪə/（形容词）附近的

–Is your home far from the school? 你家离学校远吗？
–No, it's near the school. 不远，我家离学校很近。

反义词 far 远的

neck /nek/（名词）脖子

Giraffes have long necks. 长颈鹿长着长脖子。

necklace /'neklɪs/（名词）项链

–Your necklace is pretty. 你的项链很漂亮。

–Thank you. It's made of glass. 谢谢你，它是玻璃做的。

need[1] /ni:d/（动词）需要

–Let me know if you need any help. 你需要什么帮助的话就告诉我。
–Thank you. You are so kind. 谢谢，你真好。

need[2] /ni:d/（名词）需要

–Are we going to be late? 我们会迟到吗？
–No, there's no need to hurry. 不会，不用着急。

needle /'ni:dəl/（名词）针

–Can I borrow a needle and thread? One of my buttons has come loose. 我能借用一下针线吗？我的一颗扣子松了。
–Here you are. 给你。

拓展词汇
needlework 针线活

neighbor /'neɪbə/（名词）邻居

–Do you like your new home? 你喜欢你的新家吗？
–Sure. The neighbors are very friendly. 当然啦，邻居们都很友好。

neither[1] /'naɪðə/（代词）两者都不

–There are two books here. Which one do you like? 这儿有两本书，你喜欢哪一本？
–Neither. 都不喜欢。

neither² /'naɪðə/ （连词）既不…（也不…）

–He can neither read nor write. 他不识字，也不会写字。
–But he's very clever. 但他很聪明。

nephew /'nefjuː/ （名词）侄子，外甥

–Who's this young boy? 这个小男孩儿是谁呀？
–He's my older sister's son, my nephew. 他是我姐姐的儿子，我的外甥。

nervous /'nɜːvəs/ （形容词）紧张的

–Were you nervous before the test? 你考试前紧张吗？
–No, not at all! 不，一点儿也不！

nest /nest/ （名词）巢

Many birds build their nests in trees. 很多鸟把窝建在树上。

net /net/ （名词）

1. 网，渔网
The old man threw the net into the water and caught four fish. 老人把网抛到水里，捕到了4条鱼。
2. 因特网（同 **Internet**）

拓展词汇
network 网络

never /'nevə/ （副词）从未，从不

–Have you ever failed any exams? 你考试有没有不及格过？
–No, never. 没有，从来没有过。

new /njuː/ （形容词）新的

–Who's the girl in the blue dress? 那个穿蓝色裙子的女孩是谁？
–She's our new classmate Lucy. 她是我们的新同学露西。

反义词　old 旧的

news /njuːz/ （名词）新闻，消息

–I have both good news and bad news for you. 我既有好消息也有坏消息给你。
–Oh, tell me the good news first. 哦，还是先告诉我好消息吧。

用法小贴士
news 为不可数名词，"一条消息"的说法是 a piece of news.

newspaper /'njuːspeɪpə/ （名词）报纸

–What's new in today's newspaper? 今天报纸上有什么新闻？
–A lot. Read it for yourself. 好多呢，你自己看吧。

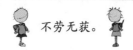
拓展词汇

daily paper 日报　morning paper 早报
evening paper 晚报

用法小贴士

在上下文清楚时，newspaper可简称为
paper。

New Year /ˌnjuː ˈjɪə/ （名词）
新年

–Happy New Year! 新年好！
–Happy New Year to you, too! 也祝
你新年好！

拓展词汇

New Year's Day 元旦
New Year's Eve 除夕
Chinese New Year 中国新年（即春节）

next /nekst/ （形容词）下一个的

–We'll have a test next week. 下礼
拜我们要考试了。
–Yes, we don't have much time to
prepare. 是啊，我们没有多少时间
准备了。

拓展词汇

next door 隔壁的

nice /naɪs/ （形容词）好的

–What do you think of your new
teacher? 你觉得你们的新老师怎么
样？
–She's a nice person. 她人挺好的。

niece /niːs/ （名词）侄女，外甥女

–Who's this lovely baby in the
picture? 照片上这个可爱的婴儿是
谁啊？

–She's my niece. She was born last
week. 是我侄女，上星期刚出生。

night /naɪt/ （名词）晚上

Bats sleep during the day and
catch food at night. 蝙蝠白天睡觉，
晚上捕食。

反义词　day 白天

拓展词汇

nightclothes 睡衣　nightlife 夜生活

nine /naɪn/ （数词）九

–What time is it now? 现在几点了？
–It's nine o'clock. 9点。

nineteen /ˌnaɪnˈtiːn/ （数词）
十九

–What's your seat number? 你的座
位号码是多少？
–Nineteen. 19。

ninety /ˈnaɪnti/ （数词）九十

My great grandma lived to ninety.
我的曾祖母活到了90岁。

no /nəʊ/ （副词）不

–Do you need any help? 你需要什
么帮助吗？
–No, thank you. 不用，谢谢！

反义词　yes 是

nobody /ˈnəʊbɒdi/（代词）没有人

–Nobody is in the classroom. Where are the students? 教室里没有人，学生们都去哪儿了？
–They are doing exercises in the playground. 他们在操场做操呢。

nod /nɒd/（动词）（过去式、过去分词 **nodded**，现在分词 **nodding**）点头

Please nod your head if you agree. 如果同意的话请点点头。

noise /nɔɪz/（名词）噪音

–Can I go into the lab? 我可以进实验室吗？
–Yes, but please don't make any noise. 可以，但是请不要发出声音。

noisy /ˈnɔɪzi/（形容词）（比较级 **noisier**，最高级 **noisiest**）吵闹的

–It's so noisy here. 这里太吵了。
–Yeah, we'd better turn down the music. 是啊，我们最好把音乐关小点。

none /nʌn/（代词）一个也没有

–How many eggs are left in the fridge? 冰箱里还有多少鸡蛋？
–None. 一个也没有了。

noodle /ˈnuːdəl/（名词）面条

–What would you like, rice or noodles? 你想吃什么，米饭还是面条？
–Noodles, please. 面条。

百科小贴士

中国的面条起源于汉代。那时面食统称为饼，因面条要在"汤"中煮熟，所以又叫汤饼。早期的面条有片状的、条状的。

noon /nuːn/（名词）中午

–Do you want to go to the post office at noon? 你中午想去邮局吗？
–No, I'll go later. 不，我晚会儿再去。

nor /nɔː/（连词）也不

–Where's Fred? 弗雷德在那里？
–I don't know. He's neither here nor there. 我不知道，他不在这里，也不在那里。

north /nɔːθ/（名词）北方

–Does the window of that room face north or south? 那间屋子的窗户是朝北还是朝南的？
–It faces north. 是朝北的。

反义词　south 南方

拓展词汇

northeast 东北　　northwest 西北

nose /nəʊz/（名词）鼻子

It's bad manners to pick your nose in public. 在公共场合挖鼻孔是不礼貌的。

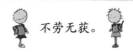

不劳无获。

拓展词汇

eagle nose 鹰钩鼻　　high nose 高鼻子

not /nɒt/ （副词）不是

–Is this your umbrella? 这是你的雨伞吗?

–No, it isn't. 不，这不是。

用法小贴士

not 往往跟动词搭配构成否定式，在口语中常用缩写形式。例如: do not 缩写为 don't，is not 缩写为 isn't。

note /nəʊt/ （名词）笔记

–Should we take notes in class? 我们上课时要记笔记吗?

–Sure. They are useful for our study. 要啊，笔记对学习很有帮助。

拓展词汇

notebook 笔记本

nothing /ˈnʌθɪŋ/ （代词）什么也没有

–What did you say? 你说什么?

–Nothing. I didn't say anything. 没有，我什么也没说。

notice /ˈnəʊtɪs/ （动词）注意到

–Have you noticed the change in the weather? 你注意到天气的变化了吗?

–Yes. It looks like rain. 注意到了，看来像要下雨。

November /nəʊˈvembə/ （名词）十一月

–How many days are there in November? 11 月有多少天?

–There are thirty days in November. 11 月有 30 天。

百科小贴士

11 月叫 November，因为这是罗马历法的第 9 个月，而拉丁文 novem 就是 9。

now /naʊ/ （副词）现在

–Are you better now? 你现在好点儿了吗?

–Much better. Thank you. 好多了。谢谢你。

number /ˈnʌmbə/ （名词）数，号码

–What's your room number? 你的房间号是多少?

–305. 305。

拓展词汇

telephone number 电话号码

nurse /nɜːs/ （名词）护士

–Are nurses all female? 护士都是女的吗?

–No. There are male nurses. 不是，也有男护士。

nut /nʌt/ （名词）坚果

–What do squirrels eat? 松鼠吃什么?

–They eat nuts. 它们吃坚果。

object /'ɒbdʒɪkt/ （名词）物体
Every object on Earth has a weight.
地球上的所有物体都有重量。

ocean /'əʊʃən/ （名词）海洋
–Which is the largest ocean on
Earth? 地球上最大的海洋是哪个？
–It's the Pacific Ocean. 是太平洋。

百科小贴士
世界上有四大洋，由大到小分别是：the
Pacific Ocean （太平洋）、the Atlantic
Ocean（大西洋）、the Indian Ocean
（印度洋）和 the Arctic Ocean （北冰
洋）。

o'clock /ə'klɒk/ （副词）…点钟
–What time is it? 几点了？
–It's five o'clock. 5 点。

用法小贴士
o'clock 只用于正点时间，且经常省略。

October /ɒk'təʊbə/ （名词）十
月
–What's the best time to visit
Beijing? 什么时候去北京游览最好？
–I'd say October. It's neither hot
nor cold. 我认为 10 月最好，
既不热也不冷。

百科小贴士
10 月叫 October，因为这是罗马历法的第
8 个月，而拉丁文的 octo 就是 8。

of /ɒv/ （介词）…的
–What's on the top of the hill?
小山顶上有什么？
–Nothing. But you can have a
good view of the city. 没有什么，
但你可以看到全城。

of course /ɒv 'kɔːs/ 当然
–Do you want to win the game?
你想赢得比赛吗？
–Of course! 当然啦！

off¹ /ɒf/ （副词）关掉
–Turn off the light when you leave.
离开的时候把灯关上。
–OK, I will. 好的。

off² /ɒf/ （介词）离开…
Keep off the grass. 勿踏草地。

office /'ɒfɪs/ （名词）办公室
Please come to my office after
class. 下课后请到我办公室来。

拓展词汇
office building 办公大楼　office hours
工作时间　post office 邮局

眼不见，心不念。

officer /ˈɒfɪsə/（名词）军官，警官

–Please give me a hand, officer.
警官，请帮我一个忙。
–What's the matter? 什么事？

often /ˈɒfən/（副词）经常

–Why is he often late for school?
他为什么上学老是迟到？
–Because he lives too far away.
因为他住得离学校太远了。

oh /əʊ/（叹词）哦，啊，哎呀

–It's Mary's birthday today. 今天是玛丽的生日。
–Oh, I almost forgot! 哎呀，我差点儿忘了！

oil /ɔɪl/（名词）

1. 油，食用油
–How do you like this dish? 这道菜怎么样？
–There's too much oil in it. 油太多了。
2. 石油
This area is rich in oil and gas. 这个地区石油和天然气很丰富。

拓展词汇

oil painting 油画　cooking oil 烹调用油 vegetable oil 植物油

OK¹ /ˌəʊˈkeɪ/（形容词）（口语）可以，好

–Is it OK if I come with you? 我能跟你一块儿去吗？
–Of course it's OK. 当然可以啦。

用法小贴士
OK 是 okay 的简写形式。

OK² /ˌəʊˈkeɪ/（叹词）好

–May I go skating today, Mom?
妈妈，今天我可以去溜冰吗？
–OK! 可以！

old /əʊld/（形容词）

1. 年老的
Some old people don't look old at all. 有的老年人看起来一点儿都不老。

2. …岁的
–How old are you? 你多大了？
–I'm twelve years old. 我 12 岁。
3. 旧的
My older brother has given me his old bike. 我哥哥把他的旧自行车给我了。

拓展词汇

old age 晚年　old people's home 养老院

Olympic Games /əˌlɪmpɪk ˈgeɪmz/（名词）奥林匹克运动会，奥运会

The Olympic Games have a long history. 奥运会历史悠久。

百科小贴士
希腊人在公元前 776 年举办了第一届奥运会。第一届现代奥运会于 1896 年 4 月在雅典举行，以后每 4 年在会员国举行一次，到 2004 年，已经举办了 28 届。2008 年第 29 届奥运会由北京主办。

 139

Out of sight, out of mind.

on /ɒn/ （介词）在…上面
There's a box on the table. The box has a picture on it. 桌上有个盒子，盒子上有图案。

once /wʌns/ （副词）
1. 一次
–Have you been to Shenzhen? 你去过深圳吗？
–I've been there once. 去过一次。
2. 曾经
She was once a shy girl, but she's now a public speaker. 她曾经是个害羞的女孩，但现在却成了公众演说家。

拓展词汇
once upon a time 从前

one¹ /wʌn/ （数词）一
–How much is your new bike? 你的新自行车多少钱？
–It's one hundred and twenty-one yuan. 121 元。

拓展词汇
one by one 一个接一个

one² /wʌn/ （代词）哪个，这个，那个
–Which one do you want, the blue one or the green one? 你想要哪个，蓝色的还是绿色的？
–The blue one, please. 请给我蓝色的。

onion /ˈʌnjən/ （名词）洋葱
–Do you like onions? 你喜欢吃洋葱吗？

–No, I don't. 不喜欢。

百科小贴士
切洋葱时，洋葱味会刺激眼睛。只要在切洋葱前把刀放在冷水里浸一会儿，再切就不会刺激眼睛了。

only¹ /ˈəʊnli/ （副词）仅仅，只是
–Are you serious? 你是认真的吗？
–Oh, no. I'm only joking. 哦，不是。我只是开玩笑。
My little dog is only one year old, but he can jump over that fence. 我的小狗只有1岁，但它可以跳过那道栅栏。

only² /ˈəʊnli/ （形容词）唯一的
–How many children do your parents have? 你父母有几个孩子？
–I'm their only child. 我是他们的独生子。

open¹ /ˈəʊpən/ （动词）打开
Open your books and turn to page 16. 打开书，翻到第16页。
反义词 close 关闭

open² /ˈəʊpən/ （形容词）开着的
–Should I close the window? 我需要把窗户关上吗？

–No. Leave it open. 不，让它开着。

反义词 closed 关着的

拓展词汇

open letter 公开信

operation /ˌɒpəˈreɪʃ(ə)l/

（名词）手术

–My grandma has just had an operation on her heart. 我奶奶刚做了心脏手术。

–I hope she's feeling better now. 我希望她现在好一些了。

or /ɔː/ （连词）或者

–Would you like black tea or green tea? 你要喝红茶还是绿茶？

–Black tea, please. 请给我红茶。

orange[1] /ˈɒrɪndʒ/ （名词）

1. 柑橘，橙子

I have an orange tree in my garden. 我的花园里有一棵橙子树。

拓展词汇

orange juice 橙汁

百科小贴士

橙子的维生素 C 和柠檬酸含量都很丰富，但一天之内食量不宜超过 3 个，吃多了反而对口腔、牙齿有害。

2. 橙黄色，橘黄色

orange[2] /ˈɒrɪndʒ/ （形容词）橙黄色的，橘黄色的

–What's the color of the box? 黑匣子是什么颜色的？

–It's orange. 是橙黄色的。

order[1] /ˈɔːdə/ （名词）命令

It's a soldier's duty to follow orders. 军人的天职是服从命令。

order[2] /ˈɔːdə/ （动词）命令

"Freeze!" the policeman ordered. "不许动！" 警察命令道。

other[1] /ˈʌðə/ （形容词）（两个中的）另外的

–Where's your other glove? 你的另一只手套呢？

–I lost it in the library yesterday. 昨天在图书馆弄丢了。

other[2] /ˈʌðə/ （代词）（两个中的）另一个，其他的人（或事物）

–Do you have any pets? 你有宠物吗？

–Yes. I have two cats. One is black and the other is white. 有。我有两只猫，一只是黑色的，另一只是白色的。

our /aʊə/ （形容词）我们的

–We finished our work on time. 我们按时完成了工作。

–We finished on time, too. 我们也按时完成了。

ours /auəz/ （代词）我们的
（东西）

–Our new house is in the country-side. How about yours? 我们的新房子在乡下，你们的呢？
–Ours is in the city. 我们的房子在城里。

ourselves /auə'selvz/ （代词）我们自己

–These kites are so lovely. Where did you buy them? 这些风筝真可爱，你们在哪里买的？
–We made them ourselves! 是我们自己做的！

out /aut/ （副词）在外面，向外

–It's sunny outside. Let's go out for a walk. 外面阳光很好，我们出去散步吧。
–OK. 好的。

outside¹ /ˌaut'saɪd/ （名词）外面

–What're the workers doing? 那些工人在干什么？
–They are cleaning the outside of the building. 他们正在清洗大楼的外面。

outside² /ˌaut'saɪd/ （副词）在外面，向外面

–It's so noisy outside. 外面真吵。
–Let's close the windows. 我们把窗户关上吧。

over¹ /'əuvə/ （介词）

1. （表示位置）在…的上面
Many birds are flying over the lake. 许多鸟在湖面上飞翔。
2. （表示数量）超过
–People under 18 are not allowed in Internet cafés. 未满 18 岁者不得进入网吧。
–I know. I'm already over 18. 我知道。我已经超过 18 岁了。

> **用法小贴士**
>
> 在英语中可以用 on、above、over 表示"在…上（面）"。on 表示表面接触，如 on the table；above 和 over 表示不与其下的表面接触，如 fly above/over the lake。

over² /'əuvə/ （形容词）结束的

–Is the game over yet? 比赛结束了吗？
–Yes. It finished half an hour ago. 结束了，半小时前结束的。

own¹ /əun/ （形容词）自己的

–Is it true? 这是真的吗？
–Of course. I saw it with my own eyes. 当然啦，是我亲眼所见。

own² /əun/ （动词）拥有

Mr. Smith owns a fruit shop. 史密斯先生拥有一家水果店。

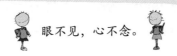

owner /ˈəʊnə/ （名词）物主，所有者

–Who's the owner of this house? 这所房子的主人是谁？

–It's Ms. Duncan. 是邓肯女士。

ox /ɒks/ （名词）（复数 **oxen** /ˈɒksən/ ）公牛

–Is this a cow or an ox? 这是头母牛还是公牛？

–It's an ox. 是头公牛。

百科小贴士

公牛极具攻击性，西班牙斗牛表演中的公牛是经过专门饲养的。

Penny wise and pound foolish.

P

Pacific Ocean /pə'sɪfɪk 'əʊʃən/
（名词）太平洋

–Is China on the west coast of the Pacific Ocean? 中国位于太平洋西岸吗？

–Yes, it is. 是的。

page /peɪdʒ/ （名词）页

–On which page is the answer to this question? 这个问题的答案在第几页？

–On page 27. 在第27页。

pain /peɪn/ （名词）痛苦

–What's wrong with you? 你哪里不舒服？

–I have a pain in my head. 我头疼。

paint /peɪnt/ （动词）绘画

Chinese paintings are painted in ink. 中国画是用墨画的。

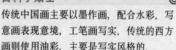

拓展词汇

paintbrush 画笔   paint box 颜料盒

painter /'peɪntə/ （名词）画家

–Is he an artist? 他是个艺术家吗？

–Yes. He's a painter. 是的，他是个画家。

painting /'peɪntɪŋ/ （名词）画

–This is a lovely painting. 这幅画很可爱。

–It's a Chinese New Year painting. 这是中国年画。

pair /peə/ （名词）一对

–I've lost one of my gloves. 我丢了一只手套。

–You've got to buy a new pair, then. 那你就得买双新的了。

palace /'pælɪs/ （名词）宫殿

–The Palace Museum was the emperor's home. 故宫曾经是皇帝的住所。

144

–It's now a public museum. 它现在是公共博物馆。

pale /peɪl/ （形容词）苍白的

–You look pale. 你看起来脸色苍白。
–I feel very tired. 我感觉很累。

panda /'pændə/ （名词）（也作 giant panda）大熊猫

–Are there many pandas in the world? 世界上的大熊猫很多吗？
–No, there are very few. 不多，数量很少。

百科小贴士

大熊猫是中国独有的珍稀、濒危动物，目前总数不到 1000 只。刚出生的大熊猫一般只有一百多克，最小的仅五十多克，最大的不超过 200 克，相当于母亲体重的千分之一左右。人工繁殖、饲养大熊猫是有效的保护措施。

paper /'peɪpə/ （名词）纸

–How many pieces of paper do you need? 你需要多少张纸？
–I need ten. 我需要 10 张。

拓展词汇

paper knife 裁纸刀　paper tiger 纸老虎

百科小贴士

造纸术、印刷术、指南针、火药是中国古代的四大发明。

pardon /'pɑ:dən/ （名词）原谅

I beg your pardon. What did you say? 请原谅，你刚才说什么？

用法小贴士

这一意思有很多个表达法，可以简单地说："Pardon?" 或者 "Pardon me?"。说的时候用升调。

parent /'peərənt/ （名词）父亲，母亲，家长

–What do your parents do? 你爸爸妈妈是做什么的？
–They are both teachers. 他们都是老师。

park¹ /pɑ:k/ （名词）公园

There are many parks in Beijing. 北京有很多公园。

park² /pɑ:k/ （动词）停车

–Can we park here? 我们能在这儿停车吗？
–No. There's a "No Parking" sign. 不行，有"禁止停车"的标志。

拓展词汇

car park（英），parking lot（美）停车场
parking ticket 违章停车罚款单

parrot /'pærət/ （名词）鹦鹉

–Can parrots speak? 鹦鹉会说话吗？
–Some of them can. 有的鹦鹉会说。

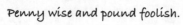*Penny wise and pound foolish.*

part /pɑ:t/ （名词）部分

–Which part of the book do you like best? 你最喜欢这本书的哪一部分？
–The last part. 最后一部分。

拓展词汇

part-time job 兼职工作

party /'pɑ:ti/ （名词）（复数 parties）聚会，派对

–What are you planning for your birthday? 你生日打算做什么？
–I want to have a birthday party. 我想开一个生日派对。

拓展词汇

dinner party 晚宴

pass /pɑ:s/ （动词）

1. 经过，路过
–Can you return this book for me? 你能帮我还这本书吗？
–Sure. I will pass the library on my way to class. 当然，我去上课的路上会经过图书馆。
2. （考试）及格
–Was the exam difficult? 考试难吗？
–Yes. Only half of the class passed. 难，全班只有一半的人及格。

past¹ /pɑ:st/ （名词）过去

–In the past, it took many days to send a letter. 过去寄一封信要好多天。
–Yes. But it takes only a few seconds now, by e-mail. 是啊，现在用电子邮件，几秒钟就好啦。

past² /pɑ:st/ （介词）过

–What time does the film begin? 电影几点开始？
–At half past seven. 7点半。

path /pɑ:θ/ （名词）小路

–What's your father doing in the garden? 你爸爸在花园里做什么呢？
–He's building a stone path. 他正在建一条石头小路。

patient¹ /'peɪʃənt/ （名词）病人

–Is this a good hospital? 这家医院好吗？
–Yes. Patients are taken good care of here. 好，病人在这里能够得到很好的照顾。

patient² /'peɪʃənt/ （形容词）耐心的

The teacher is very patient with her students. 这位老师对她的学生很耐心。

146

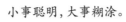

小事聪明，大事糊涂。

pay /peɪ/ （动词）（过去式、过去分词**paid** /peɪd/）付钱

–How much did you pay for the MP3 player? 你买这个MP3花了多少钱？
–It cost me 500 yuan. 500块钱。

PC /ˌpiː ˈsiː/ （名词）个人电脑

–Do you have a computer? 你有电脑吗？
–Yes, I have a PC. 是的，我有一台个人电脑。

用法小贴士
PC 的全称是 personal computer.

PE /ˌpiː ˈiː/ （名词）体育

–What did you do in the PE class today? 你们今天体育课做什么了？
–We played basketball. 我们打篮球了。

用法小贴士
PE 的全称是 physical education.

pea /piː/ （名词）豌豆

–Can you use chopsticks? 你会用筷子吗？
–Of course. I can use them to pick up peas. 当然，我能用筷子夹豌豆呢。

百科小贴士
豌豆中含有丰富的蛋白质和人体所必需的各种氨基酸，经常食用对生长发育大有益处。

peace /piːs/ （名词）和平

People all over the world love peace. 世界人民都热爱和平。

拓展词汇
world peace 世界和平

peach /piːtʃ/ （名词）（复数 **peaches**）桃

–Would you like red peaches or green ones? 你想要红桃还是绿桃？
–Red ones, please. 请给我红桃吧。

百科小贴士
桃营养丰富，富含水分、维生素C和铁，而糖分含量却很少，非常适合夏季食用。在中国，桃还被看作是长寿的象征。

peacock /ˈpiːkɒk/ （名词）孔雀

Peacocks have beautiful tail feathers. 孔雀的尾羽很漂亮。

百科小贴士
孔雀是一种热带鸟，头上有羽冠，雄孔雀的尾羽特别长，开屏时呈扇形，常见的有绿孔雀和白孔雀。

peanut /ˈpiːnʌt/ （名词）花生

Peanuts grow under the ground. 花生是长在地下的。

百科小贴士
花生开花在地面上，花儿授粉后，花托就会扎入地中，然后在地下成长为果实，就是我们吃的花生，所以花生被称为"落花生"。

P

147

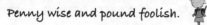
拓展词汇

peanut butter 花生酱

pear /peə/ （名词）梨

–Is this a pear tree or an apple tree? 这是棵梨树还是苹果树？
–It's a pear tree. 是梨树。

百科小贴士

梨富含水分，具有清心润肺的作用。在秋季气候干燥时，每天吃一两个梨有益健康。另外梨还可以清喉降火，食用煮好的熟梨能起到保养嗓子的作用。

pen /pen/ （名词）笔，钢笔

–Can I borrow your pen? 我能借你的笔吗？
–Sure, here you are. 可以，拿去吧。

拓展词汇

pen pal 笔友   pen name 笔名

pencil /'pensəl/ （名词）铅笔

–How many pencils are there in your pencil box? 你的铅笔盒里有多少支铅笔啊？
–There are two blue pencils and one red one. 有两支蓝铅笔和一支红铅笔。

拓展词汇

pencil box 铅笔盒
pencil sharpener 卷笔刀

people /'pi:pəl/ （名词）人，人们

–How many people live in the U.S.? 美国有多少人口？
–More than three hundred million. 超过三亿

perhaps /pə'hæps/ （副词）可能

–Where's the dog? 狗跑哪儿去了？
–I don't know. Perhaps it's behind the sofa. 不知道，可能在沙发后面吧。

person /'pɜ:sən/ （名词）人

–Do you know Andy? 你认识安迪吗？
–No. You're the only person I know here. 不认识，这儿我只认识你一个人。

pet /pet/ （名词）宠物

–Do you have any pets? 你养宠物吗？
–Yes. I have a few goldfish. 是的，我养了几条金鱼。

拓展词汇

pet shop 宠物店   pet name 昵称

phone /fəʊn/ （名词）电话

The little boy has learned to use the phone. 这个小男孩已学会用电话了。

拓展词汇

phone book 电话簿   phone card 电话卡   phone line 电话线
phone number 电话号码

photo /'fəʊtəʊ/ （名词）（复数 **photos**）照片

–Where did you take these photos? 你在哪儿照的这些照片？
–I took them in my hometown. 在我的老家照的。

physics /'fɪzɪks/ （名词）物理，物理学

–We're taking physics next year. 我们明年要开物理课了。
–It's an interesting subject. 物理是一门有趣的课。

pianist /'piːənɪst/ （名词）钢琴家

Pianists usually have long fingers. 钢琴家的手指一般都很长。

piano /pi'ænəʊ/ （名词）（复数 **pianos**）钢琴

–Mary began to play the piano when she was four. 玛丽从4岁开始弹钢琴。
–Then she must be a good player. 那她一定弹得很好。

百科小贴士
钢琴是一种键盘乐器，1709年左右由克里斯托福里在佛罗伦萨制造出来，18世纪中叶广泛流行。钢琴有各种式样和各种不同尺寸；现代钢琴的音质和触键都与以前的钢琴有很大不同。

pick /pɪk/ （动词）

1. 拾起
Please pick up the paper on the floor. 请把地上那张纸捡起来。
2. 采摘
–The apples have turned red. 苹果已经变红了。
–Let's pick them now. 我们现在就采摘吧。

picnic /'pɪknɪk/ （名词）野餐

–What are you going to do on the weekend? 你们周末打算做什么？
–We're going to have a picnic in the park. 我们要去公园野餐。

picture /'pɪktʃə/ （名词）

1. 图画
–Have you been to Guilin? 你去过桂林吗？
–Yes. It's as pretty as a picture. 去过，那儿美得像一幅画。
2. 照片
–Can we take pictures in the museum? 我们可以在博物馆里拍照吗？
–I don't think so. 我想不能。

pie /paɪ/ （名词）派，馅饼
–What smells so good? 什么东西这么香？

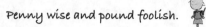
–Oh. I've just made some apple pies. 哦，我刚才做了几个苹果派。

用法小贴士

"派" 是英语 pie 的音译词。

piece /piːs/ （名词）块，片，段

–Please pass me a piece of paper. 请递给我一张纸。

–Here you are. 给你。

pig /pɪg/ （名词）（儿语 piggy /'pɪgi/ ）猪

The farmer is raising two pigs and many chickens. 这位农夫养了两头猪和许多鸡。

pigeon /'pɪdʒɪn/ （名词）鸽子

There are many pigeons in the square. 广场上有很多鸽子。

百科小贴士

鸽子分三大类：肉鸽、信鸽和观赏鸽。信鸽的记忆力很好，辨别方向的能力特别强，因此早就被人类当作传递信息的信使，纯白的鸽子还被人们视为和平的象征。

piggy bank /'pɪgi bæŋk/ （名词）储蓄罐

–How many coins are there in your piggy bank? 你的储蓄罐里有多少硬币？

–About two hundred. 大概200个。

pilot /'paɪlət/ （名词）飞行员

–What does your uncle do? 你叔叔是做什么的？

–He is a pilot. 他是个飞行员。

pineapple /'paɪnæpəl/ （名词）菠萝

–Can we eat the pineapple now? 我们现在可以吃菠萝吗？

–No, we need to put it in salty water for a while. 不行，我们得把它放在盐水里浸一会儿。

百科小贴士

菠萝又名凤梨，原产巴西，16世纪时传入中国。菠萝有七十多个品种，是岭南四大名果之一。菠萝含有大量的果糖，具有解暑止渴、消食止泻的功能。

ping-pong /'pɪŋpɒŋ/ （名词）乒乓球

–We often play ping-pong after class. 我们下课后经常打乒乓球。

–Can I join you? 我能跟你们一块儿打吗？

百科小贴士

乒乓球运动于19世纪末起源于英国，最初只是一种活动性游戏。1926年，国际乒乓球联合会正式成立，并决定举行第一届世界乒乓球锦标赛。乒乓球是中国的国球。

pink¹ /pɪŋk/ （形容词）粉色的

–What colour is your new dress? 你的新裙子是什么颜色的？

–It's pink. 是粉色的。

pink² /pɪŋk/ （名词）粉色

People say pink suits girls and blue suits boys. 人们说，粉红色适合女孩而蓝色适合男孩。

pioneer /ˌpaɪə'nɪə/ （名词）先锋，先驱

He is a pioneer of new ideas. 他是一位新思想的先锋。

pizza /'piːtsə/ （名词）比萨饼

–Where does pizza come from? 比萨饼是从什么地方传过来的？
–Italy. 意大利。

place /pleɪs/ （名词）地方

–I love this little town. 我喜欢这个小镇。
–So do I. It's a quiet, beautiful place. 我也喜欢，这个地方又安静又漂亮。

plan¹ /plæn/ （动词）计划

–What do you plan to do after the exam? 你考试完打算干什么？
–I'll have a good rest. 我要好好休息一下。

plan² /plæn/ （名词）计划

–What's your plan for the holiday? 你的假期计划是什么？
–I haven't made any plans yet. 我还没做什么计划呢。

plane /pleɪn/ （名词）飞机

–Are you going by plane or by train? 你是坐飞机还是坐火车去？
–I'm going by plane. 坐飞机去。

plant /plɑːnt/ （名词）植物

–Can plants grow without light? 植物没有光能生长吗？
–No, most plants can't. 不，大多数植物没有阳光不能生长。

拓展词汇

wild plant 野生植物
garden plant 园艺植物

plastic /'plæstɪk/ （名词）塑料

Most toys are made of plastic. 大多数玩具都是塑料做的。

plate /pleɪt/ （名词）盘子

There is a plate of meat and a bowl of soup on the table. 桌上有一盘肉、一盘汤。

play /pleɪ/ （动词）

1. 参加（体育活动或比赛）
–Can you play basketball? 你会打篮球吗？
–No, but I can play ping-pong. 不会，但我会打乒乓球。
2. 玩耍
–Where are the children? 孩子们在哪儿？
–They're playing outside. 他们在外面玩。
3. 演奏
–Mary will play the violin at my birthday party. 玛丽将在我的生日派对上拉小提琴。
–Wonderful! 太好了！

P

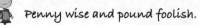
拓展词汇

playground 运动场

player 运动员，演奏者

please /pliːz/ （动词）请

–Will you please turn on the fan? It's hot here. 打开电扇好吗？这儿太热了。

–I'm sorry, but the power is out. 很抱歉，停电了。

pleased /pliːzd/ （形容词）开心的，高兴的

–I'm very pleased you can come. 你能来我真高兴。

–Thank you for inviting me. 感谢你邀请我。

pleasure /'pleʒə/ （名词）高兴

–Thank you for your help. 感谢你的帮助。

–My pleasure. 我很乐意效劳。

拓展词汇

amusement park 游乐场

plenty /'plenti/ （名词）大量，充足

–There are plenty of books in Jerry's study. 杰里的书房里有很多书。

–He always likes reading. 他一向都喜欢读书。

用法小贴士

与 a lot of 一样，plenty 既可修饰可数名词，也可修饰不可数名词，如 plenty of time（大量时间）。

plus /plʌs/ （介词）加，加上

–What is three plus one? 3加1是多少？

–It's four. 是4。

反义词 minus 减，减去

拓展词汇

plus sign 加号

p.m. /ˌpiː 'em/ 下午

–What time does the museum close? 博物馆几点关门？

–At 5 p.m. 下午5点。

用法小贴士

a.m. 表示上午。

pocket /'pɒkɪt/ （名词）口袋

The man took the keys out of his pocket. 那个人从口袋里掏出钥匙。

拓展词汇

pocketbook 口袋书，袖珍书

pocket dictionary 袖珍词典

pocket money 零花钱

poem /ˈpəʊɪm/ （名词）诗

–Mom, can you explain the poem to me? 妈妈，你能给我解释一下这首诗的意思吗？

–Yes, let me see. 好的，让我看一下。

poet /ˈpəʊɪt/ （名词）诗人

–Who's your favorite poet? 你最喜欢哪个诗人呀？

–I like Li Bai and Du Fu. 我喜欢李白和杜甫。

police /pəˈliːs/ （名词）警方，警察

Get out of here, or I'll call the police! 出去，不然我就要报警了！

拓展词汇

police station 警察局　policeman 警察
police car 警车　police dog 警犬

polite /pəˈlaɪt/ （形容词）礼貌的，客气的

It's not polite to speak with your mouth full. 嘴里塞满食物时讲话是不礼貌的。

反义词　rude　粗鲁的

pond /pɒnd/ （名词）池塘

–Are there any fish in the pond? 这个池塘有鱼吗？

–Yes, there are many here. 有好多呢。

拓展词汇

fish pond 鱼塘

pony /ˈpəʊni/ （名词）（复数 **ponies**）小马

–How do you say "small horse" in English? 怎么用英语说"小马"？

–It's a "pony." 叫 pony。

pool /puːl/ （名词）游泳池，水池

The children jumped into the pool one by one. 孩子们一个接一个地跳进了游泳池。

拓展词汇

swimming pool 游泳池

poor /pʊə/ （形容词）贫穷的，贫困的

The doctor often helps poor people. 这位医生经常帮助穷人。

反义词　rich　富有的

pop /pɒp/ （形容词）流行音乐的

–Do you know much about pop songs? 关于流行歌曲你知道得多吗？

–I have no idea. Ask John. 我不了解。你问约翰吧。

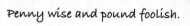

Penny wise and pound foolish.

—I'll be there in five minutes. 我5分钟后就到。

拓展词汇

pop music 流行音乐　pop song 流行歌曲　pop singer 流行歌手

popcorn /'pɒpkɔːn/ （名词）
爆米花

—You can't have popcorn as your supper. 你不能把爆米花当晚饭吃。
—But I just can't stop! 但我就是停不下来！

popular /'pɒpjʊlə/ （形容词）
流行的，受欢迎的

The teacher is very popular with students. 这位老师很受学生们的欢迎。

population /ˌpɒpjʊ'leɪʃən/
（名词）人口

China has the largest population in the world. 中国人口居世界首位。

pork /pɔːk/ （名词）猪肉

—Which do you like better, pork or beef? 你更喜欢吃猪肉还是牛肉？
—I like pork better. 我更喜欢吃猪肉。

possible /'pɒsɪbəl/ （形容词）
可能的

—Please come here as soon as possible. 请尽快赶到这儿来。

反义词　impossible　不可能的

post¹ /pəʊst/ （名词）邮件

—Is there any post for me? 有我的邮件吗？
—Sorry, there isn't. 对不起，没有。

拓展词汇

postbox 邮箱　post office 邮局
by post 邮递

post² /pəʊst/ （动词）邮寄

—Where is Sue? 休去哪里了？
—She has gone to post a letter. 她去寄信了。

用法小贴士
post是英国英语，美国英语用 mail。

postcard /'pəʊstkɑːd/ （名词）
明信片

—Remember to send us a postcard when you get there. 到了那里记着给我们寄张明信片。
—I will. 我会的。

百科小贴士
明信片的问世距今已有一百三十多年的历史，由于使用简便，邮资便宜，深受人们欢迎。中国第一套明信片由清政府发行于1896年。

154

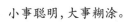

postman /'pəʊstmən/ （名词）

（复数 **postmen** /'pəʊstmən/ ）

邮递员

–Has the postman come yet? 邮递员来过了吗？

–Yes, but there's no letter for you. 来过了，但没你的信。

用法小贴士

postman是英国英语，美国英语用mailman。

pot /pɒt/ （名词）壶，罐

–I'm thirsty. 我渴了。

–There's some tea in the pot. 茶壶里有茶水。

拓展词汇

teapot 茶壶　　coffee pot 咖啡壶

potato /pə'teɪtəʊ/ （名词）

（复数 **potatoes** ）马铃薯，土豆

Potatoes grow under the ground. 土豆生长在地下。

拓展词汇

sweet potato 甘薯

pound /paʊnd/ （名词）

1. 磅（重量单位）

–What did you buy? 你买了什么？

–One pound of apples and two pounds of bananas. 一磅苹果，两磅香蕉。

2. 英镑（货币单位，符号为£）

–What money do they use in Britain? 英国使用什么货币？

–The British pound. 英镑。

百科小贴士

英镑为英国的货币单位，1英镑等于100便士（penny）。

practice¹ /'præktɪs/ （名词）

练习，实践

Practice makes perfect. 熟能生巧。

practice² /'præktɪs/ （动词）

练习

–Do you practice the piano every day? 你每天都练习弹钢琴吗？

–Yes, I practice for one hour every day. 是的。我每天练1小时。

praise¹ /preɪz/ （名词）称赞，表扬

Parents need to give their children more praise. 父母需要多表扬自己的孩子。

praise² /preɪz/ （动词）赞扬，表扬

The mother praised her children for keeping the room clean. 母亲表扬孩子们保持了房间的清洁。

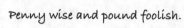 *Penny wise and pound foolish.*

prepare /prɪ'peə/ （动词）准备

–Shall we go to see a film tonight? 我们今晚去看电影好吗？
–No, I have to prepare for an exam. 不了，我得复习备考。

present¹ /'prezənt/ （形容词）在场的

–Were you present at the time? 你当时在场吗？
–No, I was at home. 不在，我当时在家里。

present² /'prezənt/ （名词）礼物

–What can I give him for a birthday present? 我送什么给他做生日礼物好呢？
–How about a book? 送本书怎么样？

president /'prezɪdənt/ （名词）总统

–Who was the first president of the United States? 谁是美国的第一任总统？
–George Washington. 乔治·华盛顿。

pretty /'prɪti/ （形容词）（比较级 **prettier**，最高级 **prettiest**）漂亮的

–You look pretty in that pink dress. 你穿那条粉色的裙子很漂亮。
–Thank you! 谢谢！

反义词 ugly 丑陋的

price /praɪs/ （名词）价格

–What's the price of this? It doesn't have a price on it. 这件东西什么价格？上面没有标明价格。
–Let me have a look. Well, it's nine dollars and ninety-nine cents. 让我看一下，喔，九元九角九分

pride /praɪd/ （名词）骄傲，自豪

She looked at her grandson with pride. 她自豪地看着她的孙子。

primary school /praɪməri skuːl/ （名词）小学

Most children enter primary school at the age of six. 大多数孩子在6岁时开始上小学。

prince /prɪns/ （名词）王子

–Does the prince have any brothers? 王子有兄弟吗？
–No, he is the king's only son. 没有，他是国王的独子。

princess /ˌprɪn'ses/ （名词）公主

Snow White is a beautiful princess. 白雪是一个美丽的公主。

prize /praɪz/ （名词）奖品

The Nobel Prize was set up by Alfred Nobel. 诺贝尔奖是阿尔弗雷德·诺贝尔设立的。

拓展词汇

prize winner 获奖者　prize money 奖金

小事聪明，大事糊涂。

problem /'prɒbləm/ （名词）
问题

–Do you have any problems at your new school? 你在新学校有什么问题吗？
–Yes. I don't have many friends yet. 有，我的朋友还不多。

produce /prə'djuːs/ （动词）
生产

–What does this factory produce? 这家工厂生产什么？
–It produces bicycles. 生产自行车。

program /'prəʊɡræm/ （名词）
节目

–What's your favorite TV program? 你最喜欢的电视节目是什么？
–I like cartoons best. 我最喜欢动画片。

拓展词汇

TV progam　电视节目
live program　实况转播

progress /'prəʊɡres/ （名词）
进步

–How did you make such progress in English? 你的英语怎么进步这么大？

–I've been talking with my friends in English every day. 我每天都用英语和我的朋友对话。

promise[1] /'prɒmɪs/ （名词）
诺言

It's wrong to break a promise. 说话不算话是不对的。

promise[2] /'prɒmɪs/ （动词）
许诺，承诺

–I won't be late next time. I promise. 我下次不会再迟到，我保证。
–OK, remember to keep your promise. 好，记得遵守你的诺言。

protect /prə'tekt/ （动词）保护
A hen always protects her children. 母鸡总是保护她的孩子。

proud /praʊd/ （形容词）骄傲的

–You've won first prize. We're so proud of you! 你得了一等奖，我们真为你骄傲！
–Thank you. 谢谢你们。

province /'prɒvɪns/ （名词）省

–Kunming is the capital of which province? 昆明是哪个省的省会？
–It's the capital of Yunnan Province. 是云南省的省会。

public¹ /'pʌblɪk/ （名词）公众

–Is the museum open to the public? 这家博物馆对公众开放吗？
–Not yet, but it will be soon. 还没有，但很快会的。

拓展词汇

public opinion 舆论

public² /'pʌblɪk/ （形容词）公众的，公共的

Everyone can borrow books from public libraries. 每个人都可以从公共图书馆借书。

pull /pʊl/ （动词）拉

–Dinner is ready. 饭做好了。
–Let's pull the chairs up to the table. 咱们把椅子拉到桌子旁边吧。

反义词 push 推

punish /'pʌnɪʃ/ （动词）惩罚

–Do your parents punish you when you do something wrong? 你做错事的时候，你父母会惩罚你吗？
–No, they tell me why I'm wrong. 不，他们会告诉我为什么我错了。

pupil /'pjuːpɪl/ （名词）小学生

–Helen and Julia are pupils in the same school. 海伦和朱莉娅是同一所学校的学生。
–They're very good friends. 她们还是很好的朋友。

purple¹ /'pɜːpəl/ （形容词）紫色的

Some grapes are green, and some are purple. 葡萄有的是绿色的，有的是紫色的。

purple² /'pɜːpəl/ （名词）紫色

–Is purple one of the colors of a rainbow? 紫色是彩虹中的颜色吗？
–Yes, it is. 是的。

push /pʊʃ/ （动词）推

–I can't open the door. 我开不了门。
–Oh, you should push it, not pull. 哦，你应该推，而不是拉。

反义词 pull 拉

put /pʊt/ （动词）（过去式、过去分词 **put**，现在分词 **putting**） 放

–Where did I put the key? 我把钥匙放哪儿了？
–Here you are. You left it in the lock! 给你，你把它忘在锁上啦！

拓展词汇

put on 穿上　　put up with 忍耐

puzzle /'pʌzəl/ （名词）难题

How dinosaurs died out is still a puzzle. 恐龙是如何灭绝的仍然是一个谜。

拓展词汇

crossword puzzle 填字游戏
jigsaw puzzle 拼图玩具

quarrel¹ /'kwɒrəl/ （动词）（过去式、过去分词 **quarreled**，现在分词 **quarreling**）吵架

–Do you quarrel with each other? 你们俩吵架吗?
–We did when we were small, but not now. 我们小时候吵，但现在不了。

用法小贴士
在美国英语中，quarrel的过去式、过去分词拼作quarreled，现在分词拼作 quarreling.

quarrel² /'kwɒrəl/ （名词）吵架

–Why don't you and Emma speak to each other? 你跟埃玛为什么不讲话?
–We had a quarrel yesterday. 我们昨天吵架了。

quarter /'kwɔːtə/ （名词）
1. 四分之一
–There are four people here. 这儿有4个人。

–So we can cut the cake into quarters. 我们可以蛋糕切成4块。
2. 一刻钟
–It's a quarter to seven now. 现在7点差一刻。
–Oh, there's still fifteen minutes to the seven o'clock news. 哦，离7点的新闻还有15分钟。

queen /kwiːn/ （名词）女王，王后

–Where does the queen live? 女王住在哪里?
–She lives in her palace. 她住在自己的宫殿里。

拓展词汇
queen bee 蜂王   queen ant 蚁王

百科小贴士
女王是对君主制国家中女性君主的称呼。君主制国家有英国、荷兰、澳大利亚、加拿大等。

question /'kwestʃən/ （名词）问题

–May I ask you a question? 我能问你一个问题吗?
–Sure. Go ahead. 当然可以了，说吧。

拓展词汇
question mark 问号

quick /kwɪk/ （形容词）快的
–Please be quick. 请快点。
–I'm coming. 我来了。

quickly /'kwɪkli/ （副词）
迅速地
–Do we have to walk so quickly?
我们非得走这么快吗？
–Yes, the film begins in five minutes. 是的，电影5分钟后就要
开始。

quiet /kwaɪət/ （形容词）安静的
–Where's Dad? 爸爸在哪儿？
–Keep quiet. Dad is asleep. 别出
声，爸爸睡着了。

quilt /kwɪlt/ （名词）被子
–Is the quilt warm enough? 被子够
暖和吗？
–It's very warm. Thank you! 很暖
和，谢谢！

quite /kwaɪt/ （副词）相当
–How's the weather in Beijing?
北京的天气怎么样？
–It's quite hot in summer and quite cold in winter. 夏天挺热，
冬天挺冷。

quiz /kwɪz/ （名词）（复数
quizzes）测验
–I'm so nervous. 我好紧张。
–Take it easy. It's only a quiz.
放轻松，这只不过是一次小测验。

用法小贴士
quiz 指测验，test 指一般考试，exam 指
比较重要的考试，如期中考试（midterm
exam）和期末考试（final exam）。

R

rabbit /'ræbɪt/ （名词）兔，家兔

Rabbits have long ears. 兔子长着长耳朵。

用法小贴士

rabbit（家兔）比 hare（野兔）体型小。儿童一般称兔子为 bunny。

race /reɪs/ （名词）赛跑

–Who won the 400-meter race? 谁赢了400米赛跑？
–Alison won first prize. 艾莉森得了第一名。

拓展词汇

racing car 赛车　　horse race 赛马
boat race 赛船

radio /'reɪdɪəʊ/（名词）（复数 **radios**）收音机

I listen to music on the radio every morning. 我每天早上都用收音机听音乐。

拓展词汇

radio station 广播电台

railway /'reɪlweɪ/ （名词）铁路，铁轨

–Why was the train late? 火车为什么晚点了？
–There was a railway accident. 铁路出事故了。

拓展词汇

railway station　火车站
railway worker　铁路工人

用法小贴士

railway 是英国英语，美国英语用 railroad。

rain¹ /reɪn/ （名词）雨

–Do you have much rain in this area? 你们这个地方下雨多吗？
–We have a lot of rain in summer, but very little rain in winter. 夏天雨多，冬天很少。

拓展词汇

rainbow 彩虹　　raincoat 雨衣
raindrop 雨滴　　rainforest 热带雨林
rainwater 雨水

rain² /reɪn/ （动词）下雨

–The air is very dry. 空气真干燥。
–Yeah, it hasn't rained for a long time. 是啊，很长时间没下雨了。

rainy /'reɪni/ （形容词）下雨的

–Bad weather, isn't it? 今天天气很不好，不是吗？
–Yes. It's windy and rainy! 是呀，又刮风又下雨的！

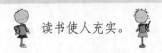

读书使人充实。

rat /ræt/ （名词）大老鼠

Cats are the biggest enemies of rats. 猫是老鼠最大的敌人。

用法小贴士

rat指比家鼠（mouse）更大的老鼠。

reach /ri:tʃ/ （动词）到达

–When will we reach the camp? 我们什么时候能到达营地？

–In an hour or so. 大约一小时吧。

用法小贴士

在表示"到达"的意思时，reach 比 get to 和 arrive at/in 正式，并且 reach 常表示用了较长时间、付出努力后到达。

read /ri:d/ （动词）（过去式、过去分词 read /red/）（阅）读

–Can you read English books? 你能读英语书吗？

–Yes, but not very difficult ones. 能，但只能读不是很难的书。

拓展词汇

reader 读者，读物　reading room 阅览室

ready /'redi/ （形容词）准备好的

–Are you ready? 准备好了吗？

–Yes. We are all ready. 是的，我们都准备好了。

real /ri:l/ （形容词）真正的，真实的

–Is the story real? 这个故事是真的吗？

–No, the writer made it up. 不是，是作者编的。

really¹ /'ri:əli/ （副词）很，非常

–I've lost my money! 我丢了钱！

–Oh, that's really bad! 啊，那太糟糕了！

really² /'ri:əli/ （叹词）（表示惊讶、怀疑、兴趣等）真的吗

–Mrs. Lee's having a baby soon. 李太太快要生孩子了。

–Really? 真的吗？

reason /'ri:zən/ （名词）原因，理由

–Do you have any reasons for doing this? 你做这件事有什么原因吗？

–I have several reasons. 我有几个原因。

receive /rɪ'si:v/ （动词）收到

–Why didn't you answer my letter? 你为什么不给我回信？

–I never received your letter. 我从来都没收到过你的信。

recent /'ri:sənt/ （形容词）最近的

Winters have been warmer in recent years. 最近几年冬天比较暖和。

recently /'riːsəntli/ （副词）最近

–I haven't seen you recently. 我最近没见到你。

–I've been ill the past few days. 我这些天病了。

red¹ /red/ （形容词）红色的

The house has yellow walls and a red roof. 这座房子的墙是黄的，房顶是红的。

拓展词汇

red card 红牌　　red light 红灯
Red Army 红军　　Red Cross 红十字会

red² /red/ （名词）红色

There's too much red in the painting. 这幅画中红色用得太多。

refuse /rɪ'fjuːz/ （动词）拒绝

–He refused my help. 他拒绝我帮忙。

–That's really strange. 真是太奇怪了。

remember /rɪ'membə/ （动词）想起，记起

–Do you remember Helen? 你记得海伦吗？

–Yes, we were classmates in primary school. 记得，我们在小学是同班同学。

repair /rɪ'peə/ （动词）修理

–My watch is broken. 我的表坏了。

–Let me take a look. I might be able to repair it. 让我看一下，也许我能修。

拓展词汇

repairman 修理工

repeat /rɪ'piːt/ （动词）重复做（或说）

–I didn't hear you. Could you please repeat it? 我没听清楚，请再说一遍好吗？

–I told you not to repeat the same mistake. 我说不要再犯同样的错误了。

reply /rɪ'plaɪ/ （动词）（第三人称单数 **replies**，过去式、过去分词 **replied**，现在分词 **replying**）回答，答复

–Why don't you reply to my question? 你为什么不回答我的问题？

–Because I don't know the answer. 因为我不知道答案。

用法小贴士

reply 和 answer 作动词表示"回答"时用法不同，reply 后面要跟 to，如 reply to a question/a letter，而 answer 不用跟 to，如 answer a question/a letter.

rest /rest/ （名词）休息

–What a busy day we've had! 今天可真忙啊！

–Oh, yes. Let's take a good rest. 哦，是啊。我们好好休息一下吧。

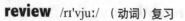

拓展词汇
restroom （美）（餐馆、电影院等中的）
洗手间

restaurant /'restərɒnt/ （名词）餐馆

–Are there Chinese restaurants in other countries? 在其他国家有中国餐馆吗？
–Yes, there are Chinese restaurants in many countries. 是的，在许多国家都有中国餐馆。

result /rɪ'zʌlt/ （名词）结果

–Did you get your exam results? 你知道考试结果了吗？
–I got high marks! 我得了高分。

return /rɪ'tɜːn/ （动词）

1. 回来
–When did they return home? 他们什么时候回到家的？
–About seven o'clock in the evening. 大约晚上7点钟。
2. 归还
–Can I borrow your bicycle? 我能借你的自行车吗？
–Sure, but please return it to me before two p.m. 行，但请在下午两点前还我。

review /rɪ'vjuː/ （动词）复习

–What are we doing in our next lesson? 我们下堂课做什么？
–We're reviewing Lesson 3. 我们复习第三课。

ribbon /'rɪbən/ （名词）丝带，缎带

She's wearing a red ribbon in her hair today. 她今天头上系着条红丝带。

拓展词汇

cut the ribbon 剪彩

rice /raɪs/ （名词）水稻，大米，米饭

–Do you grow rice or wheat here? 你们这里种水稻还是麦子？
–We grow rice. 种水稻。

拓展词汇

rice cooker 煮饭锅

rich /rɪtʃ/ （形容词）富有的

–He's the richest man in the town. 他是镇上最富有的人。
–Yes, but he wouldn't lend a penny to the poor. 是啊，但他一分钱也不肯借给穷人。

反义词 poor 贫穷的

riddle /'rɪdəl/ （名词）谜语

–Can you guess the answer to the riddle? 你能猜出这个谜语的答案吗?

–Let me think. 让我想想。

ride /raɪd/ （动词）（过去式 **rode** /rəʊd/, 过去分词 **ridden** /'rɪdən/）骑

–Can you ride a horse? 你会骑马吗?

–Yes, my father taught me to ride when I was ten. 会呀, 我10岁时爸爸就教我骑马了!

right¹ /raɪt/ （形容词）

1. 正确的

–I choose C. 我选C。

–Yes, you've got the right answer! 你选对了!

反义词 wrong 错误的

2. 右边的

–People drive on the right side of the street in many countries. 在许多国家人们都是靠右行驶。

–But in Britain and Japan people drive on the left. 但在英国和日本人们是靠左行驶的。

反义词 left 左边的

right² /raɪt/ （名词）右边

–Excuse me. How can I get to the zoo? 劳驾, 动物园怎么去?

–Go straight and it's on your right. 往前走, 就在你右手边。

反义词 left 左边

ring¹ /rɪŋ/ （名词）环, 圆圈

–What's the sign of the Olympic Games? 奥运会的标志是什么?

–Five rings locked together. 是5个交叉的环。

拓展词汇

earring 耳环　key ring 钥匙环
rings of a tree 树的年轮

ring² /rɪŋ/ （动词）（过去式 **rang** /ræŋ/, 过去分词 **rung** /rʌŋ/）（铃、钟等）响, 鸣

–The phone is ringing. 电话响了。

–I'll get it. 我来接。

rise /raɪz/ （动词）（过去式 **rose** /rəʊz/, 过去分词 **risen** /'rɪzən/）升起

–Look! The moon has risen above the mountain. 看, 月亮已经升到山头了。

–How beautiful! 多美啊!

river /'rɪvə/ （名词）河

–Jimmy can swim across the river.
吉米能游过那条河。
–He's a really good swimmer. 他真
是个游泳好手。

road /rəud/ （名词）路

–How many roads are there
between the two cities? 这两座城
市之间有几条路？
–Only one. 只有一条。

拓展词汇

road map 公路地图　road racing 公路赛

roar /rɔ:/ （动词）吼叫

–Listen, the tiger is roaring in the
cage. Is he hungry? 听，老虎在笼
子里大吼大叫的，它饿了吗？
–Perhaps he wants to go back to
the forest. 可能它想回到森林里吧。

rob /rɒb/ （动词）（过去式、
过去分词 **robbed**，现在分词
robbing）抢劫

Some thieves tried to rob the bank
last night. 昨天晚上几个窃贼企图抢
劫银行。

拓展词汇

robber 窃贼

robot /'rəubɒt/ （名词）机器人

–Can robots think? 机器人会思考
吗？
–No, they can't. 不，它们不会
思考。

百科小贴士

世界上第一个机器人是 1954 年在美国被制
造出来的。此后，机器人工业开始在欧洲
和日本发展起来。20 世纪 60 年代，第一
批工业机器人就已经同工人并肩出现在工
厂里了。

rock /rɒk/ （名词）岩石

–Do you like rock climbing? 你喜欢
攀岩吗？
–Yes. It's quite exciting. 喜欢，
很刺激。

rocket /'rɒkɪt/ （名词）火箭

–How can we push a spaceship
into space? 怎样把太空飞船发射
进太空？
–By rocket. 用火箭。

百科小贴士

火箭的发明最早是在中国，真正的火箭是
在火药发明之后出现的，其原理是火药燃
烧会产生很强的后坐力。后来，火箭武器
传入世界各国，并被大量用于战争中，如
今液体燃料的火箭在航天飞行中发挥了重
要作用。

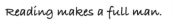
roll /rəʊl/ （动词）

1. 滚动
Roll the ball to me, please. 请把球滚给我。
2. 卷起
–How can we take the carpet out of the room? 我们怎样才能把地毯拿出房间呢？
–Roll it up and then we can take it. 把它卷起来就能拿出去了。

roof /ruːf/ （名词）屋顶

–My kite has fallen onto the roof. 我的风筝落在屋顶上了。
–I'll help you get it down. 我帮你弄下来。

room /ruːm/ （名词）房间

–This is my room. 这是我的房间。
–Oh, it's so big! 哦，真大！

拓展词汇

bedroom 卧室　bathroom 浴室
living room 起居室　reading room 阅览室　classroom 教室　dining room 餐厅

rooster /ˈruːstə/ （名词）公鸡

The farmer keeps a few roosters and more than twenty hens. 那位农民养了几只公鸡和二十多只母鸡。

root /ruːt/ （名词）根

This tree has many roots. 这棵树的根很多。

rope /rəʊp/ （名词）绳

–Do you have a jump rope? 你有跳绳吗？
–Yes, do you want to play? 有啊，你想跳吗？

拓展词汇

rope ladder　绳梯

rose /rəʊz/ （名词）玫瑰

–What colors can roses be? 玫瑰通常有什么颜色？
–Red, yellow, and white. 红色、黄色和白色。

round¹ /raʊnd/ （形容词）圆的

–Do you want a round mirror or a square one? 你想要个圆形的镜子还是方形的？
–I want a round one. 我想要圆形的。

round² /raʊnd/ （介词）围绕，环绕

–Can you round up (off) these numbers? 你能不能把这些数字调整为整数？
–Yes, 21.8 rounds up to 22, and 25.2 rounds off to 25. 行，21.8 调高到22，而25.2 调低为25。

row /rəʊ/ （名词）排

The students stood in five rows. Each row had ten people. 学生们排成5排，每排10个人。

rubber /ˈrʌbə/ （名词）

1. 橡胶

Hainan Province produces rubber.
海南省出产橡胶。

百科小贴士

人类使用天然橡胶的历史已经有好几个世纪了。哥伦布在发现新大陆的航行中发现，南美洲土著玩的一种球是用硬化了的植物汁液做成的。后来人们发现这种球能够擦掉铅笔的痕迹，因此命名为"擦子"（即rubber）。这种物质就是橡胶，这也是橡胶英文名称的由来。1903年，一位华人从马来西亚把第一株橡胶树引入了中国。

2. 橡皮（擦）

–Can I use a rubber eraser to clean pen marks? 我能用橡皮擦净钢笔痕迹吗？

–No, it won't work. 不行，擦不掉的。

拓展词汇

rubber band 橡皮筋

用法小贴士

rubber是英国英语，美国英语用 eraser。

rubbish /ˈrʌbɪʃ/ （名词）垃圾

Workers have cleared away the rubbish in the street. 工人们把街上的垃圾清理走了。

拓展词汇

rubbish recycling 废品回收

rude /ruːd/ （形容词）粗鲁的，无礼的

–Tom is a rude boy. 汤姆是个粗鲁的男孩。

–That's why he has no friends. 所以他没有朋友。

rule /ruːl/ （名词）规则，规矩

–Why did the policeman stop the driver? 警察为什么让那位司机停下？

–Because he broke a traffic rule. 因为他违反交通规则了。

ruler /ˈruːlə/ （名词）尺子

–What do we need for the mathematics test? 我们考数学时需要带什么？

–A ruler, a pencil, and an eraser. 一把尺子，一支铅笔和一块橡皮。

run /rʌn/ （动词）（过去式 ran /ræn/，过去分词 run，现在分词 running）跑

–I admire Liu Xiang very much. 我非常崇拜刘翔。

–So do I. He runs so fast. 我也很崇拜他，他跑得真快。

Russia /ˈrʌʃə/ （名词）俄罗斯

Russia is the largest country in the world. 俄罗斯是世界上最大的国家。

拓展词汇

Russian 俄罗斯的，俄罗斯人的，俄罗斯人，俄语

百科小贴士

俄罗斯是世界上面积最大的国家，地跨欧亚两个大陆。芭蕾舞是俄罗斯的国粹。

Seeing is believing.

S

sad /sæd/（比较级 **sadder**，最高级 **saddest**）（形容词）伤心的
–Mary looks sad. What's the matter? 玛丽看上去很伤心，出了什么事？
–Her cat has died. 她的猫死了。

safe /seɪf/（形容词）安全的
It's not safe to play in the street. 在马路上玩不安全。
反义词 unsafe 不安全的

safety /'seɪfti/（名词）安全
Traffic safety is very important. 交通安全很重要。
拓展词汇
safety belt 安全带　safety first 安全第一
反义词 danger 危险

sail¹ /seɪl/（名词）帆
Sails are usually white. 帆通常是白色的。

sail² /seɪl/（动词）（船）行驶，驾驶（船只）
The ship has sailed across the Atlantic many times. 这条船多次横渡大西洋。

sailor /'seɪlə/（名词）水手
–I want to be a sailor when I grow up. 我长大后想当个水手。

–You can go to many places in the world then. 那时你就能去世界上很多地方了。

拓展词汇
sailor suit （儿童穿的）水手服

salad /'sæləd/（名词）色拉
–Would you like some salad? 你要点儿色拉吗？
–Yes. I like vegetable salad. 好的，我喜欢吃蔬菜色拉。
拓展词汇
salad dressing 色拉酱
百科小贴士
色拉是一种凉拌食品，一般由香肠丁、土豆丁、水果丁或蔬菜加调味汁拌和而成。

sale /seɪl/（名词）出售
–Are these flowers for sale? 这些花卖吗？
–No. They are just for show. 不卖，它们只是用来展示的。

salt /sɔːlt/（名词）盐
–This dish doesn't have any taste. 这道菜什么味也没有。

眼见为实。

–Oh dear! I forgot to put in any salt!
哎呀，我忘了放盐啦！

salty /'sɔːlti/ （形容词）（比较级 saltier，最高级 saltiest）咸的

–Are these biscuits salty or sweet?
这些饼干是咸的还是甜的？
–They're salty. 是咸的。

same /seɪm/ （形容词）相同的

–Do you have the same classes every day? 你们每天上同样的课吗？
–No, but we have Chinese and mathematics every day. 不一样，但我们每天都会上语文和数学课。

反义词 different 不同的

sand /sænd/ （名词）沙子，沙滩

–It's nice to lie on the warm sand after swimming. 游泳后躺在暖暖的沙滩上真舒服。
–Yes. The sand here is very clean. 是啊，这儿的沙很干净。

拓展词汇

sandstorm 沙尘暴　　sand castle 沙堡

sandal /'sændəl/ （名词）凉鞋

This shop sells all kinds of sandals.
这家商店卖各种各样的凉鞋。

sandwich /'sænwɪdʒ/ （名词）（复数 sandwiches）三明治

–What did you have for lunch? 你午饭吃什么了？
–I had two sandwiches. 我吃了两个三明治。

百科小贴士
三明治这一名称源自 18 世纪英国的桑威奇（Sandwich）伯爵约翰·蒙塔古。相传他热衷赌博，为了能一边赌博一边用餐，就把牛肉饼夹在两片面包之间，三明治也因此得名。

Santa Claus /ˌsæntə 'klɔːz/ （名词）圣诞老人

Santa Claus brings presents to children on Christmas Eve. 圣诞老人在圣诞前夜给孩子们带来礼物。

百科小贴士
传说圣诞节前夜（12 月 24 日晚）圣诞老人驾着鹿拉的雪橇从北方来，由烟囱进入各家，把圣诞礼物装在袜子里挂在孩子们的床头上或壁炉旁。

satisfy /'sætɪsfaɪ/ （动词）（第三人称单数 satisfies，过去式、过去分词 satisfied，现在分词 satisfying）满意

–Are you satisfied with the exam results? 你对考试结果还满意吗？
–Yes. I made good progress in English. 满意，我的英语有很大进步。

Saturday /'sætədeɪ/ （名词）星期六

–Do you go to school on Saturdays? 你星期六上学吗？
–No, but I have a piano lesson. 不上学，但我要上钢琴课。

170

sauce /sɔːs/ （名词）酱

–Do you want some chilli sauce? 你想要点儿辣椒酱吗？
–No, I'd like some tomato sauce. 不，我想要点儿番茄酱。

sausage /'sɒsɪdʒ/ （名词）香肠

–What will we have for dinner? 晚饭我们吃什么？
–Potatoes, sausages, and vegetables. 土豆、香肠和蔬菜。

save /seɪv/ （动词）救

–How did the dog save its master? 这条狗是怎样救了它的主人？
–It barked loudly when the house was on fire. 当房子着火时它大声地叫。

say /seɪ/ （动词）（过去式、过去分词 **said** /sed/ ）说

–Sorry, what did you say just now? 对不起，你刚才说什么？
–I said I must do my homework now. 我说我现在必须做家庭作业。

scare /skeə/ （动词）感到害怕

–It's getting dark. I'm scared. 天黑了，我有点儿害怕。
–Don't be scared. We're close to home. 别害怕，我们快到家了。

school /skuːl/ （名词）学校

–Is your school big? 你们学校大吗？
–No, but it's the best school in our city. 不大，但它是我们市里最好的学校。

拓展词汇

schoolbag 书包　schoolbook 教科书
schoolchild 学童　school uniform 校服

science /saɪəns/ （名词）科学

–Do you have science classes at your school? 你们学校有科学课吗？
–Yes. I've learned to use a computer in science class. 有，我是在科学课上学会用电脑的。

拓展词汇

science fiction 科幻小说

scientist /'saɪəntɪst/ （名词）科学家

–Can you name a few famous scientists? 你能列举几个著名的科学家吗？
–I know about Newton, Einstein, and Hawking. 我知道牛顿、爱因斯坦和霍金。

scissors /'sɪzəz/ （名词）剪刀

–What did you buy for your grandma? 你给奶奶买了什么？
–A new pair of scissors. Her old pair doesn't cut well. 一把新剪刀，她那把旧剪刀不好用了。

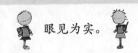
眼见为实。

score /skɔː/（名词）（比赛）得分，（考试）分数
–What was your score on the test? 你考试考了多少分？
–I don't know yet. 我还不知道。

sea /siː/（名词）海洋
About three quarters of the earth is covered by sea. 地球约 3 / 4 被海洋所覆盖。

拓展词汇

seabird 海鸟　seafood 海鲜　seagull 海鸥　seahorse 海马　sea lion 海狮　seashell 贝壳　seashore 海岸

search /sɜːtʃ/（动词）搜寻
–Did you search on the Internet? 你在因特网上搜过吗？
–Yes, and I've found a lot of useful information. 搜过，而且找到了许多有用的信息。

season /'siːzən/（名词）季节
There are four seasons in each year and three months in each season. 一年有四季，每季有三个月。

seat /siːt/（名词）座位
–Is this seat taken? 这座位有人了吗？
–No, you can sit here. 没有，你可以坐这儿。

拓展词汇

seat belt 安全带

second[1] /'sekənd/（形容词）第二的
–Have you met each other before? 你们以前见过吗？

–Yes. This is the second time we have met. 见过，这是我们第二次见面。

second[2] /'sekənd/（名词）秒
–How many seconds are there in a minute? 一分钟有多少秒？
–Sixty seconds. 60秒。

拓展词汇

second hand 秒针

secondary school /'sekəndrɪ skuːl /（名词）中学
–Are you in primary school? 你再念小学吗？
–No, I'm in secondary school now. 不是，我现在上中学了。

secret /'siːkrɪt/（名词）秘密
Jennifer keeps her age a secret. 珍妮弗对自己的年龄保密。

see /siː/（动词）（过去式 **saw** /sɔː/，过去分词 **seen** /siːn/）看见
–Did you see my glasses? 你看见我的眼镜了吗？
–No, but I'll help you look for them. 没有，但我会帮你找。

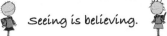
seed /si:d/ （名词）种子

–What's in your hand? 你手里是什么？
–Flower seeds. I want to plant them in the garden. 花种，我想把它们种在花园里。

seem /si:m/ （动词）好像

–Emma seems happy in kindergarten. 埃玛好像在幼儿园过得很高兴。
–Yes. She made a lot of friends there. 是啊，她在那儿交了很多朋友。

select /sɪ'lekt/ （动词）挑选

–These postcards are all very beautiful. 这些明信片都很漂亮。
–Right. It's difficult to select just one. 没错，只选一张还真难。

sell /sel/ （动词）（过去式、过去分词 **sold** /səuld/）卖

–You've got a new car! 你们买了辆新车！
–Yes. My parents sold our old car and bought this new one. 是啊，我父母把旧车卖了，买了这辆新的。
反义词 buy 购买

send /send/ （动词）（过去式、过去分词 **sent**）寄送

–Have you sent New Year cards to your friends? 你给你的朋友们寄新年贺卡了吗？
–Yes, I've sent quite a few. 是的，寄了不少。

sense /sens/ （名词）感觉

–Can you name the five senses? 你能说出5种感官的名称吗？
–Yes, they are sight, hearing, smell, taste, and touch. 可以，它们是视觉、听觉、嗅觉、味觉和触觉。

sentence /'sentəns/ （名词）句子

–Can you write English sentences? 你会用英语造句吗？
–Yes, I can write simple ones. 是的，我会造简单的句子。

separate /'sepəreɪt/ （动词）分开

–How can you tell the sugar from the salt? 你怎样区分糖和盐？
–That's easy. I separated them by taste. 很容易。我尝尝味道就区分开来。

September /sep'tembə/ （名词）九月

–When does your school begin? 你们什么时候开学？
–On September first. 9月1号。

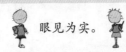

眼见为实。

set /set/ （动词）（过去式、过去分词 set）落下

The sun rises late and sets early in winter. 冬天太阳升得晚，落得早。

seven /'sevən/ （数词）七

–How many days are there in a week? 一个星期有几天？
–Seven days. 有7天。

seventeen /ˌsevən'tiːn/ （数词）十七

–How long does it take to go from Changsha to Beijing? 从长沙到北京要多长时间？
–About seventeen hours by train and two hours by air. 坐火车差不多17个小时，坐飞机两个小时。

seventy /'sevənti/ （数词）七十

–How old is your grandpa? 你爷爷多大岁数了？
–He's over seventy, but he's still working. 他七十多岁了，但还在工作。

several /'sevrəl/ （形容词）一些，几个

–You seem to know each other well. 你们好像很熟。
–Yes. We've met several times. 是的，我们见过几次了。

sex /seks/ （名词）（复数 sexes）性别

–Do you know the sex of your snake? 你知道你的蛇是什么性别吗？
–Yes, but an expert had to tell me. 能知道的，不过一名专家必须告诉我。

shake /ʃeɪk/ （动词）（过去式 shook /ʃʊk/，过去分词 shaken /'ʃeɪkən/ 摇动

Shaking hands is a common way to welcome guests. 握手是欢迎客人的常见方式。

shall /ʃæl/ （情态动词）（过去式 should /ʃʊd/）将…

–What shall we do this weekend? 这周末咱们干什么？
–We need to clean the house. 我们得把房子打扫干净。

shampoo /ʃæm'puː/ （名词）香波，洗发液

–What kind of shampoo do you need? 你需要哪种洗发液？
–Baby shampoo. 婴儿洗发液。

shape /ʃeɪp/ （名词）形状

–The hill is in the shape of an elephant. 这座小山的形状像大象。

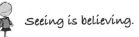

–Yes. The left part is its trunk. 对，左边的部分是大象的鼻子。

share /ʃeə/ （动词）分享

–Would you share your storybook with me? 我们一起看你的故事书好吗？
–Sure. 好的。

she /ʃi/ （代词）她

–What does your mother do? 你妈妈是做什么工作的？
–She's a nurse. 她是护士。

sheep /ʃiːp/ （名词）（复数 sheep）绵羊

–How many sheep does the farmer keep? 那位农民养了多少只羊？
–About one hundred. 大约100只。

拓展词汇

sheepdog 牧羊犬　　sheepskin 羊皮

用法小贴士

公羊为 ram，母羊为 ewe，小羊为 lamb，羊肉为 mutton，小羊肉为 lamb。

shelf /ʃelf/ （名词）（复数 shelves /ʃelvz/）架子

–Where's my English-Chinese dictionary? 我的英汉词典在哪里？
–On the second shelf. 第二层架子上。

拓展词汇

bookshelf 书架

shell /ʃel/ （名词）壳，贝壳

–Where did you get these beautiful shells? 你从哪里弄到这些漂亮的贝壳的？
–I collected them on the beach. 我在海滩上拾来的。

拓展词汇

eggshell 蛋壳　　snail shell 蜗牛壳

shine /ʃaɪn/ （动词）（过去式、过去分词 shone /ʃɒn/）照耀，发光

The sun shines on everything on Earth. 太阳照耀着地球上的万物。

ship /ʃɪp/ （名词）大船

–We're going to Australia by ship. 我们将乘船去澳大利亚。
–By ship! It must be exciting. 坐船！那肯定很刺激！

shirt /ʃɜːt/ （名词）衬衫，衬衣

–You need a new shirt. 你需要件新衬衣。
–Yes. This one's too old. 是的，这件太旧了。

拓展词汇

T-shirt T恤衫

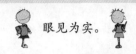

shoe /ʃuː/（名词）鞋

–I can't find my shoes. 我找不到我的鞋了。

–They're under the bed. 在床底下。

拓展词汇

shoe box 鞋盒　　shoe shop 鞋店
cloth shoes 布鞋　　sports shoes 运动鞋
running shoes 跑鞋

shop¹ /ʃɒp/（名词）商店

–Is there a shop close by? 附近有商店吗？

–Yes, there's a small shop. 是的，有个小商店。

拓展词汇

bookshop 书店

用法小贴士

shop是英国英语，美国英语用 store.

shop² /ʃɒp/（动词）（过去式、过去分词**shopped**，现在分词**shopping**）购物

–I want to go shopping tomorrow. 我明天想去商店买东西。

–I'll go with you. 我跟你去吧。

拓展词汇

shopping bag 购物袋
shopping basket 购物筐
shopping center 购物中心

short /ʃɔːt/（形容词）

1.（时间、长度、距离）短的

–The sleeves are too short. 袖子太短了。

–Well, you need a new shirt. 看来你需要一件新衬衫了。

反义词 long 长的

拓展词汇

short story 短篇小说

2. 矮的

He's the shortest boy in the class. 他是班上最矮的男生。

反义词 high 高的

shorts /ʃɔːts/（名词）短裤

–It's hot! 天真热！

–It's time to wear shorts. 可以穿短裤了。

should /ʃʊd/（情态动词）应当，应该

–We should invite Anna to the party. 我们应该邀请安娜参加派对。

–I'll call her right now. 我现在就给她打电话。

shoulder /ˈʃəʊldə/（名词）肩膀

He often carries his son on his shoulders. 他经常让儿子骑在肩上。

shout /ʃaʊt/（动词）大声说，喊叫

–Don't shout at me. 别冲我大声嚷嚷。

Seeing is believing.

–I'm sorry. It's noisy here. 对不起，这儿很吵。

show¹ /ʃəʊ/ （动词）（过去式、过去分词 showed 或 shown /ʃəʊn/）露出，给…看

–Will you show me your new pictures? 给我看看你的新照片好吗？
–Sure. 当然好啦。

show² /ʃəʊ/ （名词）展览会，表演，演出，节目

–What's the popular TV show about? 那个受欢迎的电视节目是关于什么的？
–It's about wild animals. 是关于野生动物的。

拓展词汇

show window 橱窗　　auto show 车展
talk show 脱口秀

shut /ʃʌt/ （动词）（过去式、过去分词 shut，现在分词 shutting）

1. 关（门等）
It's cold. Please shut the door. 天很冷，请关上门。
2. 闭上（眼睛等）
He shut his eyes and went to sleep. 他闭上眼睛睡了。

shy /ʃaɪ/ （形容词）羞怯的，腼腆的

–My little sister is shy. 我妹妹很腼腆。
–You should take her out more often. 你应该多带她出去。

sick /sɪk/ （形容词）生病的

–Why were you absent last week? 你上周为什么没去上学？
–I was sick. 我病了。

用法小贴士

sick是美国英语，英国英语用 ill。

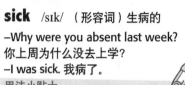

sign /saɪn/ （名词）符号，标志

–Can you see the sign? What does it say? 你能看清那个标志吗？上面写着什么？
–It says "No Smoking." 上面写着"禁止吸烟"。

silence /'saɪləns/ （名词）寂静，无声，沉默

Silence, boys and girls! 安静！孩子们。

silent /'saɪlənt/ （形容词）沉默的，安静的

–Why is everybody silent? 为什么人人都不说话？
–Because nobody knows the answer to the question. 因为没有人知道这个问题的答案。

拓展词汇

silent reading 默读

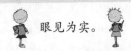

silk /sɪlk/ （名词）丝绸

–Is this shirt made of silk? 这件衬衣是丝的吗？

–No, it's made of cotton. 不是，是棉的。

百科小贴士

丝绸是中国古老文化的象征。著名的丝绸之路是汉武帝时期开创的，总长七千多公里，将古老的中国文化、印度文化、希腊文化与波斯文化联结起来，改写了整个人类的文明发展史。

silly /'sɪli/ （形容词）（比较级 **sillier**，最高级 **silliest**）愚蠢的，傻的

–Mom, can I wear my skirt? 妈妈，我能穿裙子吗？

–Don't be silly. It's cold today. 别犯傻了，今天太冷了。

simple /'sɪmpəl/ （形容词）简单的

–How was your test? 考试考得怎么样？

–It was simple. Everyone did well. 考试很简单，大家考得都不错。

since /sɪns/ （介词）自…以来

–How long have you known each other? 你们认识多久了？

–We have been friends since childhood. 我们从小就是朋友。

sing /sɪŋ/ （动词）（过去式 **sang** /sæŋ/，过去分词 **sung** /sʌŋ/）唱（歌）

–Please sing us a song. 请给我们唱首歌吧。

–Sorry. I don't have a good voice at all. 不行，我的嗓音一点儿都不好。

singer /'sɪŋə/ （名词）歌手，歌唱家

–Is she a good singer? 她是个好歌手吗？

–Oh, yes. She sings very well. 哦，是的，她唱得很好。

拓展词汇

pop singer 流行歌手

sir /sɜː/ （名词）（对男子的礼貌称呼）先生

–Can I help you, sir? 先生，您需要什么？

–A cup of coffee, please. 请给我一杯咖啡。

用法小贴士

对女士的尊称是madam。

sister /'sɪstə/（名词）姐姐，妹妹
–Do you have any sisters? 你有姐妹吗？
–Yes, I have an older sister. 有，我有一个姐姐。

拓展词汇
sister city 友好城市　sister school 友好学校

用法小贴士
英语中 sister 既可表示"姐姐"，又可表示"妹妹"。older sister 或 big sister 指"姐姐"，younger sister 或 little sister 指"妹妹"。

sit /sɪt/（动词）（过去式、过去分词 **sat**，现在分词 **sitting**）坐下，就坐
–May I sit here? 我可以坐在这里吗？
–Sorry, the seat has already been taken. 对不起，这座位已经有人了。

six /sɪks/（数词）六
Six and eight are lucky numbers in China. 6和8在中国是吉祥数字。

sixteen /ˌsɪks'tiːn/（数词）十六
My mother was sixteen when she went to college. 我妈妈上大学时16岁。

sixty /'sɪksti/（数词）六十
–What's the homework for today? 今天的家庭作业是什么？

–The exercises on page sixty. 第60页的练习题。

size /saɪz/（名词）大小，尺寸，号码
–What size shoes do you wear? 你穿多大号的鞋？
–Size 5. 5号。

skate /skeɪt/（动词）滑冰，溜冰
–Can we skate on the lake? 我们能在湖上滑冰吗？
–No, the ice is too thin. 不行，冰太薄了。

拓展词汇
skateboard 滑板

ski /skiː/（动词）滑雪
–We shall go skiing this afternoon. 我们今天下午要去滑雪。
–Oh, I wish I could ski, too. 唉，我真希望我也会滑雪。

拓展词汇
ski boots 滑雪靴

skin /skɪn/（名词）
1.（人或动物的）皮肤
My skin got burned by the sun. 我的皮肤被太阳晒伤了。
2.（水果的）表皮
Bananas have yellow skin. 香蕉的表皮是黄色的。

拓展词汇
fruit skin 果皮

skip /skɪp/（动词）（过去式、过去分词 **skipped**，现在分词 **skipping**）跳绳

–Do you know how to skip? 你知道怎样跳绳吗？
–Sure. First you hop on one foot, then on the other. 当然知道。 先用一只脚跳，再用另一只脚跳。

skirt /skɜːt/ （名词）裙子

–Alice is wearing a long skirt today. 艾丽斯今天穿着一条长裙。
–That makes her look taller! 那使她显得更高了！

拓展词汇

long skirt 长裙　short skirt 短裙

sky /skaɪ/ （名词）天，天空

–Is that a bird in the sky? 天上是只鸟吗？
–No, it's a kite. 不，那是只风筝。

拓展词汇

blue sky 蓝天　night sky 夜空

sleep¹ /sliːp/ （动词）（过去式、过去分词 slept /slept/ ）睡觉

–Did you sleep well last night? 你昨天晚上睡得好吗？
–Yes, I slept like a baby. 是的，我睡得很好。

sleep² /sliːp/ （名词）睡觉

–I'm tired. I've been reading all day. 我累了。我读了一天的书。
–You need a good sleep. 你需要好好睡一觉。

拓展词汇

sleeping bag 睡袋　sleeping car 卧铺车厢　sleepwalk 梦游

sleepy /ˈsliːpi/ （形容词）（比较级 sleepier, 最高级 sleepiest）困乏的，想睡的

–I feel sleepy after the big meal. 我大吃了一顿后觉得很困。
–So do I. 我也一样。

slipper /ˈslɪpə/ （名词）（通常用复数 slippers）拖鞋

–You shouldn't wear slippers in the classroom. 你不该在教室里穿拖鞋。
–Sorry. I won't do it again. 对不起。我以后不会那样了。

slow /sləʊ/ （形容词）慢的，缓慢的

–Mike, you're so slow. Hurry up! 迈克，你太慢了。快点儿！
–Sorry, but I'm doing my best. 对不起，但我已经尽力了。

slowly /ˈsləʊli/ （副词）慢慢地

Could you speak more slowly? I can't understand you. 能说慢点吗？我听不清。

反义词 fast 快地

Seeing is believing.

small /smɔːl/ （形容词）小的

We have a small garden at our school. 我们学校有个小花园。

反义词 big 大的

smart /smɑːt/ （形容词）

1. 时髦的，帅的
–You look very smart in that jacket. 你穿那件夹克真帅！
–Really? Thank you. 真的？谢谢。
2. 聪明的
–Lauren is very smart. 劳伦很聪明。
–She studies hard, too. 她学习也努力。

smell¹ /smel/ （名词）气味

–There's a bad smell in here. 这儿气味很难闻。
–Guess what I've found here? A dead mouse! 猜猜我发现什么了？一只死老鼠！

smell² /smel/ （动词）（过去式、过去分词 **smelled**）闻到（气味），发出气味

–Do you smell gas? 你闻到煤气味了吗？
–Oh yes! I forgot to turn off the stove! 啊，是的！我忘了关煤气！

smile¹ /smaɪl/ （动词）微笑

The teacher smiled as she spoke. 老师讲话时带着微笑。

smile² /smaɪl/ （名词）微笑

She always has a sweet smile on her face. 她总是面带甜美的微笑。

smoke¹ /sməʊk/ （名词）（燃烧产生的）烟

There is no smoke without fire. 无火不生烟，无风不起浪。
The room was full of smoke. 房子里全是烟。

smoke² /sməʊk/ （动词）抽烟，吸烟

–Does your father smoke? 你爸爸抽烟吗？
–No, he gave up smoking five years ago. 不，他5年前戒烟了。

snack /snæk/ （名词）小吃，点心

–I'm a bit hungry. 我有点儿饿了。
–Have some snacks. 吃点儿点心吧。

拓展词汇

snack shop 小吃店

snail /sneɪl/ （名词）蜗牛

Tortoises move slowly. Snails move more slowly. 乌龟爬得慢，蜗牛爬得更慢。

百科小贴士

蜗牛喜欢阴暗潮湿的环境，昼伏夜出，对冷、热、饥饿、干旱有很强的忍耐性，寿命一般在 5—6 年。蜗牛爬行后留下的痕迹是腹足分泌的黏液，避免爬行时受到损伤。

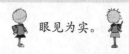
snake /sneɪk/ （名词）蛇

–What's that in the grass? 草丛里是什么？

–Look out! It's a snake! 小心，是条蛇！

snow¹ /snəʊ/ （名词）雪

We have a lot of snow this winter. 今年冬天雪下得很多。

拓展词汇

snowball 雪球　snowman 雪人　heavy snow 大雪　Snow White 白雪公主

snow² /snəʊ/ （动词）下雪

–It's snowing! 下雪了！

–Let's make a snowman! 我们堆个雪人吧！

so /səʊ/ （副词）很，非常，如此

–You've been so kind to me. 你对我一直这么好。

–You've been good to me, too. 你对我也很好呀。

It's so cold that you should wear a hat and gloves. 天很冷，你应该戴上帽子和手套。

–I had a really good time at the party. 我在聚会上玩得很开心。

–So did I. 我也是。

soap /səʊp/ （名词）肥皂

–Do you use soap in the bath? 你用肥皂洗澡吗？

–No, I use body shampoo. 不，我用沐浴液。

拓展词汇

soap bubble 肥皂泡　soap opera 肥皂剧　soap powder 洗衣粉

百科小贴士

五千多年前，埃及国王胡夫的厨师不慎将一盆油打翻在灭了火的木炭上，并发现这种油脂和炭灰混合物能够把手洗得很光滑，这就是最早的肥皂了。

soccer /'sɒkə/ （名词）足球

–Does your school have a soccer team? 你们学校有足球队吗？

–We have two, a girls team and a boys team. 我们有两个队呢，男生队和女生队。

用法小贴士

在英国英语中足球用 football 或 soccer；在美国，足球多用 soccer，而 football 则指另一种运动，即橄榄球。

百科小贴士

1863年10月26日，英国人在伦敦成立了世界上第一个足球运动组织——英国足球协会，并统一了足球规则。人们把这一天作为现代足球诞生日。中国在春秋战国时期就出现用脚踢球的活动，叫"蹴鞠"。

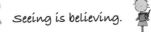
sock /sɒk/ （名词）（通常用复数 **socks**） 短袜

I like cotton socks. 我喜欢棉质袜子。

sofa /'səʊfə/ （名词）沙发

–There's no chair in this room. 这间屋里没有椅子。

–We can all sit on the big sofa. 我们可以都坐在那张大沙发上。

拓展词汇
sofabed 沙发床

百科小贴士
沙发是英语 sofa 的音译词。

soft /sɒft/ （形容词）

1. 柔软的
–Do you like a hard bed or a soft bed? 你喜欢睡硬床还是软床？
–A soft bed. 软床。

拓展词汇
soft wood 软木　　soft toy 绒毛玩具

2. 柔和的
She has a soft voice. 她的声音很柔和。

拓展词汇
soft music 轻音乐　　soft drink 软饮料（指不含酒精的饮料，如果汁）

soldier /'səʊldʒə/ （名词）士兵

–Is your brother a soldier? 你哥哥是士兵吗？

–Yes, he's been in the army for two years. 是，他已经当兵两年了。

solid /'sɒlɪd/ （名词）固体

–Water is liquid. Ice is solid. 水是液体，冰是固体。

百科小贴士
世界上的物质有固体（solid）、液体（liquid）和气体（gas）3种形态。随着温度、压力等的变化，形态会发生变化。如常温常压下的水，在 0℃ 以下结为固体的冰，100℃ 以上汽化为水蒸气。

some¹ /sʌm/ （形容词）一些

–Would you like some milk? 你要喝点儿牛奶吗？

–Yes, please. 请来点儿吧。

some² /sʌm/ （代词）一些

–Is there any juice left in the bottle? 瓶子里还剩有果汁吗？

–Yes, there's some. 是的，还剩下一些。

somebody /'sʌmbədi/ （代词）某人

–Is this your pencil box? 这是你的铅笔盒吗？

–No. It must be somebody else's. 不是，肯定是别人的。

someone /'sʌmwʌn/ （代词）某人

–Look, there is someone coming this way. 看，有个人走过来了。

–Oh, it's Tom. 哦，是汤姆。

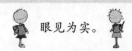

眼见为实。

something /'sʌmθɪŋ/ （代词）
某事

–Are you looking for me? 你在找我吗？

–Yes, I have something to ask you. 是的，我想问你点儿事。

sometime /'sʌmtaɪm/ （副词）
某个时候

–Shall we get together sometime this week? 我们这周什么时候聚一下好不好？

–How about sometime next week? 下周某个时间行吗？

sometimes /'sʌmtaɪmz/
（副词）有时

–Do you read English stories? 你读英语故事吗？

–Sometimes, but not often. 有时读，但不是经常。

somewhere /'sʌmweə/ （副词）
在某处

–Is your schoolbag in the bedroom? 你的书包在卧室吗？

–I've already looked there. It must be somewhere else. 我已经找过那里了，肯定在别的什么地方。

son /sʌn/ （名词）儿子

–Do you have brothers? 你有兄弟姐妹吗？

–No. I'm the only son. 没有。我是独生子。

song /sɒŋ/ （名词）歌，歌曲

–What are you going to do at the party? 派对上你们表演什么？

–We'll sing a song together. 我们会合唱一首歌。

拓展词汇

pop song 流行歌曲

soon /suːn/ （副词）不久

–It's getting colder and colder. 天越来越冷了。

–Yeah. It'll soon be winter. 是啊，很快就要到冬天了。

拓展词汇

as soon as possible 尽快

sore /sɔː/ （形容词）疼痛的

–Jim, you sound strange today. 吉姆，你的声音今天听起来有点儿奇怪。

–I've caught a cold and have a sore throat. 我感冒了，嗓子疼。

Seeing is believing.

sorry /'sɒri/ （形容词）

1. 抱歉的
–I'm sorry for calling so late. 很抱歉
这么晚给你打电话。
–That's all right. 没关系。

用法小贴士

在别人表达歉意时，要表示原谅在英语中
主要有以下4种表达方式：That's all
right./Never mind./Not at all./It doesn't
matter.

2. 难过的
–I'm sorry to hear about your
mom's illness. 听说你妈妈病了我很
难过。
–Thank you. She's getting better.
谢谢你，她正在好转。

sort /sɔːt/ （名词）种类

–What sort of books do you like?
你喜欢哪一类的书？
–All sorts. 我什么种类的都喜欢。

sound¹ /saʊnd/ （名词）声音

–What's that sound outside? 外面什
么声音？
–It's the sound of wind. 是风声。

拓展词汇

high sound 高音　　low sound 低音

sound² /saʊnd/ （动词）听起来

–You sound excited. 你听起来很
兴奋。
–I got first prize in the table tennis
match. 我得了乒乓球比赛的第一名。

soup /suːp/ （名词）汤

–Would you like some more soup?
你想再来点儿汤吗？

–No, thanks. 不用了，谢谢。

百科小贴士

饭前喝一些汤，有助于食物的消化和吸收。

sour /saʊə/ （形容词）酸的

–How do these grapes taste? 这些
葡萄味道怎么样？
–They're very sour. 太酸了。

south¹ /saʊθ/ （名词）南方

Birds fly south for the winter. 鸟儿
飞到南方过冬。

south² /saʊθ/ （形容词）南方的

–What is the weather like in South
China in summer? 夏天华南地区的
气候怎样？
–It's hot and rainy. 炎热多雨。

拓展词汇

South Africa 南非　　South America 南美洲
southeast 东南　　southwest 西南
the South Pole 南极　　south wind 南风

space /speɪs/ （名词）太空

–What does Earth look like from
space? 从太空中看地球是什么样
的？
–It looks like a blue ball. 看上去像
个蓝色的球。

拓展词汇

spaceship 宇宙飞船　　space station 宇
宙空间站　　space suit 宇航服　　space
travel 航天旅行

spare /speə/ （形容词）空闲的

–What do you do in your spare time? 空余时间你都做什么?
–I read and play volleyball. 我看书, 打排球。

speak /spi:k/ （动词）（过去式 spoke /spəuk/, 过去分词 spoken /'spəukən/）讲

–Can I speak with you for a minute? 我能跟你说会儿话吗?
–Sorry, I'm busy right now. 抱歉, 我这会儿正忙。

special /'speʃəl/ （形容词）特别的

–What's special about this dictionary? 这本词典有什么特别的?
–It's got a lot of color pictures. 它有很多彩色图片。

speech /spi:tʃ/ （名词）（复数 speeches）演讲

–There will be an English speech contest next Friday. 下个星期五将会有英语演讲比赛。
–I know, and I will make a speech, too. 我知道, 我也会参加演讲。

拓展词汇
public speech 公共演讲

speed /spi:d/ （名词）速度

A plane travels at a much higher speed than a train. 飞机的速度比火车快多了。

拓展词汇
speedboat 快艇

百科小贴士
宇宙中速度最快的是光速, 大约为 30 万千米/秒, 音速为 340 米/秒。跑得最快的动物是猎豹, 速度为 30.6 米/秒, 而世界上跑得最快的人的速度还不到 10.3 米/秒。

spell /spel/ （动词）（过去式、过去分词 spelled）拼写

–How do you spell your surname? 你的姓怎么拼写?
–Smith, s-m-i-t-h. 史密斯, s-m-i-t-h。

用法小贴士
在美国英语中, spell 的过去式、过去分词拼作 spelled。

spelling /'spelɪŋ/ （名词）拼写

–Can you spell "beautiful"? 你会拼写beautiful这个词吗?
–Sorry, my spelling is terrible. 抱歉, 我的拼写差极啦!

拓展词汇
American spelling 美式拼法　British spelling 英式拼法　spelling mistake 拼写错误

spend /spend/ （动词）（过去式、过去分词spent）

1. 花费
–How much do you spend on food

in a month? 你一个月花多少钱买食品？
–About four hundred yuan. 大约400元。

2. 度过
–Where did you spend your holiday? 你在哪里度的假？
–I visited Hong Kong. 我去了香港。

spider /'spaɪdə/ （名词）蜘蛛
–How do spiders catch food? 蜘蛛是怎么捕食的？
–By using their webs. 用它们的网。

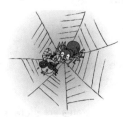

百科小贴士
一般人常将蜘蛛视为昆虫，其实蜘蛛与昆虫相差甚远。蜘蛛是八只脚的节肢动物，靠蜘蛛网捕食。蜘蛛网主要是两种丝线构成的：一种是干燥、无黏性的，一种具有黏性，可捕捉猎物。

spoon /spuːn/ （名词）勺子
We eat soup with a spoon. 我们用勺子喝汤。

sport /spɔːt/ （名词）体育运动
–What's your favorite sport? 你最喜欢的运动是什么？
–Basketball. 篮球。

sports /spɔːts/（形容词）有关运动的，适合运动的
Our school has a sports festival every year. 我们学校每年举行一次体育节。

拓展词汇
sports car 跑车　　sports meet 运动会
sports shoes 运动鞋

spring /sprɪŋ/ （名词）春天
–What's spring like in Beijing? 北京的春天是什么样的？
–It's warm but windy. 暖和，但是爱刮风。

square¹ /skweə/ （名词）
1. 广场
Tian'anmen Square is the largest square in the world. 天安门广场是世界上最大的广场。
2. 正方形
Please draw a square beside the circle. 请在圆形的旁边画一个正方形。

square² /skweə/ （形容词）正方形的
This room is square. 这个房间是正方形的。

squirrel /'skwɪrəl/ （名词）松鼠
–Where do squirrels stay in winter? 松鼠冬天呆在什么地方？
–They hide in the holes of trees. 它们藏在树洞里。

百科小贴士
松鼠属于啮齿类动物，以松子、核桃、榛子等坚果为食。松鼠还会将食物储存在树洞里或埋在地下，但有时会忘记埋藏的地方。到了第二年春天，这些坚果就会发芽，因此它们也是大森林的播种者。

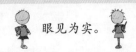

stairs /steəz/ （名词）楼梯

–The elevator isn't working. 电梯坏了。

–Let's take the stairs. 那我们就爬楼梯吧。

stamp¹ /stæmp/ （名词）邮票

–Could you give me this stamp? I collect stamps. 你能给我这张邮票吗？我集邮。

–Sorry. I collect stamps, too. 对不起，我也集邮。

百科小贴士

英国的"黑便士"是世界上第一枚邮票，发行于 1840 年 5 月 6 日，上面印有维多利亚女王的浮雕像。

stamp² /stæmp/ （动词）跺脚，踩踏

The boy stamped his feet in anger. 那男孩气得跺脚。

stand /stænd/ （动词）（过去式、过去分词 **stood** /stʊd/ ）站立

The students stood up to greet their teacher. 学生们起立向老师问好。

star /stɑː/ （名词）星星

–The stars seem to be near us. 星星好像离我们很近。

–In fact, they are very far from us. 事实上它们距离我们很远。

start /stɑːt/ （动词）开始

–When did the meeting start? 会议什么时候开始的？

–It started five minutes ago. 5 分钟前开始的。

state /steɪt/ （名词）

1. 国家

The state owns all the land. 国家拥有所有土地。

2. 州

–How many states are there in the United States? 美国有多少个州？

–Fifty. 50 个。

station /ˈsteɪʃən/ （名词）车站

–Grandma will come from our hometown tomorrow. 奶奶明天从家乡来。

–Let's meet her at the railway station. 我们去火车站接她吧。

stay /steɪ/ （动词）呆，逗留

–How long are you going to stay here? 你会在这里呆多久？

–About a week. 一个星期左右。

steak /steɪk/ （名词）牛排

–The steak smells good. 这牛排闻上去很香。

–It tastes good, too. 味道也很好。

steal /sti:l/ （动词）（过去式

stole /stəʊl/，过去分词 **stolen**

/'stəʊlən/ ）偷窃

–Why did the police take the young man away? 警察为什么带走了那个年轻人？

–Because he stole a wallet on the bus. 因为他在公共汽车上偷了一个钱包。

sticker /'stɪkə/ （名词）不干胶标签，贴画

Susan has put many pretty stickers on the wall. 苏珊在墙上贴了许多漂亮的贴画。

still /stɪl/ （副词）还是，仍然

–Mom, I'm still hungry! 妈妈，我还是饿！

–Have another piece of cake, then. 再吃块蛋糕吧。

stomach /'stʌmək/ （名词）胃，腹部

–I don't feel well. My stomach hurts. 我觉得不太舒服，肚子疼。

–You'd better see the doctor. 你最好去看医生。

stone /stəʊn/ （名词）石头

Kill two birds with one stone. 一石二鸟。

stop¹ /stɒp/ （名词）车站

–What's the next stop? 下一站是哪儿？

–It's the zoo. 是动物园。

拓展词汇

bus stop 公共汽车站

stop² /stɒp/ （动词）（过去式、过去分词 **stopped**，现在分词 **stopping** ）停止

–The rain has stopped. 雨停了。

–We can go home now. 我们现在可以回家了。

store /stɔː/ （名词）商店

There are all kinds of stores on this street. 这条街上有各种各样的商店。

拓展词汇

bookstore （美）书店

department store 百货商店

S

storm /stɔ:m/ （名词）暴风雨
The airport was closed because of a storm. 机场因为暴风雨关闭了。

story /'stɔ:ri/ （名词）（复数 **stories**）故事
–Do you want to hear a story? 你想听故事吗？
–Of course I do! 当然想听了！

straight /streɪt/ （形容词）直的
The street is wide and straight. 这条街道又宽又直。

strange /streɪndʒ/ （形容词）奇怪的
–Betty hasn't come yet. 贝蒂还没有来。
–That's strange. She's never been late before. 真奇怪，她从来没迟到过。

stranger /'streɪndʒə/ （名词）陌生人
–What should you do if a stranger knocks at the door? 如果一个陌生人敲门，你该怎么做？
–Ask him who he is. 问问他是谁。

strawberry /'strɔ:bri/ （名词）（复数 **strawberries**）草莓
–These strawberries are sweet. 这些草莓真甜。

–We grew them in our own garden. 它们是我们在自己花园种的。

百科小贴士
草莓又被称为"水果王后"，它含有丰富的维生素 C，人们把它当作活的维生素丸。

stream /stri:m/ （名词）溪流，小溪
–Can we cross the stream? 我们能跨过这条小溪吗？
–Yes, there's a bridge over there. 能，那边有座桥。

street /stri:t/ （名词）街道
–Where's the museum? 博物馆在哪儿？
–It's just across the street. 就在街对面。

strict /strɪkt/ （形容词）严格的
Our teacher is very strict with us. 我们老师对我们要求很严格。

strong /strɒŋ/ （形容词）强壮的
He has grown into a strong man. 他已长成强壮的男子汉了。

student /'stju:dənt/ （名词）学生
–Are you a student? 你是学生吗？

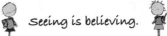
–Yes, but I will finish college soon.
是的，但我很快就要从大学毕业了。

study¹ /'stʌdi/ （动词）（第三人称单数 **studies**，过去式、过去分词 **studied**，现在分词 **studying**）学习

–It's noisy outside. I can't study. 外面太吵了，我没法学习。
–Let's close the windows. 我们把窗户关上吧。

study² /'stʌdi/ （名词）（复数 **studies**）书房

–Do you have a study of your own? 你有自己的书房吗？
–No, but I can use my parents' study. 没有，但我可以用我父母的书房。

stupid /'stjuːpɪd/ （形容词）愚蠢的

–You look unhappy. What's wrong? 你看起来不高兴，出什么事了？
–I've made a stupid mistake. 我犯了一个愚蠢的错误。

subject /'sʌbdʒɪkt/ （名词）学科

–What's your favorite subject? 你最喜欢什么科目？
–History. I've learned a lot from this subject. 历史，我从中学到了很多东西。

succeed /sək'siːd/ （动词）成功

–My dad succeeded in giving up smoking. 我爸爸成功地戒了烟。
–That's really good. 那真太好了。
反义词 fail 失败

success /sək'ses/ （名词）成功

–How was your New Year's Party? 你们的新年派对办得怎么样？
–It was a great success. 非常成功。

such /sʌtʃ/ （形容词）这么的，那么的

–Have you been to the Thousand Islands Lake? 你去过千岛湖吗？
–Yes. It's such a beautiful lake. 去过，真是美呀。

sugar /'ʃʊgə/ （名词）糖

–Do you want sugar in your coffee? 你的咖啡里要放糖吗？
–No, thank you. 不要，谢谢。
拓展词汇
brown sugar 红糖　sugar candy 冰糖
用法小贴士
sugar 一般指的是散粒的白糖或红糖；如果要表示糖果，可以用 sweet（英国英语）或 candy（美国英语）。

summer /'sʌmə/ （名词）夏天

–What sport do you do in summer? 你在夏天做什么运动？
–I like swimming. 我喜欢游泳。
拓展词汇
summer camp 夏令营　summer vacation 暑假　the Summer Palace 颐和园

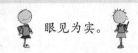

眼见为实。

sun /sʌn/ （名词）太阳

–The sun is like a big fire ball. 太阳像个大火球。

–Yes, but it is much hotter than fire. 是的，不过它可比火热得多。

拓展词汇

sunflower 向日葵　sunglasses 太阳镜

百科小贴士

太阳距离地球约 1.5 亿千米，直径约为 140 万千米，为地球体积的 130 多万倍。在太阳的组成成分中，氢占了绝大部分，按质量计，约为 71%，氦约占 27%，2% 是其他物质。

Sunday /'sʌndeɪ/ （名词）星期日，周日

There's no postal service on Sundays. 星期日没有邮政服务。

sunny /'sʌni/ （形容词）（比较级 **sunnier**，最高级 **sunniest**）阳光充足的，阳光明媚的

–What a sunny day! 天气真晴朗啊！
–Let's go out to play. 我们出去玩吧。

反义词 cloudy 多云的

supermarket /'suːpəmɑːkɪt/ （名词）超级市场

–Where do you do your shopping? 你在哪儿购物？

–At a big supermarket near my home. 在我家附近的一个大超市。

supper /'sʌpə/ （名词）晚饭

–What did you have for supper? 晚饭你吃了什么？

–Rice and vegetables. 米饭和蔬菜。

sure¹ /ʃʊə/ （形容词）确定的

–I think he's lying. 我认为他在撒谎。
–Are you sure? 你确定吗？

sure² /ʃʊə/ （副词）当然

–Could you close the window please? 请关上窗户好吗？
–Sure. 好啊。

用法小贴士

sure 表示该意时常出现在美国口语中，相当于 yes。

surname /'sɜːneɪm/ （名词）姓

Please write your surname on the first line and your first name on the second line. 请把你的姓写在第一条线上，名写在第二条线上。

surprise /sə'praɪz/ （名词）令人吃惊的事

–This violin is a birthday present for you. 这把小提琴是给你的生日礼物。

–Wow, what a big surprise! 哇，真是没想到啊！

surprised /sə'praɪzd/ （形容词）吃惊的，（觉得）奇怪的

–Tom failed the English exam. 汤姆英语考试没及格。
–I'm not surprised. He didn't work hard enough. 我不觉得奇怪，他学习不够努力。

swan /swɒn/ （名词）天鹅

The ugly duckling has grown into a beautiful swan. 丑小鸭变成了一只美丽的天鹅。

百科小贴士
天鹅体形优美，在水中滑行时神态庄重，其他水禽无论在空中或水中均不如天鹅快速。在自然中，天鹅能活 20 年，豢养的天鹅可活 50 年以上。

sweater /'swetə/ （名词）毛衣

–Your sweater looks very warm. 你的毛衣看上去很暖和。
–Yes, it's made of wool. 是的，它是羊毛的。

sweep /swi:p/ （动词）（过去式、过去分词 swept /swept/）扫，打扫

–Someone has broken the window. 有人把窗玻璃打碎了。
–Please sweep the broken glass away. 请把碎玻璃扫掉吧。

sweet¹ /swi:t/ （形容词）甜的

–Are these green apples sweet? 这些青苹果甜吗？
–No, they are a bit sour. The red ones are sweet. 不甜，有点儿酸。那些红苹果是甜的。

拓展词汇
sweet potato 甘薯　sweet corn 甜玉米
反义词 bitter 苦的

sweet² /swi:t/ （名词）

–Mom, I want some more sweets. 妈妈，我想再要些糖果。
–But you've already had a lot. 可你已经吃了好多了。

用法小贴士
sweet是英国英语，美国英语用 candy。

swim /swɪm/ （动词）（过去式 swam /swæm/，过去分词 swum /swʌm/）游泳

–Can you swim? 你会游泳吗？
–Yes, I learned to swim when I was five. 会，我 5 岁就学会游泳了。

拓展词汇
swimsuit 泳装　swimming pool 游泳池

swing /swɪŋ/ （名词）秋千

–Where's John? 约翰呢？
–He's playing on the swing in the backyard. 他在后院荡秋千。

T

table /'teɪbəl/ （名词）桌子

–Let's move the table to the middle of the room. 我们把桌子搬到屋子中间吧。

–OK. 好的。

拓展词汇

tablecloth 桌布　　table lamp 台灯
dining table 餐桌　　table manners 餐桌礼仪

table tennis /'teɪbəl tenɪs/ （名词）乒乓球

–Paul plays table tennis well. 保罗的乒乓球打得真棒。

–Sure. He practices every day. 当然了，他每天都练习。

百科小贴士

table tennis问世后，一位美国制造商以乒乓球的撞击声创造出 ping-pong这个新词，作为其产品的专利注册商标，后来成了 table tennis的另一个正式名称。当它传到中国后，人们又根据音译创造出"乒乓球"这个新语。

tail /teɪl/ （名词）尾巴

Most animals have a tail. 大多数动物都有尾巴。

take /teɪk/ （动词）（过去式 took /tʊk/, 过去分词 taken /'teɪkən/）

1. 拿

–It's going to rain. Take an umbrella with you. 就要下雨了，你带把伞吧。

–All right. 好的。

2. 搭乘（汽车、飞机等）

–How can I get to your house? 我怎么去你家？

–Take bus No. 718. 坐718路公共汽车。

3. 花费

–How long will it take to get there? 去那儿需要多长时间？

–About an hour. 大概一个小时。

tale /teɪl/ （名词）故事

–I like reading tales of adventure. 我喜欢读历险故事。

–I like tales about travel. 我喜欢游记。

拓展词汇

fairy tale 童话

talk /tɔːk/ （动词）讲话

–Did you speak to Robert? 你跟罗伯特讲话了吗？

–Yes, I talked with him for a long time. 是的，我跟他聊了很长时间。

拓展词汇

talk show 脱口秀

–You'd better take a taxi. 你最好打车去。

speak, talk, say, tell都有"说"的意思。speak泛指"讲话"，不一定有听众；talk指"与某人讲话"；say一般须指出说的内容；tell指"告诉某人某事"。

tall /tɔːl/ （形容词）高的

Basketball players are usually very tall. 篮球运动员一般都很高。

反义词 short 矮的

tape /teɪp/ （名词）磁带

Listen to the tape and write down what you hear. 认真听磁带，写下你听到的内容。

tape recorder /'teɪp rɪˌkɔːdə/
录音机

–Can I borrow your tape recorder? 我能借你的录音机吗？
–Yes, but you must use your own tape. 可以，但你得用自己的磁带。

taste¹ /teɪst/ （名词）味道

Air has no color, no taste, and no smell. 空气无色、无味、无嗅。

taste² /teɪst/ （动词）品尝

–Do you want to taste my new dish? 你想尝尝我的新菜吗？
–Of course, thank you. 当然啦，谢谢你。

taxi /'tæksi/ （名词）出租车

–How can I go to the airport? 我怎么去机场？

拓展词汇

taxi driver 出租车司机

tea /tiː/ （名词）茶

–Would you like tea or coffee? 你要茶还是咖啡？
–A cup of tea, please. 来杯茶吧。

拓展词汇

black tea 红茶　green tea 绿茶
lemon tea 柠檬茶　teacup 茶杯
teahouse 茶馆　teapot 茶壶
tea party 茶话会　tea table 茶几

百科小贴士

中国是茶的发祥地，被誉为"茶的祖国"。茶是世界三大无酒精饮料（茶叶、咖啡和可可）之一。

teach /tiːtʃ/ （过去式、过去分词
taught /tɔːt/）（动词）教

Miss Lin teaches us geography.
林小姐教我们地理。

teacher /'tiːtʃə/ （名词）老师

–This is our English teacher. 这是我们的英语老师。
–Oh, she looks very kind. 哦，她看上去很和善。

拓展词汇

Teacher's Day 教师节

195

team /tiːm/ （名词）队，团队

–Do you work together? 你们是一起工作吗？

–Yes, we work as a team. 是的，我们作为一个团队工作。

拓展词汇

teammate 队友　teamwork 团队工作

tear¹ /tɪə/ （名词）眼泪，泪水

Tears rolled down her cheeks. 眼泪顺着她的脸颊流下。

tear² /teə/ （动词）（过去式 tore /tɔː/，过去分词 torn /tɔːn/）撕，撕破

He tore the letter into pieces. 他把信撕碎了。

technology /tekˈnɒlədʒi/ （名词）科技

–Space technology can make great changes to our lives. 太空技术可以大大改变我们的生活。

–I hope it is used for peace, not war. 我希望它被运用于和平，而不是战争。

teddy bear /ˈtedi beə/ 玩具熊

–What shall we buy for Tom's birthday? 我们给汤姆买什么生日礼物？

–How about a teddy bear? 买一只玩具熊怎么样？

百科小贴士

teddy bear这一名称源自美国总统罗斯福（Theodore Roosevelt）。Theodore 的昵称是 Teddy，他喜欢猎熊，因而玩具熊就有了 teddy bear 的叫法。

telephone /ˈtelɪfəun/ （名词）电话

The telephone rang just as I was going out. 我正要出门时电话铃响了。

拓展词汇

telephone number 电话号码
telephone card 电话卡
public telephone 公用电话

television /ˈtelɪvɪʒən/ （名词）（缩写为 TV）电视

–Can I watch television for a while? 我能看会儿电视吗？

–No, you should finish your homework first. 不行，你得先做完作业。

tell /tel/ （动词）（过去式、过去分词 told）

1. 告诉

–Why didn't you tell me the good news earlier? 你为什么不把这个好消息早点儿告诉我？

–I wanted to give you a surprise. 我想给你一个惊喜呀。

2. 讲

–Can you tell me a story? 能给我讲个故事吗？

–Yes. Once upon a time... 好的，从前哪…

ten /ten/ （数词）十

–Everyone has ten fingers. 每个人都有10个手指。
–And ten toes, too. 还有10个脚趾。

tennis /'tenɪs/ （名词）网球

–Can you play tennis? 你会打网球吗？
–No, but I can play table tennis. 不会，但我会打乒乓球。

tent /tent/ （名词）帐篷

–Did you stay in a hotel on your holiday? 你们度假时住在宾馆里吗？
–No, we slept in our tents. It was fun. 不，我们在帐篷里住宿，挺好玩的。

term /tɜːm/ （名词）学期

–How many terms do you have in a year? 你们一年有几个学期？
–Two terms. 两个学期。

terrible /'terɪbəl/ （形容词）糟糕的

–How was your trip to the south? 你的南方之行怎么样？
–Terrible! It rained all the time! 糟糕透了，一直都在下雨！

test /test/ （名词）考试，测试

–Today's English test was easy. 今天的英语考试很容易。

–But I found it difficult! 可我觉得挺难的。

用法小贴士
参见 quiz 的用法小贴士。

text /tekst/ （名词）课文

Read the text carefully and then answer the questions. 认真阅读课文，然后回答问题。

than /ðæn/ （连词）比

Earth is bigger than the moon. 地球比月亮大。

thank¹ /θæŋk/ （动词）感谢

–Have you enjoyed the party? 聚会上玩得开心吗？
–Yes. Thank you. 是的，谢谢你。

thank² /θæŋk/ （名词）感谢

–Many thanks for your help. 十分感谢你的帮助。
–You are welcome. 不用客气。

用法小贴士
thank作名词总是以复数形式 thanks 出现。

that¹ /ðæt/ （形容词）那个

–Which kite is yours? 哪个风筝是你的？
–That one, with the longest tail. 尾巴最长的那个。

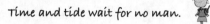
that² /ðæt/ （代词）那个

–What's that? 那是什么？
–It's a music box. 是个音乐盒。

the /ðə/ （定冠词）

1. （用于第二次提及某人或某物时）
–I watched a movie last night. 昨晚我看了一部电影。
–Was the movie interesting? 好看吗？
2. （用于特指）
–Pass me the salt, please. 请把盐递给我。
–Here you are. 给。
3. （放在形容词最高级前）
–David is so tall! 戴维真高！
–Yes, he is the tallest boy in our class. 是呀，他是我们班最高的男生。

theater /'θi:ətə/ （名词）剧院

–How often do you go to the theater? 你多久去看一次戏？
–Once a month. 每月一次。

用法小贴士
movie theater 和 cinema 都可以表示电影院，前者是美式用法，后者是英式用法。

their /ðeə/ （代词）他们的，她们的，它们的

–Don't forget our bags. 别忘了我们的包。
–These are their bags. Ours are in the car. 这是他们的包。我们的在车里。

theirs /ðeəz/ （代词）他们的，她们的，它们的（东西）

–Are these bags ours? 这些包是我们的吗？
–No, they are theirs. 不，是他们的。

them /ðem/ （代词）他们，她们，它们

–Have you told them the news? 你把消息告诉他们了吗？
–Not yet. I'll phone them later. 还没有呢，我一会儿给他们打电话。

themselves /ðəm'selvz/

（代词）他（或她、它）们自己

–What are the girls doing? 姑娘们在做什么？
–They're looking at themselves in the mirror. 她们在照镜子。

then /ðen/ （副词）

1. 然后
We visited France and then America. 我们先游览了法国，然后是美国。
2. 那么
–The key isn't in my bag. 钥匙不在我的包里。
–Then it might be in your pocket. 那可能会在你的口袋里。

there¹ /ðeə/ （代词）有

–Where can I find a restaurant? 我在哪里能找到饭店？
–There's one around the corner. 在街的拐角处有一家。

岁月不待人。

there² /ðeə/ （副词）在那里
If Tom sits here, I can sit there. 要是汤姆坐在这里，我可以坐那儿。

these¹ /ði:z/ （形容词）这些
–These photos are very good. 这些照片真漂亮。
–I took them during the holidays. 这是我度假的时候照的。

these² /ði:z/ （代词）这些
–These are Ann's books. 这些是安的书。
–Then those are mine. 那么那些就是我的了。

they /ðeɪ/ （代词）他们，她们，它们
–What's the matter? They look worried. 出了什么事？他们看起来很着急。
–They've lost their dog. 他们的狗丢了。

thick /θɪk/ （形容词）厚的
–Who's that man with thick glasses? 那位戴着厚厚的眼镜的人是谁？
–He's my father. 是我爸爸。

反义词 thin 薄的

thief /θi:f/ （名词）（复数 **thieves**）贼
–Have the police caught the car thief? 警察抓到偷车贼了吗？
–No, the thief has run away. 没有，贼已经逃跑了。

thin /θɪn/ （形容词）（比较级 **thinner**，最高级 **thinnest**）
1. 薄的
–I feel cold. 我觉得冷。
–Your coat is too thin. You need a thicker one. 你的外套太薄，你需要件厚外套。
反义词 thick 厚的
2. 瘦的
–She looks thinner than before. 她看起来比以前瘦了。
–She's been ill for two weeks. 她病了两个星期。
反义词 fat 胖的

thing /θɪŋ/ （名词）事情，东西
–What's that thing over there? 那边那个东西是什么？
–I don't know, I can't see it clearly. 不知道，我看不太清楚。

think /θɪŋk/ （动词）（过去式、过去分词 **thought** /θɔ:t/）思考，想
–Can animals think? 动物能够思考吗？
–I'm not sure. 我不太清楚。

199

拓展词汇

thinker 思想家

third /θɜːd/（形容词）第三的

–Who's the third girl from the left in the picture? 相片中左边第3个女孩子是谁?

–It's Jane. 是简。

thirsty /'θɜːsti/（形容词）（比较级 **thirstier**, 最高级 **thirstiest**）口渴的

–I'm thirsty. 我口渴。

–Drink some water, then. 那就喝点儿水吧。

thirty /'θɜːti/（数词）三十

–How many minutes is half an hour? 半个小时是多少分钟?

–Thirty minutes. 30分钟。

this¹ /ðɪs/（形容词）这个

–Is this book yours? 这本书是你的吗?

–No, it isn't. That one is mine. 不是,那本才是我的。

this² /ðɪs/（代词）这个

–What's this? 这是什么?

–It's an apple pie. 是苹果馅饼。

those¹ /ðəʊz/（形容词）那些

–Do you know those people? 你认识那些人吗?

–No, I've never seen them before. 不,我从没见过他们。

those² /ðəʊz/（代词）那些

–Are these your clothes? 这些是你的衣服吗?

–No, they aren't. Those are mine. 不是,那些才是我的。

thousand /'θaʊzənd/（数词）一千

–How many students are there in your school? 你们学校有多少学生?

–About one thousand. 大约1000人。

用法小贴士

表示两千或数千时,thousand 仍用单数形式。例如: two thousand (2000), three thousand (3000),依此类推。

thread /θred/（名词）线

–Can you give me a needle and thread? I want to sew a button onto my shirt. 你能给我针线吗? 我想往衬衫上缝个扣子。

–Here you are. 给你。

three /θriː/（数词）三

–How many people are there in your family? 你家有几口人?

–Three: my father, mother, and me. 3口人: 我爸爸、妈妈和我。

through /θruː/（介词）通过

–How did the thief get in the house? 小偷是怎么进屋的?

–He got in through the window.
他从窗户进来的。

throw /θrəʊ/ （动词）（过去式
threw /θruː/，过去分词 **thrown**
/θrəʊn/）扔，投

–Throw the ball to me, please. 请
把球扔给我。
–Catch! 接着！

thumb /θʌm/ （名词）拇指

–The thumb is shorter than the
other fingers. 大拇指比其他手指短。
–Yes. It's thicker, too. 对，它也粗
一些。

用法小贴士
大脚趾称作 big toe

thunder /'θʌndə/ （名词）雷，
雷声

–What a big storm! 好大的暴风雨啊！
–The thunder is so loud! 雷真
响！

拓展词汇
thunderstorm 雷雨

Thursday /'θɜːzdeɪ/ （名词）
星期四

–What day is today? 今天星期几？
–It's Thursday. 星期四。

ticket /'tɪkɪt/ （名词）票

–Have you bought your train
ticket? 你买火车票了吗？
–Yes. I booked it on the Internet.
买了，我是在网上预订的。

拓展词汇
ticket office 售票处

tidy /'taɪdi/ （形容词）（比较级
tidier，最高级 **tidiest**）整洁的

–Ann's room is always neat and
tidy. 安的房间总是干净整洁。
–Yes. She's a tidy person. 是的，
她是个爱干净的人。

反义词 untidy 不整洁的

tie¹ /taɪ/ （动词）（过去式、过去
分词 **tied**，现在分词 **tying**）

1. 系，拴
She tied her horse to the tree. 她把
马拴到树上。
2. 打结，系上
We are teaching Tom how to tie
a tie. 我们正在教汤姆打领带。

tie² /taɪ/ （名词）领带

–This tie doesn't look good on
you. 这条领带不适合你。
–I'll change it then. 那我就换一
条吧。

百科小贴士
领带始于罗马帝国时代。那时，士兵们脖
子上戴着一种类似围巾和领带的东西。直
到 1668 年，领带在法国才开始变为今天
这种样式，并发展成男士正装的重要组成
部分。

tiger /'taɪgə/ （名词）老虎

–Tigers are good at swimming.
老虎善于游泳。
–But they cannot climb trees.
但它们不会爬树。

time /taɪm/ （名词）

1. 时间
–What time is it? 几点了？
–It's nine o'clock. 9点整。
2. 次
–How many times have you been
to this city? 你来过这座城市多少
次？
–Oh, many times. 哦，很多次。

tire /taɪə/ （名词）轮胎

–What's wrong with your bike?
你的自行车怎么了？
–I have a flat tire. I have to change
it. 车胎没气了，得换胎。

百科小贴士
世界第一条充气轮胎是由苏格兰工程师于
1845年发明的。

tired /taɪəd/ （形容词）疲劳的

–Mom looks tired after a day's
work. 妈妈工作了一天，看起来很累。
–Let's help her do some housework. 咱们帮她做点儿家务吧。

to /tuː/ （介词）

1. 向…（方向）；到…
–Excuse me. Do you know the way
to the library? 打扰一下，你知道去
图书馆怎么走吗？
–Turn left and walk for about
five minutes. 向左转，走大约5分
钟就到。
2. 对…
–Did you talk to John about this?
你和约翰谈过这件事了吗？
–Yes, but he didn't listen to me.
谈过了，但他不听我的。

today[1] /tə'deɪ/ （副词）今天

–You look tired. 你看起来很累。
–I've been very busy today. 我今天
特别忙。

today[2] /tə'deɪ/ （名词）今天

–What day is it today? 今天星期几？
–Today is Sunday. 今天是周日。

toe /təʊ/ （名词）脚趾

–You stepped on my toe! 你踩了我
的脚趾头了。

–Oh, I'm so sorry. 哦，真对不起。

拓展词汇

toenail 脚指甲

together /təˈgeðə/ （副词）一起，共同

Families get together to eat moon cakes on Mid-Autumn Day. 中秋节时家人都聚在一起吃月饼。

toilet /ˈtɔɪlət/ （名词）洗手间，厕所，（冲洗式）马桶

–Our toilets are made to conserve water. 我们的抽水马桶安装得能节约用水。

–Good! Everybody should have those. 太好了！每个人都应配备那种装置。

拓展词汇

toilet paper 卫生纸 toilet water 花露水

tomato /təˈmɑːtəʊ/ （名词）（复数 tomatoes）番茄，西红柿

–Do you want something to drink? 你想喝点儿什么？

–Tomato juice, please. 番茄汁吧。

tomorrow¹ /təˈmɒrəʊ/ （副词）明天

–I must be going now. See you tomorrow. 我必须走了。明天见。

–See you. 再见。

tomorrow² /təˈmɒrəʊ/ （名词）明天

Tomorrow will be a fine day. 明天会是个晴天。

tongue /tʌŋ/ （名词）舌头

–Tom, it's rude to stick your tongue out at people. 汤姆，冲别人吐舌头不礼貌。

–Sorry, Mom. 对不起，妈妈。

tonight¹ /təˈnaɪt/ （副词）今晚

–Shall we do our homework together tonight? 今晚我们一起做家庭作业好吗？

–Great! I'll come to your house at seven. 太好了！我7点钟到你家来。

tonight² /təˈnaɪt/ （名词）今晚

–What's tonight's show? 今天晚上演什么节目？

–It's *The Monkey King*. 演《西游记》。

too /tuː/ （副词）

1. 也

–I'm hungry. 我饿了。

–Me too. 我也饿了。

2. 太

–How do I look in these trousers? 我穿这条裤子怎么样？

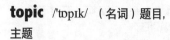
–They're too big for you. 你穿太肥大了。

tool /tu:l/ （名词）工具

I have some gardening tools. 我有一些园艺工具。

拓展词汇

toolbox 工具箱

tooth /tu:θ/ （名词）（复数 teeth /ti:θ/）牙齿

We must brush our teeth before bed. 睡觉前必须刷牙。

拓展词汇

toothbrush 牙刷　toothpaste 牙膏

百科小贴士

要保护牙齿就要从生活习惯做起，少吃高糖食品，少喝碳酸饮料，勤刷牙，用正确的刷牙方式刷牙，这样才能保持牙齿的健康。

toothache /'tu:θeɪk/ （名词）牙疼

–I've got a bad toothache. 我牙疼得厉害。
–You must see the dentist. 你得去看牙医。

top /tɒp/ （名词）顶，顶部

–I can't reach the top of the bookshelf. 我够不着书架的顶层。
–Here's a ladder. 这儿有架梯子。

topic /'tɒpɪk/ （名词）题目，主题

–What's the topic of today's meeting? 今天会议的主题是什么？
–It's about the environment. 是关于环境的。

torch /tɔ:tʃ/ （名词）（复数 torches）手电筒

–Before electricity, people lit their way with torches. 在电出现以前，人们用火炬照明。
–Wow, I can't imagine that. 哇，我真不能想象。

tortoise /'tɔ:təs/ （名词）乌龟

–What does your pet tortoise eat? 你的宠物龟吃什么食物呀？
–He likes fish. 它爱吃鱼。

用法小贴士

谈到宠物时，往往可以用人称代词。

total /'təʊtəl/ （形容词）全部的

–What's the total number of students in your school? 你们学校一共有多少学生？
–One thousand three hundred. 1300个。

touch /tʌtʃ/ （动词）摸，触摸

Don't touch the animals in the zoo. 不要触摸动物园里的动物。

toward /tə'wɔːd/ （介词）朝（着）

The boy ran toward his mother. 男孩向他妈妈跑过去。

用法小贴士

英国英语中多用 toward.

towel /tauəl/ （名词）毛巾

–The towel is very soft. 这毛巾很柔软。
–Sure, it's a new one. 当然啦，这是条新毛巾。

拓展词汇

bath towel 浴巾　　paper towel 纸巾

tower /tauə/ （名词）塔

–Have you ever climbed to the top of the tower? 你爬上过塔顶吗？
–Yes. You can see the whole town from there. 爬上过，从那儿你能看见全镇。

拓展词汇

clock tower 钟楼　　water tower 水塔
the Tower of London 伦敦塔
the Eiffel Tower 埃菲尔铁塔

town /taun/ （名词）城镇

Mary comes from a big city. Tom comes from a small town. 玛丽来自一个大城市，汤姆来自一个小镇。

拓展词汇

university town 大学城

toy /tɔɪ/ （名词）玩具

–How many toys do you have? 你有多少玩具？
–I have a toy gun, a toy car, and some others. 我有一把玩具枪，一个玩具车，还有别的玩具。

拓展词汇

soft toys 毛绒玩具　　toy shop 玩具店

traffic /'træfɪk/ （名词）交通

–Traffic jam again! 又堵车了！
–There is a lot of traffic at this time of the day. 每天这个时候车都很多。

拓展词汇

traffic light 红绿灯　　traffic jam 交通拥堵

train /treɪn/ （名词）火车

–How are you going to Shanghai? 你怎么去上海？
–I'm going by train. 我坐火车去。

trash can /trʌs kæn/ （名词）垃圾箱

–Where should I throw the empty bottle? 我该把空瓶子扔在哪儿？
–There's a trash can over there. 那边有个垃圾箱。

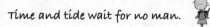

travel¹ /'trævəl/ （动词）（过去式、过去分词 **traveled**，现在分词 **traveling**）旅游，旅行

–My grandpa traveled a lot when he was young. 我爷爷年轻时经常旅行。

–No wonder he knows about many places. 难怪他知道许多地方。

用法小贴士

在美国英语中，travel 的过去式、过去分词拼作 traveled，现在分词拼作 traveling。

travel² /'trævəl/ （名词）旅行

–What's this book about? 这本书是关于什么的？

–It's about travel. 是关于旅游的。

treasure /'treʒə/ （名词）宝物，宝贝

–Can I throw away the old toys? 我能把这些旧玩具扔了吗？

–No, they are treasures for my little sister. 不行，它们可是我妹妹的宝贝。

tree /triː/ （名词）树

–Jed loved climbing trees when he was little. 杰德小时候喜欢爬树。

–He must have been very agile. 他谅必非常灵活。

拓展词汇

tree duck 树鸭

tree frog 树蛙

triangle /'traɪæŋɡəl/ （名词）三角形

–Can you draw a triangle? 你会画三角形吗？

–Yes, but I need a ruler. 会，但我需要一把尺子。

trick /trɪk/ （名词）恶作剧

The boys like playing tricks. 这些男孩们喜欢搞恶作剧。

trip /trɪp/ （名词）旅行

–I haven't seen you for a long time. 我很长时间没见到你了。

–I've made a world trip. 我去环球旅行啦。

trouble¹ /'trʌbəl/ （动词）（用于礼貌地提出请求）麻烦

–I'm sorry to trouble you, but can I borrow a pen? 很抱歉麻烦你，我能借你的钢笔吗？

–Here you are. 给你。

trouble² /'trʌbəl/ （名词）麻烦，问题

–What's the trouble? 出什么麻烦了？

–Jimmy broke the window again. 吉米又把窗户打碎了。

trousers /'traʊzəz/ （名词）裤子

–Can I wear a skirt? 我能穿裙子吗？

–You'd better wear trousers if you're riding your bike. 如果你要骑自行车就最好穿裤子。

用法小贴士
trousers是英国英语，美国英语用pants。一条裤子是 a pair of trousers，两条裤子是 two pairs of trousers，依此类推。

truck /trʌk/ （名词）卡车
Trucks can carry very heavy things. 卡车能运载很重的东西。

拓展词汇
truck driver 卡车司机

用法小贴士
truck是美国英语。

true /truː/ （形容词）真实的
–Is this a true story? 这是真事吗?
–Yes. It happened to me last year. 是的，是去年发生在我身上的事。

反义词 false 假的

trumpet /'trʌmpɪt/ （名词）喇叭
–What's that terrible noise? 那可怕的噪音是什么呀?
–Tom is practicing the trumpet. 是汤姆在练习吹喇叭。

trust /trʌst/ （动词）信任
–Can you keep a secret? 你能保密吗?

–Yes. You can trust me. 能，你可以相信我。

truth /truːθ/ （名词）事实，真理
–Are you telling the truth? 你讲的是实话吗?
–Yes, every word of it. 是，每句话都是真的。

try /traɪ/ （动词）（第三人称单数 **tries**，过去式、过去分词 **tried**，现在分词**trying**）
1. 努力
–Good luck on the exam! 祝你考试考好。
–I'll try my best! 我会尽全力。
2. 尝试
–Have you tried the new machine? 你试过那台新机器了吗?
–Yes, it worked very well. 试了，运转很好。

T-shirt /'tiːʃɜːt/ （名词）T恤衫
–These T-shirts are lovely. 这些T恤衫真好看!
–Yes, I'll buy one. 是啊，我要买一件。

Tuesday /'tjuːzdeɪ/ （名词）星期二
–Why don't you have classes on Tuesday afternoons? 星期二下午你们为什么不上课?
–Because the teachers have a meeting every Tuesday afternoon. 因为老师每周二下午都开会。

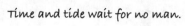
tummy /'tʌmi/ （名词）（儿语）
肚子

–The little bear has eaten too much. 小熊吃得太多了。
–Yeah. Just look at its round tummy. 是啊，看它圆鼓鼓的肚子。

turkey /'tɜːki/ （名词）火鸡

–How much does a turkey weigh? 火鸡重量能到多少？
–It can weigh as much as 50 pounds. 它能重达五十磅。

拓展词汇

Turkey 土耳其（首字母 T 大写）

百科小贴士

火鸡肉富含蛋白质、维生素 E 和 B 族维生素，而脂肪和胆固醇含量较低，非常有益健康。

turn¹ /tɜːn/ （动词）

1. 翻
–Where are the answers to these questions? 这些问题的答案在哪里？
–Turn to the next page and you'll find them. 翻到下一页就能找到。

2. 调整
–Please turn the radio down a bit. It's too loud. 请把收音机关小一点儿，声音太大了。
–I'm sorry. I'll turn it off. 对不起，我把它关了吧。

拓展词汇

turn off 关　turn on 开

turn² /tɜːn/ （名词）（轮到的）
机会

–Whose turn is it now? 轮到谁了？
–It's my turn. 轮到我了。

TV /ˌtiː'viː/ （名词）电视

–We can learn a lot from TV. 我们能够从电视中学到很多东西。
–That's true, but we shouldn't watch too much TV. 是啊，但是我们不应看太多电视。

拓展词汇

TV station 电视台
TV program 电视节目

用法小贴士

TV 的全称为 television。

百科小贴士

电视是 20 世纪人类最伟大的发明之一，第一台电视机是由苏格兰发明家约翰·洛吉·贝尔德于 1925 年发明的。

twelve /twelv/ （数词）
十二

–How many months are there in a year? 一年有几个月？
–Twelve months. 12 个月。

twenty /'twenti/ （数词）
二十

–How many boys and girls are there in your class? 你们班有多少男生，多少女生？
–We have twenty boys and twenty girls. 我们班有 20 个男生，20 个女生。

twice /twaɪs/ （副词）

1. 两次

–How often do you take piano lessons? 你多久上一次钢琴课？

–Twice a week. 每周两次。

2. 两倍

–I have twenty-five cartoon books. 我有25本卡通书。

–I have twice as many as you. 我的是你的两倍。

twin /twɪn/ （名词）双胞胎

–Do you have any brothers and sisters? 你有兄弟姐妹吗？

–I have two younger sisters. They are twins. 我有两个妹妹，她们是双胞胎。

拓展词汇

twin brothers　双胞胎兄弟

twin sisters　双胞胎姐妹

two /tuː/ （数词）二

–The math exam was too difficult. 这次数学考试太难了。

–I agree. Only two people passed. 是啊，只有两个人及格了。

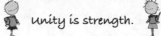

Unity is strength.

U

UFO /ˌjuː ef ˈəʊ/ （名词）不明飞行物

–What's in the sky? Is it a UFO? 天上是什么东西呀？是不明飞行物吗？
–No. It's a hot-air balloon. 不是，是个热气球。

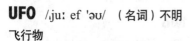

用法小贴士
UFO 是英语 unidentified flying object 的缩略形式。

ugly /ˈʌgli/ （形容词）（比较级 **uglier**，最高级 **ugliest**）丑陋的，难看的

–What an ugly painting! 这幅画可真难看！
–I agree. It's the ugliest painting I've ever seen. 没错，这是我见过的最难看的画。

umbrella /ʌmˈbrelə/ （名词）雨伞

–It looks like rain. 看起来要下雨了。

–Take an umbrella with you. 你带把伞吧。

uncle /ˈʌŋkəl/ （名词）叔叔，伯伯，舅舅

I'm going to visit Uncle Jim this weekend. 这个周末我要去看吉姆叔叔。

under /ˈʌndə/ （介词）在…下面

–What are you doing under the table? 你躲在桌子下干吗呢？
–We're playing hide-and-seek. 我们在玩捉迷藏。

underground /ˌʌndəˈgraʊnd/ （名词）地铁

–How do these trains get from one side of the city to the other? 这些火车如何从城市着一边到另一边的。
–They go through underground tunnels. 它们通过地下隧道。

用法小贴士
underground 是英国英语，美国英语用 British subway。

团结就是力量。

understand /ˌʌndə'stænd/

（动词）（过去式、过去分词

understood /ˌʌndə'stʊd/）明白，懂

–Do you understand French? 你懂法语吗？

–Yes. A little bit. 是的，懂一点儿。

uniform /'juːnɪfɔːm/ （名词）

制服

–How many school uniforms do you have? 你有几套校服？

–Two, one for spring and one for autumn. 两套，一套春季服，一套秋季服。

United Kingdom /juːˌnaɪtɪd 'kɪŋdəm/ （名词）英国

–What language do people in the United Kingdom speak? 在英国人们说什么语言？

–They speak English, of course. 他们当然说英语啦。

国是世界上最强的国家，自称"日不落帝国"，现在仍然是世界上最重要的国家之一。

United States /juːˌnaɪtɪd 'steɪts/

（名词）美国

–How many states are there in the United States? 美国有多少个州？

–There are 50 states. 有50个州。

university /ˌjuːnɪ'vɜːsɪti/

（名词）（复数 **universities**）大学

–Which university do you want to go to? 你想要上哪一所大学？

–Beijing University. 北京大学。

until[1] /ʌn'tɪl/ （介词）直到…时

–You look sleepy. 你看起来很困。

–I read until 10 o'clock last night. 昨天晚上我看书一直看到10点。

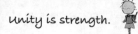

until² /ʌn'tɪl/ （连词）到…为止

–It's raining hard. 雨下得很大。
–Let's wait here until the rain stops. 我们就在这儿等到雨停吧。

up /ʌp/ （副词）往上

Susan jumped up and down when she heard the good news. 苏珊听说这个好消息后，高兴得又蹦又跳。

use /juːz/ （动词）使用

–Do you know how to use a computer? 你知道怎么用电脑吗？
–Sure. I'll show you. 当然，我用给你看。

useful /'juːsfʊl/ （形容词）有用的

This book is useful for new parents. 这本书对刚做父母的人很有用。

usual /'juːʒʊəl/ （形容词）通常的

–Mom came home earlier than usual. 妈妈比平时回家要早。
–Oh, it's Dad's birthday today! 哦，今天是爸爸的生日！

usually /'juːʒʊəli/ （副词）通常

–What time do you usually get up? 你通常什么时候起床？
–About half past six. 大约6点半。

vacation /vəˈkeɪʃən/（名词）

休假，假期

–Where are you going to spend your vacation? 你打算到哪里度假呀？

–I'm not going anywhere. 我哪儿都不去。

拓展词汇

summer vacation 暑假
winter vacation 寒假

vegetable /ˈvedʒtəbəl/（名词）

蔬菜

–What should I eat to keep healthy? 我该吃什么才能健康呢？

–Eat a lot of fresh fruits and vegetables. 多吃新鲜水果和蔬菜。

拓展词汇

green vegetable 绿色蔬菜
vegetable garden 菜园

very /ˈveri/（副词）很，非常

–Do you like the book? 你喜欢这本书吗？

–Yes, I like it very much. 是的，非常喜欢。

video /ˈvɪdiəu/（名词）

（复数 videos）录像

–Shall we go to the cinema tomorrow? 我们明天去看电影吗？

–I prefer to watch videos at home. 我更愿意在家里看录像。

拓展词汇

video game 电子游戏　videophone 可视电话　video recorder 录像机　video-tape 录像带　home video 家庭录像

view /vjuː/（名词）

1. 见解，看法

–What's your view? 你的看法是什么？

–To be honest, I don't agree with you. 说实话，我与你看法不同。

2. 视域，视野

–I can't see anything down here. 这下面什么也看不到。

–You get a good view up here. 上到这儿来就能看清楚。

village /ˈvɪlɪdʒ/（名词）村庄

–What's the book about? 这本书是关于什么的？

–It's about village life. 是关于乡村生活的。

拓展词汇

fishing village 渔村
mountain village 山村

violin /ˌvaɪəˈlɪn/（名词）

小提琴

–Is Mary a musician? 玛丽是个音乐家吗？

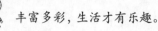丰富多彩，生活才有乐趣。

–Yes, she plays the violin very well.
是，她小提琴拉得很好。

violinist 小提琴家

visit /'vɪzɪt/（动词）参观，访问

–What did you do in Beijing? 你们在北京做什么了？
–We visited parks and museums.
我们参观了公园和博物馆。

voice mail 语音邮件

visitor /'vɪzɪtə/（名词）游客，来客

–Did you have many visitors last night? 你们昨天晚上客人多吗？
–No, just a few. 不多，只有几个人。

volleyball /'vɒlibɔːl/（名词）排球

–Peter is a volleyball player. 彼得是个排球运动员。
–I hope to watch him play sometime. 我希望什么时候看看他打球。

voice /vɔɪs/（名词）嗓音

–Who is singing upstairs? 是谁在楼上唱歌呀？
–It's Jessica. She has a good voice.
是杰西卡，她的嗓子很好。

wait /weɪt/ （动词）等待

–Wait for me! 等等我！
–Hurry up! You're already late. 快点！你已经迟到了。

waiter /'weɪtə/ （名词）
男服务员

–Waiter, can you bring me a glass of water? 服务员，请给来杯水好吗？
–OK. Just one minute. 好的，就来了。

用法小贴士
waiter指男服务员，waitress指女服务员。

wake /weɪk/ （动词）（过去式
woke /wəuk/，过去分词 **woken**
/'wəukən/）醒，醒来

–Wake up! It's already seven o'clock! 醒醒！都7点了！
–Oh no! I'll be late for school! 坏了，我上学要迟到了。

用法小贴士
美国英语中，wake 的过去式、过去分词都是 waked。

walk¹ /wɔːk/ （动词）走

–How long did it take you to get here? 你到这儿花了多长时间？
–I walked for half an hour. 我走了半小时。

walk² /wɔːk/ （名词）散步

–Let's go for a walk. 我们去散步吧。
–Good idea! 好主意！

wall /wɔːl/ （名词）墙

–Where should I put the picture? 我该把画放在哪儿？
–Hang it on the wall. 挂在墙上吧。

拓展词汇

wallpaper 墙纸　　wall painting 壁画

want /wɒnt/ （动词）想要

–What do you want to be when you're older? 你长大以后想干什么？
–I want to be a doctor. 我想当医生。

war /wɔː/ （名词）战争

–Who won the war? 谁赢得了战争？
–The new Monkey King. 新猴王。

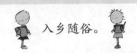
入乡随俗。

拓展词汇
the First World War 第一次世界大战
the Second World War 第二次世界大战

warm /wɔːm/ （形容词）温暖的
–It's cold outside. 外面真冷。
–Sit near the fire. It's warmer here.
靠火炉坐吧，这里暖和些。

反义词 cold 寒冷的

wash /wɒʃ/ （动词）洗
–What's Dad doing? 爸爸在做什么？
–He's washing the car. 他在洗车呢。

washing machine /'wɒʃɪŋ məʃiːn/ （名词）洗衣机
–The new washing machine saves a lot of time for everyone. 新洗衣机为大家节省了很多时间。

百科小贴士
世界上第一台电动洗衣机于1910年由美国人费希尔发明并在芝加哥制造出来。

waste /weɪst/ （动词）浪费
Eat up your rice. It's bad to waste food. 把米饭吃光，浪费粮食不好。

watch¹ /wɒtʃ/ （名词）（复数 watches）手表
–You're late again! 你又迟到了！
–Sorry, but my watch is slow.
对不起，我的手表慢了。

watch² /wɒtʃ/ （动词）看
–Would you like to play with us?
你想和我们一起玩吗？

–No, thanks. I just want to watch.
不了，谢谢。我只想看。

拓展词汇
watch TV 看电视

water /'wɔːtə/ （名词）水
–Let's swim in the river. 我们去河里游泳吧。
–Oh, no. The water is too cold.
不要，水太凉了。

拓展词汇
water bird 水鸟　　watercolor 水彩
water gun 水枪　　watermelon 西瓜
drinking water 饮用水
running water 自来水

wave /weɪv/ （动词）挥手
–Where's Tom? 汤姆在哪儿？
–Over there! He's waving to us.
在那儿！他正向我们招手呢。

way /weɪ/ （名词）路途，路线
–Do you know the way to the railway station? 你知道去火车站怎么走吗？
–Take bus No. 1 and get off at the last stop. 坐1路公交车，最后一站下车。

we /wiː/ （代词）我们
–Do you know Jack? 你认识杰克吗？

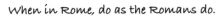

–Of course. We are good friends. 当然认识了，我们是好朋友。

weak /wiːk/ （形容词）虚弱的，无力的

–I feel weak all over. 我觉得浑身无力。
–You need some rest. 你需要休息一下。

wealth /welθ/ （名词）财富

Knowledge is the greatest wealth of your life. 知识是你一生最大的财富。

wear /weə/ （动词）（过去式 wore /wɔː/, 过去分词 worn /wɔːn/）穿，戴

–She's wearing a new dress. 她穿着新衣服。
–It's very pretty. 真漂亮。

weather /'weðə/ （名词）天气

–What will the weather be like tomorrow? 明天的天气怎么样？
–It'll be cloudy. 明天阴天。

拓展词汇

weather report 天气预报
weatherman 天气预报员

Web site /'websaɪt/ （名词）网站

This Web site has a lot of information on cars. 这个网站有许多关于轿车的信息。

拓展词汇

Web-site address 网址

wedding /'wedɪŋ/ （名词）婚礼，婚宴

–When will Miss Smith have her wedding? 史密斯小姐什么时候举办婚礼？
–Next Saturday. 下周六。

拓展词汇

wedding dress 婚纱
wedding ring 结婚戒指

Wednesday /'wenzdeɪ/ （名词）星期三

–What's the day today? 今天星期几？
–Today is Wednesday. 今天是星期三。

week /wiːk/ （名词）星期，周

There are seven days in a week. 一周有7天。

拓展词汇

this week 这周   last week 上周
next week 下周   weekday 工作日

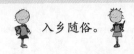
入乡随俗。

weekend /ˌwiːkˈend/ （名词）
周末

–Have a good weekend! 周末愉快！
–The same to you! 也祝你愉快！

welcome¹ /ˈwelkəm/ （动词）
欢迎

The students warmly welcomed the visitors. 学生们热情欢迎来访者。

welcome² /ˈwelkəm/ （名词）
欢迎

The rude man received a cold welcome. 那个粗鲁的人受到了冷遇。

welcome³ /ˈwelkəm/ （形容词）
受欢迎的

–Thank you for your advice. 多谢你的建议。
–You're welcome. 不用客气。

well¹ /wel/ （副词）（比较级 better，最高级 best）很好地
She plays the piano very well, but her mother plays even better. 她钢琴弹得很好，但她妈妈弹得更好。

well² /wel/ （形容词）（比较级 better，最高级 best）健康的
–How do you feel today? 你今天感觉怎样？
–I feel much better. Thank you! 我感觉好多了。谢谢你！

well³ /wel/ （叹词）噢，哦
–How do you like the film? 你觉得这部电影怎么样？
–Well, the story is good. 噢，故事情节还不错。

west /west/ （名词）西方，西部
The river flows from west to east. 这条河从西往东流。

Western /ˈwestən/ （形容词）
西方的，西洋的

–Are you interested in Western culture? 你对西方文化感兴趣吗？
–Yes, I like Western paintings. 是的，我喜欢西洋绘画。

拓展词汇

Western Europe 西欧

wet /wet/ （形容词）（比较级 wetter，最高级 wettest）湿的
–You are all wet! 你浑身都湿了！
–It's raining hard. 雨下得很大。

whale /weɪl/ （名词）鲸

The whale is the largest of all animals. 鲸是所有动物中体积最大的。

拓展词汇

blue whale 蓝鲸   killer whale 虎鲸

百科小贴士

鲸生活在海里，看起来像鱼但并不是鱼，它是哺乳动物，并且是所有动物中体积最大的。

what /wɒt/ （代词）什么

–What are you doing there? 你在那儿干什么？
–I'm looking for my ball. 我在找我的球。

wheat /wiːt/ （名词）小麦，麦子

Bread is usually made from wheat. 面包通常是用小麦做的。

拓展词汇

wheat field 麦田   wheat flour 面粉

wheel /wiːl/ （名词）车轮，轮子

–Cars have four wheels. 小轿车有4个轮子。
–Trains have many wheels. 火车有许多轮子。

拓展词汇

wheelchair 轮椅   front wheel 前轮
bicycle wheel 自行车轮

when¹ /wen/ （连词）在…的时候

–What did you do when I was away? 我不在的时候你做什么了？
–I drew a few pictures. Come take a look. 我画了几幅画，过来看一下。

when² /wen/ （副词）什么时候

–When is your birthday? 你的生日是什么时候？
–March 12. 3月12号。

where /weə/ （副词）什么地方，在哪里

–Where is the nearest bus station? 最近的公交车站在哪里？
–It's one mile away. 它在一英里以外。

whether /'weðə/ （连词）

1. 是否
–I don't know whether you like this place. 我不知道你是否喜欢这个地方。
–I certainly do. 当然喜欢啦。
2. 不管
–I must leave now whether you want to go or not. 不管你想不想走，我得离开了。
–I'll stay a little longer. 我要再呆会儿。

which¹ /wɪtʃ/ （形容词）哪一个

–Which bus should I take to the zoo? 去动物园应该坐哪一路公共汽车？
–No. 104. It's just over there. 104路，就在那边。

which² /wɪtʃ/ （代词）哪一个
–Which of these pencil boxes is yours, the blue one or the red one? 哪一个铅笔盒是你的，蓝色的还是红色的？
–The blue one. 蓝色的。

while¹ /waɪl/ （连词）当…的时候
You can go skating while I'm playing tennis. 我打网球的时候你可以去溜冰。

while² /waɪl/ （名词）一会儿
–Can you wait for a while? I'll be ready soon. 你能等一会儿吗？我很快就准备好。
–OK, but be quick. 好吧，但快一点儿。

white¹ /waɪt/ （形容词）白色的
Sam has very white teeth. 赛姆的牙齿很白。

反义词 black 黑的
拓展词汇
white ant 白蚁
the White House （美国的）白宫

white² /waɪt/ （名词）白色
These pictures are in black and white. 这些照片是黑白的。

who /huː/ （代词）谁
–Who is the speaker? 那位讲话的人是谁？
–It's our new headmaster. 是我们的新校长。

whole /həʊl/ （形容词）完整的，全部的
–You've eaten up the whole cake? 你们把整个蛋糕都吃光了？
–No, we have left a piece for you. 不，我们给你留了一块。

whom /huːm/ （代词）谁
–Whom are you talking about? 你们在谈论谁？
–Mr. Clinton, our new English teacher. 克林顿先生，我们的新英语老师。

whose /huːz/ （代词）谁的
–Whose dictionary is that? 那是谁的字典呀？
–It's mine. 是我的。

why /waɪ/ （副词）为什么
–Why are you crying? 你为什么哭啊？
–I can't find my mommy. 我找不到我妈妈了。

wide /waɪd/ （形容词）宽的，宽阔的

The main street is much wider than the side roads. 主街比边路宽多了。

反义词 narrow 窄的

wife /waɪf/ （名词）（复数 **wives** /waɪvz/）妻子

–Are you a doctor? 你是医生吗？
–No, but my wife is. 不是，但我妻子是。

拓展词汇

housewife 家庭主妇

wild /waɪld/ （形容词）野生的

Many wild animals live in this forest. 许多野生动物生活在这片森林里。

拓展词汇

wild flowers 野花　wild grass 野草
wild animals 野生动物

will /wɪl/ （情态动词）（过去式 **would** /wʊd/）

1. 将要，会
–What will you do if you get a lot of money? 如果你有很多钱你会做什么？
–I'll travel around the world. 我会周游世界。
2. 愿意
–I'm going shopping. Will you come with me? 我要去购物，你愿意和我一起去吗？
–With pleasure. 非常愿意。

用法小贴士

will 在口语中通常缩略为 'll，否定形式 will not 常缩略为 won't。

win /wɪn/ （动词）（过去式、过去分词 **won** /wʌn/，现在分词 **winning**）赢，获胜

–Who won the game? 谁赢得了比赛？
–It was our school team! 是咱们的校队！

wind /wɪnd/ （名词）风

–There is no wind today. 今天没有风。
–We can't fly kites. 我们放不了风筝了。

拓展词汇

cold wind 冷风　strong wind 大风
north wind 北风　south wind 南风
east wind 东风　west wind 西风

window /'wɪndəu/ （名词）窗户

–Do you mind if I open the window? 我打开窗户你介意吗？
–Not at all. 没关系。

windy /'wɪndi/ （形容词）（比较级 **windier**，最高级 **windiest**）多风的

–What a windy day! 风真大！
–We'd better stay at home. 我们最好呆在家里。

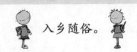
wine /waɪn/ （名词）葡萄酒

–Would you like some wine? 你来点儿葡萄酒吗?

–Yes, a little, please. 好。请来一点点。

拓展词汇

red wine 红葡萄酒　white wine 白葡萄酒　dry red 干红　dry white 干白

百科小贴士

葡萄酒是一种低酒精饮料，法国是葡萄酒的故乡。葡萄酒含有丰富的维生素，特别是维生素 B 和 C，饮用后可以帮助消化。

wing /wɪŋ/ （名词）翅膀

–Why can birds fly? 鸟儿为什么会飞?

–Because they have wings. 因为它们有翅膀。

winter /'wɪntə/ （名词）冬季

–What sports do you do in winter? 冬天你参加什么运动?

–Skiing and skating. 滑雪和溜冰。

wise /waɪz/ （形容词）明智的，聪明的

Early to bed and early to rise makes a man healthy, wealthy, and wise. 早睡早起使人健康、富裕又聪明。

反义词　foolish 愚蠢的

wish¹ /wɪʃ/ （动词）希望

I wish I could fly. 我希望我能飞。

wish² /wɪʃ/ （名词）（复数 **wishes**）愿望

–Make a wish. 许个愿吧。

–I wish I could fly in the sky. 我希望我能在天空飞翔。

witch /wɪtʃ/ （名词）（复数 **witches**）巫婆

–Are there witches in the world? 世界上有巫婆吗?

–I don't think so. 我认为没有。

百科小贴士

巫婆常出现在童话故事里，会魔法，常常骑着扫帚在天空飞行，是邪恶的象征。

with /wɪð/ （介词）同，和

–Where were you over the weekend? 周末你去哪儿了?

–I went to the beach with my parents. 我和父母一起去海边了。

without /wɪ'ðaʊt/ （介词）没有

–I've mailed the letter without a stamp. 我没贴邮票就把信投进邮箱了。

–Oh, no! 哦，真糟糕!

wolf /wʊlf/（名词）（复数 **wolves** /wʊlvz/）狼

–Did you see wolves in the zoo? 你在动物园看到狼了吗?
–Yes, they look like dogs. 看到了, 它们看起来像狗。

拓展词汇

wolf dog 狼狗

百科小贴士

狼主要包括灰狼、赤狼、郊狼、胡狼、红狼及比较接近狐狸的南极狼、南美狼。狼在西欧和北欧的很多国家绝迹了, 仅挪威、瑞典、芬兰、土耳其、希腊、意大利、西班牙和葡萄牙8个国家有狼的分布。在中国, 狼主要分布在东北、西北、内蒙以及西藏等人口密度比较小的地区。

woman /ˈwʊmən/（名词）（复数 **women** /ˈwɪmɪn/）女人

–Do you know that woman? 你认识那个女的吗?
–She's our new neighbor. 她是我们的新邻居。

拓展词汇

Women's Day 妇女节

用法小贴士

woman 与其他词构成复合名词时, 复数形式涉及两个词, 如 women teachers（女教师）、women writers（女作家）。

wonder /ˈwʌndə/（动词）想知道

–I wonder if you can lend me your dictionary. 你可以把字典借给我用一下吗?
–Of course. 当然可以。

用法小贴士

"wonder if..." 表示请求, 是一种很礼貌的用法。

wonderful /ˈwʌndəful/（形容词）精彩的

–How was the performance? 演出好看吗?
–It was wonderful! 太精彩了!

wood /wʊd/（名词）木头

–What's this table made of? 这张桌子是什么做的?
–It's made of wood. 是木头做的。

拓展词汇

woodworm 蛀木虫

word /wɜːd/（名词）

1. 词
–I can type fifty words a minute. 我一分钟能打50个单词。
–That's fast. 那是挺快的。

2. 话
–He went away without a word. 他一句话都没说就走开了。
–Oh, that's not very polite. 哦, 那可不太礼貌。

work[1] /wɜːk/（动词）工作

–You look tired. 你看起来很累。
–I've been working all day. 我工作了一整天。

work² /wɜːk/ （名词）工作

–Have you finished your work? 你做完工作了吗？

–Not yet. Don't wait for me. 还没有，别等我了。

用法小贴士

work和 job都可以指工作，但 work是不可数名词，而 job可数，如 a good job。

worker /'wɜːkə/ （名词）工人

–What does your uncle do? 你叔叔是做什么的？

–He's a worker in a car factory. 他是一家汽车厂的工人。

world /wɜːld/ （名词）世界

There are many countries in the world. 世界上有许多国家。

worm /wɜːm/ （名词）虫，蠕虫

–There's a worm in the cabbage. 卷心菜里有只虫子。

–It's eating the leaves. 它在吃菜叶呢。

拓展词汇

bookworm 书虫

worried /'wʌrid/ （形容词）焦虑的

–The old man looks worried. 那个老人看起来很着急。

–Let's ask if he needs help. 咱们去问问他是否需要帮助。

worry /'wʌri/ （动词）（第三人称单数 **worries**，过去式、过去分词 **worried**，现在分词 **worrying**）担心

–Jane hasn't come home yet. 简还没回家。

–Don't worry. She'll be back soon. 别担心，她很快就回来了。

worth /wɜːθ/ （形容词）值…钱的

–The old house is worth a lot of money. 这座老房子值很多钱。

would /wʊd/ （情态动词）（表示委婉的请求）

–Would you give me a hand? 你能帮我个忙吗？

–Sure. Just tell me what to do. 当然啦，告诉我做什么就是了。

wow /waʊ/ （叹词）哇，嚄

–This is my new car. 这是我的新车。

–Wow! It's really beautiful! 哇，真漂亮！

write /raɪt/ （动词）（过去式 **wrote** /rəʊt/，过去分词 **written** /'rɪtən/）写

–Are you doing your homework? 你在做家庭作业吗？

–No, I'm writing a letter. 不是，我在写一封信。

拓展词汇

writing 写作　　writing desk 书桌
writing paper 写字用纸

writer /ˈraɪtə/ （名词）作家

Lu Xun was a great writer in modern China. 鲁迅是中国现代一位伟大的作家。

wrong /rɒŋ/ （形容词）错误的

–May I speak to Doctor Smith? 可以请史密斯医生接电话吗？

–Sorry, you've dialed the wrong number. 对不起，你拨错号码了。

WTO /ˌdʌbəljuː tiː ˈəʊ/ （名词）世贸组织

China joined the WTO in 2002. 中国在2002年加入了世贸组织。

百科小贴士

世贸组织的全称是the World Trade Organization（世界贸易组织），它是一个国际性贸易组织，总部设在日内瓦。其主要职责是促进和规范各国间的贸易活动。

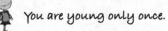

Xmas /'krɪsməs/ （名词）
圣诞节

–Oh, you've received so many Xmas cards! 啊，你收到了这么多圣诞卡！

–Yes, I've also sent out a lot. 是的，我也寄出了很多。

用法小贴士

Xmas 为 Christmas 的缩写。

X-ray /'eksreɪ/ （名词）X 射线

–I fell from the ladder and my leg hurts. 我从梯子上摔了下来，现在腿疼。

–You need to have an X-ray. 你需要做一下 X 光检查。

百科小贴士

1895 年德国物理学家威廉·康拉德·伦琴发明了 X 射线，并因此于 1901 年获得了首届诺贝尔物理学奖。当时 X 射线主要用于骨折的诊断、异物检查等方面。

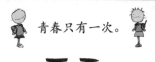

Y

yard /jɑːd/ （名词）院子

–Where's Susan? 苏珊呢？
–She's skipping in the yard. 她在院子里跳绳呢。

拓展词汇

backyard 后院　　front yard 前院

用法小贴士

yard是美国英语，英国英语用 garden。

yeah /jeə/ （副词）（**yes** 的口语形式）是的

–You're from the south, aren't you?你是南方人，对吧？
–Yeah, I'm from Guangdong. 是的，我来自广东。

year /jɪə/ （名词）

1. 年
–How long have you been learning English? 你学英语有多少年了？
–Oh, for more than five years. 哦，有5年多了。

拓展词汇

next year 明年　　the year after next 后年

2. 岁
–How old are you? 你多大了？
–I'm nine years old. 我9岁了。

yellow¹ /ˈjeləʊ/ （形容词）
黄色的

I painted my room yellow. 我把房间刷成了黄色。

拓展词汇

the Yellow River 黄河　　the Yellow Sea 黄海　　yellow card 黄牌

yellow² /ˈjeləʊ/ （名词）黄色

–What color do you like best? 你最喜欢什么颜色？
–Yellow. It's bright and lively. 黄色，它明亮、活泼。

yes /jes/ （副词）是

–Is this your bike? 这是你的自行车吗？
–Yes, it is. 是的。

yesterday¹ /ˈjestədeɪ/ （名词）
昨天

–Yesterday was my birthday. 昨天是我的生日。
–Why didn't you tell me earlier? 你为什么不早点儿告诉我呀？

yesterday² /ˈjestədeɪ/ （副词）
昨天

–Where were you yesterday morning? 昨天上午你在哪里？

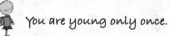

–I went to the zoo. 我去动物园了。

拓展词汇

the day before yesterday 前天

yet /jet/ （副词）还

–Have you written to your aunt?
你给你姨妈写信了吗？
–Not yet. 还没有。

用法小贴士

yet和still都是"还"、"仍然"的意思，但前者用于否定句，后者用于肯定句。例如：I'm still doing my homework.（我还在做家庭作业。）I haven't done my homework yet.（我还没做家庭作业。）

yogurt /ˈjɒɡət/ （名词）酸奶

–Do you want milk or yogurt? 你想要牛奶还是酸奶？
–Some yogurt, please. 请来点儿酸奶。

百科小贴士

酸奶是由优质牛奶经过乳酸菌发酵而成的，保存了鲜奶中所有的营养素，含有丰富的蛋白质、脂肪、矿物质，还可以降低胆固醇。

you /juː/ （代词）你，你们

–Can I sit next to you? 我能坐在你旁边吗？
–Yes, please. 可以，请坐。

用法小贴士

you没有单、复数之分，要根据上下文判断其所代表的是单数还是复数。

young /jʌŋ/ （形容词）年轻的

–Who is the pretty young woman? 那位年轻漂亮的女人是谁呀？
–She's our English teacher! 她是我们的英语老师！

your /jɔː/ （代词）你的，你们的

–Excuse me. Is this your pen? 打扰了，这是你的钢笔吗？
–Oh, yes. Thank you very much! 哦，是的。太感谢啦！

yourself /jɔːˈself/ （代词）（复数 yourselves /jɔːˈselvz/）你自己

–Can you help me do this math problem? 你能帮我做这道数学题吗？
–Try to do it yourself first. 你先试着自己做吧。

青春只有一次。

Z

zebra /'zebrə/ （名词）斑马
–Where do zebras live? 斑马生活在哪里?
–The south of Africa. 在非洲南部。

拓展词汇
zebra crossing 斑马线

百科小贴士
斑马身上的条纹是一种隐蔽色，可用来保护自己。而且，各种群之间的斑纹类形不同，根据斑纹可以识别它们所属的种群。

zero /'zɪərəʊ/ （数词）（复数 zero 或 zeros）零
–What's the score? 比分是多少?
–Three to zero. 3比0。

用法小贴士
0在号码中常读作字母 o /əʊ/。

zoo /zuː/ （名词）（复数 zoos）动物园
–My mom took me to the zoo yesterday. 我妈妈昨天带我去动物园了。
–Really? I went to the zoo, too. 真的吗? 我昨天也去动物园了。

汉英词典

CHINESE-ENGLISH

DICTIONARY

A

阿拉伯 ālābó （名词）Arab

阿司匹林 āsīpǐlín （名词）aspirin
百科小贴士
阿司匹林是英语aspirin的音译词。

阿姨 āyí （名词）aunt: 李阿姨
Aunt Li
用法小贴士
auntie是aunt的昵称。

啊 á （叹词）what: 啊，你说什
么？ What? I beg your pardon?

啊 à （叹词）ah; oh: 啊，现在我
明白了。 Ah, now I see.

哎呀 āiyā （叹词）oh no: 哎呀，
我又要迟到了！ Oh no! I'll be late
again!

埃及 āijí （名词）Egypt: 埃及人
Egyptian

挨个儿 āigèr （副词）one after
another; one by one: 挨个儿提问
学生 question the students one
after another

癌症 áizhèng （名词）cancer

矮 ǎi （形容词）short: 他又矮又
瘦。 He's short and thin.

矮个子 ǎigèzi （名词）short
person

矮小 ǎixiǎo （形容词）short and
small

艾滋病 àizībìng （名词）AIDS
百科小贴士
艾滋病的全称是获得性免疫缺陷综合征。
12月1日是世界艾滋病日。

爱 ài
1. （动词）love: 爱和平 love peace
∥爱祖国 love one's country
2. （名词）love: 孩子需要父母的
爱。 Children need their parents'
love.

爱国 àiguó （动词） love one's
country

爱好 àihào （名词）hobby: 你有
什么爱好？ What's your hobby?

爱护 àihù （动词）care for; take
good care of: 爱护视力 take
good care of one's eyesight

爱情 àiqíng （名词）love

爱人 àiren （名词）husband (or
wife)

爱屋及乌 àiwū-jíwū Love me, love my dog.

爱惜 àixī （动词）value: 爱惜生命 value one's life ∥ 爱惜时间 value one's time

安静 ānjìng （形容词）quiet: 保持安静 keep quiet

安琪儿 ānqí'ér （名词） angel

百科小贴士
安琪儿是英语angel的音译词。

安全 ānquán
1. （形容词）safe: 这里挺安全。 It's quite safe here.
2. （名词）safety: 交通安全 traffic safety

按时 ànshí （副词）on time: 按时完成作业 finish one's home-work on time ∥ 按时到达 arrive on time

岸 àn （名词）bank: 河岸 river bank

暗 àn （形容词）dark: 天色暗了。 It's getting dark.

肮脏 āngzāng （形容词）dirty: 肮脏的街道 dirty street

奥林匹克运动会 àolínpǐkè yùndòng-huì （名词）the Olympic Games

奥秘 àomì （名词）secret: 成功的奥秘 the secret of success ∥ 大自然的奥秘 the secret of nature

奥运村 àoyùncūn （名词）the Olympic Village

奥运会 àoyùnhuì （名词）the Olympic Games

澳大利亚 àodàlìyà （名词） Australia

澳门 àomén （名词）Macao

B

八 bā （数词）eight: 八八六十四。Eight times eight makes sixty-four.

八月 bāyuè （名词）August

巴黎 bālí （名词）Paris

巴士 bāshì （名词）bus: 乘巴士 take a bus

百科小贴士
巴士是英语bus的音译词.

芭蕾 bālěi （名词）ballet: 跳芭蕾 do ballet dancing

百科小贴士
芭蕾是法语ballet的音译词，为欧洲古典舞剧，以舞蹈为主要表现手段，演员舞蹈时常用脚尖着地。

拔尖儿 bájiānr （形容词）top: 他在我们班是拔尖儿的学生。He is a top student in our class.

爸爸 bàba （名词）dad; father

白 bái （形容词）white: 白衬衫 white shirt ∥ 白兔 white rabbit

白菜 báicài （名词）Chinese cabbage

白宫 báigōng （名词）the White House

百科小贴士
美国总统的官邸，在华盛顿，是一座白色建筑物，常用作美国政府的代称。

白兰地 báilándì （名词）brandy
百科小贴士
白兰地是英语brandy的音译词.

白米饭 báimǐfàn （名词）cooked rice

白日梦 báirìmèng （名词）daydream

白色 báisè
1.（形容词）white: 白色网球鞋 white tennis shoes
2.（名词）white

白薯 báishǔ（名词）sweet potato

白糖 báitáng （名词）white sugar

白天 báitiān （名词）day; daytime: 在白天 in the daytime

白蚁 báiyǐ （名词）white ant

百 bǎi （名词）hundred: 一百 one hundred ∥ 两百 two hundred

物以类聚，人以群分。

百里挑一 bǎilǐ-tiāoyī one in a hundred; one in a million

百万 bǎiwàn （数词）million: 三百万 three million

百闻不如一见 bǎi wén bùrú yī jiàn Seeing is believing.

百姓 bǎixìng （名词）ordinary people

拜拜 bàibai （动词）say goodbye; bye-bye

拜访 bàifǎng （动词）call on: 拜访老师 call on one's teacher

拜年 bàinián （动词）make a New Year visit; pay a New Year call

班 bān （名词）class: 3个班 three classes ∥ 我在三年级一班。I'm in Class One, Grade Three.

班会 bānhuì （名词）class meeting

班级 bānjí （名词）class and grade: 每个年级有4个班。Each grade has four classes.

班长 bānzhǎng （名词）class monitor

斑马 bānmǎ （名词）zebra

搬 bān （动词）move: 把桌子搬出去 move the table out

搬家 bānjiā （动词）move house: 我们下周要搬家到上海去了。We're moving to Shanghai next week.

搬运 bānyùn （动词）carry: 搬运一袋大米 carry a bag of rice

板报 bǎnbào （名词）blackboard newspaper

办法 bànfǎ （名词）way: 想出办法 find out a way

办公室 bàngōngshì （名词）office

半 bàn （数词）half: 半年 half a year ∥ 一个半月 one and a half months

半天 bàntiān （数量词）
1. half a day: 我半天就完成了全天的工作。I finished a full day's work in half a day.
2. quite a long time: 我来这儿半天了。I've been here for quite a long time.

半夜 bànyè （名词）midnight: 半夜醒来 wake up at midnight

扮演 bànyǎn （动词）play; act as: 他曾在学校演出时扮演过小丑。He once played a clown in a school play.

236

Birds of a feather flock together.

帮 bāng （动词）help: 你能帮个忙吗？Can you help me?

帮忙 bāngmáng（动词）help: 我的朋友都来帮忙了。All my friends have come to help.

帮助 bāngzhù （动词）help: 他喜欢帮助别人。He likes to help others.

绑 bǎng （动词）tie: 绑鞋带 tie one's shoelaces

棒 bàng
1.（名词）stick: 大棒 big stick
2.（形容词）wonderful; great: 太棒啦！Great! ∥ 他英语说得很棒。He speaks English very well.

棒棒糖 bàngbàngtáng （名词）lollipop

棒球 bàngqiú （名词）baseball: 打棒球 play baseball

傍晚 bàngwǎn （名词）dusk: 傍晚时分 at dusk

磅 bàng （量词）pound: 鸡蛋4美元1磅。The eggs cost four dollars a pound.

镑 bàng （名词）pound: 5镑 five pounds

包 bāo （名词）bag: 书包 schoolbag ∥ 手提包 handbag

包裹 bāoguǒ （名词）parcel

包心菜 bāoxīncài （名词）cabbage

包子 bāozi （名词）steamed stuffed bun

薄 báo （形容词）thin: 薄冰 thin ice ∥ 像纸一样薄 as thin as paper

饱 bǎo （形容词）full: 我吃饱了。I'm full.

宝宝 bǎobǎo （名词）baby

宝贝 bǎobèi （名词）darling

保持 bǎochí （动词）keep: 请保持安静！Please keep quiet! ∥ 保持健康 keep fit ∥ 保持记录 keep the record

保护 bǎohù （动词）protect: 保护视力 protect one's eyesight ∥ 保护野生动物 protect wild animals

保健 bǎojiàn （动词）keep fit: 保健饮料 health drinks ∥ 保健食品 health food

保龄球 bǎolíngqiú （名词）bowling: 去打保龄球 go bowling

保密 bǎomì （动词）keep secret: 我会保密的。I can keep it a secret.

B

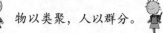

保姆 bǎomǔ （名词）nanny

保佑 bǎoyòu （动词）bless

报 bào （名词）newspaper: 晨报 morning newspaper // 晚报 evening newspaper

报道 bàodào
1. （动词）report: 报道新闻 report the news
2. （名词）report: 一篇关于奥运会的报道 a report about the Olympic Games

报告 bàogào
1. （动词）report: 向老师报告 report to the teacher
2. （名词）report; speech: 写报告 write a report // 作报告 make a speech // 成绩报告单 school report

报警 bàojǐng （动词）call the police

报纸 bàozhǐ （名词）newspaper

抱 bào （动词）hold/carry in the arms: 抱着孩子 hold a baby in one's arms

抱歉 bàoqiàn （动词）be sorry: 叫你久等了，很抱歉。 I'm very sorry to have kept you waiting.

暴风雪 bàofēngxuě （名词）snow storm

暴风雨 bàofēngyǔ （名词）rainstorm; storm

爆米花 bàomǐhuā（名词）popcorn

爆炸 bàozhà （动词）explode: 炸弹爆炸了。The bomb exploded.

杯 bēi （名词）cup; glass: 咖啡杯 coffee cup // 酒杯 wine glass // 一杯茶 a cup of tea

杯子 bēizi （名词）cup; glass

背 bēi （动词）carry on the back: 背着孩子 carry a child on one's back

悲伤 bēishāng （形容词）sad

北 běi （名词）north: 城北 north of the city // 朝北走 go north // 华北 North China

北方 běifāng （名词）north; the north: 去北方 go to the north

北美洲 běiměizhōu （名词）North America

贝壳 bèiké （名词）shell: 捡贝壳 collect shells

背 bèi （名词）back: 背疼 backache // 椅背 chair back

背包 bèibāo （名词）backpack

背后 bèihòu （名词）behind; back: 在门背后 behind the door ∥ 在山背后 at the back of the mountain ∥ 她藏在妈妈背后。 She was hiding behind her mother.

本 běn （名词）book; notebook: 练习本 exercise book

本事 běnshi （名词）ability; skill: 学点本事 learn some skills

笨 bèn （形容词）
1. stupid; foolish: 笨人 stupid person
2. slow; clumsy: 笨拙的动作 clumsy movement

笨蛋 bèndàn （名词）fool

蹦 bèng （动词）jump: 蹦下床 jump out of bed ∥ 高兴地蹦起来 jump for joy

蹦蹦跳跳 bèngbèng-tiàotiào （动词）jump up and down

蹦极 bèngjí （名词）bungee jumping
百科小贴士
蹦极是英语bungee的音译词。蹦极起源于新西兰。

鼻子 bízi （名词）nose: 高鼻子 high-bridged nose ∥ 塌鼻子 flat nose

比 bǐ （介词）
1. than: 我比弟弟高。 I am taller than my younger brother.
2. to: 我们以2比1获胜。 We won the match 2 to 1.

比分 bǐfēn （名词）score: 比分是2比1。 The score is 2 to 1.

比萨饼 bǐsàbǐng （名词）pizza
百科小贴士
比萨是英语pizza的音译词。比萨饼是意大利的特色食品。

比赛 bǐsài
1. （动词）have a match: 比赛乒乓球 have a table tennis match
2. （名词）match: 观看比赛 watch a match ∥ 举行比赛 have a match ∥ 参加比赛 take part in a match

笔 bǐ （名词）pen; pencil; brush
用法小贴士
pen指钢笔，也可指其他用墨水的笔，pencil指铅笔，brush指毛笔。

笔记 bǐjì （名词）notes:课堂笔记 classroom notes ∥ 读书笔记 reading notes

笔记本 bǐjìběn （名词）notebook

笔记本电脑 bǐjìběn diànnǎo （名词）laptop; laptop computer

笔友 bǐyǒu （名词）pen pal

B

笔直 bǐzhí （形容词）straight: 坐得笔直 sit up straight // 笔直的道路 straight road

必须 bìxū （副词）must; have to: 你明天必须来。You must come tomorrow.

毕业 bìyè （动词）graduate; finish school:小学毕业 graduate from primary school

碧绿 bìlǜ （形容词）dark green: 碧绿的田野 green fields

壁灯 bìdēng （名词）wall light

壁纸 bìzhǐ （名词）wallpaper

臂 bì （名词）arm: 挥动双臂 wave one's arms

边 biān （名词）side: 街道两边 both sides of the street // 海边 seaside // 河边 riverside

蝙蝠 biānfú （名词）bat

扁 biǎn （形容词）flat: 扁鼻子 flat nose

变 biàn （动词）change: 时代变了。Times have changed.

变成 biànchéng （动词）turn into; become: 魔术师把手帕变成了一只鸽子。The magician turned the handkerchief into a dove.

变化 biànhuà
1.（动词）change: 情况变化了。The situation has changed.
2.（名词）change: 气温变化 a change in temperature

便利店 biànlìdiàn （名词）convenience store

便士 biànshì （名词）penny: 10便士 ten pence // 他的口袋里有几个便士。There're a few pennies in his pockets.

百科小贴士
便士是英国的货币单位，100便士等于1英镑。

遍 biàn
1.（形容词）all over: 我们的朋友遍天下。We have friends all over the world.
2.（量词）time: 一遍 once // 两遍 twice // 几遍 several times

遍地 biàndì （副词）all around; everywhere: 这种花遍地都是。These flowers are everywhere.

表 biǎo （名词）watch:戴表 wear a watch // 我的表慢了两分钟。My watch is two minutes slow.

表达 biǎodá （动词）express: 表达感情 express one's feelings // 表达思想 express one's ideas

表亲 biǎoqīn （名词）cousin

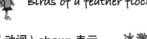

表示 biǎoshì （动词）show: 表示惊讶 show surprise // 表示愤怒 show one's anger

表演 biǎoyǎn
1. （动词）perform; play: 表演短剧 perform a short play
2. （名词）performance: 观看表演 watch a performance // 精彩的表演 wonderful performance

表扬 biǎoyáng （动词）praise: 老师表扬了大家。The teacher praised everyone.

别 bié （副词）had better not: 你最好别再那么做。You'd better not do that again.

别人 biérén （代词）someone else; other people: 你还是问别人吧。You'd better ask someone else. // 关心别人 care about other people

宾馆 bīnguǎn （名词）hotel: 五星级宾馆 five-star hotel // 住宾馆 stay in a hotel

宾客 bīnkè （名词）guest; visitor

冰 bīng （名词）ice: 冰块 ice cube // 结冰 freeze

冰棍儿 bīnggùnr （名词）ice pop; Popsicle

用法小贴士
ice pop 是英国英语，Popsicle 是美国英语。

冰激凌 bīngjīlíng （名词）ice cream

冰凉 bīngliáng （形容词）ice-cold: 她的手冰凉。Her hands were ice-cold.

冰山 bīngshān （名词）iceberg: 冰山一角 the tip of the iceberg

冰箱 bīngxiāng （名词）refrigerator; fridge

兵 bīng （名词）soldier: 当兵 join the army

饼 bǐng （名词）pancake: 玉米饼 corn flour pancakes

饼干 bǐnggān （名词）cookie; cracker: 咸饼干 salty crackers

并且 bìngqiě （连词）and; also: 他参加了会，并且讲了话。He attended the meeting and made a speech.

病 bìng （名词）disease; illness: 生病 fall ill // 她的病好了。She has recovered from her illness.

病床 bìngchuáng （名词）hospital bed

病毒 bìngdú （名词）virus: 计算机病毒 computer virus

物以类聚，人以群分。

病房 bìngfáng （名词）hospital ward

病人 bìngrén （名词）patient: 探视病人 visit a patient

波浪 bōlàng （名词）wave

玻璃 bōli （名词）glass: 一块玻璃 a sheet of glass; a piece of glass

用法小贴士
a sheet of glass指一整块大玻璃，a piece of glass 一般指摔碎的小块玻璃。

玻璃杯 bōlibēi （名词）glass

菠菜 bōcài （名词）spinach

菠萝 bōluó （名词）pineapple

播种 bōzhǒng （动词）sow seeds: 在田里播种 sow the seeds in the field

伯伯 bóbo （名词）uncle: 王伯伯 Uncle Wang

伯父 bófù （名词）uncle

伯母 bómǔ （名词）aunt

脖子 bózi （名词）neck: 长脖子 long neck

博览会 bólǎnhuì （名词）fair: 世界博览会 world's fair ∥举办博览会 hold a fair

博士 bóshì （名词）doctor: 文学博士 doctor of literature

博物馆 bówùguǎn （名词）museum: 科学博物馆 science museum ∥参观博物馆 visit a museum

捕 bǔ （动词）catch: 以捕鱼为生 fish for a living

不 bù （副词）no; not: 我不想去。 I don't want to go.

不但 bùdàn （连词）not only... （but also...）: 他不但会讲英语，还会讲法语。He can speak not only English but also French.

不对 bùduì （形容词）wrong: 这样做不对。It's wrong to do so.

不敢 bùgǎn （动词）not dare to: 不敢说实话 do not dare to tell the truth

不会 bùhuì （动词）be unable to: 我不会游泳。I can't swim.

不久 bùjiǔ （形容词）soon; before long

不客气 bùkèqi （动词）you're welcome; not at all; it's my pleasure

不明飞行物 bùmíng fēixíngwù （名词）UFO (Unidentified Flying Object)

不同 bùtóng （形容词）different: 不同种类 different kind

不许 bùxǔ （动词）not allow; must not: 这里不许抽烟。No smoking here.

布 bù （名词）cloth: 一块布 a piece of cloth ∥ 桌布 tablecloth

布丁 bùdīng （名词）pudding

布告 bùgào （名词）notice: 张贴布告 put up a notice

布娃娃 bùwáwa （名词）cloth doll

步行 bùxíng （动词）walk; go on foot: 步行上学 go to school on foot; walk to school

部队 bùduì （名词）army

部分 bùfen （名词）part: 第一部分 the first part; part one

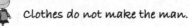

C

擦 cā （动词）wipe; clean: 擦黑板 clean the blackboard ∥ 擦眼泪 wipe the tears away

猜 cāi （动词）guess: 猜一猜 take a guess ∥ 你猜对了！You got it right!

猜测 cāicè （动词）guess

猜谜语 cāimíyǔ （动词）guess a riddle

才 cái （副词）
1. just: 电影才开始。The film has just started.
2. only: 我开始踢球的时候才5岁。I started playing football when I was only five.
3. not until: 我到11点才睡觉。I didn't go to bed until eleven.

才能 cáinéng （名词）ability; talent

财宝 cáibǎo （名词）treasure: 金银财宝 treasures

财富 cáifù （名词）wealth: 自然财富 natural wealth

财主 cáizhǔ （名词）rich man

采 cǎi （动词）pick; gather: 采花 pick flowers ∥ 采蘑菇 pick mushrooms

采摘 cǎizhāi （名词）pick: 采摘苹果 pick apples

彩笔 cǎibǐ （名词）color pencil

彩电 cǎidiàn （名词）color TV

彩虹 cǎihóng （名词）rainbow

彩色 cǎisè （名词）color: 彩色照片 color photo

菜 cài （名词）
1. vegetable: 种菜 grow vegetables
2. dish: 做几个菜 cook several dishes ∥ 川菜 Sichuan dishes

菜单 càidān （名词）menu: 看菜单 read the menu ∥ 菜单窗口 menu window

菜刀 càidāo （名词）kitchen knife

菜花 càihuā （名词）cauliflower

菜谱 càipǔ （名词）menu

人不在衣装。

菜市场 càishìchǎng （名词）vegetable market

参观 cānguān （动词）visit; look around; see: 参观博物馆 visit a museum

参加 cānjiā （动词）join; take part in; attend: 参加会议 attend a meeting ∥参加考试 go in for an exam ∥参加体育活动 take part in sports

参军 cānjūn （动词）go into/join/enter the army

餐 cān （名词）meal: 用餐 have a meal

餐馆 cānguǎn （名词）restaurant: 中餐馆 Chinese restaurant

餐巾 cānjīn （名词）cloth napkin

餐巾纸 cānjīnzhǐ （名词）paper napkin

餐厅 cāntīng （名词）dining room/hall

餐桌 cānzhuō （名词）dining/dinner table

蚕 cán （名词）silkworm: 养蚕 keep silkworms

蚕丝 cánsī （名词）silk

灿烂 cànlàn （形容词）bright: 阳光灿烂。The sun is shining brightly.

苍白 cāngbái （形容词）pale: 他脸色苍白。He looks pale.

苍老 cānglǎo （形容词）old

苍蝇 cāngying （名词）fly: 一群苍蝇 a cloud of flies

藏 cáng （动词）hide: 藏在门后 hide behind the door

操场 cāochǎng （名词）playground: 在操场上 on the playground

草 cǎo （名词）grass

草地 cǎodì （名词）lawn: 请勿践踏草地。Please keep off the grass.

草莓 cǎoméi （名词）strawberry: 摘草莓 pick strawberries

草原 cǎoyuán （名词）grassland

厕所 cèsuǒ （名词）toilet; washroom; WC

用法小贴士
WC是water closet的首字母，WC指公共场所厕所。

测验 cèyàn （动词）test: 测验英语 give a test in English

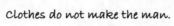
层 céng （名词）
1. layer: 这个蛋糕有3层。The cake has three layers.
2. floor: 我住顶层。I live on the top floor.

曾经 céngjīng （副词）once; at one time: 我曾经见过他。I have seen him before.

叉子 chāzi （名词）fork

差别 chābié （名词）difference: 年龄差别 difference in age

差错 chācuò （名词）mistake; error: 出差错 make a mistake ∥ 改正差错 correct a mistake

茶 chá （名词）tea: 泡茶 make tea ∥ 一杯茶 a cup of tea ∥ 浓/淡茶 strong/weak tea

茶杯 chábēi （名词）teacup

茶馆 cháguǎn （名词）teahouse

茶话会 cháhuàhuì （名词）tea party: 开茶话会 have a tea party

茶几 chájī （名词）tea table; coffee table

茶鸡蛋 chájīdàn （名词）egg boiled in tea water

茶叶 cháyè （名词）tea leaves; tea

差 chà （形容词）poor; bad: 他身体很差。He is in poor health.

蟾蜍 chánchú （名词）toad

产品 chǎnpǐn （名词）product

长 cháng （形容词）long: 长发 long hair ∥ 这条隧道有多长？How long is this tunnel? ∥ 桌子有七尺长。The table is seven feet long.

长城 chángchéng （名词）the Great Wall

百科小贴士
长城是中国古代的伟大建筑。秦统一六国后，秦始皇把各国长城连起来，西起临洮，东至辽东，绵延万余里，这就是"万里长城"名字的由来。长城于1978年被联合国教科文组织世界遗产委员会批准列入世界遗产名录。

长处 chángchù （名词）strong point: 学习别人的长处 learn from other people's strong points

长度 chángdù （名词）length

长方形 chángfāngxíng （名词）rectangle

长话短说 chánghuà-duǎnshuō make/ cut a long story short

长江 chángjiāng （名词）the Changjiang /Yangtze River

百科小贴士
长江和黄河一样，是中华民族的摇篮和文化发祥地。长江发源于青藏高原，干流总长度六千多千米，为中国第一大河，世界第三大河，仅次于非洲的尼罗河和南美洲的亚马孙河。

人不在衣装。

长久 chángjiǔ （形容词）for a long time

长裤 chángkù （名词）trousers; pants:一条长裤 a pair of trousers

长寿 chángshòu （形容词）long-lived: 这里的人大多长寿。Most of the people here can live to a very old age.

尝 cháng （动词）taste: 尝点蛋糕 try some cake; have a taste of the cake

尝试 chángshì （动词）try: 尝试各种方法 try every method // 进行尝试 have a try

常常 chángcháng （副词）often: 他上学常常迟到。He is often late for school.

厂 chǎng （名词）factory: 鞋厂 shoe factory

厂长 chǎngzhǎng （名词）factory manager

场所 chǎngsuǒ （名词）place: 公共场所 public place

唱 chàng （动词）sing

唱歌 chànggē （动词）sing (a song)

抄写 chāoxiě （动词）copy: 抄写笔记 copy notes

超级 chāojí （形容词）super: 超级大国 superpower// 超级明星 superstar

超人 chāorén （名词）superman

超市 chāoshì （名词）supermarket

巢 cháo （名词）nest: 筑巢 build a nest // 鸟巢 bird's nest

朝 cháo （动词）face: 朝北/东/南/西 face north/east/south/west // 这扇窗朝着大海。The window faces the sea.

嘲笑 cháoxiào （动词）laugh at: 嘲笑别人是不礼貌的。It's not polite to laugh at others.

潮湿 cháoshī （形容词）wet: 潮湿的天气 wet weather

吵 chǎo
1.（形容词）noisy: 这儿太吵了。It's very noisy here.
2.（动词）make a noise: 别吵了！Don't make so much noise!

吵架 chǎojià （动词）quarrel: 我跟他吵架了。I quarreled with him.

吵闹 chǎonào
1.（动词）quarrel
2.（形容词）very noisy: 吵闹的孩子们 noisy children

247

Clothes do not make the man.

吵嘴 chǎozuǐ （动词）quarrel

车 chē （名词）car: 开车 drive a car ∥ 上车 get in a car ∥ 下车 get out of a car

车祸 chēhuò （名词）traffic accident; car accident

车轮 chēlún （名词）wheel

车票 chēpiào （名词）ticket

车胎 chētāi （名词）tire: 车胎瘪了 have a flat tire

车站 chēzhàn （名词）station; stop

沉 chén
1.（形容词）heavy: 这桌子真沉。 The table is heavy.
2.（动词）sink: 沉入水中 sink under water

沉甸甸 chéndiàndiàn （形容词）heavy

沉重 chénzhòng （形容词）heavy

晨练 chénliàn （名词）morning exercise/practice

衬衫 chènshān （名词）shirt: 穿上衬衫 put on a shirt

趁热打铁 chènrè-dǎtiě strike while the iron is hot; make hay while the sun shines

称呼 chēnghu （动词）call: 用姓称呼某人 call somebody by his/her last name

称赞 chēngzàn （动词）praise

成功 chénggōng （动词）succeed; be a success: 成功之路 way to success ∥ 会议开得很成功。 The meeting was a great success.

成绩 chéngjì （名词）result: 取得好成绩 get a good result ∥ 考试成绩 exam results

成人 chéngrén （名词）adult

成为 chéngwéi （动词）become; turn into: 成为歌唱家/作家 grow into a singer/writer

成员 chéngyuán （名词）member: 家庭成员 family member

诚实 chéngshí （形容词）honest

城堡 chéngbǎo （名词）castle

城墙 chéngqiáng （名词）city wall

城市 chéngshì （名词）city; town: 建设城市 build a city ∥ 城市生活 city life ∥ 旅游城市 tourist city

乘 chéng （动词）take: 乘出租车 take a taxi ∥ 乘船 take a boat ∥ 乘电梯 take an elevator ∥ 乘飞机 take a plane; travel by air; fly ∥ 乘公交车 take a bus ∥ 乘火车 take a train

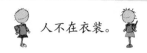

人不在衣装。

乘客 chéngkè （名词）passenger: 火车乘客 train passengers

乘凉 chéngliáng （动词）enjoy the cool: 在树荫下乘凉吧。Enjoy the shade under the tree.

惩罚 chéngfá （动词）punish: 小偷受到了惩罚。The thieves were punished.

橙色 chéngsè
1.（形容词）orange
2.（名词）orange

橙汁 chéngzhī （名词）orange juice: 一杯橙汁 a glass of orange juice

橙子 chéngzi （名词）orange

吃 chī （动词）eat: 吃饭 have a meal ∥ 吃药 take medicine ∥ 在家吃 eat in ∥ 在外面吃 eat out

吃惊 chījīng （动词）be surprised: 听到这消息我很吃惊。I am surprised at the news. ∥ 他吃惊地看着我。He looked at me in surprise.

池塘 chítáng （名词）pond; pool

迟到 chídào （动词）be/come/arrive late: 上学迟到 be late for school ∥ 校车迟到了10分钟。The school bus arrived ten minutes late.

迟钝 chídùn （形容词）slow: 思维迟钝 be slow in thinking

迟早 chízǎo （副词）sooner or later: 他迟早会明白的。He'll understand sooner or later.

尺寸 chǐcùn （名词）size: 量尺寸 take the measurements

尺子 chǐzi （名词）ruler: 用尺子量 measure with a ruler

耻辱 chǐrǔ （名词）shame

翅膀 chìbǎng （名词）wing: 鸟靠翅膀飞行。Birds fly with their wings.

虫子 chóngzi （名词）insect; worm

重复 chóngfù （动词）do again; repeat

重新 chóngxīn （副词）again: 重新考虑 think twice ∥ 重新开始工作 go back to work

宠物 chǒngwù （名词）pet: 宠物猫 pet cat ∥ 宠物店 pet shop ∥ 宠物食品 pet food ∥ 宠物医院 pet hospital

仇人 chóurén （名词）enemy

绸子 chóuzi （名词）silk

Clothes do not make the man.

丑八怪 chǒubāguài （名词）very ugly person: 他真是个丑八怪。 He's really ugly.

丑陋 chǒulòu （形容词）ugly: 丑陋的面孔 ugly face

出丑 chūchǒu （动词）make a fool of oneself

出发 chūfā （动词）set off: 出发去旅行 set off on a journey

出国 chūguó （动词）go abroad

出名 chūmíng
1. （动词）become famous: 她出名很早。 She became famous early.
2. （形容词）famous: 这个演员很出名。The actor is very famous.

出去 chūqù （动词）go out: 出去散步 go out for a walk.

出生 chūshēng （动词）be born: 你什么时候出生的？ When were you born?

出售 chūshòu （动词）sell: 出售各种商品 sell all kinds of goods

出席 chūxí （动词）attend: 出席会议 attend a meeting

出洋相 chūyángxiàng （动词）make a fool of oneself: 当众出洋相 make a fool of oneself in public

出院 chūyuàn （动词）leave the hospital

出租车 chūzūchē （名词）taxi: 坐出租车 take a taxi

初 chū
1. （形容词）early: 初春 early spring // 初冬 early winter
2. （名词）beginning: 这个月初 the beginning of this month

初学者 chūxuézhě （名词）beginner

初中 chūzhōng （名词）middle school: 初中生 middle student

除夕 chúxī （名词）New Year's Eve: 除夕守岁 stay up all night on New Year's Eve to see in the New Year

厨房 chúfáng （名词）kitchen

厨师 chúshī （名词）cook

橱窗 chúchuāng （名词）store window

橱柜 chúguì （名词）cabinet

处理 chǔlǐ （动词）handle: 处理日常工作 handle day-to-day work

触角 chùjiǎo （名词）feeler: 蜗牛长着两只触角。A snail has two feelers.

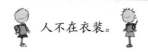
触摸 chùmō （动词）touch: 轻轻触摸 touch gently

穿 chuān （动词）
1. put on; wear: 穿衣服 put on one's clothes ∥我应该穿什么去参加派对？ What should I wear to the party?
2. cross: 穿过马路 cross the street

穿越 chuānyuè （动词）cross: 穿越边境 cross the border ∥穿越时空 travel across the space

传真 chuánzhēn （名词）fax: 发传真 send a fax

船 chuán （名词）boat; ship: 帆船 sailing boat ∥渔船 fishing boat

窗 chuāng （名词）window: 擦窗 clean a window ∥售票窗 ticket window

窗户 chuānghu （名词）window

窗帘 chuānglián （名词）curtain

床 chuáng （名词）bed: 铺床 make the bed ∥单人床 single bed ∥上床睡觉 go to bed

床单 chuángdān （名词）bed sheet: 换床单 change the bed sheets

床头灯 chuángtóudēng （名词）bedside lamp

床头柜 chuángtóuguì （名词）night table

创造 chuàngzào （动词）create: 创造美好生活 create a better life

吹 chuī （动词）blow: 吹泡泡 blow bubbles ∥吹泡泡糖 blow bubble gum ∥吹气球 blow up a balloon

吹牛 chuīniú （动词）talk big; talk tall

锤子 chuízi （名词）hammer

春风 chūnfēng （名词）spring breeze

春节 chūnjié （名词）Spring Festival; Chinese New Year: 过春节 celebrate the Spring Festival

春雷 chūnléi （名词）spring thunder

春天 chūntiān （名词）spring: 春天到了。Spring is here.

春雨 chūnyǔ（名词） spring rain

词 cí （名词）word: 新词 new words

Clothes do not make the man.

词典 cídiǎn （名词）dictionary: 查词典 look up in a dictionary // 英汉词典 English-Chinese dictionary

瓷器 cíqì （名词）china: 一件瓷器 a piece of china

磁带 cídài （名词）tape: 听磁带 listen to a tape // 放磁带 play a tape

磁盘 cípán （名词）disk: 软磁盘 floppy disk

匆忙 cōngmáng （形容词）in a hurry: 匆忙回答 reply in a hurry

葱 cōng （名词）spring onion

聪明 cōngming （形容词）bright; clever; smart

从 cóng （介词）from: 从东到西 from east to west // 从北京出发 start off from Beijing

从来 cónglái （副词）always, at all times: 他从来如此。He's always like this. // 我从来没见过他。I've never seen him before.

用法小贴士

"从来"用于否定句时，英语要用表示否定的副词，如第2个例句中的"never"。

从前 cóngqián （名词）the past: 在从前 in the past

粗心 cūxīn （形容词）careless: 粗心的孩子 a careless child

村民 cūnmín （名词）villager; village people

村庄 cūnzhuāng （名词）village

存钱 cúnqián （动词）save money

存钱罐 cúnqiánguàn （名词）money box; piggy bank

错 cuò （形容词）wrong: 对不起，我错了。 I'm sorry I was wrong.

错误 cuòwù
1.（名词）mistake: 发现错误 find a mistake
2.（形容词） wrong: 错误答案 wrong answer

D

答应 dāying （动词）
1. answer; reply: 问你呢，怎么不答应？I was asking you a question. Why didn't you answer?
2. promise: 她答应来。She promised she would come.

答案 dá'àn （名词）answer; key: 问题的答案 the answer/key to a question

答卷 dájuàn
1. （名词） answer sheet
2. （动词） answer exam questions

打 dǎ （动词）
1. beat; knock: 打人 hit somebody ∥ 你打你弟弟是不对的。It's wrong for you to beat your little brother.
2. play: 打扑克 play cards ∥ 打排球 play volleyball
3. open: 打开盒子 open a box

打的 dǎdī （动词）take a taxi

打电话 dǎdiànhuà （动词）call: 到了请给我打电话。Please call me when you arrive.

打赌 dǎdǔ （动词）bet: 你敢打赌吗？Do you dare to bet?

打架 dǎjià （动词）fight: 小猫和小狗在打架。The kitten is fighting with the dog.

打开 dǎkāi （动词）open: 打开窗户 open the window ∥ 打开心扉 open one's heart

打猎 dǎliè （动词）go hunting

打扫 dǎsǎo （动词）clean; sweep: 打扫房间 clean the room

打算 dǎsuàn
1. （动词）plan: 你今天晚上打算做什么？What are you planning to do tonight?
2. （名词）plan: 你假期有什么打算？What's your plan for the vacation?

打仗 dǎzhàng （动词）fight a battle: 打败仗 lose a battle ∥ 打胜仗 win a battle

打招呼 dǎzhāohu （动词）greet; say hello to: 她笑着跟我打了个招呼。She greeted me with a smile.

大 dà （形容词）
1. big; large: 这件衬衫我穿太大了。This shirt is too big for me.

2. old: 你多大了? How old are you?

大地 dàdì （名词）earth: 大地母亲 Mother Earth

大家 dàjiā （代词）all of us; everybody: 大家都很开心。All of us are happy.

大街 dàjiē （名词）main street; avenue

大量 dàliàng （形容词）many; much: 大量事实 many facts ∥大量工作 much work

大陆 dàlù （名词）mainland: 中国大陆 the mainland of China

大米 dàmǐ （名词）rice

大人 dàren （名词）adult

大声 dàshēng （名词）loud voice: 大声呼救 cry out for help ∥他冲我大声叫嚷。He shouted at me.

大腕 dàwàn （名词）big shot

大小 dàxiǎo （名词）size: 它们大小一样。They're the same size.

大学 dàxué （名词）university: 大学老师 university teacher ∥大学生 university student

逮 dǎi （动词）catch: 逮小偷 catch a thief ∥逮老鼠 catch mice

大夫 dàifu （名词）doctor

代词 dàicí （名词）pronoun

带 dài （动词）take; bring: 带伞 take an umbrella ∥可以带朋友一起来吗? Can I bring a friend with me?

带领 dàilǐng （动词）lead: 他带领我们度过了那段困难时期。He led us through that difficult period.

袋鼠 dàishǔ （名词）kangaroo

戴 dài （动词）put on; wear: 戴上眼镜 put on （a pair of）glasses ∥戴项链 wear a necklace

担心 dānxīn （动词）worry: 不要为我担心。Don't worry about me.

单词 dāncí （名词）word

单独 dāndú （形容词）alone; by oneself: 单独旅行 travel alone

单亲 dānqīn （名词）single parent: 单亲家庭 single parent family

单人床 dānrénchuáng （名词）single bed

胆量 dǎnliàng （名词）courage

但是 dànshì （连词）but; yet: 他虽然小, 但是懂得很多。He is young but knows a lot.

诞生 dànshēng （动词）be born: 新中国诞生于1949年。New China was born in 1949.

淡 dàn （形容词）weak; light: 淡茶 weak tea ∥ 淡蓝色 light blue

淡水 dànshuǐ （名词）freshwater: 淡水鱼 freshwater fish

蛋 dàn （名词）egg: 鸟蛋 bird egg ∥ 恐龙蛋 dinosaur egg

蛋白 dànbái （名词）egg white

蛋糕 dàngāo （名词）cake: 烤蛋糕 bake a cake ∥ 巧克力蛋糕 chocolate cake

蛋黄 dànhuáng （名词）yolk

蛋壳 dànké （名词）eggshell

当 dāng （介词）when: 当我上床时，已经12点了。When I went to bed, it was already twelve o'clock.

当然 dāngrán （副词）certainly; of course: "我可以把窗户打开吗？" "当然可以。""Can I open the window?" "Certainly."

当时 dāngshí （名词）that time; then: 当时我很生气。I was very angry at that time.

当心 dāngxīn （动词）be careful; take care: 过马路要当心。Watch

out when you're crossing the street.

党 dǎng （名词）party: 中国共产党 Communist Party of China

党员 dǎngyuán（名词）party member

刀 dāo （名词）knife: 菜刀 kitchen knife

刀叉 dāochā （名词）knives and forks

导盲犬 dǎomángquǎn （名词）guide dog; seeing-eye dog

用法小贴士
guide dog是英国英语，seeing-eye dog是美国英语。

岛 dǎo （名词）island: 海南岛 Hainan Island

岛屿 dǎoyǔ （名词）islands

捣乱 dǎoluàn （动词）make trouble: 别给我捣乱。Don't make trouble for me.

倒 dǎo （动词）
1. fall: 摔倒在地上 fall to the ground
2. change: 倒车 change trains/buses

到 dào （动词）
1. arrive; reach: 到站 reach one's stop ∥ 你什么时候到北京的？

When did you arrive in Beijing?
2. go to: 到伦敦去 go to London

到处 dàochù （副词）at all places; everywhere: 到处都是游客。You can see tourists everywhere.

到达 dàodá （动词）arrive; reach: 按时到达 arrive on time

盗窃 dàoqiè （动词）steal

盗贼 dàozéi （名词）robber; thief

道路 dàolù （名词）road; way: 修筑道路 build a road

道歉 dàoqiàn （动词）apologize; make an apology: 我向你道歉。I apologize to you.

道谢 dàoxiè （动词）thank; say thanks: 说几句道谢的话 say a few words of thanks

稻子 dàozi （名词）rice

得 dé （动词）get: 得满分 get full marks ∥ 得头奖 win first prize

得病 débìng （动词）become ill; fall ill

得到 dédào （动词）get: 他想得到的都得到了。He's got all he wanted.

德国 déguó （名词）Germany

德语 déyǔ （名词）German

灯 dēng （名词）light; lamp: 开灯 turn on the light ∥ 关灯 turn off the light

灯光 dēngguāng （名词）lamplight; light: 明亮的灯光 bright light

灯泡 dēngpào （名词）bulb

灯塔 dēngtǎ （名词）lighthouse

登场 dēngchǎng （动词）go on stage

登陆 dēnglù （动词）go on shore; land: 台风登陆了。The typhoon has reached land.

登录 dēnglù （动词）log on: 登录网站 log onto a web site

等待 děngdài （动词）wait: 我们不能再等待下去了。We can't wait anymore.

等到 děngdào （连词）when: 等到我们赶到，他们已经走了。They had left when we arrived.

凳子 dèngzi （名词）stool; bench

低声 dīshēng （名词）low voice: 低声唱 sing in a low voice

的士 dīshì （名词）taxi: 的士司机 taxi driver

Do not teach fish to swim.

迪斯科 dísikē （名词）disco

迪斯尼乐园 dísiní lèyuán （名词）Disneyland

敌人 dírén （名词）enemy: 我们战胜了敌人。We have defeated the enemy.

底下 dǐxia （名词）under; below: 桌子底下 under the desk

地方 dìfang （名词）
1. place: 遥远的地方 a far-away place // 你是什么地方人？Where are you from?
2. room: 桌子没地方放。There is no room for the table.

地理 dìlǐ （名词）geography: 地理课 geography class

地球 dìqiú （名词）Earth

地球村 dìqiúcūn （名词）global village

地球仪 dìqiúyí （名词）globe

地铁 dìtiě （名词）subway; underground

地图 dìtú （名词）map: 旅游地图 tourist map // 市区地图 city map // 世界地图 map of the world

地下 dìxià （名词）underground: 地下商场 underground shopping mall

地震 dìzhèn （名词）earthquake: 大地震 big earthquake

地址 dìzhǐ （名词）address: 家庭地址 home address // 电子邮箱地址 e-mail address // 网络地址 Web-site address

弟弟 dìdi （名词）younger brother; little brother

弟兄 dìxiong （名词）brothers: 他们弟兄俩是双胞胎。They are twin brothers.

第二次世界大战 dì-èr cì shìjiè dàzhàn （名词）Second World War; World War II

第三世界 dì-sān shìjiè（名词）Third World: 第三世界国家 Third World countries

第一 dì-yī （数）first: 获得第一名 win first place

第一次世界大战 dì-yī cì shìjiè dàzhàn （名词）First World War; World War I

第一夫人 dì-yī fūrén （名词）First Lady

点 diǎn（名词）
1. point: 两条直线交于一点。Two lines meet at a point.
2. o'clock: 8点 eight o'clock

点名 diǎnmíng（动词）call the roll

点燃 diǎnrán（动词）light: 点燃蜡烛 light a candle

点头 diǎntóu（动词）nod: 点头致意 nod a greeting

点心 diǎnxin（名词）refreshments; snacks

点子 diǎnzi（名词）idea: 新点子 a fresh idea // 好点子 a good idea

电冰箱 diànbīngxiāng（名词）refrigerator; fridge

电车 diànchē（名词）tram; street car: 无轨电车 trolley

电灯 diàndēng（名词）lamp; light

电话 diànhuà（名词）telephone; phone: 打电话 make a phone call // 接电话 answer the phone // 电话号码 phone number // 电话卡 phone card // 电话簿 phone book

电话亭 diànhuàtíng（名词）telephone box

电脑 diànnǎo（名词）computer: 打开/关闭电脑 turn on/off a computer // 个人电脑 personal computer（PC）

电脑游戏 diànnǎo yóuxì（名词）computer game: 打电脑游戏 play computer games

电视 diànshì（名词）television; TV: 看电视 watch TV // 电视机 TV set

电视剧 diànshìjù（名词）TV drama

电梯 diàntī（名词）elevator: 乘电梯 take the elevator

用法小贴士
lift是英国英语，elevator是美国英语。

电影 diànyǐng（名词）film; movie: 看电影 see a film; go to the cinema // 演电影 act in a film // 电影演员 film actor/actress

用法小贴士
film是英国英语，movie是美国英语。

电影院 diànyǐngyuàn（名词）cinema

电子邮件 diànzǐ yóujiàn（名词）e-mail: 发送电子邮件 send an e-mail // 电子邮件地址 e-mail address

钓鱼 diàoyú（动词）go fishing

掉 diào（动词）drop; fall: 掉到地板上 fall onto the floor

跌 diē （动词）fall: 跌倒 fall down

碟子 diézi （名词）small plate; saucer

盯 dīng （动词）stare at; gaze: 盯着某人看 stare at somebody

钉子 dīngzi （名词）nail: 拔钉子 pull out a nail ∥ 钉钉子 hammer in a nail

丢 diū （动词）lose: 我丢了钱包。I've lost my wallet.

丢脸 diūliǎn （动词）lose face: 为自己的错误道歉并不丢脸。You won't lose face to apologize for your mistake.

丢人 diūrén （动词）lose face: 你做那样的事会丢人的。You'll lose face if you do that.

东 dōng （名词）east: 城市的东边 east of the city ∥ 东风 east wind

东北 dōngběi （名词）northeast: 东北风 northeast wind

东道国 dōngdàoguó （名词）host country

东道主 dōngdàozhǔ （名词）host: 做东道主 act as host; play host

东方 dōngfāng （名词）east: 太阳从东方升起。The sun rises in the east.

东南 dōngnán （名词）southeast

东西 dōngxi （名词）thing: 你手里拿着什么东西？What's that thing in your hand?

冬季 dōngjì （名词）winter: 在冬季 in winter

冬季奥运会 dōngjì àoyùnhuì （名词）Winter Olympic Games

冬眠 dōngmián（动词）hibernate: 熊在冬眠。The bears are hibernating.

冬天 dōngtiān （名词）winter: 在冬天 in winter

动词 dòngcí （名词）verb

动画片 dònghuàpiān （名词）cartoon

动物 dòngwù （名词）animal: 野生动物 wild animals

动物园 dòngwùyuán （名词）zoo: 去动物园 go to the zoo

动植物 dòngzhíwù （名词）animals and plants

洞 dòng （名词）hole: 挖洞 dig a hole

洞穴 dòngxué （名词）cave; hole

都 dōu （副词）all; both: 一切都准备好了。Everything is ready. ∥

不要班门弄斧。

两个人都来了。Both of them have come.

兜 dōu （名词）pocket: 后兜 back pocket

斗牛 dòuniú （名词）bullfight

豆腐 dòufu （名词）tofu

豆子 dòuzi （名词）bean; pea

都市 dūshì （名词）city: 大都市 big city

毒品 dúpǐn （名词）drug: 吸食毒品 take/use drugs

独生子女 dúshēng zǐnǚ （名词）only child

独自 dúzì （副词）alone; by one-self: 独自生活 live alone

读书 dúshū （动词）read; study

读物 dúwù （名词）reader: 儿童读物 readers for children

读者 dúzhě （名词）reader

肚子 dùzi （名词）belly: 饿肚子 go hungry

度过 dùguò （动词）spend; pass: 共同度过美好时光 spend a good time together

端午节 duānwǔjié （名词）Dragon Boat Festival

短 duǎn （形容词）short: 短发 short hair

短裤 duǎnkù （名词）shorts

短裙 duǎnqún （名词）short skirt

短信 duǎnxìn （名词）text message: 我会给你发短信。I'll text you.

断 duàn （动词）break: 他的腿断了。His leg is broken.

堆 duī （动词）pile: 堆雪人 build/make a snowman

队 duì （名词）
1. line: 插队 jump the line ∥ 排队 line up
2. team; group: 组成一个队 organize into a team

队长 duìzhǎng （名词）group/team leader

对 duì （形容词）right; correct: 这题我回答对了。I answered this question correctly.

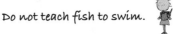

对不起 duìbùqǐ （动词）sorry; I'm sorry

对话 duìhuà （名词）dialogue

吨 dūn （名词）ton

盹 dǔn （名词）nap: 打盹儿 take a nap

多 duō
1.（形容词）much; many; a lot of: 朋友多 have many friends ∥ 时间不多 have little time
2.（形容词）more than; over: 他六十多岁了。He is over sixty.
3.（副词）how: 你多大了？How old are you?
4.（副词）how; what: 多可爱的小狗啊！What a lovely puppy!

多多益善 duōduō-yìshàn the more, the better

多么 duōme（副词）how; what: 多么美丽的景色啊！What a beautiful scene!

多少 duōshao（代词）how many/how much: 屋里有多少人？How many people are there in the room? ∥ 这本书多少钱？How much is this book?

多云 duōyún（形容词）cloudy: 多云的天气 a cloudy day

躲 duǒ （动词）hide: 躲在门背后 hide behind the door

躲藏 duǒcáng （动词）hide

俄罗斯 éluósī （名词）Russia: 俄罗斯人 Russian

俄语 éyǔ （名词）Russian: 说俄语 speak Russian

鹅 é （名词）goose

额头 étóu （名词）forehead

饿 è （形容词）hungry: 又累又饿 be tired and hungry ∥ 我饿了。I'm hungry.

儿歌 érgē （名词）children's song

儿女 érnǚ （名词）children: 养儿育女 raise children

儿孙 érsūn （名词）children and grandchildren

儿童 értóng （名词）children: 学龄前儿童 preschool children

儿童节 értóngjié （名词）Children's Day

儿子 érzi （名词）son

而且 érqiě （连词）...but also: 这些学生不但学习好，而且体育也很好。These students are good not only at study but also at sports.

用法小贴士

but also（而且）常与not only（不但）连用。

耳朵 ěrduo （名词）ear

耳机 ěrjī （名词）earphones; headphones

二 èr （数词）two: 第二 the second ∥ 一加一等于二。One plus one is two.

二胡 èrhú （名词）*erhu*（a Chinese two-stringed musical instrument played with a bow）: 拉二胡 play the *erhu*

百科小贴士

二胡是一种中国传统乐器，又名"胡琴"，唐代已出现，音色优美、表现力强。阿炳是近代杰出的二胡演奏家；著名的二胡乐曲有《二泉映月》等。

二手 èrshǒu （形容词）secondhand: 二手车 secondhand car

二月 èryuè （名词）February

F

发财 fācái （动词）get rich

发疯 fāfēng （动词）go crazy; go mad: 气得发疯 be mad with anger

发火 fāhuǒ （动词）get angry; lose one's temper

发明 fāmíng
1. （名词）invention: 最新发明 the newest invention
2. （动词）invent: 贝尔1876年发明了电话。 Bell invented the telephone in 1876.

发怒 fānù （动词）get angry

发烧 fāshāo （动词）have a fever: 发高烧 have a high fever

发生 fāshēng （动词）happen; take place: 发生交通事故 have a traffic accident ∥ 发生了什么事？ What's up?

发现 fāxiàn （动词）find (out); discover: 发现秘密 find out a secret

发言 fāyán （动词）speak; make a speech: 在会上发言 speak at the meeting

法官 fǎguān （名词）judge

法律 fǎlù （名词）law: 制定法律 make a law ∥ 遵守法律 obey the law

帆船 fānchuán （名词）sailing boat

番茄 fānqié （名词）tomato: 番茄酱 tomato sauce; ketchup

翻 fān （动词）turn; turn over: 翻到下一页。 Turn to the next page. ∥ 小猫把牛奶打翻了。 The kitten knocked over the milk.

烦恼 fánnǎo （形容词）worried: 我真为这事烦恼。 I'm really worried about this.

繁忙 fánmáng （形容词）busy: 繁忙的交通 heavy traffic

返回 fǎnhuí （动词）return; come/go back: 返回地球 return to earth (or Earth)

饭 fàn （名词）meal: 饭前/后 before/after a meal ∥ 吃饭 have a meal

饭菜 fàncài （名词）meal: 简单的饭菜 simple meal

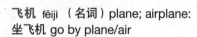

饭碗 fànwǎn （名词）bowl

方 fāng （形容词）square: 方脸 square face

方便面 fāngbiànmiàn （名词）instant noodles

方法 fāngfǎ （名词）way; method: 学习方法 study method

房 fáng （名词）house: 建房 build a house

房屋 fángwū （名词）house; building: 修建房屋 build a house

房子 fángzi （名词）house; building: 盖房子 build a house

访问 fǎngwèn （动词）visit: 访问欧洲 visit Europe

放 fàng （动词）put; place: 请把花瓶放在桌子上。Please put the vase on the table.

放学 fàngxué （动词）dismiss students from school: 放学啦！School is over!

飞 fēi （动词）fly: 在天上飞 fly in the sky ∥ 飞机正飞往巴黎。The plane is flying to Paris.

飞碟 fēidié （名词）UFO

用法小贴士
UFO 是 unidentified flying object（不明飞行物）的缩写形式。

飞机 fēijī （名词）plane; airplane: 坐飞机 go by plane/air

飞翔 fēixiáng （动词）fly: 鸟儿在天空自由地飞翔。Birds are flying freely in the sky.

飞行 fēixíng （动词）fly: 飞行服 flying suit

非常 fēicháng （副词）very: 非常聪明 very clever ∥ 学习非常努力 study very hard

非典 fēidiǎn （名词）SARS

百科小贴士
2003年流行的一种由新型冠状病毒引起的传染性非典型肺炎，发病急，传染性强，主要症状是发热、干咳、呼吸困难、乏力等，病死率较高。

非洲 fēizhōu （名词）Africa: 非洲人 African

肥胖 féipàng （形容词）fat

肥皂 féizào （名词）soap: 一块肥皂 a bar of soap

废话 fèihuà （名词）nonsense: 别说废话！Don't talk nonsense!

费用 fèiyòng （名词）cost: 生产费用 production cost ∥ 生活费用 living cost

分 fēn
1.（动词）divide: 把全班分成8个小组。Divide the class into eight groups.

2.（量词）minute: 3点45分 a quarter to four

3.（量词）point: 他得了90分。 He got ninety points out of one hundred.

分数 fēnshù （名词）mark; point

分享 fēnxiǎng （动词）share: 分享快乐 share joys

粉笔 fěnbǐ （名词）chalk: 一支粉笔 a piece of chalk // 彩色粉笔 colored chalk

粉红 fěnhóng （形容词）pink

愤怒 fènnù （形容词）angry

风 fēng （名词）wind: 东/南/西/北风 east/south/west/north wind // 起风了。The wind rose. // 风刮得很大。The wind is blowing hard.

风景 fēngjǐng （名词）scenery: 美丽的风景 beautiful scenery

风水 fēngshuǐ （名词）*feng shui*

百科小贴士
在中国旧时指宅基地、墓地等所处的地理形势，迷信认为风水的好坏可以影响家族的兴衰和吉凶。

风俗 fēngsú （名词）custom: 地方风俗 local custom

疯狂 fēngkuáng （形容词）crazy; mad

疯子 fēngzi （名词）madman

锋利 fēnglì （形容词）sharp: 锋利的刀子 sharp knife

蜂蜜 fēngmì （名词）honey: 采集蜂蜜 gather honey

夫妇 fūfù （名词）husband and wife

夫妻 fūqī （名词）husband and wife

夫人 fūrén （名词）madam; lady; Mrs: 第一夫人 First Lady

肤色 fūsè （名词）skin color; color: 各种肤色的人 people of all colors

扶手椅 fúshǒuyǐ （名词）armchair

服务 fúwù （动词）serve: 服务中心 service center // 免费服务 free service // 我们乐意为您服务。We are happy to serve you.

服务员 fúwùyuán （名词）waiter; waitress

服装 fúzhuāng （名词）clothing: 服装款式 clothing style // 服装店 clothing store

符号 fúhào （名词）mark; symbol: 重音符号 stress mark

斧头 fǔtou （名词）ax

失败是成功之母。

父母 fùmǔ （名词）father and mother; parents

父亲 fùqīn （名词）father

付款 fùkuǎn （动词）pay

妇女 fùnǚ （名词）woman: 妇女和儿童 women and children

妇女节 fùnǚjié （名词）Women's Day

附近 fùjìn
1.（形容词）nearby: 附近的商店 a nearby shop
2.（名词）附近有没有邮局？Is there a post office around here?

复习 fùxí （动词）go over; review: 复习功课 go over/review one's lessons

副词 fùcí （名词）adverb

富人 fùrén （名词）a rich person; rich people: 穷人和富人 the rich and the poor

富翁 fùwēng （名词）a very rich person; moneybags

富有 fùyǒu （形容词）rich

富裕 fùyù （形容词）rich

腹部 fùbù （名词）stomach; belly

G

咖喱 gālí （名词）curry

百科小贴士

咖喱是英语curry的音译词。

该 gāi （动词）
1. should: 你不该那样做。You shouldn't have done that. ∥ 我该走了。I must be off now. ∥ 我的大衣该洗了。My coat needs cleaning.
2. be one's turn: 该我了。It's my turn.

改变 gǎibiàn （动词）change: 改变方向 change direction ∥ 改变主意 change one's mind

改正 gǎizhèng （动词）correct: 改正错误 correct one's mistakes

盖子 gàizi （名词）lid; cover: 打开盖子 open the lid ∥ 盖上盖子 put the lid on

干 gān （形容词）dry: 干柴 dry wood ∥ 感到口干 feel thirsty

干净 gānjìng （形容词）clean: 把衣服洗干净 clean the clothes ∥ 把厨房打扫干净 clean the kitchen

干洗 gānxǐ （动词）dry-clean: 把衣服送去干洗 have the clothes dry-cleaned

干燥 gānzào （形容词）dry: 干燥的气候 dry climate

甘薯 gānshǔ （名词）sweet potato

甘甜 gāntián （形容词）sweet

赶 gǎn （动词）
1. catch up with: 我想赶上他。I want to catch up with him.
2. (try to) catch: 赶火车 try to catch the train

赶集 gǎnjí （动词）go to a fair/market

赶紧 gǎnjǐn （副词）quickly; hurriedly: 赶紧离开/上楼 hurry away/upstairs

赶快 gǎnkuài （副词）quickly; immediately: 赶快！要不然就赶不上汽车了。Hurry up, or we'll miss the bus.

感恩节 gǎn'ēnjié （名词）Thanksgiving Day

感觉 gǎnjué
1. （名词）sense; feeling: 不安的感觉 uneasy feeling ∥ 幸福的感觉 happiness
2. （动词）feel: 感觉饿 feel hungry

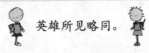

英雄所见略同。

感冒 gǎnmào （名词）cold: 患感冒 catch/have a cold ∥ 重感冒 a bad/heavy cold

感谢 gǎnxiè （动词）thank: 感谢光临！Thank you for coming! ∥ 非常感谢。Thank you very much. / Thanks a lot. / Many thanks.

干活儿 gànhuór （动词）work: 我正在干活儿。I'm working.

刚 gāng （副词）just: 天刚黑。It has just gotten dark. ∥ 她刚满16岁。She's just turned sixteen.

刚才 gāngcái （副词）just now: 刚才我见过他。I saw him just now.

钢笔 gāngbǐ （名词）fountain pen; pen

钢琴 gāngqín （名词）piano: 弹钢琴 play the piano ∥ 钢琴家 pianist

高 gāo （形容词）high: 高山 high mountain ∥ 高楼大厦 high buildings

高大 gāodà （形容词）tall and big; tall

高尔夫球 gāo'ěrfūqiú （名词）golf: 打高尔夫球 play golf ∥ 高尔夫球场 golf course

百科小贴士
高尔夫是英语golf的音译词。

高科技 gāokējì （名词）high technology

高速公路 gāosù gōnglù （名词）superhighway: 信息高速公路 information superhighway

高兴 gāoxìng （形容词）happy; glad: 见到你很高兴。I'm very glad to meet you.

高中 gāozhōng （名词）senior high school

糕点 gāodiǎn （名词）pastry: 糕点房 bakery

告别 gàobié （动词）say goodbye to

告诉 gàosu （动词）tell; say; let know: 谁告诉你的？Who told you that?

哥哥 gēge （名词）older brother

胳膊 gēbo （名词）arm: 左胳膊 left arm ∥ 右胳膊 right arm

鸽子 gēzi （名词）pigeon; dove: 和平鸽 dove of peace

歌唱 gēchàng （动词）sing: 放声歌唱 sing loudly

歌唱家 gēchàngjiā （名词）singer

Great minds think alike.

歌曲 gēqǔ （名词）song: 流行歌曲 pop song // 电影歌曲 theme song of a film

歌手 gēshǒu （名词）singer: 流行歌手 pop singer // 青年歌手 young singer

歌舞 gēwǔ （名词）songs and dances

隔壁 gébì （名词）next door: 隔壁邻居 next-door neighbor // 住在隔壁 live next door

隔墙有耳 géqiáng-yǒu'ěr walls have ears

各 gè （代词）each; every; all: 各国人民 people of all nations

各个 gègè （代词）each; every; all: 各个部分 all the parts

给 gěi （动词）give: 请给我那本书。Please give me that book.

根 gēn （名词）root: 这棵树有许多根。This tree has many roots.

跟 gēn
1.（介词）with: 我跟你一起去。I'll go with you.
2.（连词）and: 他跟我是好朋友。He and I are good friends.
3.（介词）as: 爸爸跟妈妈一样高。Mom is as tall as Dad.
4.（动词）follow: 请跟我读。Read after me, please.

更 gèng （副词）more; even: 更好 even better // 兄弟俩都高，弟弟更高些。Both the brothers are tall. The younger brother is even taller.

更加 gèngjiā （副词）more; even more: 更加漂亮 even more beautiful

工程师 gōngchéngshī （名词）engineer

工具 gōngjù （名词）tool

工人 gōngrén （名词）worker

工资 gōngzī （名词）salary; wage

用法小贴士
salary通常指按月发给职员的工资，wage通常指按周发给工人的工资。

工作 gōngzuò
1.（名词）job; work: 你爸爸是做什么工作的？What does your dad do?
2.（动词）work: 在医院工作 work in a hospital

弓箭 gōngjiàn （名词）bow and arrow

公厕 gōngcè （名词）toilet

公共汽车 gōnggòng qìchē （名词）bus: 1路公共汽车 bus No. 1 // 公共汽车站 bus stop

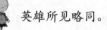
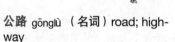

公路 gōnglù （名词）road; high-way

公牛 gōngniú （名词）bull

公平 gōngpíng （形容词）fair: 对每个人都公平 be fair to everybody

公司 gōngsī （名词）company

公园 gōngyuán （名词）park

公主 gōngzhǔ （名词）princess

功夫 gōngfu （名词）kung fu

百科小贴士
kung fu是功夫的音译词。

功课 gōngkè （名词）homework: 做功课 do homework

宫殿 gōngdiàn （名词）palace

共产党 gòngchǎndǎng （名词）Communist Party: 中国共产党 Communist Party of China

篝火 gōuhuǒ （名词）bonfire; campfire: 燃起篝火 make a bonfire // 篝火晚会 campfire party

狗 gǒu （名词）dog: 猎狗 hunting dog

购买 gòumǎi （动词）buy: 购买房子 buy a house

购物 gòuwù （动词）go shopping: 购物袋 shopping bag

够 gòu
1. （副词）enough: 我吃够了。I've had enough. // 已经够好了。It's good enough.
2. （动词）be enough: 时间不够 do not have enough time

姑姑 gūgu （名词）aunt

用法小贴士
姑姑、姨妈都称aunt，如果要区别，可以用paternal aunt（姑姑）和maternal aunt（姨妈）。

姑娘 gūniang （名词）girl: 小姑娘 little girl // 年轻姑娘 young girl

古 gǔ （形容词）ancient: 古埃及 ancient Egypt // 古罗马 ancient Rome

古代 gǔdài （名词）ancient times

古国 gǔguó （名词）ancient country

古籍 gǔjí （名词）ancient books

古老 gǔlǎo （形容词）ancient: 古老的文化 ancient culture

古诗 gǔshī （名词）ancient poetry; classical poetry

谷物 gǔwù （名词）grain: 各种谷物 all kinds of grains

骨头 gǔtou （名词）bone: 鱼骨头 fish bone

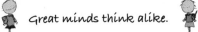
鼓 gǔ （名词）drum: 打鼓 beat a drum

鼓励 gǔlì （动词）encourage: 鼓励某人好好学习 encourage somebody to study hard

固体 gùtǐ （名词）solid

故宫 gùgōng （名词）the Forbidden City; the Palace Museum

故事 gùshi （名词）story: 讲故事 tell a story

故乡 gùxiāng （名词）hometown

顾客 gùkè （名词）customer

瓜 guā （名词）melon: 甜瓜 honeydew melon ∥西瓜 watermelon

呱呱叫 guāguājiào （形容词）terrific: 他的英语呱呱叫。His English is terrific!

挂 guà （动词）hang: 把画挂在墙上 hang the picture on the wall ∥把帽子挂起 hang up one's hat ∥挂断电话 hang up

怪 guài
1. （形容词）strange: 怪梦 strange dream ∥怪人 strange person
2. （动词）blame: 这事不能怪她。We can't blame her for this.

关 guān （动词）
1. close; shut: 关抽屉 shut a drawer ∥关门 close the door
2. turn off: 关电视 turn off the TV ∥请关灯。Please turn off the light.

关闭 guānbì （动词）
1. close; shut: 门窗都关闭着。Both the door and the windows are closed.
2. close down: 公司关闭了。The company has closed down.

关心 guānxīn （动词）care for: 关心自己 care for oneself ∥关心他人 care for others

观点 guāndiǎn （名词）view; opinion: 持不同观点 hold different views ∥你的观点是什么？What's your opinion?

观看 guānkàn （动词）watch: 观看比赛 watch a match ∥观看演出 see a performance

观众 guānzhòng （名词）audience: 电影观众 film audience ∥电视观众 TV audience

冠词 guàncí （名词）article

冠军 guànjūn （名词）champion: 获得冠军 win a championship ∥世界冠军 world champion ∥乒乓球冠军 table tennis champion

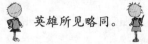

英雄所见略同。

罐头 guàntou （名词）canned food: 肉罐头 canned meat

罐子 guànzi （名词）pot: 两罐子蜂蜜 two pots of honey

光明 guāngmíng
1.（形容词）bright: 光明前途 bright future
2.（名词）light: 太阳给我们带来光明。The sun gives us light.

光盘 guāngpán （名词）CD
用法小贴士
CD是compact disk的缩写形式。

光线 guāngxiàn （名词）light: 不要在光线不好的地方看书。Don't read in poor light.

光阴 guāngyīn （名词）time: 一寸光阴一寸金。Time is money.

光阴似箭 guāngyīn-sìjiàn time flies

广播 guǎngbō
1.（动词）broadcast: 广播新闻 broadcast news
2.（名词）broadcast: 收听外语广播 listen to foreign language broadcast

广阔 guǎngkuò （形容词）wide; broad: 广阔的世界 wide world

归还 guīhuán （动词）return: 按时归还 return something on time

龟 guī （名词）tortoise: 龟壳 tortoise shell

鬼 guǐ （名词）ghost: 讲鬼故事 tell a ghost story // 你相信有鬼吗? Do you believe in ghosts?

柜子 guìzi （名词）cupboard

滚 gǔn （动词）
1. roll: 硬币滚到桌子下面去了。The coin rolled under the table.
2. get out: 你给我滚！Get out!

棍 gùn （名词）stick: 木棍 wooden stick

锅 guō （名词）pan; pot: 炒菜锅 frying pan // 电饭锅 electric cooker

国 guó （名词）country; nation: 爱国 love one's country // 救国 save the country // 外国 foreign countries

国歌 guógē （名词）national anthem

国际 guójì （形容词）international: 国际关系 international relations // 国际奥林匹克委员会 the International Olympic Committee

国家 guójiā （名词）country; nation: 西方国家 Western nations

国旗 guóqí （名词）national flag

272

国庆 guóqìng （名词）National Day: 庆祝国庆 celebrate the National Day

国王 guówáng （名词）king

果酱 guǒjiàng （名词）jam: 一瓶果酱 a jar of jam

果实 guǒshí （名词）fruit: 结果实 produce/bear fruit

果汁 guǒzhī （名词）fruit juice: 新鲜果汁 fresh fruit juice ∥ 果汁饮料 fruit drink

过 guò （动词）
1. cross: 过河 cross the river ∥ 过马路 cross the street
2. spend: 周末你打算怎么过? How are you going to spend the weekend?

3. pass: 现在是 8 点过 10 分。It's ten past eight.

过错 guòcuò （名词）fault: 这不是他的过错。This is not his fault.

过来 guòlái （动词）come over; come here: 快过来! Come over here, quick!

过年 guònián （动词）celebrate the New Year

过去
1. guòqu（动词）go over; pass by: 你在这里等着，我过去看看。You wait here; I'll go over and see. ∥ 从我身边过去 pass me by
2. guòqù（名词）past: 忘记过去 forget the past

H

哈哈 hāhā （叹词）aha; ha ha: 哈哈，我猜对了！Aha, I've got it.

蛤蟆 háma （名词）toad

还 hái （副词）still; yet: 我还在做家庭作业。I'm still doing my homework. ‖ 爸爸还没回来。Dad hasn't come back yet.

用法小贴士
still 和 yet 都表示"还"，但前者用于肯定句，后者用于否定句。

还是 háishi
1.（副词）still: 你看起来还是那么年轻。You still look very young.
2.（连词）or: 你想喝什么，水还是果汁？What would you like, water or juice?

孩子 háizi （名词）child: 她有两个孩子。She has two children.

海 hǎi （名词）sea: 南海 South China Sea ‖ 海水 sea water

海岸 hǎi'àn （名词）sea coast; shore

海豚 hǎitún （名词）dolphin

海鲜 hǎixiān （名词）seafood

海洋 hǎiyáng （名词）seas and oceans; ocean: 浩瀚的海洋 vast ocean

害怕 hàipà （动词）fear; be afraid: 许多人都害怕蛇。Many people are afraid of snakes.

害羞 hàixiū （动词）be shy: 刚开始那个男孩有些害羞。The little boy was a bit shy at the beginning.

寒假 hánjià （名词）winter vacation

寒冷 hánlěng （形容词）cold: 寒冷的冬季 cold winter

喊 hǎn （动词）
1. shout; cry out: 他大喊："救命！救命！" He cried out, "Help! Help!"
2. call: 有人在外边喊我。Someone is calling me outside.

喊叫 hǎnjiào （动词）shout; cry out: 愤怒地喊叫 shout angrily

汉堡包 hànbǎobāo （名词）hamburger

百科小贴士
汉堡包是英语 hamburger 的音译词。

汉语 hànyǔ （名词）Chinese: 汉语拼音 *pinyin*

汉字 hànzì （名词）Chinese character

汉族 hànzú （名词）Han ethnic group

行 háng （名词）line; row: 站成一行 stand in a line ∥ 几行树 several rows of trees

航行 hángxíng （动词）sail: 船在逆风航行。The ship is sailing against the wind.

好 hǎo （形容词）good; nice; fine: 好朋友 good friend ∥ 好吃 delicious ∥ 天气真好！The weather is really nice!

好久 hǎojiǔ （形容词）long: 好久以前 a long time ago

好看 hǎokàn （形容词）
1. good-looking; pretty: 这件衬衫真好看。The shirt is really pretty.
2. interesting: 节目很好看。The show was really interesting.

好像 hǎoxiàng （副词）seem; be like: 好像要下雨。It looks like rain.

好笑 hǎoxiào （形容词）funny: 有什么好笑的? What's so funny?

号 hào （名词）
1. date: 今天几号？What's the date today?
2. size: 大号 large size ∥ 小号 small size

号码 hàomǎ （名词）number: 电话号码 telephone number

好 hào （动词）like; love: 他很好学。He likes studying.

耗子 hàozi （名词）mouse; rat: 猫捉耗子。Cats catch mice.

喝 hē （动词）drink: 喝茶 drink tea

和 hé
1. （连词）and: 只有我和你知道。Only you and I know it.
2. （介词）with: 我和你一起去。I'll go with you.

和蔼 hé'ǎi （形容词）kind: 和蔼的老奶奶 a kind grandma

和平 hépíng （名词）peace: 和平鸽 dove of peace ∥ 热爱和平 love peace

河 hé （名词）river: 江河湖海 rivers, lakes, and seas

河流 héliú （名词）river

河马 hémǎ （名词）hippo

盒 hé （名词）box: 火柴盒 match box ∥铅笔盒 pencil box

贺卡 hèkǎ （名词）greeting card: 寄贺卡 send a greeting card ∥电子贺卡 e-card ∥生日贺卡 birth-day card

贺年卡 hèniánkǎ （名词）New Year card

褐色 hèsè
1. （形容词）brown: 褐色的头发 brown hair
2. （名词）brown

黑 hēi （形容词）
1. black: 他穿着一双黑鞋子。He is wearing a pair of black shoes.
2. dark: 天要黑了。It's getting dark.

黑暗 hēi'àn （形容词）dark: 黑暗的角落 dark corner ∥四周一片黑暗。It's dark everywhere.

黑白 hēibái （名词）black and white: 黑白电视机 black-and-white television

黑客 hēikè （名词）hacker: 电脑黑客 computer hacker

百科小贴士
黑客是英语hacker的音译词。

黑面包 hēimiànbāo （名词）brown bread

黑人 hēirén （名词）Black people

黑色 hēisè
1. （形容词）black: 黑色的鞋子 black shoes
2. （名词）black: 她穿了一身黑色衣服。She is dressed in black.

黑市 hēishì （名词）black market

嘿 hēi （叹词）hey: 嘿，当心啊！Hey, be careful!

很 hěn （副词）very; very much: 跑得很快 run very fast ∥工作很努力 work very hard ∥我很喜欢它。I like it very much.

狠心 hěnxin （形容词）heartless: 你太狠心了！You are so heartless!

恨 hèn （动词）hate: 你对我说谎，我恨你。You lied to me. I hate you.

恒星 héngxīng （名词）star: 太阳是一颗恒星。The sun is a star.

烘烤 hōngkǎo （动词）bake: 烘烤蛋糕 bake cakes ∥烘烤面包 bake bread

红 hóng （形容词）red: 红地毯 red carpet

红包 hóngbāo （名词）red packet (with money in it): 给红包作为新年礼物 give a red packet as a New Year present

红茶 hóngchá （名词）black tea: 你想喝红茶还是绿茶？Do you like black tea or green tea?

红军 hóngjūn （名词）the Red Army

红领巾 hónglǐngjīn （名词）
1. Young Pioneer's neckerchief
2. Young Pioneer

红绿灯 hónglǜdēng （名词）traffic lights

红旗 hóngqí （名词）red flag

红色 hóngsè
1.（形容词）red: 红色的头发 red hair
2.（名词）red: 鲜艳的红色 bright red

红十字会 hóngshízìhuì （名词）the Red Cross: 中国红十字会 the Red Cross Society of China

红薯 hóngshǔ （名词）sweet potato: 烤红薯 baked sweet potatoes

红糖 hóngtáng （名词）brown sugar

洪水 hóngshuǐ （名词）flood

猴子 hóuzi （名词）monkey: 金丝猴 golden monkey

后来 hòulái （副词）afterward: 后来我再也没有见过他。I have never seen him again after that.

后门 hòumén （名词）back door

后面 hòumiàn （名词）back: 在后面 at the back

后年 hòunián （名词）the year after next; two years from now

后天 hòutiān （名词）the day after tomorrow: 大后天 three days from today

厚 hòu （形容词）thick: 厚脸皮 thick-skinned ∥厚衣服 thick clothes

呼喊 hūhǎn （动词）cry out; shout: 高声呼喊 shout at the top of one's lungs

呼救 hūjiù （动词）cry for help

呼吸 hūxī （动词）breathe: 呼吸新鲜空气 breathe in fresh air ∥深呼吸 breathe deeply

忽然 hūrán （副词）suddenly: 他忽然想到了一个好主意。All of a sudden, a good idea came to him.

狐狸 húli （名词）fox: 狐狸犬 fox dog ∥狐狸尾巴总是要露出来的。A fox cannot hide its tail.

胡萝卜 húluóbo （名词）carrot

胡子 húzi （名词）beard: 白胡子 white beard

壶 hú （名词）kettle; pot: 茶壶 tea pot // 暖壶 hot water bottle

湖 hú （名词）lake: 湖水 lake water // 西湖 the West Lake

蝴蝶 húdié （名词）butterfly

蝴蝶结 húdiéjié （名词）bow; bow tie

虎 hǔ （名词）tiger: 猛虎 fierce tiger

互联网 hùliánwǎng （名词）Internet

互相 hùxiāng （副词）each other: 互相帮助 help each other // 互相依赖 depend on each other

户外 hùwài （名词）outdoor: 户外运动 outdoor sports

护士 hùshi （名词）nurse: 护士长 head nurse // 护士节 Nurses' Day

花 huā
1.（名词）flower: 野花 wild flowers // 浇花 water flowers // 种花 grow flowers
2.（动词）spend: 花钱 spend money // 花时间 spend time

花白 huābái （形容词）gray: 花白胡子 gray beard

花草 huācǎo （名词）flowers and plants: 请勿践踏花草！Keep off the flowers and plants!

花朵 huāduǒ （名词）flowers

花篮 huālán （名词）flower basket

花生 huāshēng （名词）peanut: 花生酱 peanut butter // 花生油 peanut oil

> **用法小贴士**
> 花生在英语中也可以叫做groundnut，也就是"地下的坚果"。

花椰菜 huāyēcài （名词）cauliflower

花园 huāyuán （名词）garden

划船 huáchuán （动词）row a boat; go boating

华人 huárén （名词）Chinese people: 美籍华人 Chinese American

滑冰 huábīng （动词）skate; go skating

滑雪 huáxuě （动词）ski; go skiing: 滑雪衫 ski suit // 滑雪鞋 ski boots

化学 huàxué （名词）chemistry: 化学变化 chemical change

画 huà
1. （名词）picture; drawing; painting: 中国画 Chinese painting ∥ 油画 oil painting
2. （动词）draw; paint: 画水彩画 paint in watercolors ∥ 画一条直线 draw a straight line

画板 huàbǎn （名词）drawing board

画笔 huàbǐ （名词）paintbrush

画画 huàhuà （动词）draw a picture

画家 huàjiā （名词）painter

话 huà （名词）word; talk: 和某人说几句话 have a talk with somebody

坏 huài （形容词）bad: 坏消息 bad news ∥ 做坏事 do bad things

坏事 huàishì （名词）bad things

欢呼 huānhū （动词）cheer: 为胜利而欢呼 cheer for the victory

欢乐 huānlè （形容词）happy: 欢乐的人群 happy crowd ∥ 欢乐的时光 happy times

欢迎 huānyíng （动词）welcome: 欢迎来中国！Welcome to China!

还 huán （动词）return: 还书 return a book

环球 huánqiú （名词）around the world: 环球旅行 around-the-world travel

缓慢 huǎnmàn （形容词）slow

唤醒 huànxǐng （动词）wake up: 明天早晨7点把我唤醒。Wake me up at seven tomorrow morning.

皇帝 huángdì （名词）emperor: 秦始皇是中国的第一位皇帝。Qinshihuang was the first emperor of China.

皇宫 huánggōng （名词）palace: 紫禁城是明清两朝的皇宫。The Forbidden City was the palace of the Ming and Qing dynasties.

皇后 huánghòu （名词）empress

黄 huáng （形容词）yellow

黄瓜 huánggua （名词）cucumber: 新鲜的黄瓜 fresh cucumbers

黄河 huánghé （名词）the Yellow River

黄金 huángjīn （名词）gold

黄牌 huángpái （名词）yellow card: 吃了一张黄牌 get a yellow card ∥ 亮黄牌 show a yellow card to someone

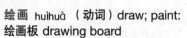
黄色 huángsè
1.（形容词）yellow
2.（名词）yellow

黄油 huángyóu （名词）butter: 黄油面包片 bread and butter

谎话 huǎnghuà （名词）lie: 说谎话 tell a lie

灰尘 huīchén （名词）dust: 地板布满灰尘。The floor is covered in dust.

灰色 huīsè
1.（形容词）gray
2.（名词）gray

回答 huídá
1.（动词）answer; reply: 回答问题 answer a question
2.（名词）answer; reply: 这就是我的回答。This is my answer.

回去 huíqù （动词）go back; return: 早点回去！Go back early!

回头 huítóu （动词）turn one's head

回信 huíxìn （动词）write back; write in reply

会见 huìjiàn （动词）meet with: 会见客人 meet with guests

会议 huìyì （名词）meeting: 参加会议 attend a meeting

绘画 huìhuà （动词）draw; paint: 绘画板 drawing board

昏暗 hūn'àn （形容词）dim: 昏暗的灯光 dim light

婚礼 hūnlǐ （名词）wedding: 参加婚礼 attend a wedding // 举行婚礼 hold a wedding

浑身 húnshēn （副词）all over the body: 冻得浑身发抖 shiver all over with cold

馄饨 húntun （名词）wonton: 馄饨汤 wonton soup // 包馄饨 make wontons

活动 huódòng （名词）activity: 户外活动 outdoor activities // 体育活动 sports

活泼 huópo （形容词）lively: 活泼的孩子 a lively child

火 huǒ （名词）fire: 玩火 play with fire

火柴 huǒchái （名词）match: 火柴棒 match stick // 火柴盒 match box

火车 huǒchē （名词）train: 乘坐火车 take a train // 上/下火车 get on/off a train // 火车票 train ticket // 火车站 train/railway station

火箭 huǒjiàn （名词）rocket

欲速则不达。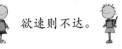

火腿 huǒtuǐ （名词）ham

火焰 huǒyàn （名词）flame: 跳跃的火焰 dancing flames

伙伴 huǒbàn （名词）very good friend (mate)

或者 huòzhě （连词）or: 我们今天或者明天去都行。We can go today or tomorrow.

获胜 huòshèng （动词）win: 比赛获胜 win a match

J

几乎 jīhū （副词）almost; nearly: 我们几乎误了火车。We almost missed the train.

饥饿 jī'è （形容词）hungry: 感到饥饿 feel hungry

机场 jīchǎng （名词）airport: 国际机场 international airport

机关枪 jīguānqiāng （名词）machine gun

机灵 jīling （形容词）clever; smart: 机灵的孩子 a clever child

机器 jīqì （名词）machine: 修理机器 repair a machine

肌肉 jīròu （名词）muscle: 结实的肌肉 strong muscles

鸡 jī （名词）chicken: 公鸡 rooster // 母鸡 hen // 小鸡 chick // 烧鸡 roast chicken

鸡蛋 jīdàn （名词）egg: 煎鸡蛋 fry eggs

鸡尾酒 jīwěijiǔ （名词）cocktail

基因 jīyīn （名词）gene: 人类基因 human gene

百科小贴士
基因是英语 gene 的音译词。

激动 jīdòng （动词）be excited: 人们听到好消息很激动。People were excited at the good news.

激光 jīguāng （名词）laser

及时 jíshí （副词）in time: 及时赶到 arrive in time

吉普车 jípǔchē （名词）jeep

百科小贴士
吉普车是英语 jeep 的音译词.

极 jí （副词）very: 极为重要 very important // 我们中的极少数人 very few of us

急 jí （动词）worry: 别急，我来帮你。Don't worry. I'll help you.

急忙 jímáng （形容词）in a hurry: 急忙离开 leave in a hurry

疾病 jíbìng （名词）illness: 严重疾病 serious illness

集市 jíshì （名词）market: 乡村集市 village market

时间还没到，不要作判断。

集邮 jíyóu （动词）collect stamps: 集邮册 stamp album

几 jǐ （数词）how many: 你有几本书？ How many books do you have? ∥ 几点了？ What's the time? ∥ 你几岁了？ How old are you?

几个 jǐgè （数词）a few; several: 几个同学 a few classmates ∥ 几个问题 several questions

计划 jìhuà （名词）plan: 学习计划 study plan ∥ 做计划 make a plan

计算机 jìsuànjī （名词）computer: 个人计算机 personal computer; PC

记 jì （动词）write down: 记笔记 take notes ∥ 记日记 keep a diary

记录 jìlù
1. （动词）record; keep a record: 记录日期 record the date
2. （名词）notes; record: 打破记录 break a record

技术 jìshù （名词）technology: 采用新技术 use new technology

系 jì （动词）tie: 系鞋带 tie one's shoelaces ∥ 系着红领巾 wear a Young Pioneer's neckerchief

季节 jìjié （名词）season: 收获季节 harvest season

季军 jìjūn （名词）third place (in a match); bronze winner

继续 jìxù （动词）go on: 继续工作 go on working

寄 jì （动词）mail; send; post: 寄信 post a letter ∥ 寄包裹 send a parcel

寂静 jìjìng （形容词）quiet; silent: 寂静的街道 quiet street ∥ 寂静的夜晚 silent night

寂寞 jìmò （形容词）lonely: 感到寂寞 feel lonely

加 jiā （动词）add: 加盐 add salt

加拿大 jiānádà （名词）Canada

加入 jiārù （动词）
1. add: 把糖加入牛奶里 add sugar to milk
2. join: 加入足球队 join a football team ∥ 我可以加入你们的活动吗？ May I join you?

加油 jiāyóu （动词）come on: 杰克，加油！ Come on, Jack!

夹克 jiākè （名词）jacket: 皮夹克 leather jacket

百科小贴士
夹克是英语jacket的音译词。

家 jiā （名词）home; family: 呆在家里 stay at home ∥ 三口之家 a family of three

283

家具 jiājù （名词）furniture: 一件家具 a piece of furniture ∥一套家具 a set of furniture

用法小贴士

furniture是不可数名词，因而没有复数形式。

家属 jiāshǔ （名词）family member

家庭 jiātíng （名词）family: 幸福的家庭 a happy family

家庭影院 jiātíng yǐngyuàn （名词）home cinema

家务 jiāwù （名词）housework: 做家务 do housework

家乡 jiāxiāng （名词）hometown

家长 jiāzhǎng （名词）parent: 家长会 parents' meeting

甲虫 jiǎchóng （名词）beetle

假如 jiǎrú （连词）if: 假如她不在，就留个口信。Please leave a message if she isn't in.

假装 jiǎzhuāng （动词）pretend: 假装睡着了 pretend to be asleep

价钱 jiàqian （名词）price: 价钱是多少？What's the price?

驾驶 jiàshǐ （动词）drive: 驾驶汽车 drive a car

驾驶员 jiàshǐyuán （名词）driver: 公共汽车驾驶员 bus driver

架 jià （名词）shelf: 书架 bookshelf

假期 jiàqi （名词）holiday; vacation: 度假期 spend a holiday/vacation

假日 jiàrì （名词）holiday: 假日旅游 travel on holidays ∥在假日里 during the holidays

尖 jiān
1. （形容词）sharp: 尖头铅笔 sharp pencil
2. （名词）point: 针尖 the point of a needle

尖子生 jiānzishēng （名词）top student

坚果 jiānguǒ （名词）nut

坚强 jiānqiáng （形容词）strong: 坚强的团队 a strong team

坚硬 jiānyìng （形容词）hard: 坚硬的甲壳 hard shell

肩膀 jiānbǎng （名词）shoulder: 宽肩膀 broad shoulders ∥窄肩膀 narrow shoulders

艰苦 jiānkǔ （形容词）difficult; hard: 艰苦的比赛 difficult match ∥艰苦的工作 hard work

捡 jiǎn （动词）pick up: 小女孩儿从地板上捡起自己的玩具。The little girl picked up her toy from the floor.

检查 jiǎnchá （动词）examine; check

剪刀 jiǎndāo （名词）scissors: 一把剪刀 a pair of scissors

简单 jiǎndān （形容词）simple: 简单的问题 simple question

简朴 jiǎnpǔ （形容词）simple: 简朴的生活 simple life

见 jiàn （动词）
1. see: 亲眼所见 see with one's own eyes
2. meet; see: 明天见！See you tomorrow! // 你们以前见过吗？Have you met each other before?

见面 jiànmiàn （动词）meet; see: 你们经常见面吗？Do you often see each other?

建议 jiànyì （动词）advise: 医生建议他戒烟。The doctor advised him to give up smoking.

建造 jiànzào （动词）build: 建造房屋 build a house

建筑 jiànzhù
1.（动词）build: 建筑桥梁 build a bridge

2.（名词）building: 高大的建筑 large buildings

剑 jiàn （名词）sword: 利剑 sharp sword

健康 jiànkāng
1.（名词）health: 保持健康 keep fit // 有益健康 good for health
2.（形容词）healthy: 健康食品 healthy food

渐渐 jiànjiàn （副词）little by little: 雪渐渐融化了。Little by little the snow melted.

毽子 jiànzi （名词）shuttlecock: 踢毽子 play/kick the shuttlecock

箭 jiàn （名词）arrow: 射箭 shoot an arrow

箭头 jiàntóu （名词）arrowhead

江 jiāng （名词）river: 长江 the Changjiang/Yangtze River

江河 jiānghé （名词）rivers

将军 jiāngjūn （名词）general

将来 jiānglái （名词）future: 在不久的将来 in the near future

姜 jiāng （名词）ginger: 姜汁 ginger juice

讲话 jiǎnghuà
1.（动词）speak; talk: 会上大家都

讲话了。Everybody spoke at the meeting.
2.（名词）speech; talk: 发表讲话 give a speech

奖杯 jiǎngbēi （名词）cup: 赢得奖杯 win the cup

奖牌 jiǎngpái （名词）medal: 赢得奖牌 win a medal

交 jiāo （动词）hand in: 交作业 hand in one's homework ∥ 交卷 hand in the exam paper

交警 jiāojǐng （名词）traffic police

交谈 jiāotán （动词）talk with each other; chat: 用英语交谈 talk with each other in English

交通 jiāotōng （名词）traffic: 繁忙的交通 heavy traffic ∥ 交通堵塞 traffic jam

郊游 jiāoyóu （动词）go on an outing

浇 jiāo （动词）water: 浇花 water flowers

骄傲 jiāo'ào （形容词）proud: 为…而骄傲 be proud of... ∥ 十分骄傲 as proud as a peacock

胶布 jiāobù （名词）tape: 一卷胶布 a roll of tape

胶卷 jiāojuǎn （名词）film: 一卷胶卷 a roll of film ∥ 黑白/彩色胶卷 black and white/color film

胶水 jiāoshuǐ （名词）glue: 一瓶胶水 a bottle of glue

教 jiāo （动词）teach: 教英语 teach English

教书 jiāoshū （动词）teach: 在中学教书 teach in a secondary school

焦急 jiāojí （形容词）anxious; worried: 我十分焦急。I was deeply worried.

角 jiǎo （名词）
1. horn: 牛角 ox horn
2. angle: 锐角 sharp angle ∥ 直角 right angle

角落 jiǎoluò （名词）corner: 在房间的角落 in a corner of the room

饺子 jiǎozi （名词）*jiaozi*; Chinese dumpling: 包饺子 make Chinese dumplings

百科小贴士
饺子在三国时就已出现，宋代称饺子为"角儿"，元朝称饺子为"扁食"。清朝时，出现了诸如"饺儿"、"水点心"、"煮饽饽"等有关饺子的新的称谓。饺子一般要在年三十晚上12点以前包好，待到半夜时吃，取"更岁交子"之意，"子"为"子时"，交与"饺"谐音。

脚 jiǎo （名词）foot: 一双脚 a pair of feet ∥ 赤脚 bare-footed

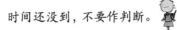

脚步 jiǎobù （名词）footstep: 沉重的脚步 heavy footsteps

脚趾 jiǎozhǐ （名词）toe: 大脚趾 big toe

搅拌 jiǎobàn （动词）mix: 把黄油和糖搅拌在一起 mix butter and sugar ∥ 搅拌机 blender

叫 jiào （动词）
1. cry; shout: 大叫一声 give a loud cry ∥ 疼得大声叫 cry out in pain
2. call: 叫警察/医生 call the police/a doctor

叫嚷 jiàorǎng （动词）shout: 大声叫嚷 shout at the top of one's voice ∥ 对着某人叫嚷 shout at somebody

轿车 jiàochē （名词）car

教科书 jiàokēshū （名词）textbook

教师 jiàoshī （名词）teacher: 尊重教师 respect teachers ∥ 大学教师 university teacher

教师节 jiàoshījié （名词）Teachers' Day: 庆祝教师节 celebrate Teachers' Day

教室 jiàoshì （名词）classroom: 打扫教室 clean the classroom ∥ 在教室里 in the classroom

教堂 jiàotáng （名词）church: 去教堂做礼拜 go to church

教学 jiàoxué （名词）teaching

教育 jiàoyù （名词）education: 基础教育 basic education ∥ 学校教育 school education

接 jiē （动词）
1. receive: 接到一封信 receive a letter ∥ 接电话 answer the phone
2. meet; welcome: 到火车站接人 meet someone at the railway station
3. catch; get hold of: 接球 catch the ball

接二连三 jiē'èr-liánsān one after another

接受 jiēshòu （动词）accept: 接受礼物 accept a gift ∥ 接受邀请 accept an invitation

街道 jiēdào （名词）street: 穿过街道 cross the street ∥ 拥挤的街道 crowded street

节目 jiémù （名词）program: 电视节目 TV program

节日 jiérì （名词）festival: 庆祝节日 celebrate a festival ∥ 传统节日 traditional festival

节约 jiéyuē （动词）save: 节约时间 save time ∥ 节约用水 save water

Judge nothing before the time.

洁白 jiébái （形容词）pure white: 洁白的雪 pure white snow

结婚 jiéhūn （动词）marry; get married

结束 jiéshù （动词）end; finish: 这个学期将在1月10日结束。This term will end on January 10.

姐姐 jiějie （名词）older sister

解答 jiědá （动词）explain; answer: 解答问题 answer questions

解释 jiěshì （动词）explain: 解释原因 explain the reason

介词 jiècí （名词）preposition

介绍 jièshào （动词）introduce: 自我介绍 introduce oneself

介意 jièyì （动词）mind: 一点儿也不介意 do not mind at all ∥我打开窗你介意吗？Do you mind if I open the window?

戒酒 jièjiǔ （动词）give up/stop drinking

戒烟 jièyān （动词）give up/stop smoking

戒指 jièzhi （名词）ring: 结婚戒指 wedding ring ∥戴戒指 wear a ring

借 jiè （动词）
1. borrow: 我可以借一下你的自行车吗？Can I borrow your bicycle?
2. lend: 他从不借钱给别人。He never lends money.

借口 jièkǒu （名词）excuse: 找借口 make an excuse

今后 jīnhòu （名词）from now on

今年 jīnnián （名词）this year

今天 jīntiān （名词）today: 今天的报纸 today's newspaper ∥今天是我的生日。Today is my birthday.

金 jīn （名词）gold: 纯金 pure gold ∥金币 gold coin ∥金项链 gold necklace

金牌 jīnpái （名词）gold medal: 获得金牌 win a gold medal

金钱 jīnqián （名词）money: 时间就是金钱。Time is money.

金秋 jīnqiū （名词）autumn; fall

用法小贴士
autumn是英国英语，fall是美国英语。

金属 jīnshǔ （名词）metal

金丝猴 jīnsīhóu （名词）golden monkey

百科小贴士
金丝猴是中国特有的猴类，其尾巴的长度和身体的长度大体相同，背部有金黄色光亮的长毛，属国家一级保护动物。

金鱼 jīnyú （名词）goldfish

金子 jīnzi （名词）gold

仅仅 jǐnjǐn （副词）only: 我仅仅迟到了3分钟。 I was only late by three minutes.

尽快 jǐnkuài （副词）as soon as possible: 请尽快回复！ Please reply as soon as possible!

尽早 jǐnzǎo （副词）as early/soon as possible: 尽早回来。 Come back as soon as possible.

紧张 jǐnzhāng（形容词）nervous; anxious: 我很紧张。 I felt very nervous.

尽头 jìntóu （名词）end: 在…的尽头 at the end of... ∥ 走到…尽头 walk to the end of...

进步 jìnbù
1.（名词）progress: 在学习上取得进步 make progress in one's study
2.（动词）improve: 他的英语进步了。 His English has improved.

进来 jìnlái （动词）come in: 进来吧！ Come in!

进入 jìnrù （动词）enter; get into: 进入大厅 enter the hall

近 jìn （形容词）close; near: 离得近 be close/near to

近代 jìndài （名词）modern times: 在近代 in modern times

近视 jìnshì （形容词）near-sighted

京剧 jīngjù （名词）Peking opera: 唱京剧 sing Peking opera ∥ 看京剧 watch Peking opera

经常 jīngcháng （副词）often: 我们经常出去吃饭。 We often eat out.

经过 jīngguò （动词）pass; go through: 这汽车经过动物园吗？ Does this bus pass the zoo?

经理 jīnglǐ （名词）manager

惊奇 jīngqí （形容词）surprised

惊讶 jīngyà （形容词）surprised: 她听到这个消息感到很惊讶。 She felt surprised at the news.

精彩 jīngcǎi （形容词）wonderful: 精彩的表演 wonderful performance

精力 jīnglì （名词）energy: 将精力用于学习 devote one's energy to study

鲸鱼 jīngyú （名词）whale: 一群鲸鱼 a school of whales

井 jǐng （名词）well: 挖井 dig a well

景色 jǐngsè （名词）scenery: 美丽的景色 beautiful scenery

警察 jǐngchá （名词）police; policeman: 女警察 policewoman

警察局 jǐngchájú （名词）police station

警车 jǐngchē （名词）police car

警卫 jǐngwèi （名词）guard

竞赛 jìngsài （名词）contest: 参加竞赛 go in for/enter a contest

敬佩 jìngpèi （动词）admire

静悄悄 jìngqiāoqiāo （形容词）very quiet

镜子 jìngzi （名词）mirror: 照镜子 look in the mirror

究竟 jiūjìng （副词）on earth: 你究竟在干什么？What on earth are you doing?

九 jiǔ （数词）nine

九月 jiǔyuè （名词）September

久 jiǔ （形容词）long; for a long time: 好久不见。Long time no see.

酒 jiǔ （名词）alcoholic drink: 白酒 spirits ∥ 啤酒 beer ∥ 葡萄酒 wine ∥ 戒酒 give up drinking

用法小贴士
不同的酒有不同的英文名称。

酒吧 jiǔbā （名词）bar

酒店 jiǔdiàn （名词）hotel: 五星级酒店 five-star hotel

旧 jiù （形容词）old; second-hand: 旧房子 old house ∥ 旧书 second-hand/old book

救护车 jiùhùchē （名词）ambulance

救命 jiùmìng （动词）save somebody's life: 大叫救命 cry out for help

舅舅 jiùjiu （名词）uncle

舅妈 jiùmā （名词）aunt

居住 jūzhù （动词）live: 在郊区居住 live in the suburbs

鞠躬 jūgōng （动词）bow: 向某人鞠躬 bow to somebody

举 jǔ （动词）lift; raise: 举起一个笨重的箱子 lift a heavy box

举办 jǔbàn （动词）hold: 举办奥运会 hold the Olympic Games ∥ 举办派对 hold a party

举例 jǔlì （动词）give an example: 举例来说 for example; for instance

举手 jǔshǒu （动词）raise one's hand; put up one's hand: 有问题请举手。Raise your hand if you have any questions.

巨大 jùdà （形容词）huge; great: 巨大的成功 great success

巨人 jùrén （名词）giant

句号 jùhào （名词）period

句型 jùxíng （名词）sentence pattern: 练习句型 practice sentence patterns

句子 jùzi （名词）sentence: 造句子 make a sentence

拒绝 jùjué （动词）refuse: 拒绝改变主意 refuse to change one's mind

俱乐部 jùlèbù （名词）club: 加入高尔夫俱乐部 join a golf club

剧院 jùyuàn （名词）theater: 去剧院看戏 go to the theater

距离 jùlí （名词）distance: 近距离 short distance ∥ 远距离 long distance

聚会 jùhuì （名词）party: 生日聚会 birthday party

聚集 jùjí （动词）gather: 广场上聚集了很多人。A large crowd gathered in the square.

卷笔刀 juǎnbǐdāo （名词）pencil sharpener

卷心菜 juǎnxīncài （名词）cabbage

决定 juédìng
1.（动词）decide; make up one's mind: 我决定去那儿。I decided to go there.
2.（名词）decision: 作出决定 make a decision

角色 juésè （名词）role; part: 扮演一个重要角色 play an important role/part

觉得 juéde （动词）
1. feel: 觉得冷 feel cold ∥ 觉得有点累 feel a bit tired
2. think; feel: 你觉得这部电影怎么样？What do you think of the film?

爵士乐 juéshìyuè （名词）jazz: 弹奏爵士乐 play jazz

百科小贴士
爵士是英语jazz的音译词。

军队 jūnduì （名词）army

军官 jūnguān （名词）officer: 陆军军官 army officer ∥ 海军军官 navy officer ∥ 空军军官 air officer

军人 jūnrén （名词）soldier

俊俏 jùnqiào （形容词）pretty: 俊俏的姑娘 a pretty girl

Kill two birds with one stone.

K

咖啡 kāfēi （名词）coffee: 请给我来两杯咖啡。Two coffees, please.

百科小贴士
咖啡是英语 coffee 的音译词。

卡 kǎ （名词）card: 电话卡 telephone card ∥ 生日卡 birthday card

卡车 kǎchē （名词）truck

用法小贴士
lorry 是英国英语，truck 是美国英语。

卡拉 OK kǎlā OK （名词）karaoke: 唱卡拉 OK sing karaoke ∥ 卡拉 OK 厅 karaoke bar

百科小贴士
卡拉 OK 是 karaoke 的音译词。

卡片 kǎpiàn （名词）card

卡通 kǎtōng （名词）cartoon

百科小贴士
卡通是英语 cartoon 的音译词。

开 kāi （动词）
1. open: 开门 open the door
2. turn on: 开电视 turn on the TV
3. drive: 开车 drive a car

开会 kāihuì （动词）attend a meeting

开火 kāihuǒ （动词）open fire; fire: 向敌人开火 fire at the enemy

开始 kāishǐ （动词）begin; start: 9 点开始上课。Class begins at nine o'clock.

开水 kāishuǐ （名词）boiled water

开头 kāitóu
1. （动词）begin; start: 以大写字母开头 begin with a capital letter
2. （名词）beginning; start: 这只是故事的开头。This is only the beginning of the story.

开玩笑 kāiwánxiào （动词）joke; make a joke: 我只是在开玩笑。I was only joking.

开心 kāixīn （形容词）happy: 我一点儿也不开心。I'm not happy at all. ∥ 玩得很开心 have a good time

开学 kāixué （动词）school begins: 学校 9 月 1 日开学。School begins on September 1.

看 kān （动词）look after; take care of: 看孩子 look after a child

292

一石二鸟。

看管 kānguǎn （动词）look after:
看管行李 look after the luggage

看家 kānjiā （动词）look after
the house

砍 kǎn （动词）cut: 砍树 cut
down a tree

看 kàn （动词）
1. see; watch; look at: 看电视
watch TV ∥ 看电影 see a film ∥ 看
比赛 watch a game
2. read: 看书 read a book

看病 kànbìng （动词）see a
doctor; go to a doctor

看法 kànfǎ （名词）view;
opinion: 你的看法如何？What's
your opinion?

看见 kànjiàn （动词）see: 我看不
见你。I can't see you.

看起来 kànqǐlái （动词）seem;
look like: 他看起来很高兴。He
seems very happy. ∥ 看起来要下
雨了。It looks like rain.

看望 kànwàng （动词）visit; see:
看望病人 visit a patient

康乃馨 kāngnǎixīn （名词）
carnation

百科小贴士
康乃馨是英语carnation的音译词。它象
征慈祥、温馨、真挚、无价的母爱，是母
亲节送给母亲的最好花卉.

考 kǎo （动词）take an exam: 我
们明天要考英语。We have an
English exam tomorrow.

考试 kǎoshì
1.（动词）take an exam
2.（名词）exam; test: 参加考试
take an exam ∥ 期末考试 final
exam ∥ 通过考试 pass an exam

烤 kǎo （动词）bake; roast: 烤蛋
糕 bake a cake

烤鸭 kǎoyā （名词）roast duck:
北京烤鸭 Beijing roast duck

靠 kào （动词）lean against: 靠
在墙上 lean against the wall

科学 kēxué （名词）science: 科
学技术 science and technology

科学家 kēxuéjiā （名词）scientist

壳 ké （名词）shell: 花生壳
peanut shell ∥ 鸡蛋壳 eggshell

咳嗽 késou （动词）cough: 咳嗽
得很厉害 cough badly

可爱 kě'ài （形容词）lovable;
lovely: 活泼可爱 lively and lovable

可口 kěkǒu （形容词）delicious:
可口的饭菜 delicious meal

可能 kěnéng
1.（形容词）possible: 这是可能的。
It's possible.

293

2.（副词）may; might: 他可能会来。He may come.

可怕 kěpà （形容词）terrible: 可怕的梦 a terrible dream

可是 kěshì （连词）but; however: 这件衣服很漂亮，可是太贵。This dress is very nice, but too expensive.

可笑 kěxiào （形容词）funny: 吉姆戴那顶帽子很可笑。Jim looks funny in that cap.

可以 kěyǐ
1.（动词）may; can: 我可以进来吗？May I come in? // 你可以随时来。You can come any time.
2.（形容词）not bad: 他的英语学得还可以。He's not bad at English.

渴 kě （形容词）thirsty: 感到口渴 feel thirsty // 又饥又渴 be both hungry and thirsty

克隆 kèlóng （动词）clone: 克隆羊 cloned sheep // 克隆技术 cloning technology

刻 kè （名词）quarter: 现在是5点差一刻。It is a quarter to five now.

刻苦 kèkǔ （形容词）hardworking: 刻苦学习 study hard // 刻苦的学生 a hardworking student

客气 kèqi （形容词）polite: 王先生对人很客气。Mr. Wang is very polite to people.

客人 kèrén （名词）guest

客厅 kètīng （名词）sitting room

课 kè （名词）
1. class: 一堂数学课 a math class // 上课 have a class // 今天上午有4节课。There are four classes this morning.
2. lesson: 第一课 Lesson One

课本 kèběn （名词）textbook: 英语课本 English textbook

课程 kèchéng （名词）course: 通过一门课程 pass a course // 我们这学期有6门课程。We have six courses this term.

课程表 kèchéngbiǎo （名词）school timetable

课间休息 kèjiān xiūxi （名词）break: 在课间休息的时候 during the break

课堂 kètáng （名词）classroom; schoolroom: 课堂作业 classroom work // 课堂讨论 classroom discussion

课文 kèwén （名词）text: 背诵课文 recite a text // 读课文 read a text

课桌 kèzhuō （名词）classroom desk: 课桌椅 classroom desks and chairs

肯定 kěndìng
1.（动词）be sure: 你肯定吗？ Are you sure?
2.（副词）certainly: 我肯定不会骗你。 I certainly won't cheat you.

坑 kēng （名词）hole: 挖一个坑 dig a hole

空 kōng （形容词）empty: 空盒子 empty box

空军 kōngjūn （名词）air force

空气 kōngqì （名词）air: 新鲜空气 fresh air

空中 kōngzhōng （名词）air: 在空中 in the air

孔雀 kǒngquè （名词）peacock: 孔雀舞 peacock dance ∥快看！孔雀开屏了！ Look! The peacock is spreading its tail!

孔子 kǒngzǐ （名词）Confucius

百科小贴士
孔子是春秋末期思想家、政治家、教育家，儒家学说的创始人，"孔孟之道" 中的 "孔" 即孔子.

恐惧 kǒngjù （形容词）scared; frightened: 感到恐惧 feel frightened

恐龙 kǒnglóng （名词）dinosaur

恐怕 kǒngpà （副词）
1. for fear of: 我恐怕要迟到了。 I am afraid that I'll be late.
2. perhaps: 恐怕火车要晚点了。 Perhaps the train will be late.

空儿 kòngr （名词）spare time: 我没空儿。 I don't have time.

空闲 kòngxián （名词）free time: 在空闲时间 in one's spare time

口袋 kǒudai （名词）pocket: 外衣口袋 coat pocket ∥口袋书 pocket book

口渴 kǒukě （形容词）thirsty: 感到口渴 feel thirsty

口香糖 kǒuxiāngtáng （名词）chewing gum: 嚼口香糖 chew gum

口信 kǒuxìn （名词）message: 请给汤姆带个口信。 Please take a message to Tom.

口语 kǒuyǔ （名词）spoken language: 英语口语 spoken English

扣子 kòuzi （名词）button: 扣子松了。 A button has come loose.

枯燥 kūzào （形容词）boring: 枯燥的讲座 boring lecture ∥感到很枯燥 feel bored

哭 kū （动词）cry: 哭笑不得 do not know whether to cry or to laugh

哭鼻子 kūbízi （动词）cry

窟窿 kūlong （名词）hole: 冰窟窿 ice hole

苦 kǔ （形容词）bitter: 味道苦 taste bitter

裤子 kùzi （名词）trousers; pants: 一条裤子 a pair of trousers

用法小贴士
trousers是英国英语，pants是美国英语.

酷 kù （形容词）cool: 吉姆戴上太阳镜很酷。Jim looks cool in his sunglasses.

夸奖 kuājiǎng （动词）praise: 老师经常夸奖学生。The teacher often praises her students.

块 kuài （量词）
1. piece: 一块面包 a piece of bread ∥ 一块肥皂 a bar of soap
2. yuan: 100块钱 one hundred yuan

快 kuài
1.（形容词）fast; quick: 跑得快 run fast
2.（副词）soon: 他很快就到。He'll soon be here.
3.（动词）hurry up: 快！我们已经迟到了！Hurry up! We're already late!

快餐 kuàicān （名词）fast food: 西式快餐 Western fast food

快活 kuàihuo （形容词）happy: 感到快活 feel happy

快乐 kuàilè （形容词）happy: 快乐的童年 happy childhood ∥ 生日快乐！Happy birthday!

筷子 kuàizi （名词）chopsticks: 一双筷子 a pair of chopsticks

宽 kuān （形容词）wide; broad: 七尺宽 seven feet wide

宽带 kuāndài （名词）broadband: 宽带网 broadband network

筐 kuāng （名词）basket: 废纸筐 wastepaper basket ∥ 购物筐 shopping basket ∥ 自行车筐 bicycle basket

狂 kuáng （形容词）mad: 发狂 go mad ∥ 狂人 madman

昆虫 kūnchóng （名词）insect

困 kùn （形容词）sleepy: 每天晚上9点钟我就困了。I get sleepy at nine o'clock every night.

困难 kùnnan
1.（形容词）difficult: 困难的局面 a difficult situation
2.（名词）difficulty: 克服困难 overcome difficulty ∥ 遇到困难 get into difficulties

Love me, love my dog.

L

垃圾 lājī （名词）rubbish: 清扫垃圾 clean away rubbish

垃圾食品 lājī shípǐn （名词）junk food: 垃圾食品有害健康。Junk food is bad for your health.

垃圾桶 lājītǒng （名词）trashcan: 请将废纸扔进垃圾桶。Please throw waste paper into the trashcan.

垃圾邮件 lājī yóujiàn （名词）junk mail

拉 lā （动词）pull: 拉开门 pull the door open

喇叭 lǎba （名词）trumpet: 吹喇叭 blow a trumpet

蜡烛 làzhú （名词）candle: 点蜡烛 light a candle ∥生日蜡烛 birthday candles

辣 là （形容词）hot: 辣椒 hot pepper ∥这道菜太辣了。This dish is too hot.

来 lái （动词）come: 公共汽车来了！Here comes the bus.

来自 láizì （动词）come from: 这些名画来自意大利。These famous paintings come from Italy.

蓝色 lánsè
1.（形容词）blue: 蓝色的天空 blue sky
2.（名词）blue: 蓝色是我最喜欢的颜色。Blue is my favorite color.

篮球 lánqiú （名词）basketball: 篮球运动员 basketball player ∥打篮球 play basketball ∥篮球筐 basketball basket

篮子 lánzi （名词）basket: 菜篮子 vegetable basket

懒 lǎn （形容词）lazy: 懒虫 lazybones ∥懒学生 lazy student

狼 láng （名词）wolf: 狼狗 wolf dog ∥一群狼 a pack of wolves

朗读 lǎngdú （动词）read aloud: 朗读课文 read aloud the text

浪费 làngfèi （动词）waste: 不要浪费水。Don't waste water.

劳动 láodòng
1.（名词）work; labor: 体力劳动 physical labor
2.（动词）work: 在地里劳动 work in the field

劳动节 láodòngjié （名词）International Labor Day; May Day

劳驾 láojià （动词）excuse me:
劳驾，请问洗手间在哪儿？Excuse
me, where is the rest room?

老 lǎo
1.（形容词）old: 变老 grow old ∥
老婆婆 old lady
2.（形容词）old: 老朋友 old
friend
3.（副词）always: 他老是犯错。
He always makes mistakes.

老板 lǎobǎn （名词）boss: 大老
板 big boss

老大妈 lǎodàmā （名词）granny;
old lady

老大爷 lǎodàye （名词）grandpa;
old man

老公 lǎogōng （名词）husband

老虎 lǎohǔ （名词）tiger

老家 lǎojiā （名词）hometown

老婆 lǎopo （名词）wife

老人 lǎorén （名词）an old person; old people: 尊敬老人 respect
old people

老师 lǎoshī （名词）teacher: 英语
老师 English teacher

老鼠 lǎoshǔ （名词）mouse; rat
用法小贴士
作宠物饲养的小老鼠用mouse一词；像垃
圾堆边那种又大又脏令人厌恶的老鼠用rat
一词。

老太太 lǎotàitai （名词）old lady

老头儿 lǎotóur （名词）old man:
白胡子老头儿 a white-bearded
old man

老外 lǎowài （名词）foreigner

姥姥 lǎolao （名词）grandmother;
grandma
用法小贴士
姥姥或外婆指妈妈的妈妈，奶奶指爸爸的
妈妈，英语却没有这种区别。如果一定要
区分，可以说maternal grandmother
（姥姥），paternal grandmother（奶奶）。

姥爷 lǎoye （名词）grandfather;
grandpa
用法小贴士
maternal grandfather（姥爷），paternal
grandfather（爷爷）。

乐 lè
1.（形容词）happy: 他乐坏了。
He's extremely happy.
2.（动词）laugh: 你乐什么呀？
What are you laughing at?

乐趣 lèqù （名词）pleasure; joy:
生活的乐趣 the joys of life

乐意 lèyì （动词）be willing; be ready: 我们很乐意帮忙。We're willing to help.

乐园 lèyuán （名词）amusement park; playground: 迪斯尼乐园 Disneyland // 儿童乐园 children's playground

雷 léi （名词）thunder

雷达 léidá （名词）radar

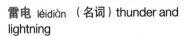
百科小贴士
雷达是英语radar的音译词。

雷电 léidiàn （名词）thunder and lightning

雷雨 léiyǔ （名词）thunderstorm

垒球 lěiqiú （名词）softball: 打垒球 play softball

百科小贴士
垒球多为女子运动项目，与棒球相比，所使用的球较大且软。

泪水 lèishuǐ （名词）tear: 擦去泪水 wipe away one's tears // 忍住泪水 keep one's tears back

类 lèi （名词）kind: 人类 human kind // 同类的动物 animals of the same kind

类型 lèixíng （名词）kind; sort: 我不喜欢那种类型的人。I don't like that kind of people.

累 lèi （形容词）tired: 你累不累? Are you tired?

冷 lěng （形容词）cold: 天渐渐冷起来了。It's getting colder.

冷饮 lěngyǐn （名词）cold drink

冷战 lěngzhàn （名词）cold war

离开 líkāi （动词）leave: 请离开这里！Please leave!

梨 lí （名词）pear: 梨树 pear tree

礼貌 lǐmào （名词）manners: 没有礼貌 have no manners; be impolite

礼品 lǐpǐn （名词）gift; present: 礼品店 gift shop

礼堂 lǐtáng （名词）hall

礼物 lǐwù （名词）present; gift: 收到一份礼物 receive a gift

里边 lǐbian （名词）inside: 老师在里边。The teacher is inside.

理发 lǐfà （动词）get a haircut; have one's hair cut

理发店 lǐfàdiàn （名词）hairdresser's

理发师 lǐfàshī （名词）hairdresser

理解 lǐjiě （动词）understand: 难以理解 difficult to understand // 感谢你的理解。Thank you for your understanding.

理想 lǐxiǎng （名词）dream: 我的理想是当一名宇航员。My dream is to be an astronaut.

历史 lìshǐ （名词）history: 有着悠久历史的国家 a country with a long history

历险 lìxiǎn （动词）have adventures

立即 lìjí （副词）immediately; at once: 放学后立即回家 go home immediately after school

立刻 lìkè （副词）immediately; right away: 我立刻就来。I'm coming right away.

利用 lìyòng （动词）use; make use of: 利用一切机会 make use of every opportunity

例如 lìrú （动词）take for example

例子 lìzi （名词）example: 举几个例子 give some examples

联欢 liánhuān （动词）have a party: 师生联欢 a student-teacher party

聊天 liáotiān （动词）chat: 聊天室 chat room

了解 liǎojiě （动词）know; understand: 老师很了解我。The teacher knows me well.

猎狗 liègǒu （名词）hunting dog

猎人 lièrén （名词）hunter

邻居 línjū （名词）neighbor: 隔壁邻居 next-door neighbor

铃 líng （名词）bell: 铃响了。There goes the bell.

零 líng （数词）zero: 二零零六年 the year 2006 // 比分是零比二。The score is zero to two.

零花钱 línghuāqián （名词）pocket money

零钱 língqián （名词）change: 零钱不用找了。Keep the change, please.

领带 lǐngdài （名词）tie

领导 lǐngdǎo
1.（名词）leader: 一个很有能力的领导 an able leader
2.（动词）lead: 领导和平运动 lead a peace movement

领袖 lǐngxiù （名词）leader: 伟大的领袖 a great leader

另外 lìngwài （代词）other; another: 另外一个人 another person

留 liú （动词）stay: 独自留在家里 stay at home alone

留神 liúshén （动词）be careful; watch out: 留神脚下！Watch your step!

留学 liúxué （动词）study abroad: 在英国留学 study in Britain // 留学生 students studying abroad; overseas students

用法小贴士
students studying abroad 指本国学生在国外学习，overseas students 指到本国学习的外国学生。

留言 liúyán （动词）leave a message: 妈妈不在家。你想留言吗？Mom's not in. May I take a message?

流动 liúdòng （动词）flow: 河水流动很慢。The river flows very slowly.

流感 liúgǎn （名词）flu: 得流感 get the flu // 禽流感 bird flu

流利 liúlì （形容词）fluent: 英语说得很流利 speak English fluently

流露 liúlù （动词）show: 他的脸上流露出失望的神情。His face showed his disappointment.

流水 liúshuǐ （名词）flowing water

流星 liúxīng （名词）meteor: 流星雨 meteor shower

流行 liúxíng （动词）be popular: 流行歌曲 popular songs // 他的歌现在很流行。His songs are very popular these days.

六 liù （数词）six

六月 liùyuè （名词）June

龙 lóng （名词）dragon: 龙王 Dragon King

龙船 lóngchuán （名词）dragon boat: 划龙船 row a dragon boat

聋 lóng （形容词）deaf: 他一只耳朵聋了。He's deaf in one ear.

聋哑 lóngyǎ （形容词）deaf-mute: 聋哑儿童 deaf-mute children

笼子 lóngzi （名词）cage: 鸟笼子 bird cage

楼 lóu （名词）
1. building: 教学楼 classroom building // 办公楼 office building
2. floor; story: 一楼 ground floor // 二楼 first floor

楼房 lóufáng （名词）building: 一座八层高的楼房 an eight-story building

楼梯 lóutī （名词）stairs: 爬楼梯 climb the stairs

搂 lǒu （动词）hug; hold in one's arms: 妈妈把小女孩搂在怀里。The mother held her little girl in her arms.

陆地 lùdì （名词）land: 地球大约仅有1/4的面积是陆地。Only about one-fourth of Earth is land.

录 lù （动词）record: 录歌曲 record songs // 把他的话录下来。Record what he has to say.

录像 lùxiàng （名词）video: 录像带 videotape; video // 看录像 watch a video

录像机 lùxiàngjī （名词）video recorder

录音 lùyīn （动词）record

录音机 lùyīnjī （名词）tape recorder

鹿 lù （名词）deer

路 lù （名词）road; way: 马路 street // 问路 ask the way // 指路 show the way

路过 lùguò （动词）pass by/through: 我每天都要路过那家书店。I pass by the bookstore every day. // 她上周路过上海。She passed through Shanghai last week.

路上 lùshang （名词）
1. on the road: 路上停着一辆车。There is car parking on the road.
2. on the way: 在回家的路上 on the way home

露水 lùshuǐ （名词）dew

驴 lǘ （名词）donkey

旅馆 lǚguǎn （名词）hotel: 住旅馆 stay in a hotel // 三星级旅馆 three-star hotel

旅客 lǚkè （名词）passenger: 火车旅客 train passengers

旅行 lǚxíng （动词）travel; take a journey: 环球旅行 travel around the world // 旅行包 travel bag

旅游 lǚyóu （动词）travel: 到全国各地旅游 travel around the country

律师 lǜshī （名词）lawyer

绿 lǜ （形容词）green: 淡绿 light green // 深绿 dark green

绿茶 lǜchá （名词）green tea

绿灯 lǜdēng （名词）green light: 要等到绿灯才可以过马路。You shall not cross the road until the light turns green.

绿卡 lǜkǎ （名词）green card

百科小贴士
绿卡指美国授予外国人的永久居住权，因其在持有人护照上的标识为绿色，故称绿卡。

绿色 lǜsè
1.（形容词）green: 绿色的田野 green field
2.（名词）green

绿色食品 lǜsèshípǐn （名词）organic food

乱 luàn （形容词）untidy; in a mess: 屋子很乱。The room is in a mess.

轮 lún （动词）take turns: 轮到我了。It's my turn.

轮船 lúnchuán （名词）ship: 乘坐轮船 take a ship

轮流 lúnliú （动词）by turns; in turn: 轮流休息 take a rest by turns

轮胎 lúntāi （名词）tire: 轮胎瘪了 have a flat tire

轮椅 lúnyǐ （名词）wheelchair: 推轮椅 push a wheelchair ∥ 坐轮椅 use a wheelchair

萝卜 luóbo （名词）radish

骡子 luózi （名词）mule

骆驼 luòtuo （名词）camel

落 luò （动词）
1. fall; drop: 树叶落了。The leaves have fallen from the trees.
2. set: 太阳从西方落下。The sun sets in the west.

落后 luòhòu （动词）fall behind: 在学习上落后 fall behind in one's study

M

妈妈 māma （名词）mother; mom

麻烦 máfan
1.（名词）trouble: 遇到麻烦 get into trouble
2.（动词）trouble: 麻烦某人 trouble somebody

麻雀 máquè （名词）sparrow

马 mǎ （名词）horse: 骑马 ride a horse

马车 mǎchē （名词）carriage: 赶马车 drive a carriage

马大哈 mǎdàhā （名词）careless person

马虎 mǎhu （形容词）careless

马拉松 mǎlāsōng （名词）marathon: 参加马拉松赛跑 run a marathon

马路 mǎlù （名词）road; street: 过马路 cross a road

马上 mǎshàng （副词）at once; right away: 我马上回来。I'll be back right away.

马戏 mǎxì （名词）circus: 昨天我们去看了场马戏表演。We went to the circus yesterday.

马戏团 mǎxìtuán （名词）circus

蚂蚁 mǎyǐ （名词）ant: 像热锅上的蚂蚁 like a cat on hot bricks

买 mǎi （动词）buy: 我花了300元买了这辆自行车。I bought this bike for 300 yuan.

买单 mǎidān （动词）pay the bill: 谁买单呀？Who will pay the bill?

麦克风 màikèfēng （名词）microphone; mike: 对着麦克风唱歌 sing to a microphone

麦子 màizi （名词）wheat: 播种麦子 sow wheat ∥ 收割麦子 harvest wheat

卖 mài （动词）sell: 卖菜 sell vegetables ∥ 卖光 sell out

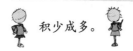
馒头 mántou （名词）steamed bread; *mantou*

百科小贴士
*mantou*是馒头的拼音。

满 mǎn （形容词）full; filled: 杯子里装满了水。The cup is full of water.

满分 mǎnfēn （名词）full marks: 得满分 get full marks

满意 mǎnyì （动词）be satisfied: 对…感到满意 be satisfied with/by...

漫长 màncháng （形容词）very long: 漫长的岁月 long years

漫画 mànhuà （名词）cartoon: 画漫画 draw a cartoon ∥漫画书 comic book

慢 màn （形容词）slow: 他跑得慢。He is a slow runner. ∥我的手表慢了15分钟。My watch is fifteen minutes slow.

芒果 mángguǒ （名词）mango

百科小贴士
芒果是英语mango的音译词。

忙 máng （形容词）busy: 我忙着做作业。I am busy with/doing my homework. ∥他正忙着回信。He is busy answering letters.

忙碌 mánglù （形容词）busy

盲人 mángrén （名词）blind person: 盲人学校 blind school

猫 māo （名词）cat; kitty; kitten

用法小贴士
kitty是儿语，kitten指小猫。

毛 máo （名词）hair

毛笔 máobǐ （名词）Chinese writing brush

毛病 máobìng （名词）trouble: 我的自行车出毛病了。There is something wrong with my bike.

毛巾 máojīn （名词）towel: 洗脸毛巾 hand towel ∥洗澡毛巾 bath towel

毛衣 máoyī （名词）sweater

帽子 màozi （名词）hat; cap: 戴上帽子 put on a hat/cap ∥戴着帽子 wear a hat/cap ∥摘下帽子 take off one's hat/cap

没有 méiyǒu （动词）do not have; there is not: 我没有零花钱。I don't have any pocket money. ∥教室里没有学生。There isn't any student in the classroom.

玫瑰 méigui （名词）rose: 一束玫瑰 a bunch of roses ∥红玫瑰 red roses

眉毛 méimao （名词）eyebrow: 画眉毛 draw one's eyebrows with an eyebrow pencil

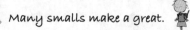
煤 méi （名词）coal: 无烟煤 smokeless coal

煤矿 méikuàng （名词）coal mine

煤气 méiqì （名词）gas: 打开/关上煤气 turn on/off the gas // 煤气灶 gas stove

每 měi （代词）every; each; per: 以每小时100公里的速度 at the speed of 100 km per hour // 这药每天吃3次。Take this medicine three times a day.

每次 měicì （副词）every time; each time

每天 měitiān （副词）every day; each day

美 měi （形容词）beautiful: 多美的风景！What a beautiful sight!

美国 měiguó （名词）America; United States of America; U.S.: 美国英语 American English // 美国人 American // 美国在北美洲。The United States is in North America.

美好 měihǎo （形容词）fine; good; happy: 过着美好的生活 lead a happy life

美丽 měilì （形容词）beautiful; pretty: 美丽如画 as pretty as a picture

美人 měirén （名词）beauty: 睡美人 Sleeping Beauty

美术 měishù （名词）fine arts: 美术馆 art museum

美元 měiyuán （名词）American dollar

妹妹 mèimei （名词）younger sister

门 mén （名词）door; gate: 开/关门 open/close the door // 敲门 knock at the door

门铃 ménlíng （名词）doorbell: 按门铃 ring the doorbell

梦 mèng
1.（名词）dream: 做梦 have a dream
2.（动词）dream: 梦见 dream about

梦话 mènghuà （名词）sleep-talking: 说梦话 talk in one's sleep

梦想 mèngxiǎng
1.（名词）dream: 梦想成真。A dream has come true.
2.（动词）dream of: 我梦想成为一名教师。I dream of becoming a teacher.

迷 mí （名词）fan: 体育迷 sports fan

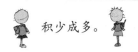

迷宫 mígōng （名词）maze: 穿过迷宫 go through a maze

迷路 mílù （动词）lose one's way; get lost: 恐怕我们迷路了。I'm afraid we've lost our way.

迷你裙 mínǐqún （名词）mini-skirt

百科小贴士
迷你是英语 mini 的音译词。

谜语 míyǔ （名词）riddle: 猜谜语 solve a riddle

米饭 mǐfàn （名词）rice: 一碗米饭 a bowl of rice ∥ 我们晚饭吃鱼和米饭。We're having fish and rice for supper.

秘密 mìmì （名词）secret: 保守秘密 keep a secret ∥ 泄露秘密 let out a secret

密码 mìmǎ （名词）password; PIN: 输入密码 enter the password

百科小贴士
PIN 是 personal identification number（个人识别号码）的缩写，指银行卡的个人密码。

蜜 mì （名词）honey: 酿蜜 make honey

蜜蜂 mìfēng （名词）bee

蜜月 mìyuè （名词）honeymoon

绵羊 miányáng （名词）sheep

棉花 miánhua （名词）cotton: 种棉花 grow cotton ∥ 摘棉花 pick cotton

棉花糖 miánhuātáng （名词）cotton candy

免费 miǎnfèi （动词）be free: 午餐免费。The lunch is free.

面包 miànbāo （名词）bread: 一片面包 a piece/slice of bread ∥ 烤面包 bake/toast bread

面粉 miànfěn （名词）flour: 把面粉和鸡蛋混合起来 mix flour with eggs

面条 miàntiáo （名词）noodle: 煮面条 cook noodles

面子 miànzi （名词）face: 保全面子 save face ∥ 丢面子 lose face

喵 miāo （拟声词）meow; mew: 猫在喵喵叫。The cat is mewing.

用法小贴士
meow 指猫引起注意或发出警告的叫声，mew 指小猫的叫声或猫不高兴时的叫声。

秒 miǎo （名词）second: 3分14秒 three minutes fourteen seconds

秒针 miǎozhēn （名词）second hand

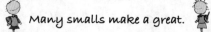

妙 miào （形容词）wonderful: 妙极了！That's wonderful!

灭 miè （动词）go out: 火灭了。The fire went out.

灭火 mièhuǒ （动词）put out a fire

灭亡 mièwáng （动词）become extinct; be wiped out

民歌 míngē （名词）folk song

民族 mínzú （名词）
1. nation: 民族文化 national culture
2. ethnic group: 少数民族 minority ethnic group

名 míng
1. （名词）name; given name: 名和姓 first name and surname
2. （形容词）famous: 名画 famous paintings

名词 míngcí （名词）noun

名单 míngdān （名词）name list

名牌 míngpái （名词）famous brand

名人 míngrén （名词）famous person

名著 míngzhù （名词）classics

名字 míngzi （名词）name; first name and surname: （给某人）起名字 give a name (to somebody)

明白 míngbai （动词）know; understand: 你明白了吗？Do you understand?

明亮 míngliàng （形容词）bright: 明亮的教室 a bright classroom

明年 míngnián （名词）next year

明天 míngtiān （名词）tomorrow: 明天晚上 tomorrow evening

明信片 míngxìnpiàn （名词）post-card: 寄明信片 send a postcard

明星 míngxīng （名词）star: 电影明星 film star

命 mìng （名词）life: 救命 save somebody's life ∥ 丧命 lose one's life

命令 mìnglìng
1. （动词）order: 警察命令司机停车。The policeman ordered the driver to stop.
2. （名词）order: 听从命令 follow orders

命名 mìngmíng （动词）name; give a name: 新船还没有命名。The new ship hasn't been named yet.

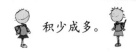
摸 mō （动词）feel; touch: 她轻轻地摸了一下婴儿。She touched the baby gently.

模范 mófàn （名词）model; example: 模范学生 model student

模特 mótè （名词）model
百科小贴士
模特是英语model的音译词。

模型 móxíng （名词）model: 做飞机模型 make a model plane

摩登 módēng （形容词）modern
百科小贴士
摩登是英语modern的音译词。

摩托车 mótuōchē （名词）moped; motorbike: 骑摩托车 ride a moped
百科小贴士
摩托是英语motor的音译词。

蘑菇 mógu （名词）mushroom: 采蘑菇 pick mushrooms

魔术 móshù （名词）magic: 变魔术 perform magic // 魔术师 magician

陌生人 mòshēngrén （名词）stranger

墨 mò （名词）Chinese ink

墨绿 mòlǜ （名词）dark green

墨镜 mòjìng （名词）sunglasses; dark glasses: 戴墨镜 wear sunglasses

墨水 mòshuǐ （名词）ink: 一瓶红墨水 a bottle of red ink

默默 mòmò （副词）quietly; in silence: 默默地坐着 sit in silence

默写 mòxiě （动词）write from memory: 默写生词 write out the new words from memory

某人 mǒurén （名词）someone; somebody

母鸡 mǔjī （名词）hen: 母鸡下蛋啦！The hen has laid an egg!

母牛 mǔniú （名词）cow

母亲 mǔqīn （名词）mother: 慈爱的母亲 a loving mother

母语 mǔyǔ （名词）mother tongue; native language: 说母语 speak one's mother tongue

木柴 mùchái （名词）wood: 劈木柴 chop wood

木匠 mùjiàng （名词）carpenter

木乃伊 mùnǎiyī （名词）mummy
百科小贴士
木乃伊是古代埃及人用防腐剂、香料等处理后保存下来的不会腐烂的尸体。

木偶 mù'ǒu （名词）puppet: 木偶戏 puppet show

木头 mùtou （名词）wood; log: 一块木头 a piece of wood ∥ 木头椅子 wooden chair

目标 mùbiāo （名词）goal: 生活目标 goals in life

目前 mùqián （名词）present moment; now: 到目前为止 so far

沐浴 mùyù （动词）take a bath

牧童 mùtóng （名词）shepherd boy

牧羊犬 mùyángquǎn （名词）sheepdog

牧羊人 mùyángrén （名词）shepherd

N

拿 ná （动词）hold; take: 谁拿走了我的帽子？ Who's taken my hat?

拿出 náchū （动词）take out:从口袋里拿出票 take out the ticket from the pocket

哪个 nǎge （代词）which; which one: 哪个最好？ Which one is the best?

哪里 nǎli （代词）where: 你刚才去哪里了？ Where have you been?

哪儿 nǎr （代词）where: 你在哪儿看见他了？ Where did you see him?

哪些 nǎxiē （代词）which; what: 哪些是你的？ Which ones are yours?

那 nà （代词）that: 那本书 that book

那个 nàge （代词）that: 那个比这个好。 That one is better than this one.

那里 nàli （代词）there: 在那里 over there // 去那里 go there

那么 nàme （代词）like that; so: 简是那么喜欢她的小猫。 Jane likes her cat so much.

那些 nàxiē （代词）those: 那些是什么？ What are those?

那样 nàyàng （代词）like that; of that kind: 你不能那样对我！ You can't treat me like that!

纳闷 nàmèn （动词）feel puzzled: 这事让我纳闷。 I'm puzzled by this.

奶 nǎi （名词）milk: 喝奶 drink milk

奶茶 nǎichá （名词）tea with milk

百科小贴士
奶茶指掺了砖茶的牛奶、羊奶或马奶，是蒙古族和藏族地区常见的饮品。

奶粉 nǎifěn （名词）milk powder: 冲杯奶粉 make a cup of milk with milk powder

奶酪 nǎilào （名词）cheese: 一块奶酪 a piece of cheese // 奶酪蛋糕 cheese cake

奶奶 nǎinai （名词）grandmother; grandma

麻烦没找你，就别自找麻烦。

奶牛 nǎiniú （名词）cow: 奶牛场 dairy farm

奶油 nǎiyóu （名词）cream: 奶油蛋糕 cream cake ∥ 奶油巧克力 chocolate cream

耐心 nàixīn （形容词）patient: 对…有耐心 be patient with... ∥ 耐心等待 wait patiently

男孩子 nánháizi （名词）boy: 淘气的男孩子 a naughty boy

男朋友 nánpéngyou （名词）boyfriend

男人 nánrén （名词）man

男生 nánshēng （名词）schoolboy; male student: 我们班有20个男生。There are twenty boys in our class.

男性 nánxìng （名词）male

男子汉 nánzǐhàn （名词）man

南 nán （名词）south: 朝南 face south ∥ 南风 south wind

南方 nánfāng （名词）south: 中国南方 the south of China ∥ 在南方 in the south ∥ 南方人 southerner

南瓜 nánguā （名词）pumpkin: 南瓜子 pumpkin seed ∥ 蜡烛放在南瓜里边。 pumpkin light (candle placed inside a pumpkin)

南极 nánjí （名词）South Pole

南极洲 nánjízhōu （名词）Antarctica

南美洲 nánměizhōu （名词）South America

难 nán（形容词）difficult; hard: 很难在一天内完成这项任务。It is difficult to finish the task in one day.

难过 nánguò （形容词）sad; sorry: 感到难过 feel sorry

难看 nánkàn （形容词）bad-looking; ugly: 这衣服真难看！ What an ugly dress!

难受 nánshòu （形容词）
1. uncomfortable; ill: 感到难受 feel uncomfortable
2. sad; sorry; unhappy: 他考试没及格，心里很难受。He felt very unhappy because he had failed the exam.

恼火 nǎohuǒ（形容词）angry: 学生没完成作业，老师很恼火。The teacher was angry because the students did not finish their homework.

脑袋 nǎodai （名词）head: 耷拉着脑袋 hang one's head

脑筋 nǎojīn （名词）brains; mind; head: 动脑筋 use one's brains/head

闹哄哄 nàohōnghōng （形容词）noisy: 孩子们闹哄哄的。The children were noisy.

闹钟 nàozhōng（名词）alarm clock: 把闹钟定到早晨6点 set the alarm clock for 6 a.m. // 闹钟在7点响了。The alarm clock went off at seven o'clock.

内 nèi （名词）inside; within: 几天之内 within a few days

内部 nèibù （名词）inside

内疚 nèijiù （形容词）guilty: 感到内疚 feel guilty

内心 nèixīn （名词）heart: 发自内心 come from one's heart // 内心深处 deep in one's heart

能 néng （动词）
1. can; be able to: 能读会写 be able to read and write
2. can/could please: 你能告诉我几点了吗? Could you tell me the time?

能够 nénggòu （动词）can; be able to: 我能够照顾自己了。I can take care of myself.

能力 nénglì（名词）ability: 提高能力 improve one's ability // 阅读能力 reading ability

能源 néngyuán （名词）energy: 节约能源 save energy

泥 ní （名词）mud

泥巴 níba （名词）mud

泥土 nítǔ （名词）earth; soil: 一把泥土 a handful of soil

你 nǐ （代词）you

你们 nǐmen（代词）you

年 nián （名词）year: 新的一年 a new year// 在年底 at the end of the year

年代 niándài （名词）age: 在和平年代 in times of peace // 在90年代 in the nineties

年级 niánjí（名词）grade; year: 二年级小学生 second-year pupils // 我在五年级二班。I'm in Class Two, Grade Five.

年纪 niánjì （名词）age: 年纪一样大 be of the same age // 你多大年纪? How old are you?

年龄 niánlíng （名词）age: 入学年龄 starting-school age

年轻 niánqīng （形容词）young: 年轻人 young people ∥ 看起来年轻 look young

念 niàn （动词）read: 念一篇文章 read an article

念书 niànshū （动词）study: 我在第一中学念书。I study in No. 1 Secondary School.

念头 niàntou （名词）idea; thought

鸟 niǎo （名词）bird: 喂鸟 feed birds

您 nín （代词）you: 您好！How do you do!

宁静 níngjìng （形容词）peaceful: 宁静的湖泊 a peaceful lake

柠檬 níngméng （名词）lemon: 柠檬茶 lemon tea ∥ 柠檬汁 lemon juice

凝视 níngshì （动词）gaze at; stare: 凝视着窗外 gaze out of the window

牛 niú （名词）cattle; cow; ox: 两头牛 two heads of cattle ∥ 牛角 ox horn

用法小贴士
cattle 是牛的总称，cow 指母牛，ox 指公牛。

牛奶 niúnǎi （名词）milk: 喝牛奶 drink milk ∥ 挤牛奶 milk a cow ∥ 鲜牛奶 fresh milk

牛排 niúpái （名词）beef steak: 烤牛排 cook steak

牛肉 niúròu （名词）beef

牛仔裤 niúzǎikù （名词）jeans: 穿牛仔裤 wear jeans

扭 niǔ （动词）turn around: 扭过头去 turn one's head

纽扣 niǔkòu （名词）button: 扣上/解开大衣纽扣 button/unbutton one's coat

农场 nóngchǎng （名词）farm: 在农场工作 work on a farm ∥ 农场主 farm owner

农村 nóngcūn （名词）countryside: 在农村 in the countryside

农活 nónghuó （名词）farm work: 干农活 do farm work

农具 nóngjù （名词）farm tool

农民 nóngmín （名词）peasant; farmer

农田 nóngtián （名词）farmland

农作物 nóngzuòwù （名词）crops

浓 nóng （形容词）thick; strong: 浓汤 thick soup ∥ 浓咖啡 strong coffee

努力 nǔlì（动词）make an effort: 努力学习 study hard ∥ 尽最大努力 do one's best

女儿 nǚ'ér （名词）daughter

女孩子 nǚháizi （名词）girl

女朋友 nǚpéngyou （名词）girl-friend

女人 nǚrén （名词）woman

女生 nǚshēng （名词）schoolgirl; female student: 我们班有30个女生。There are thirty girls in our class.

女士 nǚshì （名词）lady: 女士优先！Ladies first!

女王 nǚwáng （名词）queen: 伊丽莎白女王 Queen Elizabeth

女性 nǚxìng（名词）female

女子 nǚzǐ （名词）woman:女子篮球 women's basketball ∥女子双打 women's doubles ∥女子学校 girls' school

暖和 nuǎnhuo （形容词）warm: 感觉暖和 feel warm ∥暖和的天气 warm weather

诺言 nuòyán （名词）promise: 许下诺言 make a promise ∥信守诺言 keep one's promise ∥违背诺言 break a promise

One is never too old to learn. 活到老学到老。

哦 ó （叹词）oh: 哦，是真的吗? Oh, really?

欧元 ōuyuán （名词）euro

百科小贴士
欧盟统一货币，于2002年1月1日正式流通。

欧洲 ōuzhōu （名词）Europe: 欧洲国家 European countries

Practice makes perfect.

P

爬 pá （动词）climb: 爬山 climb a mountain // 爬树 climb a tree

怕 pà （动词）fear; be afraid of: 老鼠怕猫。Mice are afraid of cats. // 他什么都不怕。He fears nothing.

拍照 pāizhào （动词）take a picture: 给某人拍照 take a picture of somebody

排 pái
1.（名词）row; line: 站成一排 stand in a row // 前排 front row // 后排 back row
2.（量词）row; line: 一排房子 a row of houses

排队 páiduì （动词）stand in line 排队等候 wait in line

排球 páiqiú （名词）volleyball: 打排球 play volleyball // 沙滩排球 beach volleyball

派 pài
1.（动词）send: 派人去请医生 send for the doctor
2.（名词）pie: 草莓派 strawberry pie

派对 pàiduì （名词）party: 生日派对 birthday party

百科小贴士
派对是英语 party 的音译词。

攀登 pāndēng （动词）climb

盘子 pánzi （名词）plate: 塑料盘子 plastic plate

判断 pànduàn （动词）judge: 根据事实判断 judging by the fact

盼望 pànwàng （动词）look forward to; expect: 我盼望你的来访。I look forward to your visit.

旁 páng （名词）side: 道路两旁 on both sides of the street

旁边 pángbiān （名词）side: 坐在某人旁边 sit at/by somebody's side

螃蟹 pángxiè （名词）crab

胖 pàng （形容词）fat: 他越来越胖了。He is getting fatter.

胖乎乎 pànghūhū （形容词）chubby: 胖乎乎的小男孩 a chubby little boy

胖子 pàngzi（名词）fat person

跑 pǎo （动词）run: 跑得快 run fast // 跑上楼 run upstairs

跑步 pǎobù （动词）jog: 我每天早晨在公园里跑步。I go jogging in the park every morning.

泡 pào （名词）bubble: 肥皂泡 soap bubble // 吹泡泡 blow bubbles

泡茶 pàochá （动词）make tea

泡泡糖 pàopaotáng （名词）bubble gum;chewing gum: 吹泡泡糖 blow bubble gum

炮 pào （名词）cannon: 开炮 fire off a cannon

炮火 pàohuǒ （名词）gunfire

陪伴 péibàn （动词）keep somebody company

培训 péixùn （动词）train: 培训课 training course

佩服 pèifú （动词）admire: 佩服某人 admire somebody

喷泉 pēnquán （名词）fountain

盆 pén （名词）basin; pot: 花盆 flowerpot // 洗脸盆 washbasin

烹饪 pēngrèn （动词）cook (dishes): 擅长烹饪 be good at cooking // 中式烹饪 Chinese cooking

朋友 péngyou （名词）friend: 好朋友 good friend // 交朋友 make friends

捧 pěng （动词）hold/carry something in both hands: 捧着奖杯 hold the cup in both hands

碰 pèng （动词）
1. knock: 碰倒某人 knock somebody down // 碰翻某物 knock something over
2. meet; run into: 碰到某人 meet somebody; run into somebody

碰面 pèngmiàn （动词）meet: 我们8点钟在电影院碰面。We'll meet at the cinema at eight o'clock.

皮 pí （名词）leather: 皮包 leather handbag // 皮带 leather belt // 皮鞋 leather shoes

皮肤 pífū （名词）skin: 皮肤白 have fair skin // 皮肤黑 have dark skin

疲劳 píláo （形容词）tired: 感到疲劳 feel tired

啤酒 píjiǔ （名词）beer: 一杯啤酒 a glass of beer // 喝啤酒 drink/have some beer

琵琶 pípá （名词）Chinese lute

百科小贴士
琵琶是中国传统乐器，有4根弦，琴身呈瓜子形。秦朝时就已经出现，著名的琵琶曲有《十面埋伏》等。

便宜 piányi （形容词）cheap: 这本书真便宜。This book is really cheap.

片 piàn （名词）piece: 玻璃片 pieces of glass ∥一片面包 a piece of bread

骗 piàn （动词）cheat: 骗人 cheat somebody ∥受骗 be cheated

骗子 piànzi （名词）cheater

漂浮 piāofú （动词）float: 天空中漂浮着一朵白云。A white cloud was floating in the sky.

飘扬 piāoyáng （动词）wave; fly: 五星红旗迎风飘扬。The Chinese national flag is waving in the wind.

票 piào （名词）ticket: 买票 buy a ticket ∥火车票 train ticket

漂亮 piàoliang （形容词）pretty; beautiful: 漂亮的衣服 pretty clothes

拼写 pīnxiě （动词）spell: 拼写单词 spell words ∥拼写错误 spelling mistakes

拼音 pīnyīn （名词）*Pinyin*

百科小贴士
*Pinyin*是"拼音"的拼音写法，已被收入一些英文原版词典。

贫民 pínmín （名词）poor people

贫穷 pínqióng （形容词）poor: 过着贫穷的生活 live/lead a poor life

品尝 pǐncháng （动词）taste: 品尝不同菜肴 taste different dishes

品德 pǐndé （名词） moral character: 品德教育 moral education

品牌 pǐnpái （名词）brand: 知名品牌 famous brand

乒乓球 pīngpāngqiú （名词）ping-pong; table tennis: 打乒乓球 play ping-pong/table tennis ∥乒乓球拍 table tennis bat

平 píng （形容词）flat: 平地 flat ground

平安 píng'ān （形容词）safe and sound: 平安到达 arrive safe and sound

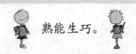

熟能生巧。

平等 píngděng（形容词）equal: 法律面前，人人平等。All are equal before the law.

平静 píngjìng（形容词）calm; quiet: 平静的夜晚 quiet night

平时 píngshí（名词）usual: 像平时一样 as usual

苹果 píngguǒ（名词）apple: 摘苹果 pick apples

瓶 píng（名词）bottle: 酒瓶 wine bottle ∥ 一瓶牛奶 a bottle of milk ∥ 把瓶子倒空 empty a bottle

破 pò（形容词）broken; torn: 瓶子破了。The bottle was broken.

破坏 pòhuài（动词）destroy; harm

扑克 pūkè（名词）poker; playing cards: 打扑克 play cards

百科小贴士
扑克是英语 poker 的音译词。

铺床 pūchuáng（动词）make the bed

葡萄 pútáo（名词）grape: 葡萄汁 grape juice

葡萄酒 pútáojiǔ（名词）wine: 白葡萄酒 white wine ∥ 红葡萄酒 red wine

普通 pǔtōng（形容词）ordinary; common: 普通人 the general public

瀑布 pùbù（名词）waterfall

320

七 qī （数词）seven: 七点钟 seven o'clock ∥ 第七 the seventh

七月 qīyuè （名词）July

妻子 qīzi （名词）wife

期待 qīdài （动词）look forward to: 我们期待你早日答复。We look forward to your early reply.

期末 qīmò （名词）end of a term: 期末考试 final exam

期中 qīzhōng （名词）midterm: 期中考试 midterm exam

欺骗 qīpiàn （动词）cheat: 欺骗某人 cheat somebody

其实 qíshí （副词）in fact; as a matter of fact: 其实考试并不难。In fact, the exam wasn't difficult.

其他 qítā （代词）other; else: 其他事情 other things ∥ 看到其他人了吗？Did you see anybody else?

奇怪 qíguài （形容词）strange: 奇怪的声音 strange noise

奇观 qíguān （名词）natural wonder; wonder of Nature: 世界奇观 world wonders

奇迹 qíjì （名词）miracle; wonder: 我们的成功真是奇迹！Our success is really a miracle!

奇妙 qímiào （形容词）wonderful: 奇妙的世界 wonderful world

骑 qí （动词）ride: 骑马 ride a horse ∥ 骑自行车 ride a bike

棋子 qízǐ （名词）chess piece

旗 qí （名词）flag: 升旗 raise a flag ∥ 降旗 lower a flag

旗帜 qízhì （名词）flag: 旗帜迎风飞扬。The flags are flying in the wind.

企鹅 qǐ'é （名词）penguin

企业 qǐyè （名词）enterprise

起床 qǐchuáng （动词）get up; get out of bed: 起床早 get up early

起飞 qǐfēi （动词）take off: 飞机准点起飞。The plane took off on time.

起来 qǐlai （动词）站起来 stand up:拣起来 pick up // 太阳升起来。The sun rises.

起立 qǐlì （动词）stand up: 全体起立！Everybody, stand up!

气愤 qìfèn（形容词）angry: 感到气愤 be/feel angry

气功 qìgōng （名词）qigong: 练气功 practice qigong

百科小贴士
qigong是气功的拼音。气功是我国一种传统的健身方法，主要是通过调节呼吸以祛病强身。

气球 qìqiú（名词）balloon: 吹气球 blow up a balloon // 热气球 hot-air balloon

气体 qìtǐ （名词）gas: 散发气体 give off gas // 吸入气体 take in gas

气味 qìwèi （名词）smell: 带有某种气味 have a smell of something // 散发气味 give off a smell // 气味难闻 bad smell

气温 qìwēn （名词）temperature: 气温下降/上升 the temperature falls/rises // 零下/零上5度的气温 temperature of 5°C below/above zero

汽车 qìchē （名词）car: 乘坐汽车 take a car // 开汽车 drive a car // 停放汽车 park a car

汽水 qìshuǐ （名词）soda

汽油 qìyóu（名词） gas

用法小贴士
美国多用 gas，英国多用 petrol.

千 qiān （数词）thousand: 一千 one thousand // 几千人 several thousand people

千方百计 qiānfāng-bǎijì in every way possible

千克 qiānkè （名词）kilogram; kilo; kg

千米 qiānmǐ （名词）kilometer; km

牵 qiān （动词）pull; lead along: 牵着一头牛往地里走 lead an ox to the fields

铅笔 qiānbǐ （名词）pencil: 铅笔盒 pencil box // 铅笔刀 pencil sharpener // 用铅笔写 write in pencil

前 qián （名词）front: 前门 front door

前面 qiánmian （名词）front: 房子前面有棵树。There is a tree in front of the house.

前年 qiánnián （名词）the year before last

前期 qiánqī（名词）early days: 19世纪前期 in the early nineteenth century

前天 qiántiān （名词）the day before yesterday

前线 qiánxiàn （名词）front: 上前线 go to the front

钱 qián （名词）money: 付钱 pay for something ∥ 花钱 spend money ∥ 向某人借钱 borrow money from somebody ∥ 借钱给某人 lend money to somebody ∥ 多少钱？How much is it?

钱包 qiánbāo （名词）wallet: 丢钱包 lose one's wallet ∥ 捡钱包 pick up a wallet

钱财 qiáncái （名词）wealth; money: 浪费钱财 waste money

浅 qiǎn （形容词）shallow: 浅水 shallow water

枪 qiāng （名词）gun: 开枪 fire a gun/open fire

强大 qiángdà （形容词）strong: 强大的国家 a strong nation

强盗 qiángdào （名词）robber

强国 qiángguó （名词）strong nation: 世界强国 world power

强壮 qiángzhuàng （形容词）strong

墙 qiáng （名词）wall

抢 qiǎng （动词）rob: 抢银行 rob a bank

抢劫 qiǎngjié （动词）rob: 抢劫犯 robber

悄悄 qiāoqiāo （副词）quietly: 悄悄离开 leave quietly

跷跷板 qiāoqiāobǎn （名词）see-saw: 玩跷跷板 play on a seesaw

敲 qiāo （动词）knock: 敲门 knock at the door

桥 qiáo （名词）bridge: 搭桥 build a bridge ∥ 过桥 cross a bridge

瞧 qiáo （动词）look; see: 瞧一眼 have a look at ∥ 等着瞧吧。Wait and see.

瞧不起 qiáobuqǐ （动词）look down upon/on

有志者事竟成。要成功靠恒心。

巧克力 qiǎokèlì （名词）chocolate: 一块巧克力 a bar of chocolate ∥ 巧克力蛋糕 chocolate cake

百科小贴士
巧克力是英语 chocolate 的音译词

巧妙 qiǎomiào （形容词）clever: 巧妙的回答 a clever answer

茄子 qiézi （名词）eggplant; aubergine

用法小贴士
eggplant 是美国英语，aubergine 是英国英语。

钦佩 qīnpèi （动词）admire: 极为钦佩 admire very much

亲爱 qīn'ài （形容词）dear; loved: 亲爱的朋友 dear friend

亲密 qīnmì （形容词）close: 亲密的朋友 a close friend

亲切 qīnqiè （形容词）kind; warm: 亲切的握手 shake hands warmly ∥ 待人亲切 be kind to people

亲吻 qīnwěn （动词）kiss: 亲吻脸颊 kiss somebody on the cheek

勤快 qínkuài （形容词）hardworking: 他很勤快。He is a hardworking person.

勤劳 qínláo （形容词）hardworking: 勤劳的人民 hardworking people

寝室 qǐnshì （名词）bedroom: 打扫寝室 clean one's bedroom

青春 qīngchūn （名词）youth; youthfulness: 充满青春活力 full of youthful energy

青年 qīngnián （名词）
1. youth; youthful days: 从青年到老年 from youth to old age
2. youth; young people: 现代青年 modern youth

青少年 qīngshàonián （名词）teenagers; teens: 青少年教育 teenage education

青蛙 qīngwā （名词）frog

轻 qīng （形容词）light: 重量轻 be light in weight ∥ 轻如羽毛 as light as a feather

轻音乐 qīngyīnyuè （名词）light music: 听轻音乐 listen to light music

清楚 qīngchu
1. （形容词）clear: 发音清楚 pronounce clearly ∥ 看清楚 see clearly
2. （动词）know; understand: 这个问题你清楚吗？Do you understand this question?

清洁 qīngjié （形容词）clean: 保持房间清洁 keep the room clean ∥ 清洁工 cleaner

清静 qīngjìng （形容词）quiet: 过清静的生活 lead a quiet life

情谊 qíngyì （名词）friendship: 师生情谊 friendship between teachers and students

晴朗 qínglǎng （形容词）fine; sunny; clear: 晴朗的天空 clear skies // 晴朗的早晨 a fine morning // 天气晴朗 fine sunny weather

请 qǐng （动词）
1. ask: 请人帮忙 ask somebody for help // 请他进来。Ask him to come in.
2. invite; ask: 请人吃饭 invite somebody for dinner
3. please: 请坐。Take a seat, please. // 请稍候。Please wait a minute.

请假 qǐngjià （动词）ask for leave: 我病了，请了一天假。I was ill and asked for a day's sick leave.

请求 qǐngqiú （动词）ask: 请求帮助 ask for help

请问 qǐngwèn （动词）excuse me; please: 请问去图书馆怎么走？Excuse me, how can I get to the library?

庆祝 qìngzhù （动词）celebrate: 庆祝新年 celebrate the New Year // 庆祝生日 celebrate somebody's birthday

穷 qióng （形容词）poor: 穷人 poor people // 穷国 poor country

秋 qiū （名词）autumn; fall: 秋去冬来。Winter comes after autumn.

秋千 qiūqiān （名词）swing: 我们去荡秋千玩吧。Let's go on the swings.

秋天 qiūtiān （名词）autumn; fall

用法小贴士
autumn 是英国英语，fall 是美国英语。

求 qiú （动词）ask; beg: 求人原谅 beg for forgiveness

求助 qiúzhù （动词）ask somebody for help

球 qiú （名词）ball: 踢球玩 kick a ball around // 球赛 ball game // 雪球 snowball

球场 qiúchǎng （名词）playing field: 足球场 football field

球迷 qiúmí （名词）(ball game) fan: 足球迷 football fan

去 qù （动词）go to; leave for: 去买东西 go shopping // 爸爸昨天去上海了。Dad went to Shanghai yesterday.

去年 qùnián （名词）last year

有志者事竟成。要成功靠恒心。

去世 qùshì（动词）die; pass away: 因病去世 die of an illness // 他爷爷两年前去世了。His grandfather passed away two years ago.

用法小贴士
pass away 是比较委婉的表达。

趣味 qùwèi（名词）interest: 我觉得那本书很有趣味。The book is of great interest to me.

圈 quān（名词）circle: 画个圈儿 draw a circle

全部 quánbù（形容词）all; whole: 全部时间 all one's time // 我知道全部真相。I know the whole truth.

全国 quánguó（名词）whole country: 全国各地 all over the country // 全国冠军 national champion // 闻名全国 be famous in the whole country

全家福 quánjiāfú（名词）family photo: 照全家福 take a family photo

全球 quánqiú（名词）the whole world: 享誉全球 be famous all over the world

全体 quántǐ（名词）all; everyone: 学校全体师生 all the teachers and students of the school

泉水 quánshuǐ（名词）spring water: 清澈的泉水 clear spring water

拳头 quántou（名词）fist: 举起拳头 raise one's fist

劝告 quàngào（名词）advice: 一个劝告 a piece of advice

缺点 quēdiǎn（名词）shortcoming; weakness: 改正缺点 correct one's shortcomings // 指出缺点 point out somebody's shortcomings

缺席 quēxí（动词）be absent: 上课缺席 be absent from a class // 今天两个学生缺席。Two students are absent today.

却 què（副词）but; yet: 他很穷，却很快乐。He is poor, but happy.

裙子 qúnzi（名词）skirt; dress
用法小贴士
skirt指半裙，dress指连衣裙。

R

然而 rán'ér（连词）but; however: 他病了，然而仍坚持上学。He was ill, but he still went to school.

然后 ránhòu（词）then; after that: 先右拐，然后左拐。First turn right, then left.

燃烧 ránshāo（动词）burn: 燃烧的大火 burning fire

嚷嚷 rāngrang（动词）shout: 安静！别嚷嚷。Be quiet! Don't shout.

让 ràng（动词）let; allow: 让我去吧。Let me go.

让座 ràngzuò（动词）give up one's seat to somebody: 给老人让座 give up one's seat to the elderly

热 rè
1.（形容词）hot: 天很热。It's hot. // 我又热又渴。I'm hot and thirsty.
2.（动词）heat (up); warm (up): 把牛奶在炉子上热一热。Warm up the milk on the stove.
3.（名词）fever: 发热 have a fever

热爱 rè'ài（动词）love: 热爱祖国 love one's country // 热爱中国文化 love Chinese culture

热狗 règǒu（名词）hot dog

热乎乎 rèhūhū（形容词）warm: 热乎乎的饭菜 hot meals // 心里热乎乎的 be moved/touched

热闹 rènao（形容词）lively: 热闹的场面 a lively scene // 热闹的街道 a busy street

热情 rèqíng（形容词）warmhearted: 他待人很热情。He is a warm-hearted person.

热线 rèxiàn（名词）hotline: 打热线 phone a hotline // 市长热线 the mayor's hotline // 投诉热线 a complaint hotline

热心 rèxīn（形容词）warmhearted: 热心人 warmhearted people

热饮 rèyǐn（名词）hot drink: 一杯热饮 a cup of hot drink

人 rén（名词）person; people: 我家有3口人。There are three people in my family.

人才 réncái（名词）talent

人口 rénkǒu（名词）population: 中国是世界上人口最多的国家。China has the largest population in the world.

人类 rénlèi（名词）mankind: 人类的进步 human progress // 人类文明 human civilization

人们 rénmen（名词）people: 好心的人们 kind people

人民 rénmín（名词）the people: 为人民服务 serve the people // 劳动人民 ordinary working people // 中国人民 Chinese people

人民币 rénmínbì（名词）renminbi (RMB) (Chinese currency)

人权 rénquán（名词）human rights: 基本人权 basic human rights // 保护人权 protect human rights

人人 rénrén（副词）everyone; everybody: 人人都可以参加。Everybody can take part.

人生 rénshēng（名词）life: 享受人生 enjoy one's life // 虚度人生 waste one's life

认错 rèncuò（名词）admit one's mistakes: 他终于认错了。He finally admitted that he was wrong.

认得 rènde（动词）know: 我不认得路。I don't know the way.

认识 rènshi（动词）know: 你认识他吗？Do you know him?

认为 rènwéi（动词）think: 你认为这部电影怎么样？What do you think of this film?

认真 rènzhēn（形容词）serious: 我是认真的。I'm serious.

任何 rènhé（形容词）any: 任何人 anybody // 任何事 anything // 任何地方 anywhere

任务 rènwu（名词）task: 完成任务 finish a task

扔 rēng（动词）throw: 扔石头 throw a stone // 扔掉 throw away

仍然 réngrán（副词）still: 这件毛衣很旧了，但我仍然喜欢它。This sweater is very old, but I still like it.

日报 rìbào（名词）daily newspaper: 《中国日报》 China Daily // 《人民日报》 People's Daily

日本 rìběn（名词）Japan: 日本人 Japanese

日常 rìcháng（形容词）everyday: 日常生活 everyday life // 日常用语 everyday words and expressions

日出 rìchū（名词）sunrise: 看日出 watch the sunrise

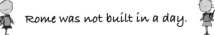

日记 rìjì（名词）diary: 记日记 keep a diary

日期 rìqī（名词）date: 出生日期 date of birth ∥ 考试日期 date of the exam

日圆 rìyuán（名词）Japanese yen

日子 rìzi（名词）
1. day: 幸福的日子 happy days
2. life: 过好日子 live a happy life

绒毛玩具 róngmáo wánjù（名词）soft toy

容貌 róngmào（名词）looks: 容貌美丽 have good looks

容易 róngyì（形容词）easy: 说起来容易做起来难。It's easier said than done.

柔道 róudào（名词）judo

百科小贴士
柔道是 judo 的音译词。

柔软 róuruǎn（形容词）soft: 柔软的床 soft bed ∥ 柔软的头发 soft hair

肉 ròu（名词）meat: 鱼肉 fish ∥ 肉丸子 meat ball ∥ 肉饼 meat pancake

如此 rúcǐ（代词）so; such: 如此昂贵 so expensive ∥ 如此美丽 so beautiful ∥ 这幅画是如此美丽。The picture is so beautiful.

如果 rúguǒ（连词）if: 如果明天不下雨，我就去公园。If it doesn't rain tomorrow, I'll go to the park.

如何 rúhé（代词）how; how about: 你考得如何？How was your examination? ∥ 明天如何？How about tomorrow?

如今 rújīn（名词）nowadays; now; these days: 如今坐飞机是平常事。Air travel is commonplace nowadays.

乳牛 rǔniú（名词）dairy cow

入睡 rùshuì（动词）fall asleep

入伍 rùwǔ（动词）join the army

软 ruǎn（形容词）soft: 软床 soft bed

软件 ruǎnjiàn（名词）software: 开发软件 develop software

软盘 ruǎnpán（名词）floppy disk

软糖 ruǎntáng（名词）soft sweets/candies

用法小贴士
sweet 是英国英语，而且一般用复数形式，candy 是美国英语。

罗马非一日建成。

软饮料 ruǎnyǐnliào（名词）soft drinks

百科小贴士
软饮料指不含酒精的饮料。

弱点 ruòdiǎn（名词）weakness:
改正弱点 correct one's weakness

弱小 ruòxiǎo（形容词）small and weak

Strike while the iron is hot.

S

赛 sài
1.（动词）have a sports match: 网球比赛 have a tennis match
2.（名词）match; game: 足球赛 football game

赛车 sàichē
1.（动词）have a car race
2.（名词）race car: 赛车模型 model race car

赛点 sàidiǎn（名词）match point

赛马 sàimǎ（动词）horse race

赛跑 sàipǎo（动词）run a race: 参加赛跑 run a race // 长距离赛跑 long-distance race // 环城赛跑 round-the-city race

赛艇 sàitǐng（名词）racing boat

三 sān（数词）three: 三匹马 three horses

三八妇女节 sān-bā fùnǚjié（名词）International Women's Day

三角形 sānjiǎoxíng（名词）triangle: 画三角形 draw a triangle

三明治 sānmíngzhì（名词）sandwich: 果酱三明治 jam sandwich // 火腿三明治 ham sandwich

百科小贴士
三明治是英语 sandwich 的音译词。

三天两头 sāntiān-liǎngtóu almost every day: 他三天两头地迟到。He's late almost every day.

三月 sānyuè（名词）March

伞 sǎn（名词）umbrella: 撑伞 open an umbrella // 今天有雨，带把伞。It's going to rain today. Take an umbrella with you.

散步 sànbù（动词）take a walk: 去散步 go for a walk // 你想和我一起散散步吗？Would you like to join me for a walk?

嗓子 sǎngzi（名词）throat: 我嗓子疼。I've got a sore throat.

扫 sǎo（动词）sweep: 地扫过了吗？Have you swept the floor?

扫地 sǎodì（动词）sweep the floor

色彩 sècǎi（名词）color: 鲜艳的色彩 bright colors

331

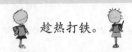
色拉 sèlā（名词）salad: 拌色拉 prepare a salad // 水果色拉 fruit salad // 蔬菜色拉 green salad

百科小贴士
色拉是英语salad的音译词.

森林 sēnlín（名词）forest: 保护森林 protect the forest // 森林火灾 forest fire

杀 shā（动词）kill: 杀虫 kill insects

杀害 shāhài（动词）kill: 杀害野生动物 kill wild animals

杀手 shāshǒu（名词）killer

沙 shā（名词）sand: 黄沙 yellow sand

沙尘暴 shāchénbào（名词）sandstorm

沙袋 shādài（名词）sandbag

沙发 shāfā（名词）sofa: 沙发床 sofa bed

百科小贴士
沙发是英语sofa的音译词.

沙漠 shāmò（名词）desert: 沙漠动物 desert animal // 沙漠植物 desert plant // 撒哈拉大沙漠 Sahara Desert

沙滩 shātān（名词）beach: 沙滩排球 beach volleyball // 沙滩鞋 beach shoes

沙子 shāzi（名词）sand

鲨 shā（名词）shark: 食人鲨 man-eating shark // 白鲨 white shark

鲨鱼 shāyú（名词）shark

傻 shǎ（形容词）stupid; silly: 傻小子 silly boy // 傻姑娘 silly girl

傻瓜 shǎguā（名词）fool: 大傻瓜 big fool

山 shān（名词）hill; mountain: 登山 climb a mountain // 上山 go up a hill // 下山 go down a hill // 高山 high mountains

用法小贴士
hill指小山, mountain指大山、高山.

山城 shānchéng（名词）mountain city

山村 shāncūn（名词）mountain village

山顶 shāndǐng（名词）top of a mountain; hilltop

山洞 shāndòng（名词）cave

山歌 shāngē（名词）folk song: 唱支山歌 sing a folk song

山花 shānhuā（名词）mountain flower

山林 shānlín（名词）mountain forest

山泉 shānquán（名词）mountain spring

山羊 shānyáng（名词）goat

闪电 shǎndiàn（名词）lightning

闪烁 shǎnshuò（动词）twinkle: 闪烁的星星 twinkling stars

扇子 shànzi（名词）fan: 一把扇子 a fan

善良 shànliáng（形容词）kind-hearted; kind: 她心地善良。She is kindhearted.

善于 shànyú（动词）be good at: 善于演说 be good at public speaking

擅长 shàncháng（动词）be good at: 擅长英语 be good at English

伤 shāng（名词）wound: 重伤 serious wound

伤害 shānghài（动词）hurt: 你的话伤害了她的感情。Your words have hurt her feelings.

伤心 shāngxin（形容词）sad: 我感到很伤心。I felt very sad.

商场 shāngchǎng（名词）shopping center: 逛商场 go shopping

商店 shāngdiàn（名词）shop; store: 儿童用品商店 children's store ∥ 百货商店 department store

商人 shāngrén（名词）business-people; merchant

上班 shàngbān（动词）go to work: 他上班去了。He has gone to work.

上半场 shàngbànchǎng（名词）first half (of a game, concert, etc.): 上半场我们以7分领先。We won by seven points in the first half.

上床 shàngchuáng（动词）go to bed

上帝 shàngdì（名词）god: 顾客就是上帝。The customer is always right.

上来 shànglái（动词）come up: 快点上来。Come up quickly.

上面 shàngmian（名词）the top of: 那本书就在我的书桌上面。The book is on my desk.

上升 shàngshēng（动词）rise; go up: 气温在上升。The temperature is going up.

上网 shàngwǎng（动词）go online: 我正在上网。I'm surfing the Internet.

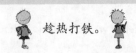

上午 shàngwǔ（名词）morning: 上午10点 ten o'clock in the morning ∥ 明天上午 tomorrow morning

上学 shàngxué（动词）go to school

上演 shàngyǎn（动词）perform; stage: 今晚上演什么节目？What's on tonight?

上涨 shàngzhǎng（动词）go up; rise: 河水正在上涨。The river is rising. ∥ 物价上涨了。Prices have gone up.

烧烤 shāokǎo（名词）barbecue: 举行烧烤野餐 have a barbecue

勺 sháo（名词）spoon: 一勺盐 a spoon of salt

少 shǎo（形容词）few; little: 去的人很少。Few people went. ∥ 时间很少。There is little time.

用法小贴士
few 用来修饰可数名词，little 用来修饰不可数名词。

少年儿童 shàonián értóng（名词）children

少年宫 shàoniángōng（名词）children's palace

少先队员 shàoxiān duìyuán（名词）Young Pioneer

舌头 shétou（名词）tongue: 小男孩儿吐舌头做鬼脸。The little boy stuck out his tongue to make faces.

蛇 shé（名词）snake

谁 shéi（代词）who: 你找谁？Who are you looking for? ∥ 这是谁的书？Whose book is this?

身份证 shēnfènzhèng（名词）ID card

身高 shēngāo（名词）height: 他有六英尺高。He is six feet tall.

身体 shēntǐ（名词）body: 身体健康 in good health

深 shēn（形容词）deep: 深水 deep water ∥ 深呼吸 deep breath

什么 shénme（代词）what: 你找什么？What are you looking for?

神 shén（名词）god

神秘 shénmì（形容词）mysterious: 神秘的宇宙 mysterious universe

升旗 shēngqí（动词）raise a flag

升起 shēngqǐ（动词）rise: 太阳从东方升起。The sun rises in the east.

Strike while the iron is hot.

升学 shēngxué（动词）go to the next level of school: 升学考试 entrance exam

生病 shēngbìng（动词）fall ill/sick: 我生病了，不能上学。I cannot go to school because I am ill.

生动 shēngdòng（形容词）lively: 生动的表演 a lively performance

生活 shēnghuó
1.（动词）live: 在一起幸福地生活 live happily together
2.（名词）life: 日常生活 daily life

生命 shēngmìng（名词）life: 挽救生命 save a life ∥失去生命 lose one's life

生气 shēngqì（动词）get angry: 生某人的气 be angry with somebody

生日 shēngrì（名词）birthday: 祝你生日快乐！Happy birthday to you! ∥生日派对 birthday party

生长 shēngzhǎng（动词）grow: 生长在田地里 grow in the field

生字 shēngzì（名词）new word: 记生字 learn new words by heart

声音 shēngyīn（名词）voice; sound: 发出声音 make a sound ∥提高声音 raise one's voice

绳子 shéngzi（名词）rope: 一根绳子 a piece of rope

省 shěng
1.（动词）save: 省时间 save time ∥省钱 save money
2.（名词）province: 河北省 Hebei Province

圣诞 shèngdàn（名词）Christmas (Day): 圣诞节前夜 Christmas Eve ∥圣诞快乐！Merry Christmas! ∥圣诞卡 Christmas card ∥圣诞老人 Father Christmas; Santa Claus ∥圣诞树 Christmas tree

失败 shībài（动词）fail; lose: 在比赛中失败 lose a match

失火 shīhuǒ（动词）catch fire; be on fire: 商店失火了！The shop is on fire!

失去 shīqù（动词）lose: 失去耐心 lose one's patience

失望 shīwàng
1.（动词）disappoint: 他令我失望。He has disappointed me.
2.（形容词）disappointed: 感到失望 be/feel disappointed

失业 shīyè（动词）lose one's job

诗 shī（名词）poem: 朗诵诗 recite a poem

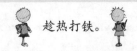
诗人 shīrén（名词）poet

狮子 shīzi（名词）lion: 狮子王 Lion King ∥母狮子 lioness

湿 shī（形容词）wet: 湿衣服 wet clothes

湿透 shītòu（形容词）wet all over: 他浑身湿透了。He is wet all over.

十 shí（数词）ten: 十点十分 ten past ten

十二月 shí'èryuè（名词）December

十分 shífēn（副词）very; most: 十分高兴 be very pleased

十一月 shíyīyuè（名词）November

十月 shíyuè（名词）October

十字路口 shízì lùkǒu（名词）crossroad: 在第一个十字路口 at the first crossroad

石头 shítou（名词）stone; rock: 一堆石头 a pile of stones ∥像石头一样坚硬 as hard as stone

石油 shíyóu（名词）oil

时常 shícháng（副词）often: 我时常去那里。I often go there.

时代 shídài（名词）times: 时代变了。Times have changed.

时候 shíhou（名词）time: 每天这个时候 at this time every day ∥时候不早了。It's getting late.

时间 shíjiān（名词）time: 节省时间 save time ∥业余时间 spare time

时刻表 shíkèbiǎo（名词）timetable: 列车时刻表 railway timetable

时针 shízhēn（名词）hour hand (of a clock)

识字 shízì（动词）learn to read: 读书识字 read and write

实话 shíhuà（名词）truth: 说实话 tell the truth

实验 shíyàn（名词）experiment; test: 做实验 do/make an experiment

实验室 shíyànshì（名词）laboratory; lab

食品 shípǐn（名词）food: 绿色食品 organic food ∥婴儿食品 baby food

食堂 shítáng（名词）dining room/hall: 学生食堂 students' dining hall

食物 shíwù（名词）food: 冷冻食物 frozen food ∥食物链 food chain

使 shǐ（动词）make: 运动使人更健康。Exercise makes people healthier.

使用 shǐyòng（动词）use: 使用工具 use tools

士兵 shìbīng（名词）soldier

世纪 shìjì（名词）century: 一个世纪 one century ∥世纪之交 at the turn of the century ∥21世纪 twenty-first century

世界 shìjiè（名词）world: 世界闻名 be world-famous ∥世界冠军 world champion

世界杯 shìjièbēi（名词）World Cup: 赢得世界杯 win the World Cup

世贸组织 shìmào zǔzhī（名词）WTO (World Trade Organization): 加入世贸组织 join the WTO ∥世贸组织成员 WTO member

市场 shìchǎng（名词）market: 市场经济 market economy

事 shì（名词）matter; thing: 跟你说件事。I have something to tell you. ∥发生什么事了？What's up?/What's the matter?

事故 shìgù（名词）accident: 交通事故 traffic accident

事情 shìqíng（名词）matter: 事情的真相 the truth of something

事实 shìshí（名词）fact: 事实胜于雄辩。Facts speak louder than words. ∥事实上 in fact

试 shì（动词）try: 试衣服 try on clothes ∥试一试 have a try

试卷 shìjuàn（名词）exam paper: 交试卷 hand in an exam paper

试题 shìtí（名词）exam/test questions

试验 shìyàn（动词）test; experiment

视力 shìlì（名词）sight; eyesight: 保护视力 protect one's eyesight ∥检查视力 have one's eyes tested ∥视力差 have poor eyesight

是 shì（动词）be: 我是学生，他是老师。I'm a student. He's a teacher.

用法小贴士
be 与不同人称和单复数主语搭配时有不同的形式：I am, you are, he/she is, they are.

是否 shìfǒu（副词）whether; if: 我不知他是否会来。I don't know whether/if he is coming.

室内 shìnèi（名词）inside of a building; indoors

室外 shìwài（名词）outside of a building; outdoors: 室外活动 outdoor activities

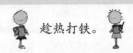

逝世 shìshì（动词）pass away; die

用法小贴士

pass away 是 die 的委婉表达.

收到 shōudào（动词）receive; get: 收到一份礼物 receive a present

收集 shōují（动词）collect: 收集邮票 collect stamps

收拾 shōushi（动词）put in order; tidy up: 收拾屋子 tidy up the room // 收拾床铺 make the bed

收音机 shōuyīnjī（名词）radio: 听收音机 listen to the radio

手 shǒu（名词）hand: 手拉手 hand in hand

手臂 shǒubì（名词）arm: 上臂 upper arm // 下臂 lower arm

手表 shǒubiǎo（名词）wristwatch

手机 shǒujī（名词）mobile phone: 手机号 cell phone number

手绢 shǒujuàn（名词）handkerchief

手枪 shǒuqiāng（名词）handgun: 玩具手枪 toy gun

手术 shǒushù（名词）operation: 接受手术 have an operation

手套 shǒutào（名词）gloves: 一副手套 a pair of gloves // 拳击手套 boxing gloves

手提包 shǒutíbāo（名词）handbag

手指 shǒuzhǐ（名词）finger: 手指甲 fingernail

首都 shǒudū（名词）capital: 北京是中国的首都。Beijing is the capital of China.

首先 shǒuxiān（副词）first: 首先发言 be the first to speak

寿命 shòumìng（名词）life: 寿命长/短 have a long/short life

受伤 shòushāng（动词）be wounded: 他在战争中受伤了。He was wounded in the war.

售货员 shòuhuòyuán（名词）shop assistant: 我妈妈是售货员。My mother is a shop assistant.

售票处 shòupiàochù（名词）ticket office

瘦 shòu（形容词）thin: 又高又瘦 tall and thin // 他瘦了。He has lost weight.

瘦小 shòuxiǎo（形容词）thin and small

瘦子 shòuzi（名词）a thin person

书 shū（名词）book: 历史书 history book // 买书 buy a book

书包 shūbāo（名词）schoolbag

Strike while the iron is hot.

书店 shūdiàn（名词）bookstore

书法 shūfǎ（名词）calligraphy

书房 shūfáng（名词）study

书架 shūjià（名词）bookshelf

书桌 shūzhuō（名词）desk: 收拾书桌 clear up the desk

叔叔 shūshu（名词）uncle: 李叔叔 Uncle Li

用法小贴士

英语没有"叔叔"和"舅舅"之分，都称作 uncle。如果一定要区分，可以用 paternal uncle 指"叔叔"，maternal uncle 指"舅舅"。

梳子 shūzi（名词）comb

舒服 shūfu（形容词）
1. comfortable: 舒服的椅子 a comfortable chair
2. feel well: 今天我有点不舒服。I don't feel well today./I am not myself today.

输 shū（动词）lose: 我们的队输了比赛。Our team lost the game.

蔬菜 shūcài（名词）vegetable: 新鲜蔬菜 fresh vegetables ∥ 蔬菜和水果 fruits and vegetables

熟 shú（形容词）
1. cooked; done: 肉熟了。The meat is done.
2. ripe: 熟透的苹果 ripe apples

熟练 shúliàn（形容词）skilled: 熟练工 a skilled worker

熟能生巧 shúnéngshēngqiǎo Practice makes perfect.

熟悉 shúxī（动词）know well; be familiar with: 我对他不熟悉。I don't know him well.

暑假 shǔjià（名词）summer vacation

鼠标 shǔbiāo（名词）mouse: 击鼠标 click the mouse

数 shǔ（动词）count: 学数数儿 learn how to count

薯条 shǔtiáo（名词）French fries

用法小贴士

French fries 是美国英语，chips 是英国英语。

束 shù（量词）bunch: 一束花 a bunch of flowers

树 shù（名词）tree: 爬树 climb a tree ∥ 植树 plant trees

树林 shùlín（名词）woods

数 shù（名词）number: 学生数 the number of students

数码相机 shùmǎ xiàngjī（名词）digital camera

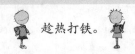

数学 shùxué（名词）mathematics; math: 数学老师 math teacher ∥数学题 math problem

数字 shùzì（名词）figure

刷 shuā
1.（名词）brush: 鞋刷 shoe brush
2.（动词）brush: 刷衣服 brush one's clothes

刷牙 shuāyá（动词）brush one's teeth

摔 shuāi（动词）
1. fall: 摔倒在地 fall to the ground ∥摔了一跤 have a fall
2. break: 盘子掉在地上摔碎了。The plate fell to the ground and broke to pieces.

帅 shuài（形容词）handsome: 帅小伙 handsome young man

双 shuāng
1.（形容词）two; both: 双目失明 blind in both eyes
2.（量词）pair: 一双筷子 a pair of chopsticks ∥两双袜子 two pairs of socks

双胞胎 shuāngbāotāi（名词）twins: 双胞胎姐妹 twin sisters

双人床 shuāngrénchuáng（名词）double bed

霜 shuāng（名词）frost

霜叶 shuāngyè（名词）red leaves

水 shuǐ（名词）water: 一杯水 a cup of water ∥喝水 drink some water

水彩 shuǐcǎi（名词）watercolor: 水彩颜料 watercolors ∥水彩画 watercolor painting

水稻 shuǐdào（名词）rice: 种水稻 grow rice ∥水稻田 rice field

水果 shuǐguǒ（名词）fruit: 新鲜水果 fresh fruit ∥水果刀 fruit knife ∥水果色拉 fruit salad

水手 shuǐshǒu（名词）sailor

水灾 shuǐzāi（名词）flood

睡 shuì（动词）sleep: 睡得好 sleep well ∥早睡早起 early to bed and early to rise

睡觉 shuìjiào（动词）sleep: 上床睡觉 go to bed ∥睡个好觉 have a good sleep ∥睡觉晚 stay up late ∥该睡觉了。It's time to go to bed.

睡梦 shuìmèng（名词）sleep; dream

睡醒 shuìxǐng（动词）wake up: 7点钟睡醒 wake up at seven o'clock

睡着 shuìzháo（动词）fall asleep

说 shuō（动词）speak; talk; say: 说英语 speak English ∥ 说实话 tell the truth

说话 shuōhuà（动词）say; speak; talk: 大声说话 speak loudly

说谎 shuōhuǎng（动词）tell a lie; lie: 他从不说谎。He never tells a lie.

司机 sījī（名词）driver: 出租车司机 taxi driver ∥ 公共汽车司机 bus driver

丝绸 sīchóu（名词）silk

思考 sīkǎo（动词）think: 认真思考 think carefully

思念 sīniàn（动词）miss: 思念家人 miss one's family

死 sǐ（动词）die: 冻死 die of cold ∥ 死于心脏病 die of a heart attack

死亡 sǐwáng（动词）die

四 sì（数词）four: 第四次 the fourth time

四处 sìchù（名词）everywhere: 四处张望 look around

四季 sìjì（名词）four seasons: 这个城市一年四季如春。It's like spring all year round in the city.

四周 sìzhōu（名词）all sides; all around

似乎 sìhū（副词）as if: 似乎要下雨了。It looks like rain.

松 sōng（形容词）loose: 鞋带松了。The shoelace has come loose.

松鼠 sōngshǔ（名词）squirrel

送 sòng（动词）
1. give: 送生日礼物 give somebody a birthday gift
2. see somebody off: 送某人回家 see somebody home ∥ 把客人送到门口 see a guest to the door

搜查 sōuchá（动词）search

速度 sùdù（名词）speed: 以每小时60公里的速度 at the speed of sixty miles an hour

宿舍 sùshè（名词）dormitory: 学生宿舍 students' dormitory

塑料 sùliào（名词）plastic: 塑料袋 plastic bag ∥ 塑料玩具 plastic toy

酸 suān（形容词）sour: 酸苹果 sour apple

酸奶 suānnǎi（名词）yogurt

蒜 suàn（名词）garlic: 一头蒜 a head of garlic

算术 suànshù（名词）math

用法小贴士
math 是美国英语，math 是英国英语。

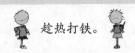

算数 suànshù（动词）count: 他4岁就学会算数了。He learned to count when he was only four.

虽然 suīrán（连词）though: 他虽然年纪小，却很懂事。Though he is young, he is thoughtful.

随身听 suíshēntīng（名词）Walkman: MP3 随身听 MP3 player

随时 suíshí（副词）at any time: 随时随地 at any time and in any place ∥ 公交车随时都会来。The bus may come at any moment.

岁 suì（量词）year: 10岁 ten years old

碎 suì（动词）break: 玻璃杯掉到地上摔碎了。The glass fell to the floor and broke into pieces. ∥ 窗户碎了。The window is broken.

孙女 sūnnǚ（名词）granddaughter

孙子 sūnzi（名词）grandson

所以 suǒyǐ（连词）so: 因为找不到你，所以我走了。I couldn't find you so I left.

所有 suǒyǒu（形容词）all: 所有的人 all the people

锁 suǒ
1.（名词）lock
2.（动词）lock (up): 锁门 lock the door

T

他 tā（代词）he; him: 他是警察。He is a policeman. ∥ 我很久没见到他了。I haven't seen him for a long time.

他们 tāmen（代词）they; them: 他们是双胞胎兄弟。They are twin brothers.

它 tā（代词）it: 别把它弄丢了。Don't lose it.

它们 tāmen（代词）they; them: 故事书在那边，请把它们拿过来。The storybooks are over there, please bring them over. ∥ 沙发上有两只猫，它们都是奶奶养的。There are two cats on the sofa; they belong to Grandma.

她 tā（代词）she; her: 她是我们的音乐老师。She is our music teacher. ∥ 我很久没见到她了。I haven't seen her for a long time.

她们 tāmen（代词）they; them: 我有两个姐姐，她们都是舞蹈家。I have two sisters; they are both dancers.

塔 tǎ（名词）tower: 电视塔 TV tower ∥ 水塔 water tower

台灯 táidēng（名词）desk lamp

台风 táifēng（名词）typhoon

百科小贴士
台风是英语 typhoon 的音译词.

台阶 táijiē（名词）step: 上台阶 go up the steps ∥ 下台阶 go down the steps

抬 tái（动词）raise; lift: 抬头 raise one's head ∥ 抬胳膊 lift up one's arm ∥ 请抬一下你的椅子。Please lift up your chair a bit.

太 tài（副词）too; so: 你真是太好了。You are so kind. ∥ 菜太好吃了。The dish was so delicious.

太极拳 tàijíquán（名词）tai chi (chuan): 爷爷每天早上都打太极拳。Grandpa does tai chi every morning.

太空 tàikōng（名词）space: 太空船 spaceship ∥ 太空人 spaceman ∥ 太空行走 spacewalk

太阳 tàiyáng（名词）sun: 太阳光 sunlight ∥ 太阳镜 sunglasses

两人智慧胜一人。

谈话 tánhuà（动词）talk; chat: 小声谈话 talk in a low voice // 老师要找你谈话。The teacher wants to talk with you.

谈论 tánlùn（动词）discuss; talk about: 谈论问题 discuss a question // 谈论天气 chat about the weather

弹奏 tánzòu（动词）play: 弹奏钢琴 play the piano // 弹奏一支曲子 play a piece of music

坦克 tǎnkè（名词）tank: 轻型/重型坦克 light/heavy tank

 百科小贴士
坦克是英语 tank 的音译词。

毯子 tǎnzi（名词）blanket

汤 tāng（名词）soup: 热汤 hot soup // 牛肉汤 beef soup // 鸡汤 chicken soup

汤匙 tāngchí（名词）soup spoon

唐诗 tángshī（名词）Tang poetry

糖 táng（名词）sugar; sweets: 白糖 white sugar // 红糖 brown sugar // 一块糖 a sweet

糖果 tángguǒ（名词）sweets: 一盒糖果 a box of sweets

躺 tǎng（动词）lie: 躺在床上 lie in bed // 仰躺着 lie on one's back

逃学 táoxué（动词）play truant

桃 táo（名词）peach

淘气 táoqì（形容词）naughty: 淘气的男孩 a naughty boy

讨论 tǎolùn（动词）discuss: 讨论问题 discuss a problem

特别 tèbié
1.（形容词）special: 特别的一天 a special day // 特别的礼物 a special gift
2.（副词）especially: 今年冬天特别冷。It's especially cold this winter.

疼 téng（动词）ache; hurt: 嗓子疼 have a sore throat // 头疼 have a headache

疼爱 téng'ài（动词）love dearly: 疼爱孩子 love one's children dearly

梯子 tīzi（名词）ladder: 爬梯子 climb a ladder

踢 tī（动词）kick: 踢球，开球 kick a ball

踢球 tīqiú（动词）play soccer

提问 tíwèn（动词）ask a question: 老师在课堂上提问了吗？Did the teacher ask any questions in the class?

 344

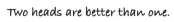
题 tí（名词）question; problem: 数学题 math problem ∥ 试题 examination questions

题目 tímù（名词）subject; title; topic:作文题目 the title of the composition ∥ 演讲题目 the topic of the speech

体操 tǐcāo（名词）gymnastics: 做体操 do gymnastics ∥ 练习体操 practice gymnastics

体温 tǐwēn（名词）temperature: 量体温 measure one's temperature ∥ 他的体温在升高。His temperature is going up.

体育 tǐyù（名词）
1. physical education (PE): 体育老师 PE teacher
2. sports: 体育节目 sports program

体育场 tǐyùchǎng（名词）sports stadium

体重 tǐzhòng（名词）weight: 称体重 weigh oneself

天安门 tiān'ānmén（名词）Tian'anmen: 天安门广场 Tian'anmen Square

天鹅 tiān'é（名词）swan

天空 tiānkōng（名词）sky: 仰望天空 look up into the sky ∥ 晴朗的天空 clear sky

天气 tiānqì（名词）weather: 恶劣的天气 bad weather ∥ 好天气 fine weather

天使 tiānshǐ（名词）angel

天堂 tiāntáng（名词）heaven; paradise: 人间天堂 heaven on earth

天天 tiāntiān（名词）every day; each day: 好好学习，天天向上。Study hard and make progress every day.

添 tiān（动词）add: 添水 add water (to) ∥ 添衣服 put on more clothes

田 tián（名词）field; farmland: 麦田 wheat field ∥ 稻田 rice field

田野 tiányě（名词）fields: 广阔的田野 vast fields

甜 tián（形容词）sweet: 甜汤 sweet soup

甜点 tiándiǎn（名词）dessert

甜蜜 tiánmì（形容词）sweet; happy: 甜蜜的梦 a sweet dream ∥ 甜蜜的生活 a sweet/happy life

甜食 tiánshí（名词）sweet; dessert

两人智慧胜一人。

挑选 tiāoxuǎn（动词）choose; select; pick (out): 细心挑选 carefully select/choose // 这家商店有品种繁多的货物可供挑选。The store has a wide selection of goods.

调皮 tiáopí（形容词）naughty: 调皮的孩子 a naughty child

跳 tiào（动词）jump: 跳到地上 jump onto the ground // 跳起来 jump into the air // 跳上跳下 jump up and down

跳高 tiàogāo（名词）high jump

跳绳 tiàoshéng（动词）jump rope: 我们一起跳绳吧。Let's jump rope.

跳舞 tiàowǔ（动词）dance

跳远 tiàoyuǎn（名词）long jump

铁路 tiělù（名词）railway; railroad: 铁路警察 railway police

听 tīng（动词）listen to; hear: 听故事 listen to a story // 听广播 listen to the radio // 听音乐 listen to music

用法小贴士
listen指"听"的动作，hear指"听见"。

听见 tīngjiàn（动词）hear: 我听了一会儿，什么也没听见。I listened for a while, but heard nothing.

听讲 tīngjiǎng（动词）listen to a lecture: 仔细听讲 listen to a lecture carefully // 一面听讲，一面记笔记 take notes while listening to a lecture

停止 tíngzhǐ（动词）stop: 停止工作 stop working // 停止谈话 stop talking

挺 tǐng（副词）very; quite; pretty: 挺好 pretty good // 考试挺难的。The examination was quite difficult.

通常 tōngcháng（副词）usually: 他通常7点起床。He usually gets up at seven.

通红 tōnghóng（形容词）very red: 她两眼哭得通红。Her eyes are red from crying.

通宵 tōngxiāo（名词）all night: 通宵派对 all-night party

同 tóng
1.（动词）be the same: 形状相同 be of the same shape // 同名 have the same name
2.（介词）with: 同我一起来吧。Come with me.
3.（连词）and: 我同他都来自南方。He and I both come from the south.

同班 tóngbān（动词）be in the same class: 同班同学 classmate // 迈克和我同班。Mike and I are in the same class.

346

Two heads are better than one.

同伴 tóngbàn（名词）companion

同窗 tóngchuāng（名词）schoolmate; classmate

同归于尽 tóngguīyújìn die together: 与敌人同归于尽 die together with the enemy

同时 tóngshí（名词）same time: 同时发生 happen at the same time

同岁 tóngsuì（形容词）of the same age: 我俩同岁。We're of the same age.

同屋 tóngwū（名词）roommate: 我有3个同屋。I have three roommates.

同学 tóngxué（名词）classmate: 新同学 new classmate // 他是我的同学。He is my classmate.

同样 tóngyàng（形容词）same: 同样的价格 same price // 同样大小 be of the same size

同意 tóngyì（动词）agree: 我同意。I agree. // 他不同意我的观点。He doesn't agree with me.

同桌 tóngzhuō（名词）classmate sharing the same desk at school

童话 tónghuà（名词）fairy tale: 讲童话故事 tell fairy tales

童年 tóngnián（名词）childhood: 快乐的童年 a happy childhood

童星 tóngxīng（名词）child star

桶 tǒng（名词）bucket: 一桶水 a bucket of water

痛 tòng（动词）ache: 头痛 have a headache // 牙痛 have a toothache // 胃痛 have a stomachache

偷 tōu（动词）steal: 偷钱包 steal somebody's wallet

头 tóu（名词）
1. head: 点头 nod one's head // 摇头 shake one's head // 从头到脚 from head to foot
2. beginning: 从头至尾 from beginning to end

头发 tóufa（名词）hair: 长头发 long hair // 白头发 white hair

头脑 tóunǎo（名词）brains; mind: 头脑聪明 have a brilliant mind // 头脑冷静 have a cool head

头痛 tóutòng（动词）have a headache: 我头痛得很厉害。I have a bad headache.

投递 tóudì（动词）deliver: 投递邮件 deliver mail

突然 tūrán（副词）suddenly: 突然下雨了。Suddenly it started to rain.

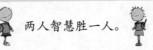
两人智慧胜一人。

图画 túhuà（名词）picture: 画一幅图画 draw a picture

图书 túshū（名词）books: 科技图书 science books ∥ 外文图书 foreign language books

图书馆 túshūguǎn（名词）library: 学校图书馆 school library ∥ 国家图书馆 national library

土 tǔ（名词）soil: 黑土 black soil ∥ 红土 red soil

土地 tǔdì（名词）land: 肥沃的土地 rich land ∥ 贫瘠的土地 poor land

土豆 tǔdòu（名词）potato: 土豆泥 mashed potato

吐司 tǔsī（名词）toast: 一片吐司 a piece of toast

百科小贴士
吐司是英语 toast 的音译词。

兔 tù（名词）rabbit; hare: 家兔 rabbit ∥ 野兔 hare ∥ 小白兔 white bunny

兔子 tùzi（名词）rabbit; hare

团队 tuánduì（名词）team: 团队精神 team spirit ∥ 旅游团队 tourist group

推 tuī（动词）push: 推开门 push the door open

腿 tuǐ（名词）leg: 鸡腿 chicken legs ∥ 桌子腿 desk legs ∥ 裤腿 trousers legs

拖把 tuōbǎ（名词）mop: 一把拖把 a mop

脱 tuō（动词）take...off: 脱大衣 take off one's coat

Walls have ears.

W

挖 wā（动词）dig: 挖洞 dig a hole

哇哇 wāwā（拟声词）wail: 哇哇大哭 wail; cry loudly

蛙人 wārén（名词）frogman

娃娃 wáwa（名词）baby; child: 洋娃娃 doll ∥ 布娃娃 rag doll ∥ 娃娃脸 baby face

袜 wà（名词）socks: 棉袜 cotton socks

袜子 wàzi（名词）socks: 一双袜子 a pair of socks

外边 wàibian（名词）outside: 请在外边等。Please wait outside. ∥ 外边很冷。It's cold outside.

外宾 wàibīn（名词）foreign guest

外公 wàigōng（名词）grandfather; grandpa

用法小贴士
英语没有"外公"和"爷爷"的区别，可以用 maternal grandfather 指外公，paternal grandfather 指爷爷。

外国 wàiguó（名词）foreign country: 外国留学生 foreign student ∥ 外国友人 foreign friend ∥

外国语 foreign language ∥ 外国人 foreigner

外面 wàimian（名词）outside: 到外面走走 take a walk outside

外婆 wàipó（名词）grandmother; grandma

用法小贴士
英语没有"外婆"和"奶奶"的区别，可以用 maternal grandmother 指外婆，paternal grandmother 指奶奶。

外甥 wàisheng（名词）nephew

外孙 wàisūn（名词）grandson

外孙女 wàisūnnǚ（名词）granddaughter

外衣 wàiyī（名词）coat

外语 wàiyǔ（名词）foreign language: 你会说几门外语？How many foreign languages can you speak?

豌豆 wāndòu（名词）pea

完 wán（动词）complete; finish: 我吃完了。I've finished eating.

349

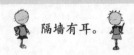

完成 wánchéng（动词）complete; finish: 我的作业还没完成。I haven't finished my homework yet.

完全 wánquán（副词）completely; totally: 完全相同 exactly the same ∥ 我完全同意你的看法。I totally agree with you.

完整 wánzhěng（形容词）complete: 一个完整的句子 a complete sentence

玩 wán（动词）play: 玩积木 play with the building blocks ∥ 玩牌 play cards ∥ 玩电脑游戏 play computer games

玩具 wánjù（名词）toy: 玩具店 toy store ∥ 玩具枪 toy gun

玩耍 wánshuǎ（动词）play: 在户外玩耍 play outdoors

玩笑 wánxiào（名词）joke: 跟某人开玩笑 play a joke on someone

顽皮 wánpí（形容词）naughty: 顽皮的男孩 a naughty boy

晚 wǎn
1.（名词）evening; night: 昨晚 last night ∥ 从早到晚 from morning till night
2.（形容词）late: 太晚了！It's too late!

晚安 wǎn'ān（动词）Good night!

晚报 wǎnbào（名词）evening paper

晚饭 wǎnfàn（名词）supper; dinner: 吃晚饭 have supper ∥ 准备晚饭 prepare supper

晚会 wǎnhuì（名词）party: 参加晚会 go to a party

晚礼服 wǎnlǐfú（名词）evening dress: 一件漂亮的晚礼服 a beautiful evening dress

晚上 wǎnshang（名词）evening; night: 在晚上 at night ∥ 昨天晚上 last night

碗 wǎn（名词）bowl: 玻璃碗 glass bowl ∥ 汤碗 soup bowl

碗柜 wǎnguì（名词）cabinet

万 wàn（数词）ten thousand: 一万两千 twelve thousand ∥ 十万 a hundred thousand

万里长城 wànlǐ chángchéng（名词）the Great Wall

万里长征 wànlǐ chángzhēng（名词）the Long March

王八 wángba（名词）tortoise

王妃 wángfēi（名词）princess: 戴安娜王妃 Princess Diana

王冠 wángguān（名词）crown

王后 wánghòu （名词）queen

用法小贴士

"王后"和"女王"都称作 queen。

王子 wángzǐ （名词）prince: 查尔斯王子 Prince Charles

网 wǎng （名词）
1. net: 渔网 fishing net
2. Internet: 上网 go online ∥ 网上购物 Internet shopping

网吧 wǎngbā （名词）Internet café

网球 wǎngqiú （名词）tennis: 打网球 play tennis ∥ 网球明星 tennis star

网页 wǎngyè （名词）web page: 打开网页 open a web page ∥ 制作网页 make a web page

网友 wǎngyǒu （名词）chat buddy

网站 wǎngzhàn （名词）Web site: 访问一个网站 visit a Web site

网址 wǎngzhǐ （名词）web address

往 wǎng
1. （动词）go: 人来人往。People come and go.
2. （介词）to: 飞往伦敦 fly to London

往往 wǎngwǎng （副词）often: 老人往往健忘。Old people are often forgetful.

忘 wàng （动词）forget: 我忘了带雨伞。I forgot to bring my umbrella.

忘记 wàngjì （动词）forget: 别忘记关灯。Don't forget to turn off the light.

危害 wēihài （动词）harm: 抽烟危害健康。Smoking harms your health.

危险 wēixiǎn
1. （形容词）dangerous: 玩火危险。It's dangerous to play with fire.
2. （名词）danger: 面临危险 be faced with a danger

威士忌 wēishìjì （名词）whiskey: 一瓶威士忌 a bottle of whiskey

百科小贴士

威士忌是英语 whiskey 的音译词。

微风 wēifēng （名词）gentle breeze

微笑 wēixiào
1. （动词）smile: 我们都对着相机微笑。We all smiled into the camera.
2. （名词）smile: 面带微笑 with a smile on one's face

围巾 wéijīn （名词）scarf: 一条红围巾 a red scarf

唯一 wéiyī （形容词）only: 他是家里唯一的孩子。He is the only child in the family.

隔墙有耳。

维生素 wéishēngsù（名词）
vitamin: 富含维生素 be rich in
vitamins ∥维生素A vitamin A

伟大 wěidà（形容词）great: 伟大
的发现 great discovery ∥伟大的
国家 great country

伟人 wěirén（名词）great person

尾巴 wěiba（名词）tail

卫兵 wèibīng（名词）guard

卫生间 wèishēngjiān（名词）toilet;
lavatory; washroom; restroom:
上卫生间 go to the toilet ∥男卫生
间 Gents' ∥女卫生间 Ladies'

卫生纸 wèishēngzhǐ（名词）toilet
paper

卫星 wèixīng（名词）satellite: 人
造卫星 man-made satellite

为了 wèile（介词）for; in order to:
为了明天早起，我得早睡。In order
to get up early tomorrow, I must
go to bed early.

为什么 wèishénme（副词）why: 为
什么不试一试？Why not have a
try? ∥你为什么迟到了？Why are
you late?

未来 wèilái（名词）future: 在未来
in the future

位置 wèizhi（名词）
1. place: 把它放回原来的位置。
Put it back in its place.
2. position: 替代某人的位置 take
somebody's place

位子 wèizi（名词）seat; place:
换位子 change seats

味道 wèidao（名词）taste; flavor:
尝味道 taste the flavor ∥我不喜欢
洋葱的味道。I don't like the taste
of onions.

喂 wèi
1.（动词）feed: 用肉喂狗 feed a
dog meat / feed meat to a dog
2.（叹词）hello; hey: 喂，能找一
下王先生吗？（打电话用语）Hello,
may I speak to Mr. Wang?

温 wēn（形容词）warm: 温水
warm water

温度 wēndù（名词）temperature:
最低/高温度 the lowest/highest
temperature

温暖 wēnnuǎn（形容词）warm: 温
暖的家庭 warm family ∥温暖的天
气 warm weather ∥温暖如春 be
as mild as spring

温泉 wēnquán（名词）hot spring

温室 wēnshì（名词）greenhouse

文化 wénhuà（名词）culture: 古老的文化 an ancient culture

文章 wénzhāng（名词）article: 写文章 write an article

闻 wén（动词）smell: 菜闻起来很香。The dish smells delicious.

闻名 wénmíng（动词）be famous: 闻名全国 be famous across the country

蚊子 wénzi（名词）mosquito

吻 wěn（动词）kiss: 吻别 kiss somebody goodbye

问 wèn（动词）ask: 问老师问题 ask the teacher a question

问题 wèntí（名词）question; problem: 回答问题 answer a question ∥ 解决问题 solve a problem

窝 wō（名词）nest: 筑窝 build a nest ∥ 蚂蚁窝 ants' nest

蜗牛 wōniú（名词）snail: 慢如蜗牛 be as slow as a snail

我 wǒ（代词）I; me: 我是学生。I'm a student. ∥ 告诉我 tell me ∥ 听我说 listen to me ∥ 这本书是你的还是我的? Is the book yours or mine?

我们 wǒmen（代词）we; us: 我们是好朋友。We are good friends. ∥ 他问了我们一个问题。He asked us a question. ∥ 哪张桌子是我们的? Which table is ours?

握手 wòshǒu（动词）shake hands: 和某人握手 shake hands with somebody

卧室 wòshì（名词）bedroom: 有3个卧室的房子 a house with three bedrooms

乌龟 wūguī（名词）tortoise

乌鸦 wūyā（名词）crow

乌云 wūyún（名词）black/dark cloud: 乌云蔽日。Black clouds have covered the sun. ∥ 乌云笼罩 be darkened by black clouds

污染 wūrǎn（动词）pollute: 废水污染了河流。Waste water has polluted the river. ∥ 空气污染 air pollution

屋顶 wūdǐng（名词）roof: 修屋顶 repair a roof ∥ 在屋顶上 on the roof

屋子 wūzi（名词）room: 打扫屋子 clean the room

无聊 wúliáo（形容词）dull; bored: 我觉得无聊。I'm bored.

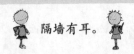

无声 wúshēng（动词）be silent; be soundless: 无声电影 silent film∥到处寂静无声。All was silent.

无忧无虑 wúyōu-wúlǜ carefree: 过着无忧无虑的生活 live a carefree life∥无忧无虑的女孩子 a carefree girl

五 wǔ（数词）five: 五个苹果 five apples∥五路公共汽车 No. 5 bus∥第五个 the fifth∥一周工作五天 work five days a week

五星红旗 wǔxīng hóngqí（名词）Five-Star Red Flag; the Chinese national flag

午饭 wǔfàn（名词）lunch: 吃午饭 have lunch∥留下吃午饭 stay for lunch∥午饭吃什么? What's for lunch?

午觉 wǔjiào（名词）nap after lunch: 睡午觉 take a nap after lunch

武器 wǔqì（名词）weapon; arms: 放下武器 lay down arms∥携带武器 carry a weapon

武术 wǔshù（名词）martial arts; kung fu: 一套武术 a set of kung fu∥练武术 practice kung fu

百科小贴士
kung fu 是功夫的音译词。

舞蹈 wǔdǎo（名词）dance: 舞蹈班 dance class∥舞蹈家 dancer

舞会 wǔhuì（名词）dance party; ball: 参加舞会 go to a dance∥举行舞会 hold a dance

物理 wùlǐ（名词）physics

物体 wùtǐ（名词）object

雾 wù（名词）fog: 一场大雾 a heavy fog∥浓雾 thick fog∥雾散了。The fog has cleared.∥起雾了。A fog has come down.

Xmas comes but once a year.

X

夕阳 xīyáng （名词）evening sun; setting sun: 看夕阳西下 watch the sunset

西 xī（名词）west: 朝西走 go west ∥向西拐 turn west ∥西风 west wind

西北 xīběi（名词）northwest: 朝向西北 face the northwest ∥中国西北部 northwest of China

西餐 xīcān（名词）Western food: 吃西餐 have Western food

西方 xīfāng（名词）
1. west: 太阳从西方落下。The sun sets in the west.
2. the West: 西方国家 Western countries

西服 xīfú（名词）Western clothes; suit

西瓜 xīguā （名词）watermelon: 一块西瓜 a slice of watermelon ∥西瓜汁 watermelon juice ∥西瓜子 watermelon seed

西红柿 xīhóngshì（名词）tomato

西南 xīnán（名词）southwest: 向西南飞行 fly southwest

西药 xīyào（名词）Western medicine: 吃西药 take Western medicine

吸毒 xīdú（动词）take drugs: 吸毒者 drug user

吸烟 xīyān（动词）smoke: 禁止吸烟。No smoking. ∥吸烟有害健康。Smoking is harmful to your health.

希望 xīwàng
1.（名词）wish; hope: 放弃希望 give up hope ∥满怀希望 be full of hope
2.（动词）hope; wish; expect: 他希望长大了当医生。He hopes to become a doctor when he grows up. ∥希望如此。I hope so.

熄灭 xīmiè（动词）go out: 灯光熄灭了。The lights went out.

膝盖 xīgài（名词）knee

蟋蟀 xīshuài（名词）cricket

习惯 xíguàn
1.（动词）get/be/become used to: 习惯早起 be used to getting up early
2.（名词）habit: 保持好习惯 keep a good habit ∥改掉坏习惯 get rid

of a bad habit ∥ 养成习惯 get into a habit

洗 xǐ（动词）wash: 洗脸 wash one's face ∥ 洗碗 do the washing up

洗发液 xǐfàyè（名词）shampoo

百科小贴士
洗发液又称洗发香波，香波是英语shampoo的音译词。

洗衣机 xǐyījī（名词）washing machine

洗澡 xǐzǎo（动词）have/take a bath/shower

喜欢 xǐhuan（动词）like; love: 喜欢动物 like animals ∥ 喜欢游泳 like swimming

戏剧 xìjù（名词）play: 上演戏剧 put on a play

细心 xìxīn
1.（形容词）careful: 细心的人 a careful person
2.（副词）carefully: 细心挑选 carefully choose

虾 xiā（名词）shrimp

瞎 xiā（动词）be blind: 瞎了一只眼 be blind in one eye

瞎子 xiāzi（名词）blind person

狭窄 xiázhǎi（形容词）narrow: 狭窄的街道 a narrow street

下 xià
1.（介词）under: 床下 under the bed ∥ 坐在树下 sit under the tree
2.（形容词）next: 下个星期 next week ∥ 下个世纪 next century
3.（动词）get down; go down: 下楼 go downstairs ∥ 下火车 get off a train
4.（动词）make: 下决心 make up one's mind

下班 xiàbān（动词）finish: 6点下班 finish work at six

下车 xiàchē（动词）get off: 下公共汽车 get off the bus

下次 xiàcì（名词）next time

下降 xiàjiàng（动词）fall: 温度下降了10度。The temperature fell by 10°C.

下课 xiàkè（动词）finish class: 下课了。Class is over.

下来 xiàlái（动词）come/get down: 从楼上下来 come downstairs

下午 xiàwǔ（名词）afternoon: 明天下午 tomorrow afternoon ∥ 星期三下午 Wednesday afternoon ∥ 下午好！Good afternoon!

下雨 xiàyǔ（动词）rain: 在下大雨。It's raining heavily. ∥ 看起来要下雨。It looks like rain.

夏令营 xiàlìngyíng（名词）summer camp: 参加夏令营 join a summer camp

356

夏天 xiàtiān（名词）summer: 前年夏天 the summer before last

先 xiān（副词）first; before: 如果你先完成，你可以回家。If you finish first, you can go home. ∥ 他比我先到。He arrived earlier than I did.

先生 xiānsheng（名词）Mr.: 王先生 Mr. Wang

鲜 xiān（形容词）
1. fresh: 鲜花 fresh flower ∥ 鲜肉 fresh meat ∥ 鲜鱼 fresh fish
2. bright: 鲜红 bright red; scarlet

鲜血 xiānxuè（名词）blood

鲜艳 xiānyàn（形容词）brightly colored: 鲜艳的五星红旗冉冉升起。The bright Chinese national flag is raised slowly.

闲 xián（形容词）at leisure: 闲着没事干 have nothing to do

咸 xián（形容词）salty: 海水又苦又咸。Seawater tastes bitter and salty. ∥ 咸菜 pickles

显微镜 xiǎnwēijìng（名词）microscope

现代 xiàndài（名词）modern times: 在现代 in modern times

现在 xiànzài（名词）now: 直到现在 till now ∥ 从现在起 from now on

线 xiàn（名词）
1. thread: 一根线 a piece of thread
2. wire: 电话线 telephone wire ∥ 钓鱼线 fishing line

乡村 xiāngcūn（名词）village; countryside: 乡村音乐 country music

乡下 xiāngxia（名词）countryside; village: 住在乡下 live in the countryside

相互 xiānghù（副词）each other: 相互帮助 help each other ∥ 相互学习 learn from each other

相同 xiāngtóng（形容词）same: 大小相同 be of the same size

相信 xiāngxìn（动词）believe; trust: 难以相信。It's hard to believe. ∥ 请相信我。Please trust me.

香 xiāng（形容词）
1. fragrant: 这些花真香。The flowers smell fragrant.
2. delicious: 菜真香啊！What a delicious dish!

香槟酒 xiāngbīnjiǔ（名词）champagne

百科小贴士
香槟是英语 champagne 的音译词。

香波 xiāngbō（名词）shampoo

百科小贴士

香波是英语shampoo的音译词。

香肠 xiāngcháng（名词）sausage

香港 xiānggǎng（名词）Hong Kong

香蕉 xiāngjiāo（名词）banana

香水 xiāngshuǐ（名词）perfume

香皂 xiāngzào（名词）soap

箱子 xiāngzi（名词）box: 搬箱子 carry a box // 一箱子苹果 a box of apples

响 xiǎng
1.（形容词）loud: 很响的声音 loud sounds
2.（动词）make a sound; ring: 电话铃在响。The telephone is ringing. // 闹钟响了。The alarm clock went off.

响亮 xiǎngliàng（形容词）loud and clear

想 xiǎng（动词）
1. think: 认真想想 think carefully // 想出办法 find a way
2. want to: 我想吃点东西。I want to eat something.
3. miss: 你走了以后，我们都很想你。After you left, we all missed you.

想法 xiǎngfǎ（名词）idea: 有了一个想法 have an idea

想念 xiǎngniàn（动词）miss: 我很想念我的奶奶。I miss my grandma very much.

想象 xiǎngxiàng（动词）imagine: 想象未来 imagine the future

想象力 xiǎngxiànglì（名词）imagination: 丰富的想象力 rich imagination

向 xiàng（介词）to; toward: 向东流 flow east // 向某人学习 learn from somebody // 向上看 look upward

项链 xiàngliàn（名词）necklace: 钻石项链 diamond necklace

相机 xiàngjī（名词）camera: 数码相机 digital camera

相片 xiàngpiàn（名词）photo: 彩色相片 color photo

象棋 xiàngqí（名词）Chinese chess: 下象棋 play Chinese chess // 国际象棋 chess

像 xiàng（动词）look like; take after: 她长得像她妈妈。She takes after her mother.

橡胶 xiàngjiāo（名词）rubber: 橡胶树 rubber tree

橡皮 xiàngpí（名词）eraser; rubber eraser

用法小贴士

eraser是美国英语，rubber是英国英语。

消息 xiāoxi（名词）news: 一条消息 a piece of news ∥ 好消息 good news ∥ 坏消息 bad news

小 xiǎo（形容词）
1. small; little: 小房间 small room
2. young: 他比我小两岁。He is two years younger than I.

小丑 xiǎochǒu（名词）clown: 演小丑 play a clown ∥ 马戏团小丑 circus clown

小狗 xiǎogǒu（名词）puppy

小孩 xiǎohái（名词）child; kid

小鸡 xiǎojī（名词）chick

小姐 xiǎojiě（名词）Miss: 王小姐 Miss Wang

小麦 xiǎomài（名词）wheat: 小麦粉 wheat flour

小猫 xiǎomāo（名词）kitten

小朋友 xiǎopéngyǒu（名词）little boy; little girl; little fellow/kid: 小朋友，你在找什么呢？What are you looking for, my little fellow?

小时 xiǎoshí（名词）hour: 一个小时 an hour ∥ 一个半小时 one and a half hours

小时候 xiǎoshíhou（名词）childhood: 小时候的照片 childhood photo

小提琴 xiǎotíqín（名词）violin: 拉小提琴 play the violin ∥ 小提琴手 violinist

小偷 xiǎotōu（名词）thief: 抓小偷 catch a thief

小心 xiǎoxīn
1.（动词）take care; be careful: 过马路要小心。Be careful when you cross the street.
2.（形容词）careful: 我当时不够小心。I wasn't careful then.

小学 xiǎoxué（名词）primary school

小学生 xiǎoxuéshēng（名词）student

小组 xiǎozǔ（名词）group: 学习小组 study group

校 xiào（名词）school: 校车 school bus ∥ 全校师生 the whole school ∥ 按时到校 get to school on time

校服 xiàofú（名词）school uniform

校园 xiàoyuán（名词）campus: 在校园里 on campus

校长 xiàozhǎng（名词）headmaster

笑 xiào（动词）smile; laugh

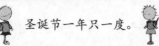

圣诞节一年只一度。

笑话 xiàohuà
1.（名词）joke: 讲笑话 tell a joke
2.（动词）laugh at: 请别笑话我。
Please don't laugh at me.

笑容 xiàoróng（名词）smile: 面带笑容 have a smile on one's face

歇 xiē（动词）rest; have a rest: 歇一歇 have a rest

鞋 xié（名词）shoe: 一双鞋 a pair of shoes // 穿鞋 put on one's shoes // 脱鞋 take off one's shoes

写 xiě（动词）write: 写作文 write a composition // 在黑板上写 write on the blackboard

写作 xiězuò（动词）write: 练习写作 practice writing

谢谢 xièxie（动词）thank you: 谢谢你的礼物。Thank you for your present.

心 xīn（名词）heart: 他的心跳得很快。His heart was beating fast.

心愿 xīnyuàn（名词）wish; dream: 良好心愿 good wishes

心脏 xīnzàng（名词）heart: 心脏病 heart disease

辛苦 xīnkǔ（形容词）hard: 辛苦的工作 hard work

辛勤 xīnqín（形容词）hardworking: 辛勤劳动 work hard

新 xīn（形容词）new: 新车 new car // 新同学 new student

新年 xīnnián（名词）new year: 新年快到了。The New Year is coming. // 新年快乐！Happy New Year!

新手 xīnshǒu（名词）new hand

新闻 xīnwén（名词）news: 新闻报道 news report // 一条新闻 a piece of news

新鲜 xīnxiān（形容词）fresh: 新鲜空气 fresh air // 新鲜面包 fresh bread // 新鲜蔬菜 fresh vegetables

信 xìn
1.（名词）letter: 写信 write a letter // 收到信 receive a letter
2.（动词）believe; trust: 信不信由你。It's up to you to believe it or not.

信封 xìnfēng（名词）envelope: 拆开信封 open an envelope // 在信封上写地址 address an envelope

信任 xìnrèn（动词）trust: 我信任你。I trust you.

信箱 xìnxiāng（名词）mailbox; letterbox

兴奋 xīngfèn（形容词）excited: 感到兴奋 feel excited

星期 xīngqī（名词）week: 上星期 last week ∥ 下星期 next week ∥ 3个星期 three weeks ∥ 星期一 Monday ∥ 星期二 Tuesday ∥ 星期三 Wednesday ∥ 星期四 Thursday ∥ 星期五 Friday ∥ 星期六 Saturday ∥ 星期日 Sunday

星星 xīngxing（名词）star: 闪烁的星星 twinkling stars

行动 xíngdòng
1.（动词）act: 立即行动 act at once
2.（名词）act; action: 奇怪的行动 strange act

行李 xíngli（名词）baggage; luggage: 一件行李 a piece of luggage ∥ 收拾行李 pack one's bags

行驶 xíngshǐ（动词）travel; go; run: 高速行驶 travel at a high speed

形容词 xíngróngcí（名词）adjective

形状 xíngzhuàng（名词）shape: 形状相同 be of the same shape

醒 xǐng（动词）wake up: 从梦中醒来 wake up from a dream

兴趣 xìngqù（名词）interest: 感兴趣 be interested in

幸福 xìngfú（形容词）happy: 幸福的家庭 a happy family ∥ 幸福的生活 a happy life

幸运 xìngyùn（形容词）lucky: 幸运数字 lucky number

姓 xìng（名词）surname; family name: 你姓什么？ What's your family name? ∥ 我姓李。 My family name is Li.

姓名 xìngmíng（名词）name

兄弟 xiōngdì（名词）brothers: 孪生兄弟 twin brothers

胸 xiōng（名词）chest; breast

胸膛 xiōngtáng（名词）chest; breast

熊 xióng（名词）bear: 玩具熊 teddy bear

熊猫 xióngmāo（名词）panda

休息 xiūxi（动词）have a rest

修 xiū（动词）repair; fix; mend: 修表 repair a watch ∥ 修车 repair a car

修建 xiūjiàn（动词）build: 修建马路 build a road

修理 xiūlǐ（动词）repair: 修理收音机 repair a radio ∥ 修理自行车 repair bicycles

嗅 xiù（动词）smell: 你嗅到烟味儿了吗？ Do you smell cigarette smoke?

361

嗅觉 xiùjué （名词）sense of smell: 狗的嗅觉很灵敏。Dogs have a sharp sense of smell.

需要 xūyào （动词）need: 需要帮忙 need help ∥我需要好好休息一下。I need a good rest.

许多 xǔduō（形容词）many; much; a lot of: 许多人 many people ∥许多时间 much time ∥我有许多朋友。I've got a lot of friends.

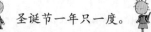

用法小贴士
many 只能修饰可数名词，much 只能修饰不可数名词，a lot of 可以修饰两者。

选 xuǎn （动词）choose: 他选了最大的蛋糕。He chose the biggest cake.

选举 xuǎnjǔ （动词）elect: 选举班长 elect a class monitor ∥选举总统 elect a president

选择 xuǎnzé
1.（动词）choose: 从这两个中选一个。Choose one from these two.
2.（名词）choice: 没有选择 have no choice ∥作选择 make a choice

靴子 xuēzi （名词）boots: 一双靴子 a pair of boots

学 xué （动词）learn: 学英语 learn English ∥学钢琴 learn to play the piano

学期 xuéqī （名词）term: 上学期 the first term ∥下学期 the second term

学生 xuésheng （名词）student; pupil: 小学生 pupil ∥中学生 middle school student ∥大学生 university student

学习 xuéxí （动词）
1. study: 努力学习 study hard ∥学习文化 learn to read and write
2. learn from: 向某人学习 learn from somebody ∥向雷锋学习 learn from Lei Feng

学校 xuéxiào （名词）school: 艺术学校 art school

雪 xuě （名词）snow: 第一场雪 the first snow ∥大雪 heavy snow ∥下雪了。It's snowing.

雪白 xuěbái（形容词）snow-white: 雪白的头发 snow-white hair

雪花 xuěhuā（名词）snowflake: 雪花飞舞。Snowflakes are swirling.

雪球 xuěqiú（名词）snowball: 扔雪球 throw snowballs

雪人 xuěrén（名词）snowman: 堆雪人 make a snowman

寻找 xúnzhǎo （动词）look for: 小女孩在寻找妈妈。The little girl was looking for her mother.

迅速 xùnsù（形容词）quick

Y

丫头 yātou（名词）girl: 她是个可爱的丫头。She's a lovely girl.

压岁钱 yāsuìqián（名词）gift of money to children for Chinese New Year

呀 yā（叹词）oh no: 呀，我又把语文课本忘在家里了！Oh no! I left my Chinese textbook at home again!

鸭 yā（名词）duck: 烤鸭 roast duck ∥ 小鸭子 duckling ∥《丑小鸭》The Ugly Duckling

牙 yá（名词）tooth: 乳牙 milk tooth ∥ 刷牙 brush one's teeth

牙齿 yáchǐ（名词）tooth

牙膏 yágāo（名词）toothpaste: 挤牙膏 squeeze toothpaste

牙刷 yáshuā（名词）toothbrush

牙疼 yáténg（名词）toothache: 我牙疼。I've got a toothache.

牙医 yáyī（名词）dentist

亚运村 yàyùncūn（名词）Asian Games Village

亚运会 yàyùnhuì（名词）Asian Games

亚洲 yàzhōu（名词）Asia: 亚洲人 the Asians

烟 yān（名词）
1. smoke: 浓烟 heavy smoke
2. cigarette: 吸烟 smoke; smoke cigarettes

烟花 yānhuā（名词）fireworks: 放烟花 set off fireworks

严格 yángé（形容词）strict: 老师们对我们很严格。The teachers are very strict with us.

炎黄子孙 yánhuáng zǐsūn（名词）Chinese people

盐 yán（名词）salt: 海盐 sea salt ∥ 食盐 table salt ∥ 请把盐递给我。Please pass me the salt.

颜色 yánsè（名词）color: 鲜艳的颜色 bright colors ∥ 你的新鞋子是什么颜色的？What color are your new shoes?

眼镜 yǎnjìng（名词）glasses: 一副眼镜 a pair of glasses ∥ 戴眼镜 wear glasses

人不可貌相。

眼睛 yǎnjing（名词）eye: 又大又亮的眼睛 big bright eyes // 睁开眼睛 open one's eyes // 闭上眼睛 close one's eyes

眼泪 yǎnlèi（名词）tear: 擦干眼泪 wipe away one's tears

演 yǎn（动词）act: 演杂技 perform acrobatics

演唱 yǎnchàng（动词）sing: 演唱歌曲 sing a song

演出 yǎnchū
1.（动词）perform; put on a performance: 登台演出 perform on the stage
2.（名词）performance: 观看演出 watch a performance

演讲 yǎnjiǎng
1.（动词）make a speech: 她擅长演讲。She is good at making speeches.
2.（名词）speech: 英语演讲赛 English speech contest

演员 yǎnyuán（名词）actor; actress

羊 yáng（名词）sheep; goat: 绵羊 sheep // 山羊 goat

阳光 yángguāng（名词）sunshine: 明媚的阳光 bright sunshine

洋 yáng
1.（名词）ocean: 太平洋 the Pacific Ocean
2.（形容词）foreign: 洋文 foreign language

洋葱 yángcōng（名词）onion

洋人 yángrén（名词）foreigner

样 yàng（名词）kind: 你喜欢什么样的音乐？What kind of music do you like?

要求 yāoqiú
1.（动词）require; demand: 老师要求大家安静。The teacher demanded that everyone be quiet.
2.（名词）demand: 合理要求 reasonable demand

腰带 yāodài（名词）belt

邀请 yāoqǐng（动词）invite: 邀请朋友参加聚会 invite friends to a party

摇 yáo（动词）shake: 摇头 shake one's head

咬 yǎo（动词）bite: 咬嘴唇 bite one's lip // 咬指甲 bite one's fingernail

药 yào（名词）medicine: 吃药 take medicine

要 yào
1.（动词）want: 我要一个新台灯。I want a new desk lamp.
2. should: 饭前要洗手。You should wash your hands before you eat.

364

钥匙 yàoshi（名词）key: 一串钥匙 a bunch of keys

爷爷 yéye（名词）grandfather; grandpa

也 yě（副词）too: 他12岁，我也12岁。He is twelve. I'm twelve, too.

也许 yěxǔ（副词）maybe; perhaps: 也许明天会下雨。Perhaps it will rain tomorrow.

野 yě（形容词）wild: 野果 wild fruit∥野花 wild flower∥野马 wild horse

野餐 yěcān（动词）have a picnic

野兽 yěshòu（名词）wild animal

叶 yè（名词）leaf: 绿叶 green leaves∥红叶 red leaves

叶子 yèzi（名词）leaf

页 yè（名词）page: 这本书有90页。The book has ninety pages.∥请翻到第10页。Please turn to page ten.

页码 yèmǎ（名词）page number

夜里 yèli（名词）night-time: 夜里很冷。It was very cold at night.

夜市 yèshì（名词）night market

夜晚 yèwǎn（名词）night

一 yī（数词）one: 一分钟 one minute

一半 yíbàn（数词）half: 一半人 half of the people

一辈子 yíbèizi（名词）all one's life: 他做了一辈子好事。He has done good deeds all his life.

一边 yìbiān（副词）at the same time: 他一边吃饭，一边说话。He was eating and talking at the same time.

一共 yígòng（副词）in total: 我们学校一共有1000名学生。There are one thousand students in our school in total.

一起 yìqǐ（副词）together: 一起来 come together

一切 yìqiè（代词）all; everything: 一切都很好。All is well.

一天到晚 yìtiān-dàowǎn from morning till night: 一天到晚学习 study from morning till night

一些 yìxiē（数量词）some: 一些人在读书，一些人在看报。Some people were reading books; some were reading newspapers.

一样 yíyàng（形容词）same: 他和我一样高。He is as tall as I am.

一月 yīyuè（名词）January

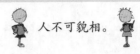

衣服 yīfu （名词）clothes: 新衣服 new clothes // 换衣服 change clothes

医生 yīshēng （名词）doctor: 看医生 see a doctor

医院 yīyuàn （名词）hospital: 去医院看病 go to the hospital

姨妈 yímā （名词）aunt

用法小贴士
英语没有"姨妈"和"姑妈"之分，可以用 maternal aunt 表示"姨妈"，用 paternal aunt 表示"姑妈"。

移动 yídòng （动词）move: 移动脚步 move one's feet

颐和园 yíhéyuán （名词）the Summer Palace

已经 yǐjing （副词）already: 他已经走了。 He's already left.

以后 yǐhòu （名词）later: 两年以后 two years later

以前 yǐqián （名词）ago; before: 10年以前 ten years ago // 我和她以前没见过。 I've never met her before.

以为 yǐwéi （动词）think: 我以为我是对的。 I think I'm right.

椅子 yǐzi （名词）chair: 扶手椅 armchair

亿 yì （数词）a hundred million

艺术 yìshù （名词）art

艺术家 yìshùjiā （名词）artist

意见 yìjiàn （名词）opinion; view: 你是什么意见？ What's your opinion?

因特网 yīntèwǎng （名词）Internet

百科小贴士
因特网是英语 Internet 的音意合译词。是目前全球最大的由众多计算机网络互联而成的网络，覆盖一百五十多个国家。

因为 yīnwèi （连词）because: 我迟到了，因为我起晚了。 I was late because I got up late.

音乐 yīnyuè （名词）music: 听音乐 listen to music // 古典音乐 classical music // 流行音乐 pop music

银行 yínháng （名词）bank: 中国人民银行 People's Bank of China // 中国银行 Bank of China // 世界银行 World Bank

饮料 yǐnliào （名词）drink: 软饮料 soft drink

饮食 yǐnshí （名词）food and drink

应该 yīnggāi （副词）should: 你应该早点来。 You should come here earlier.

英镑 yīngbàng （名词）British pound

英国 yīngguó （名词）Britain; the United Kingdom

英雄 yīngxióng （名词）hero: 民族英雄 national hero

英语 yīngyǔ （名词）English: 说英语 speak English

婴儿 yīng'ér （名词）baby: 婴儿食品 baby food

影片 yǐngpiàn （名词）film: 外国影片 foreign film

硬 yìng （形容词）hard: 硬木 hard wood ∥ 硬座 hard seat

硬币 yìngbì （名词）coin

硬件 yìngjiàn （名词）hardware

硬盘 yìngpán （名词）hard disk

拥抱 yōngbào （动词）hug: 他与到场的每个人拥抱。He hugged everyone present.

永远 yǒngyuǎn （副词）forever: 我会永远记住你。I will remember you forever.

泳衣 yǒngyī （名词）bathing suit

勇敢 yǒnggǎn （形容词）brave: 勇敢的战士 brave soldiers

勇气 yǒngqì （名词）courage: 有勇气 have courage

用 yòng （动词）use: 我可以用一下你的钢笔吗？May I use your pen?

优点 yōudiǎn （名词）strong point: 学习别人的优点 learn from the strong points of other people

由于 yóuyú （连词）because: 由于太晚了，我就没出去。I didn't go out because it was too late.

邮局 yóujú （名词）post office

邮票 yóupiào （名词）stamp: 收集邮票 collect stamps ∥ 贴邮票 put stamps on the envelope

百科小贴士

世界上第一枚邮票于1840年在英国发行，中国的第一套邮票是"大龙邮票"，于1878年由清政府发行。

油 yóu （名词）oil: 动物油 animal oil ∥ 石油 oil ∥ 植物油 vegetable oil

油漆 yóuqī （名词）paint: 油漆未干！Wet paint!

游客 yóukè （名词）visitor: 游客止步！No visitors!

游览 yóulǎn （动词）visit: 游览长城 visit the Great Wall

Y

游乐园 yóulèyuán （名词）amusement park: 儿童游乐园 children's amusement park

游戏 yóuxì （名词）game: 玩游戏 play games // 电子游戏 video games

游戏机 yóuxìjī （名词）video game player

游泳 yóuyǒng （动词）swim: 去游泳 go swimming

游泳池 yóuyǒngchí （名词）swimming pool: 室内游泳池 indoor swimming pool // 室外游泳池 outdoor swimming pool

友好 yǒuhǎo （形容词）friendly: 友好的微笑 friendly smile

友人 yǒurén （名词）friend: 国际友人 foreign friend

友谊 yǒuyì （名词）friendship: 深厚友谊 deep friendship

有 yǒu （动词）
1. have: 你有宠物吗？ Do you have any pets?
2. there is/are: 我们班有45个学生。There are forty-five students in our class.

有名 yǒumíng （形容词）famous; well-known: 这家餐馆很有名。The restaurant is very famous.

有趣 yǒuqù （形容词）funny; interesting: 有趣的故事 interesting story

有时 yǒushí （副词）sometimes: 天气有时冷，有时热。It's sometimes cold and sometimes hot.

有些 yǒuxiē （代词）some: 有些地方 some places // 有些人 some people

又 yòu （副词）
1. again: 他又来了。He's come again.
2. both...and: 又唱又跳 sing and dance // 又累又饿 be both tired and hungry

右 yòu （名词）right: 向右转 turn right

幼儿 yòu'ér （名词）small children

幼儿园 yòu'éryuán （名词）nursery; kindergarten

幼小 yòuxiǎo （形容词）young

于是 yúshì （连词）so: 我很困，于是早早睡觉了。I was sleepy, so I went to bed early.

鱼 yú （名词）fish: 两条鱼 two fish // 鱼塘 fish pond // 鱼缸 fish tank

愉快 yúkuài （形容词）happy; pleasant: 祝你旅途愉快！Have a good trip!

You cannot judge a book by its cover.

愚蠢 yúchǔn（形容词）foolish; stupid: 愚蠢的错误 foolish mistake ∥ 愚蠢的想法 stupid idea

宇航 yǔháng （动词）travel in space

宇航服 yǔhángfú（名词）space suit

宇航员 yǔhángyuán（名词）astronaut

宇宙 yǔzhòu（名词）universe: 宇宙的奥秘 secrets of the universe

宇宙飞船 yǔzhòu fēichuán（名词）spaceship

百科小贴士

宇宙飞船是航天器的一种，从地球上发射出去，能在宇宙空间航行，分为卫星式载人飞船和登月载人飞船。中国第一艘载人宇宙飞船于 2003 年 10 月 15 日发射上天。

羽毛 yǔmáo（名词）feather: 羽毛扇 fan made of feathers

羽毛球 yǔmáoqiú （名词）badminton: 打羽毛球 play badminton

雨 yǔ（名词）rain: 春雨 spring rain ∥ 大雨 heavy rain ∥ 小雨 light rain

雨林 yǔlín（名词）rainforest: 雨林气候 rainforest climate

雨伞 yǔsǎn （名词）umbrella: 打雨伞 open an umbrella

雨鞋 yǔxié（名词）rain boots

雨衣 yǔyī（名词）raincoat

语法 yǔfǎ （名词）grammar: 英语语法 English grammar

语文 yǔwén（名词）
1. language
2. Chinese: 语文课 Chinese class

语言 yǔyán（名词）language: 学习语言 learn a language

语音 yǔyīn （名词）pronunciation: 标准语音 standard pronunciation

玉米 yùmǐ（名词）corn: 玉米面 corn flour

浴巾 yùjīn（名词）bath towel

浴帽 yùmào （名词）shower cap

浴室 yùshì （名词）bathroom

预备 yùbèi（动词）prepare for: 预备考试 prepare for an exam

预习 yùxí（动词）prepare for one's lessons

遇到 yùdào（动词）meet: 我是一年前第一次遇到他的。I first met him a year ago.

元 yuán （名词）yuan: 10元钱 ten yuan

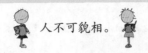

人不可貌相。

元旦 yuándàn （名词）New Year's Day

元宵节 yuánxiāojié（名词） Lantern Festival

百科小贴士

元宵节是中国传统节日，在农历正月十五。这天晚上民间有观灯的习俗。

园丁 yuándīng（名词）
1. gardener
2. teacher

原谅 yuánliàng （动词）forgive：请原谅我。Please forgive me.

原因 yuányīn （名词）reason：他迟到的原因是没赶上公交车。The reason he was late was that he missed the bus.

原子 yuánzǐ（名词）atom：原子弹 atom bomb

圆 yuán （形容词） round：圆脸 round face ∥圆桌 round table

圆圈 yuánquān（名词）circle：画一个圆圈 draw a circle

圆珠笔 yuánzhūbǐ（名词） ballpoint pen

猿猴 yuánhóu（名词）apes and monkeys

猿人 yuánrén（名词）ape man：北京猿人 Peking Man

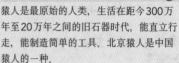
百科小贴士

猿人是最原始的人类，生活在距今300万年至20万年之间的旧石器时代，能直立行走，能制造简单的工具。北京猿人是中国猿人的一种。

远 yuǎn（形容词）far：那地方离这儿很远。The place is very far from here.

愿望 yuànwàng（名词）wish；hope：我的愿望是去爬上长城。I wish to climb the Great Wall.

愿意 yuànyì（动词）be willing；be ready：他总是愿意帮忙。He is always ready to help others.

月 yuè（名词）
1. moon：一轮圆月 a full moon
2. month：一年有十二个月。There are twelve months in a year.

月饼 yuèbīng（名词）moon cake

月光 yuèguāng（名词）moonlight：明亮的月光 bright moonlight

月亮 yuèliang （名词）moon

月球 yuèqiú （名词）moon

乐队 yuèduì（名词）band：校乐队 school band

阅读 yuèdú （动词）read：阅读书报 read books and newspapers ∥仔细阅读 read carefully

阅览室 yuèlǎnshì （名词）reading room

云 yún （名词）cloud

云彩 yúncai （名词）cloud

允许 yǔnxǔ （动词）allow: 我不允许猫进入卧室。I don't allow the cat in the bedroom.

运动 yùndòng （名词）sports; exercises: 参加运动 do sports // 经常进行运动 take regular exercises

运动会 yùndònghuì （名词）sports meet; games: 举行运动会 hold a sports meet

运动鞋 yùndòngxié （名词）sneakers: 一双运动鞋 a pair of sneakers

运动员 yùndòngyuán （名词）athlete; sportsman; sportswoman; player: 足球运动员 football player

运气 yùnqi （名词）luck: 好运气 good luck

Z

杂志 zázhì（名词）magazine: 儿童杂志 children's magazine

灾难 zāinàn（名词）disaster

栽 zāi（动词）plant; grow: 栽花 grow flowers

栽种 zāizhòng（动词）plant; grow

再 zài（副词）
1. again: 再说一遍。Say it again.
2. then: 吃完饭再玩。Eat your dinner and then you can play.

再见 zàijiàn（动词）goodbye; bye-bye; see you

在 zài
1.（动词）be: 他在教室里。He is in the classroom.
2.（副词）be doing something: 他在打篮球。He is playing basketball.
3.（介词）at: 在机场 at the airport

在乎 zàihu（动词）care: 人家怎么说，我才不在乎呢。I don't care what people say.

在家 zàijiā（动词）be at home; be in

赞美 zànměi（动词）praise

脏 zāng（形容词）dirty: 脏手 dirty hands∥脏衣服 dirty clothes

脏话 zānghuà（名词）dirty words: 说脏话 use dirty words

早 zǎo
1.（形容词）early: 还早呢。It's still early.∥火车早到了几分钟。The train was a few minutes early.
2.（副词）a long time ago: 我早知道了。I knew that a long time ago.

早安 zǎo'ān（名词）good morning

早操 zǎocāo（名词）morning exercises: 做早操 do morning exercises

早晨 zǎochen（名词）morning

早饭 zǎofàn（名词）breakfast: 吃早饭 have breakfast

早上 zǎoshang（名词）morning: 早上好！Good morning!

澡堂 zǎotáng（名词）bathhouse

造 zào（动词）make; build: 造船 build a ship

造句 zàojù（动词）make a sentence

造纸 zàozhǐ（动词）make paper

噪音 zàoyīn（名词）noise: 制造噪音 make noises

贼 zéi（名词）thief: 捉贼 catch a thief

怎么 zěnme（代词）how; what; why: 怎么啦？What's up? ∥他怎么还不回来？Why isn't he back yet?

怎样 zěnyàng（代词）how; what: 你觉得这本书怎样？What do you think of the book?

曾祖父 zēngzǔfù（名词）great-grandfather

曾祖母 zēngzǔmǔ（名词）great-grandmother

增加 zēngjiā（动词）increase

炸弹 zhàdàn（名词）bomb: 定时炸弹 time bomb

摘 zhāi（动词）pick: 摘花 pick flowers ∥摘水果 pick fruits

窄 zhǎi（形容词）narrow: 路很窄。The road is very narrow.

战场 zhànchǎng（名词）battlefield

战斗 zhàndòu
1.（名词）fight; battle: 激烈的战斗 fierce battle
2.（动词）fight: 战斗到底 fight to the end

战舰 zhànjiàn（名词）battleship

战士 zhànshì（名词）soldier: 解放军战士 PLA soldiers

战争 zhànzhēng（名词）war: 战争结束。The war ended.

站 zhàn
1.（动词）stand: 站起来 stand up
2.（名词）stop; station: 公共汽车站 bus stop ∥火车站 railway station

站立 zhànlì（动词）stand

张 zhāng（量词）一张纸 a piece of paper ∥一张桌子 a table

长 zhǎng
1.（名词）head; leader: 队长 team leader ∥校长 head teacher
2.（动词）grow: 长得快 grow fast
3.（动词）begin to grow: 长胡子 grow a beard ∥长叶子 grow leaves

长大 zhǎngdà（动词）grow up

丈夫 zhàngfu（名词）husband

账单 zhàngdān（名词）bill

All work and no play makes Jack a dull boy.

招呼 zhāohu（动词）greet: 招呼某人 greet somebody; say hello

着急 zháojí（形容词）worried: 我真的很着急。I'm really worried.

着凉 zháoliáng（动词）catch cold: 当心着凉。Be careful not to catch cold.

找 zhǎo（动词）look for: 找工作 look for a job

找到 zhǎodào（动词）find: 我找不到回家的路。I couldn't find my way home.

照顾 zhàogù（动词）look after: 照顾好孩子 take good care of the children

照片 zhàopiàn（名词）photo; picture: 拍照片 take a picture // 彩色照片 color photo // 黑白照片 black-and-white photo

照相 zhàoxiàng（动词）take a picture

照相机 zhàoxiàngjī（名词）camera: 使用照相机 use a camera // 修理照相机 repair a camera

这 zhè（代词）this: 这匹马 this horse // 这是李先生。This is Mr. Li.

这边 zhèbian（代词）this side; here: 到这边来。Come over here.

这次 zhècì（代词）this time

这个 zhège（代词）this: 这个问题 this problem

这里 zhèlǐ（代词）here: 乔治在这里吗? Is George here?

这么 zhème（代词）such; so: 今天这么热。It's so hot today.

这儿 zhèr（代词）here

这些 zhèxiē（代词）these: 这些书 these books

针 zhēn（名词）needle

针线 zhēnxiàn（名词）needle and thread: 针线活 needlework

侦探 zhēntàn（名词）detective: 侦探故事 detective story

真 zhēn
1.（形容词）true; real: 真话 truth
2.（副词）really: 她真勇敢。She's really brave.

真实 zhēnshí（形容词）true: 真实的故事 true story

真正 zhēnzhèng（形容词）true; real: 真正的朋友 true friend

睁 zhēng（动词）open: 睁开眼睛 open one's eyes

374

只会用功不玩耍，聪明孩子也变傻。

整个 zhěnggè（形容词）whole: 整个国家/世界 the whole nation/world

整天 zhěngtiān（名词）all day

整夜 zhěngyè（名词）all night: 我整夜未眠。I was awake all night.

正确 zhèngquè（形容词）correct: 正确的答案 correct answer

只 zhī（量词）一只鸡 a chicken ∥ 两只老虎 two tigers

枝条 zhītiáo（名词）branch

知道 zhīdào（动词）know: 他知道的事情很多。He knows a lot.

知识 zhīshi（名词）knowledge: 知识就是力量。Knowledge is power.

蜘蛛 zhīzhū（名词）spider

直 zhí（形容词）straight

直线 zhíxiàn（名词）straight line

侄女 zhínǚ（名词）niece

侄子 zhízi（名词）nephew

值日 zhírì（动词）be on duty: 今天我值日。I'm on duty today.

植物 zhíwù（名词）plant

只 zhǐ（副词）only: 只剩一个了。There's only one left.

只有 zhǐyǒu（副词）only; alone: 只有他知道这件事。Only he knows about it.

纸 zhǐ（名词）paper: 一张纸 a piece of paper

纸杯 zhǐbēi（名词）paper cup

纸巾 zhǐjīn（名词）paper towel

指甲 zhǐjiɑ（名词）nail: 剪指甲 cut one's nails

指南针 zhǐnánzhēn（名词）compass

指头 zhǐtou（名词）finger

制造 zhìzào（动词）make: 中国制造 made in China

中 zhōng（名词）center; middle

中餐 zhōngcān（名词）Chinese meal/food

中东 zhōngdōng（名词）the Middle East

中国 zhōngguó（名词）China: 中国人 Chinese

中国共产党 zhōngguó gòngchǎndǎng（名词）Communist Party of China (CPC)

中华 zhōnghuá（名词）China: 爱我中华 love my homeland China

中华民族 zhōnghuá mínzú（名词）Chinese nation

中华人民共和国 zhōnghuá rénmín gònghéguó（名词）People's Republic of China

中间 zhōngjiān（名词）
1. center; middle: 她坐在前排中间。She sat in the middle of the front row.
2. among: 在我们中间 among us

中年 zhōngnián（名词）middle age: 中年人 middle-aged people

中秋节 zhōngqiūjié（名词）Mid-autumn Festival

百科小贴士
中秋节在农历八月十五那一天。

中文 zhōngwén（名词）Chinese

中午 zhōngwǔ（名词）noon: 在中午 at noon

中心 zhōngxīn（名词）center: 市中心 city center

中学 zhōngxué（名词）secondary school; high school

用法小贴士
secondary school 是英国英语，high school 是美国英语。

中央 zhōngyāng（名词）center: 在湖的中央 at the center of the lake ∥中央政府 central government

钟表 zhōngbiǎo（名词）clocks and watches

钟头 zhōngtóu（名词）hour: 3个半钟头 three and a half hours

种 zhǒng（量词）kind; type: 两种选择 two choices

种类 zhǒnglèi（名词）kind; type: 花的种类很多。There are all kinds of flowers.

种 zhòng（动词）grow; plant: 种树 plant trees ∥种庄稼 grow crops

种植 zhòngzhí（动词）grow; plant: 种植玫瑰 grow roses

重 zhòng（形容词）
1. heavy: 这箱子太重了，我搬不动。This box is too heavy for me to move.
2. serious: 重病 serious illness

重要 zhòngyào（形容词）important: 重要的会议 important meeting

重音 zhòngyīn（名词）stress; accent: 这个单词有两个重音。The word has two stresses.

周 zhōu（名词）week: 本/上/下周 this/last/next week // 每周工作40个小时 work forty hours a week

周末 zhōumò（名词）weekend: 在周末 on the weekend

周日 zhōurì（名词）Sunday

昼夜 zhòuyè（名词）day and night

猪 zhū（名词）pig: 养猪 keep pigs

猪肉 zhūròu（名词）pork

竹林 zhúlín（名词）bamboo forest

竹子 zhúzi（名词）bamboo; bamboo tree

主人 zhǔrén（名词）host: 女主人 hostess

主席 zhǔxí（名词）chairman; chairwoman; chair; chairperson: 中华人民共和国主席 President of the People's Republic of China

主页 zhǔyè（名词）home page

主意 zhǔyi（名词）
1. idea: 好主意 good idea
2. decision: 打定主意 make a decision; make up one's mind // 改变主意 change one's mind

主语 zhǔyǔ（名词）subject

煮 zhǔ（动词）boil; cook: 煮鸡蛋 boil eggs // 煮米饭 cook rice

住 zhù（动词）live: 住在北京 live in Beijing // 你住在哪儿？Where do you live?

祝贺 zhùhè（动词）congratulate: 祝贺你的成功！Congratulations on your success!

祝愿 zhùyuàn（动词）wish: 祝愿你梦想成真。I wish your dream will come true.

著名 zhùmíng（形容词）famous

抓 zhuā（动词）catch: 抓小偷 catch a thief

庄稼 zhuāngjia（名词）crops: 种庄稼 grow crops // 收庄稼 harvest crops

壮 zhuàng（形容词）strong

准备 zhǔnbèi（动词）prepare: 准备饭菜 prepare a meal // 准备考试 prepare for an exam

捉 zhuō（动词）catch: 捉蝴蝶 catch butterflies // 猫头鹰白天睡觉，晚上捉老鼠。Owls sleep by day and hunt rats by night.

桌子 zhuōzi（名词）table; desk: 放在桌子上 put something on the table ∥ 坐在桌子旁 sit at the table

子弹 zǐdàn（名词）bullet

子女 zǐnǚ（名词）sons and daughters; children

仔细 zǐxì（形容词）careful: 仔细观察 observe carefully

紫色 zǐsè（名词）purple

自从 zìcóng（介词）since; from: 自从去年秋天到现在 from last autumn till now

自动取款机 zìdòng qǔkuǎnjī（名词）ATM (automatic teller machine)

自豪 zìháo（形容词）proud: 他为儿子感到自豪。He is proud of his son.

自己 zìjǐ（代词）oneself: 她什么事都自己做。She does everything herself.

自然 zìrán（名词）nature: 大自然 Mother Nature

自行车 zìxíngchē（名词）bicycle; bike: 骑自行车 ride a bicycle

字 zì（名词）word: 认字 be able to read

字典 zìdiǎn（名词）dictionary: 在字典里查一下这个词。Look up the word in the dictionary.

字母 zìmǔ（名词）letter: 英语字母表 the English alphabet

棕色 zōngsè
1.（形容词）brown
2.（名词）brown

总是 zǒngshì（副词）always; all the time: 太阳总是从东方升起。The sun always rises in the east.

走 zǒu（动词）
1. walk: 走回家 walk home
2. leave: 他刚走。He's just left.

走路 zǒulù（动词）walk; go on foot: 我走路上学。I walk to school.

足够 zúgòu（形容词）enough: 足够的时间 enough time

足球 zúqiú（名词）football: 踢足球 play football ∥ 足球赛 football game ∥ 足球队 football team ∥ 足球运动员 footballer ∥ 足球场 football field

组 zǔ（名词）group; team: 兴趣小组 interest group

祖父 zǔfù（名词）grandfather

祖国 zǔguó（名词）homeland; motherland: 热爱祖国 love one's country

祖母 zǔmǔ（名词）grandmother

嘴 zuǐ（名词）mouth: 张开嘴 open one's mouth ∥ 闭上嘴 close/shut one's mouth

最 zuì（副词）most: 最大 the biggest ∥ 最有趣 the most interesting

最好 zuìhǎo
1.（形容词）best: 最好的办法 the best way
2.（副词）had better: 你今天最好不要游泳。You'd better not go swimming today.

最佳 zuìjiā（形容词）best: 最佳方案 the best plan

最近 zuìjìn（副词）recently: 你最近去过动物园吗？Have you been to the zoo recently?

尊敬 zūnjìng（动词）respect: 尊敬父母 respect one's parents

昨天 zuótiān（名词）yesterday

左边 zuǒbian（名词）left; left side: 坐在我的左边 sit on my left

作家 zuòjiā（名词）writer

作文 zuòwén（名词）composition: 写作文 write a composition

作业 zuòyè（名词）homework; schoolwork: 做作业 do one's homework

作者 zuòzhě（名词）author; writer

坐 zuò（动词）
1. sit: 坐下 sit down ∥ 这张桌子可坐4个人。This table seats four.
2. travel by: 坐飞机 by air/plane ∥ 坐火车/公共汽车 by train/bus

座号 zuòhào（名词）seat number

座位 zuòwèi（名词）seat: 靠窗户的座位 window seat

做 zuò（动词）
1. do: 做功课 do one's homework ∥ 做实验 carry out experiments
2. make: 做飞机模型 make a model airplane ∥ 做裙子 make a skirt

做饭 zuòfàn（动词）cook; do the cooking; prepare a meal

做梦 zuòmèng（动词）have a dream: 做个好梦！Have a good dream! ∥ 白日做梦 daydream

附 录

APPENDICES

· 时间 Time ·

What time is it? / Can you tell me the time? / Do you have the time?

It's one.
It's one o'clock.
注：在整点后，既可以加上 o'clock，也可以不加。

It's a quarter past one.
It's one fifteen.
注：past 表示 "超过"。

It's half past one.
It's one thirty.
注：half 表示 "半个小时"。

It's a quarter to two.
It's one forty-five.
注：to 表示 "不到"。

· 日期 Dates ·

When is Children's Day?
It's on June 1/June 1ˢᵗ/1 June/1ˢᵗ June.
注：在英国英语中，日期放在月份前；在美国英语中，通常月份在前。日期既可以用基数词，也可以用序数词。

When were you born?
I was born on September 10, 1998 / 10 September 1998.
注：年份应放在最后。如果将日期放在月份后，需要用逗号将年份与日期分开。

383

· 日 Days ·

星期一　Monday
星期二　Tuesday
星期三　Wednesday
星期四　Thursday
星期五　Friday
星期六　Saturday
星期日　Sunday

· 月份 Months ·

一月　　January
二月　　February
三月　　March
四月　　April
五月　　May
六月　　June
七月　　July
八月　　August
九月　　September
十月　　October
十一月　November
十二月　December

384

亚洲　　Asia

非洲　　Africa

北美洲　North America

南美洲　South America

南极洲　Antarctica

欧洲　　Europe

大洋洲　Oceania

太平洋　Pacific Ocean

大西洋　Atlantic Ocean

印度洋　Indian Ocean

北冰洋　Arctic Ocean

附录 3 节日

·中国节日 Chinese Holidays·

春节	Chinese New Year/Spring Festival
元宵节	Lantern Festival
植树节	Arbor Day
清明节	Tomb-sweeping Day
端午节	Dragon-boat Festival
中秋节	Mid-autumn Festival
教师节	Teacher's Day
国庆节	National Day

·国际节日 International Holidays·

元旦	New Year's Day
国际妇女节（3月8日）	International Women's Day
国际劳动节（5月1日）	International Labor Day
国际儿童节（6月1日）	International Children's Day

·西方节日 Western Holidays·

情人节（2月14日）	Valentine's Day
愚人节（4月1日）	April Fool's Day
复活节（春分后第一个星期日）	Easter
母亲节（5月的第二个星期日）	Mother's Day
父亲节（6月的第三个星期日）	Father's Day
鬼节（万圣节前夜，10月31日夜）	Halloween
万圣节（11月1日）	All Saints' Day
感恩节（11月最后一个星期四）	Thanksgiving
圣诞节（12月25日）	Christmas Day

1	one	一	1st	first	第一
2	two	二	2nd	second	第二
3	three	三	3rd	third	第三
4	four	四	4th	fourth	第四
5	five	五	5th	fifth	第五
6	six	六	6th	sixth	第六
7	seven	七	7th	seventh	第七
8	eight	八	8th	eighth	第八
9	nine	九	9th	ninth	第九
10	ten	十	10th	tenth	第十
11	eleven	十一	11th	eleventh	第十一
12	twelve	十二	12th	twelfth	第十二
13	thirteen	十三	13th	thirteenth	第十三
14	fourteen	十四	14th	fourteenth	第十四
15	fifteen	十五	15th	fifteenth	第十五
16	sixteen	十六	16th	sixteenth	第十六
17	seventeen	十七	17th	seventeenth	第十七
18	eighteen	十八	18th	eighteenth	第十八
19	nineteen	十九	19th	nineteenth	第十九
20	twenty	二十	20th	twentieth	第二十
30	thirty	三十	30th	thirtieth	第三十
40	forty	四十	40th	fortieth	第四十
50	fifty	五十	50th	fiftieth	第五十
60	sixty	六十	60th	sixtieth	第六十
70	seventy	七十	70th	seventieth	第七十
80	eighty	八十	80th	eightieth	第八十
90	ninety	九十	90th	ninetieth	第九十
100	hundred	百	100th	hundredth	第一百
1,000	thousand	千	1,000th	thousandth	第一千
1,000,000	million	百万	1,000,000th	millionth	第一百万

387

· 男孩的名字 Boys' Names ·

拼写	发音	中文译名	含义
Adam	/'ædəm/	亚当	世界上第一个男人
Alan	/'ælən/	艾伦	和谐的；英俊的
Andrew	/'ændru:/	安德鲁	有阳刚气质的；无畏的
Bill	/bɪl/	比尔	勇猛的卫士
Bob	/bɒb/	鲍勃	好的名望；盛名
Brian	/'braɪən/	布赖恩	有力的领袖；出身显贵
Carl	/kɑ:l/	卡尔	伟大的人物
Charles	/tʃɑ:lz/	查尔斯	男子汉
Chris	/krɪs/	克里斯	基督的信使
Daniel	/'dænjəl/	丹尼尔	上帝是我的最高审判者
David	/'deɪvɪd/	戴维	可爱的人；朋友
Dennis	/'denɪs/	丹尼斯	从酒神Dionysus名字而来
Donald	/'dɒnəld/	唐纳德	世界之王
Douglas	/'dʌɡləs/	道格拉斯	深灰色的
Edward	/'edwəd/	爱德华	富有的人
Eric	/'erɪk/	埃里克	领导者
Frank	/fræŋk/	弗兰克	自由人
Fred	/fred/	弗雷德	强大而富有的；和平的统治者
George	/dʒɔ:dʒ/	乔治	耕种者
Henry	/'henri/	亨利	家里的管事者
Jack	/dʒæk/	杰克	上帝仁慈的恩赐
James	/dʒeɪmz/	詹姆斯	代替他人的人
Jason	/'dʒeɪsən/	贾森	治疗者；饱学之士
Jeff	/dʒef/	杰夫	神圣的和平

拼写	发音	中文译名	含义
Jim	/dʒɪm/	吉姆	代替他人的人
John	/dʒɒn/	约翰	上帝仁慈的给予
Johnson	/dʒɒnsən/	约翰逊	约翰之子
Joseph	/dʒəʊzɪf/	约瑟夫	愿上帝再添（一子）
Kevin	/kevɪn/	凯文	出身很好的；圣人
Louis	/luːi/	路易斯	战功显赫的
Mark	/mɑːk/	马克	战神
Martin	/mɑːtɪn/	马丁	好战的
Matthew	/mæθjuː/	马修	上帝的赐予
Michael	/maɪkəl/	迈克尔	酷似上帝的人
Nick	/nɪk/	尼克	胜利者
Patrick	/pætrɪk/	帕特里克	身份高贵的；贵族
Paul	/pɔːl/	保罗	小家伙
Peter	/piːtə/	彼得	坚强的人
Phillip	/fɪlɪp/	菲利普	爱马的人；战士
Richard	/rɪtʃəd/	理查德	勇敢的
Robert	/rɒbət/	罗伯特	盛名
Roy	/rɔɪ/	罗伊	国王
Sam	/sæm/	萨姆	上帝之名
Samuel	/sæmjʊəl/	塞缪尔	上帝之名
Stephen	/stiːvən/	斯蒂芬	王冠
Steven	/stiːvən/	史蒂文	王冠
Thomas	/tɒməs/	托马斯	太阳神
Tom	/tɒm/	汤姆	太阳神
William	/wɪljəm/	威廉	强有力的战士

· 女孩的名字 Girls' Names ·

拼写	发音	中文译名	含义
Alice	/ˈælɪs/	艾丽斯	尊贵的；和善的
Amy	/ˈeɪmi/	埃米	钟爱的
Ann	/æn/	安	优美的
Barbara	/ˈbɑːbərə/	芭芭拉	陌生人
Betty	/ˈbeti/	贝蒂	上帝的誓约
Catherine	/ˈkæθərɪn/	凯瑟琳	纯洁的人
Christina	/krɪsˈtiːnə/	克里斯蒂娜	基督的信徒
Daisy	/ˈdeɪzi/	黛西	雏菊
Diana	/daɪˈænə/	黛安娜	月亮
Doris	/ˈdɒrɪs/	多丽丝	海洋女神
Elizabeth	/ɪˈlɪzəbəθ/	伊丽莎白	上帝的誓约
Ellen	/ˈelən/	埃伦	火炬
Emily	/ˈemɪli/	埃米莉	金嗓子；和蔼可亲的
Fiona	/fiˈəʊnə/	菲奥娜	美貌的
Grace	/greɪs/	格雷丝	优雅的
Hannah	/ˈhænə/	汉娜	优雅的
Helen	/ˈhelən/	海伦	光彩照人的女孩
Jane	/dʒeɪn/	简	上帝是仁慈的
Jennifer	/ˈdʒenɪfə/	珍妮弗	白色的波浪
Jessica	/ˈdʒesɪkə/	杰茜卡	上帝的恩宠
Joan	/dʒəʊn/	琼	上帝仁慈的赐予
Judy	/ˈdʒuːdi/	朱迪	赞美
Julia	/ˈdʒuːliə/	朱莉娅	头发柔软的
Julie	/ˈdʒuːli/	朱莉	头发柔软的

390

拼写	发音	中文译名	含义
Karen	/'kærən/	卡伦	纯正
Kate	/keɪt/	凯特	纯洁的人
Kelly	/'keli/	凯莉	女战士
Laura	/'lɔːrə/	劳拉	月桂树
Lily	/'lɪli/	莉莉	百合花
Linda	/'lɪndə/	琳达	美丽的人
Lisa	/'liːsə/	莉萨	上帝的誓约
Maria	/mə'riːə/	玛丽亚	悲苦的
Martha	/'mɑːθə/	玛莎	家里的女主人
Mary	/'meəri/	玛丽	海之女
May	/meɪ/	梅	少女
Michelle	/mɪ'ʃel/	米歇尔	紫菀花
Monica	/'mɒnɪkə/	莫妮卡	指导者
Nancy	/'nænsi/	南希	优雅
Nina	/'niːnə/	尼娜	有权势的
Pamela	/'pæmələ/	帕梅拉	爱捣蛋却令人怜的小孩
Rachel	/'reɪtʃəl/	雷切尔	小羊
Rebecca	/rɪ'bekə/	丽贝卡	迷人之美
Sarah	/'seərə/	萨拉	公主
Sophia	/səʊ'fiːə/	索菲娅	智者
Susan	/'suːzən/	苏珊	小百合
Tina	/'tiːnə/	蒂娜	娇小玲珑
Tracy	/'treɪsi/	特蕾西	通往集市的小路
Vivian	/'vɪviən/	薇薇安	活泼的
Wendy	/'wendi/	温迪	勇于冒险的少女

ability /əˈbɪlɪti/（名）能力，才能

abroad /əˈbrɔːd/（副）到国外；在国外

absence /ˈæbsəns/（名）不在，缺席

accent /ˈæksənt/（名）口音，音调

according to /əˈkɔːdɪŋ tuː/ 按照，根据

account /əˈkaʊnt/（名）描述；账户

achieve /əˈtʃiːv/（动）达到，取得

acrobatics /ˌækrəˈbætɪks/（名）杂技

actual /ˈæktʃʊəl/（形）实际的

AD /ˌeɪ ˈdiː/（副）公元

addition /əˈdɪʃən/（名）加（算数用语）

adjective /ˈædʒɪktɪv/（名）形容词

admire /ədˈmaɪə/（动）钦佩；羡慕

admission /ædˈmɪʃən/（名）准入，接纳

advance /ædˈvɑːns/（动）前进

advantage /ædˈvɑːntɪdʒ/（名）优点，好处

adverb /ˈædvɜːb/（名）副词

advertise /ˈædvətaɪz/（动）为…做广告

advertisement /ædˈvɜːtɪsmənt/（名）广告

advise /ædˈvaɪz/（动）忠告，劝告，建议

affair /əˈfeə/（名）事，事情

affect /əˈfekt/（动）影响

afford /əˈfɔːd/（动）负担得起（的费用）

African /ˈæfrɪkən/ 1.（形）非洲的；非洲人的 2.（名）非洲人

afterward /ˈɑːftəwəd/（副）后来

aggression /əˈgreʃən/（名）侵略

aggressive /əˈgresɪv/（形）侵略的；咄咄逼人的

agreement /əˈgriːmənt/（名）协议

agricultural /ˌægrɪˈkʌltʃərəl/（形）农业的

agriculture /ˈægrɪkʌltʃə/（名）农业，农学

aim /eɪm/ 1.（名）目的；目标 2.（动）计划，打算；瞄准；针对

aircraft /ˈeəkrɑːft/（名）飞机（单复数同）

airline /ˈeəlaɪn/（名）航空公司

airmail /ˈeəmeɪl/（名）航空邮件

airplane /ˈeəpleɪn/（名）（美）飞机

alarm /əˈlɑːm/（名）警报

album /ˈælbəm/（名）相册，集邮册

alcoholic /ˌælkəˈhɒlɪk/（形）（含）酒精的

alive /əˈlaɪv/（形）活着的，存在的

alone /əˈləʊn/（形）单独的，孤独的

along /əˈlɒŋ/ 1.（副）向前；和…一同 2.（介）沿着，顺着

aloud /əˈlaʊd/（副）大声地

although /ɔːlˈðəʊ/（连）虽然，尽管

altogether /ˌɔːltəˈgeðə/（副）总共

amaze /əˈmeɪz/（动）使惊奇，使惊叹

ambulance /ˈæmbjʊləns/（名）救护车

American /əˈmerɪkən/ 1.（形）美国的；美国人的 2.（名）美国人

amuse /əˈmjuːz/（动）逗笑，逗乐

amusement /əˈmjuːzmənt/（名）娱乐

ancestor /ˈænsestə/（名）祖宗，祖先

anger /ˈæŋgə/（名）怒，愤怒

announce /əˈnaʊns/（动）宣布，宣告

announcement /əˈnaʊnsmənt/（名）通告，通知

annoy /əˈnɔɪ/（动）使烦恼

Antarctic /æntˈɑːktɪk/（形）南极的 the Antarctic 南极

Antarctica /æntˈɑːktɪkə/（名）南极洲

antique /ænˈtiːk/（名）古董

anxious /ˈæŋkʃəs/（形）忧虑的，焦急的

anybody /ˈenibɒdi/（代）任何人，无论谁

anyhow /ˈenihaʊ/（副）不管怎样

anyone /ˈeniwʌn/（代）任何人，无论谁

anyway /ˈeniweɪ/（副）不管怎样

anywhere /ˈeniweə/（副）任何地方

ape /eɪp/（名）类人猿

apology /əˈpɒlədʒi/（名）道歉，歉意

appear /əˈpɪə/（动）出现

appearance /əˈpɪərəns/（名）出现，露面；容貌

application /ˌæplɪˈkeɪʃən/（名）申请

apply /əˈplaɪ/（动）申请

appointment /əˈpɔɪntmənt/（名）约会

appreciate /ə'pri:ʃieɪt/（动）欣赏；感激

Arab /'ærəb/ 1.（形）阿拉伯的 2.（名）阿拉伯人

Arabic /'ærəbɪk/ 1.（形）阿拉伯语的 2.（名）阿拉伯语

Arctic /'ɑːktɪk/（形）北极的
　the Arctic 北极
　the Arctic Ocean 北冰洋

area /'eərɪə/（名）面积；地域，地方，区域；范围，领域

argue /'ɑːgjuː/（动）争辩，争论

argument /'ɑːgjʊmənt/（名）争论，辩论

arise (arose, arisen) /ə'raɪz/（动）起来

arithmetic /ə'rɪθmɪtɪk/（名）算术

arm /ɑːm/ 1.（动）以…装备，武装起来 2.（名）武器

arrange /ə'reɪndʒ/（动）安排，布置

arrangement /ə'reɪndʒmənt/（名）安排，布置

arrival /ə'raɪvəl/（名）到来，到达

article /'ɑːtɪkəl/（名）文章

ash /æʃ/（名）灰；灰末

ashamed /ə'ʃeɪmd/（形）惭愧的，害臊的

Asian /'eɪʒən/ 1.（形）亚洲的；亚洲人的 2.（名）亚洲人

aside /ə'saɪd/（副）在旁边

assistant /ə'sɪstənt/（名）助手，助理

astonish /ə'stɒnɪʃ/（动）使惊讶

astronomy /ə'strɒnəmi/（名）天文学

athlete /'æθliːt/（名）运动员

Atlantic /ət'læntɪk/（形）大西洋的
　the Atlantic Ocean 大西洋

atmosphere /'ætməsfɪə/（名）大气；气氛

atom /'ætəm/（名）原子

attack /ə'tæk/（动）攻击，袭击

attempt /ə'tempt/（动）试图，尝试

attentively /ə'tentɪvli/（副）注意地

attitude /'ætɪtjuːd/（名）态度

attract /ə'trækt/（动）吸引

attractive /ə'træktɪv/（形）有吸引力的

aubergine /'əʊbəʒiːn/（名）茄子

audience /'ɔːdɪəns/（名）观众，听众

aunt /'ɑːnt/（名）阿姨

Australian /ɒs'treɪlɪən/ 1.（形）澳大利亚的；澳大利亚人的 2.（名）澳大利亚人

automatic teller machine /ɔːtəmætɪk telə mə'ʃiːn/（名）自动取款机

avenue /'ævɪnjuː/（名）大道

average /'ævərɪdʒ/（形）平均的

avoid /ə'vɔɪd/（动）避免，躲开，逃避

award /ə'wɔːd/（名）奖品，奖励

backache /'bækeɪk/（名）背痛

background /'bækgraʊnd/（名）背景

backward /'bækwəd/（副）向后

backyard /ˌbæk'jɑːd/（名）后院

bacon /'beɪkən/（名）咸猪肉，熏猪肉

bacteria /bæk'tɪərɪə/（名）细菌

badly /'bædli/（副）坏，恶劣地

bakery /'beɪkəri/（名）面包店；糕点房

balance /'bæləns/（名）平衡

balcony /'bælkəni/（名）阳台；楼座

ball /bɔːl/（名）舞会

ballpoint = ballpoint pen /'bɔːlpɔɪnt/（名）圆珠笔

ban /bæn/ 1.（名）禁令 2.（动）禁止，取缔

bandage /'bændɪdʒ/（名）绷带

bang /bæŋ/（叹）砰

bank account（名）银行账户

bar /bɑː/（名）条；（长方）块，棒，横木

barbecue /'bɑːbɪkjuː/（名）烤肉野餐

bargain /'bɑːgɪn/（动）讨价还价

base /beɪs/（名）根据地，基地；（棒球）垒

basement /'beɪsmənt/（名）地下室

basic /'beɪsɪk/（形）基本的

bat /bæt/（名）（棒球、板球的）球棒

bathe /beɪð/（动）洗澡；游泳

bathhouse /ˈbɑːθhaʊs/（名）澡堂

bathrobe /ˈbɑːθrəʊb/（名）浴衣

bathroom /ˈbɑːruːm/（名）浴室，盥洗室

bathtub /ˈbɑːθtʌb/（名）澡盆

battery /ˈbætəri/（名）电池

battleground /ˈbætəlɡraʊnd/（名）战场

bay /beɪ/（名）湾，海湾

BC /ˌbiː ˈsiː/（副）公元前

beam /biːm/（名）平衡木

bean curd /ˈbiːnkɜːd/（名）豆腐

bear /beə/（动）承受，负担，承担；忍受，容忍

beat (beat,beaten) /biːt/ 1.（动）敲打；跳动；打赢 2.（名）（音乐）节拍

beauty /ˈbjuːti/（名）美丽；美人

bedclothes /ˈbedkləʊðz/（名）铺盖（被褥等）

bedroom /ˈbedruːm/（名）寝室，卧室

beehive /ˈbiːhaɪv/（名）蜂箱

beetle /ˈbiːtəl/（名）甲虫

beg /beɡ/（动）请求，乞求；乞讨

beginning /bɪˈɡɪnɪŋ/（名）开始，开端

behave /bɪˈheɪv/（动）守规矩；表现

behavior /bɪˈheɪvjə/（名）行为，举止

being /ˈbiːɪŋ/（名）物；生物；人

Belgium /ˈbeldʒəm/（名）比利时

belief /bɪˈliːf/（名）信念

belly /ˈbeli/（名）肚子

belong /bɪˈlɒŋ/（动）属于，附属

belt /belt/（名）（皮）带

bend (bent,bent) /bend/（动）使弯曲

beneath /bɪˈniːθ/（介）在…下方，在…下面

besides /bɪˈsaɪdz/（介）除了…还有

best seller /ˌbest ˈselə/（名）畅销书

beyond /bɪˈjɒnd/（介）（表示位置）在…的那边

biology /baɪˈɒlədʒi/（名）生物（学）

birdcage /ˈbɜːdkeɪdʒ/（名）鸟笼

birth /bɜːθ/（名）出生，诞生

birthplace /ˈbɜːθpleɪs/（名）出生地；故乡；发祥地

bit /bɪt/（名）一点，一些，少量

bite (bit,bitten) /baɪt/（动）咬，叮

blame /bleɪm/（名，动）责备，责怪

blank /blæŋk/ 1.（名）空白 2.（形）空的

bleed /bliːd/（动）出血，流血

blender /ˈblendə/（名）搅拌机

bless /bles/（动）保佑，降福

block /blɒk/ 1.（名）街区；积木 2.（动）阻塞

blood /blʌd/（名）血，血液

blouse /blaʊz/（名）宽罩衫；（妇女、儿童穿的）短上衣

blow /bləʊ/（名）击；打击

board /bɔːd/（名）木板；布告牌；委员会

boat race（名）划船比赛

boating /ˈbəʊtɪŋ/（名）划船（游玩），泛舟

bodybuilding /ˈbɒdibɪldɪŋ/（名）健美运动

boil /bɔɪl/（动）沸腾；烧开；煮…

bookcase /ˈbʊkkeɪs/（名）书橱

bookmark /ˈbʊkmɑːk/（名）书签

bookshelf /ˈbʊkʃelf/（名）书架

bookshop /ˈbʊkʃɒp/（名）书店

bookstore /ˈbʊkstɔː/（名）（美）书店

booth /buːð/（名）岗；（为某种用途而设的）亭，小隔间

　telephone booth 电话亭

border /ˈbɔːdə/（名）国界

born /bɔːn/（形）出生的

botany /ˈbɒtəni/（名）植物；植物学

bottom /ˈbɒtəm/（名）底部，底

bound¹ /baʊnd/（形）被绑的

bound² /baʊnd/（动，名）跳跃

bow /baʊ/（动，名）鞠躬，弯腰行礼

bowling /ˈbəʊlɪŋ/（名）保龄球

boxing /ˈbɒksɪŋ/（名）拳击（运动）

brake /breɪk/ 1.（名）闸 2.（动）刹车

branch /brɑːntʃ/（名）树枝；分枝；分公司，分店；支部

brandy /'brændi/（名）白兰地

bravery /'breɪvəri/（名）勇气

break /breɪk/（名）间隙

breath /breθ/（名）气息，呼吸

breathe /briːð/（动）呼吸

brick /brɪk/（名）砖，砖块

bride /braɪd/（名）新娘

bridegroom /'braɪdɡruːm/（名）新郎

breeze /briːz/（名）微风

brief /briːf/（形）简洁的

Britain /'brɪtən/（名）英国

British /'brɪtɪʃ/（形）英国的
　the British（名）英国国民

broad /brɔːd/（形）宽的，宽大的

broadband /'brɔːdˌbænd/（名）宽带

broadcast (broadcast, broadcast或-ed, -ed) /'brɔːdkɑːst/ 1.（动）广播 2. 广播节目

broken /'brəʊkən/（形）弄坏了的

bronze /brɒnz/（名）青铜

buddy /'bʌdi/（名）伙伴

broom /bruːm/（名）扫帚

brotherhood /'brʌðəhʊd/（名）兄弟般的关系

brunch /brʌntʃ/（名）早午饭（早饭和午饭并作一顿吃）

bucket /'bʌkɪt/（名）铲斗；桶

Buddhism /'bʊdɪzəm/（名）佛教

Buddhist /'bʊdɪst/（名）佛教徒

buddy /'bʌdi/（名）伙伴

bulb /bʌlb/（名）灯泡

bullfight /'bʊlfaɪt/（名）斗牛

bun /bʌn/（名）小圆面包

bunch /bʌntʃ/（名）束

bungee jumping /'bʌndʒi dʒʌmpɪŋ/（名）蹦极

bunny /'bʌni/（名）兔子

burial /'beriəl/（名）埋葬

burst /bɜːst/（动）突然发生；突然发作

bury /'beri/（动）埋，葬

bush /bʊʃ/（名）灌木丛，矮树丛

business /'bɪznɪs/（名）生意

businessman /'bɪznɪsmæn/（名）男商人，男企业家

businesswoman /'bɪznɪswʊmən/（名）女商人，女企业家

butcher /'bʊtʃə/ 1.（名）肉商；屠夫 2.（动）屠宰（动物）；残杀（人）

cab /kæb/（名）出租车

cafeteria /ˌkæfɪ'tɪəriə/（名）自助餐厅

calm /kɑːm/ 1.（形）镇静的，沉着的 2.（动）使镇静，使沉着

campus /'kæmpəs/（名）（大学）校园

Canadian /kə'neɪdiən/ 1.（形）加拿大的；加拿大人的 2.（名）加拿大人

canal /kə'næl/（名）运河；水道

cancel /'kænsəl/（动）取消

cancer /'kænsə/（名）癌

cannon /'kænən/（名）大炮

cannot=can't /'kænɒt/（情态动）不能，不会

canteen /kæn'tiːn/（名）餐厅，食堂

carbon /'kɑːbən/（名）碳

card games 纸牌游戏

carefully /'keəfʊli/（副）认真地

careless /'keələs/（形）粗心的；漫不经心的

carnation /kɑː'neɪʃən/（名）康乃馨

carpenter /'kɑːpɪntə/（名）木匠

carve /kɑːv/（动）刻；雕刻

case /keɪs/（名）情况；病例；案件

cash /kæʃ/ 1.（名）现金，现钞 2.（动）兑现

cast (cast, cast) /kɑːst/（动）扔，抛，撒

cathedral /kə'θiːdrəl/（名）（天主教）大教堂

cattle /'kætəl/（名）牛（总称）；家畜

cauliflower /ˈkɒliflaʊə/（名）菜花

CD-ROM（名）只读光盘（compact disk read-only memory的缩写）

ceiling /ˈsiːlɪŋ/（名）天花板，顶棚

celebrate /ˈselɪbreɪt/（动）庆祝

celebration /ˌselɪˈbreɪʃən/（名）庆祝；庆祝会

cell /sel/（名）细胞

cellar /ˈselə/（名）地窖

centigrade /ˈsentɪɡreɪd/（形）摄氏的

centimeter /ˈsentɪmiːtə/（名）公分，厘米

central /ˈsentrəl/（形）中心的，中央的

certain /ˈsɜːtən/（形）确定的

certificate /səˈtɪfɪkət/（名）证明，证明书

chain /tʃeɪn/（名）链；链条

chain store（名）连锁店

chairman /ˈtʃeəmən/（名）主席，会长；议长

chairperson /ˈtʃeəpɜːsən/（名）主席，会长；主持人

chairwoman /ˈtʃeəwʊmən/（名）女主席，女会长；女议长

challenge /ˈtʃælɪndʒ/（名）挑战（性）

challenging /ˈtʃælɪndʒɪŋ/（形）具有挑战性的

champagne /ʃæmˈpeɪn/（名）香槟

champion /ˈtʃæmpiən/（名）冠军

championship /ˈtʃæmpiənʃɪp/（名）锦标赛；冠军称号

chance /tʃɑːns/（名）机会，可能性

change /tʃeɪndʒ/ 1.（名）零钱；找头 2.（动）改变，变化；更换；兑换

changeable /ˈtʃeɪndʒəbəl/（形）易变的，变化无常的

channel /ˈtʃænəl/（名）水渠

character /ˈkærɪktə/（名）（汉）字；性格

charge /tʃɑːdʒ/（名）价钱

chapter /ˈtʃæptə/（名）章

chart /tʃɑːt/（名）图表

chase /tʃeɪs/（动）追赶

cheat /tʃiːt/（名）作弊，欺骗

check (noun) /tʃek/（名）支票

check (verb) /tʃek/（动）检查；批改

cheek /tʃiːk/（名）面颊，脸蛋

cheer /tʃɪə/（名，动）欢呼，喝彩

Cheer up! 振作起来！提起精神！

cheerful /ˈtʃɪəfʊl/（形）兴高采烈的，快活的

cheers /tʃɪəz/（叹）干杯；（英口语）谢谢，再见

cheese /tʃiːz/（名）奶酪

chemical /ˈkemɪkəl/ 1.（形）化学的 2.（名）化学品

chemist /ˈkemɪst/（名）药剂师；化学家

chest /tʃest/（名）胸部

chew /tʃuː/（动）咀嚼

chewing gum /ˈtʃuːɪŋ ɡʌm/（名）口香糖

chick /tʃɪk/（名）小鸡

chief /tʃiːf/（形）主要的

chimney /ˈtʃɪmni/（名）烟囱，烟筒

Chinese /tʃaɪˈniːz/ 1.（形）中国的；中国人的；汉语的 2.（名）中国人；汉语

choice /tʃɔɪs/（名）选择，抉择

choke /tʃəʊk/（名，动）窒息

choose (chose, chosen) /tʃuːz/（动）选择

chop /tʃɒp/（动）劈，砍

Christian /ˈkrɪstʃən/（名）基督徒

Christmas Eve /ˌkrɪsməs ˈiːv/ 圣诞（前）夜

chubby /ˈtʃʌbi/（形）丰满的，圆圆胖胖的

cigar /sɪˈɡɑː/（名）雪茄烟

citizen /ˈsɪtɪzən/（名）公民，居民

civil /ˈsɪvəl/（形）国内的

clap /klæp/（动）拍手，鼓掌

classic /ˈklæsɪk/（名）名著

classical /ˈklæsɪkəl/（形）传统的；古典的

cleaner /ˈkliːnə/（名）清洁工

clear /klɪə/（形）清晰的；明亮的；清楚的

clearly /'klɪəli/（副）清楚地

clerk /klɑːk/（名）职员

click /klɪk/（动）点击（计算机用语）

climate /'klaɪmət/（名）气候

clinic /'klɪnɪk/（名）诊所

cloth /klɒθ/（名）布

clothing /'kləʊðɪŋ/（名）衣服（总称）

club /klʌb/（名）俱乐部；纸牌中的梅花

clumsy /'klʌmzi/（形）笨拙的

coal /kəʊl/（名）煤

cock /kɒk/（名）公鸡

cocktail /'kɒkteɪl/（名）鸡尾酒

cocoa /'kəʊkəʊ/（名）可可粉

cold-blooded /ˌkəʊld'blʌdɪd/（形）（动物）冷血的

collar /'kɒlə/（名）衣领

colleague /'kɒliːg/（名）同事

collect /kə'lekt/（动）收集，搜集

collection /kə'lekʃən/（名）收藏品

comb /kəʊm/ 1.（名）梳子 2.（动）梳

combine /kəm'baɪn/（动）使联合，使结合

comedy /'kɒmədi/（名）喜剧

comfort /'kʌmfət/（名）安慰；慰问

comic /'kɒmɪk/（名）连环画

comma /'kɒmə/（名）逗号

command /kə'mɑːnd/（名，动）命令

comment /'kɒment/（名）评论

common /'kɒmən/（形）普通的

commonplace /'kɒmənpleɪs/（名）平常事

communicate /kə'mjuːnɪkeɪt/（动）联络，沟通

communication /kəˌmjuːnɪ'keɪʃən/（名）沟通；通讯

communism /'kɒmjʊnɪzəm/（名）共产主义

communist /'kɒmjuːnɪst/ 1.（名）共产主义者 2.（形）共产党的；共产主义的

companion /kəm'pænjən/（名）同伴；同事

compare /kəm'peə/（动）比较，对照

compass /'kʌmpəs/（名）指南针

compete /kəm'piːt/（动）比赛，竞赛

competition /ˌkɒmpɪ'tɪʃən/（名）比赛，竞赛

competitor /kəm'petɪtə/（名）竞赛者，比赛者

complete /kəm'pliːt/ 1.（形）完成的 2.（动）完成，结束

completely /kəm'pliːtli/（副）完全地

compressed /kəm'prest/（形）压缩的

computer game /kəm'pjuːtə ɡeɪm/ 电子游戏

comrade /'kɒmreɪd/（名）同志

conceited /kən'siːtɪd/（形）骄傲自满的

concert /'kɒnsət/（名）音乐会，演奏会

conclude /kən'kluːd/（动）完成，结束

conclusion /kən'kluːʒən/（名）结论；结束

condition /kən'dɪʃən/（名）条件，状况

conduct /kən'dʌkt/（动）引导，带领

conductor /kən'dʌktə/（名）管理人；指导者；（车上的）售票员，列车员；乐队指挥

conference /'kɒnfrəns/（名）（正式的）会议；讨论会

congratulate /kən'grætʃuleɪt/（动）祝贺

connect /kə'nekt/（动）连接

connection /kə'nekʃən/（名）连接物；接触，联系

conservation /ˌkɒnsə'veɪʃən/（名）（自然资源的）保护

conservative /kən'sɜːvətɪv/（形）保守的

consider /kən'sɪdə/（动）考虑

considerate /kən'sɪdərət/（形）体贴的

consideration /kənˌsɪdə'reɪʃən/（名）考虑；关心

consist /kən'sɪst/（动）包含，组成，构成

constant /'kɒnstənt/（形）经常的，不断的

construct /kən'strʌkt/（动）构筑；建造，建设

construction /kən'strʌkʃən/（名）建造，建设；建筑物

contain /kən'teɪn/（动）包含；包括；能容纳

container /kən'teɪnə/（名）容器

content¹ /kən'tent/（形）满意的

content² /'kɒntent/（名）内容

continent /'kɒntɪnənt/（名）大陆，大洲；陆地

continue /kən'tɪnjuː/（动）继续

contrary /'kɒntrəri/ 1.（名）相反 2.（形）相反的

contribution /ˌkɒntrɪ'bjuːʃn/（名）贡献

control /kən'trəʊl/（动，名）控制

convenience /kən'viːniəns/（名）便利

convenient /kən'viːniənt/（形）便利的，方便的

conversation /ˌkɒnvə'seɪʃən/（名）谈话，交谈

cop /kɒp/（名）（口语）警察

coral /'kɒrəl/（名）珊瑚

cordless /'kɔːdləs/（形）无线的

correction /kə'rekʃən/（名）改正

correspond /ˌkɒrɪ'spɒnd/（动）（与人）通信

cost /kɒst/ 1.（名）价格 2.（动）值（多少钱）

cottage /'kɒtɪdʒ/（名）（郊外的）小屋

could /kʊd/（情态动）（can的过去式）可以…；（表示许可或请求）可以…，行

count /kaʊnt/（动）数，点数

counter /'kaʊntə/（名）柜台，结账处

countryside /'kʌntrisaɪd/（名）乡下，农村

couple /'kʌpəl/（名）夫妇

courage /'kʌrɪdʒ/（名）勇气，胆略

court /kɔːt/（名）法庭，法院

courtyard /'kɔːtjɑːd/（名）庭院，院子

cover /'kʌvə/ 1.（名）盖子 2.（动）覆盖

cowboy /'kaʊbɔɪ/（名）（美国）牛仔；牧场骑士

coworker /kəʊ'wɜːkə/（名）同事

crab /kræb/（名）螃蟹

crawl /krɔːl/（动）爬

crazy /'kreɪzi/（形）疯狂的

create /kri'eɪt/（动）创造；造成

credit /'kredɪt/（名）信誉

crime /kraɪm/（名）（法律上的）罪，犯罪

criminal /'krɪmɪnəl/（名）罪犯

crew /kruː/（名）全体船员

crossing /'krɒsɪŋ/（名）十字路口；人行横道

crowd /kraʊd/ 1.（名）人群 2.（动）拥挤，群聚

crowded /'kraʊdɪd/（形）拥挤的

cruel /'kruːəl/（形）残忍的，残酷的；无情的

cube /kjuːb/（名）立方体

cubic /'kjuːbɪk/（形）立方体的，立方形的

cure /kjʊə/（名，动）治疗

curious /'kjʊəriəs/（形）好奇的；奇异的

currency /'kʌrənsi/（名）货币；现金

curtain /'kɜːtən/（名）窗帘

cushion /'kʊʃən/（名）垫子

custom /'kʌstəm/（名）风俗，习惯

customer /'kʌstəmə/（名）（商店等的）顾客，主顾

customs /'kʌstəmz/（名）海关，关税

cycle /'saɪkəl/（动）骑自行车

cyclist /'saɪklɪst/（名）骑自行车的人

daily /'deɪli/ 1.（形）每日的，日常的 2.（副）每天 3.（名）日报

dairy /'deəri/（名）乳制品

dam /dæm/（名）水坝，堰堤

damage /'dæmɪdʒ/（名，动）毁坏，损害

damp /dæmp/ 1.（形）潮湿的 2.（名）潮湿

danger /'deɪndʒə/（名）危险

dangerous /'deɪndʒərəs/（形）危险的

darkness /'dɑ:knɪs/（名）黑暗，阴暗

dash /dæʃ/（动，名）快跑，冲刺，短跑

data /'deɪtə/（名）资料，数据

database /'deɪtəbeɪs/（名）资料库，数据库

date /deɪt/（名）枣

dawn /dɔ:n/（名）黎明，拂晓

daydream /'deɪdri:m/（名）白日梦

daylight /'deɪlaɪt/（名）日光，白昼；黎明

deadline /'dedlaɪn/（名）最后期限，截止日期

deaf-mute /ˌdef'mju:t/（形）聋哑的

deal /di:l/（名）数量

dear /dɪə/（叹）（表示惊愕等）哎呀，唷

death /deθ/（名）死亡

debate /dɪ'beɪt/（名，动）讨论，辩论

debt /det/（名）债务；欠款

decision /dɪ'sɪʒən/（名）决定；决心

declare /dɪ'kleə/（动）声明；断言

decorate /'dekəreɪt/（动）装饰，修饰

decoration /ˌdekə'reɪʃən/（名）装饰，修饰

deed /di:d/（名）行为；事迹

deeply /'di:pli/（副）深深地

defeat /dɪ'fi:t/（动）击败，战胜

defence (美 defense) /dɪ'fens/（名）防御；防务

defend /dɪ'fend/（动）防守；保卫

degree /dɪ'gri:/（名）程度

delay /dɪ'leɪ/（动，名）拖延，耽搁

delete /dɪ'li:t/（动）删去

delight /dɪ'laɪt/（名）快乐，乐事

delighted /dɪ'laɪtɪd/（形）高兴的，快乐的

deliver /dɪ'lɪvə/（动）投递（信件、邮包等）

demand /dɪ'mɑ:nd/（动）要求

department /dɪ'pɑ:tmənt/（名）部门

departure /dɪ'pɑ:tʃə/（名）离开，启程

depend /dɪ'pend/（动）依靠

depth /depθ/（名）深，深度

describe /dɪ'skraɪb/（动）描写，叙述

description /dɪ'skrɪpʃən/（名）描述，描写

desert /dɪ'zɜ:t/（动）舍弃，遗弃

design /dɪ'zaɪn/ 1.（动）设计 2.（名）图案，设计

desire /dɪ'zaɪə/（动，名）要求；期望

dessert /dɪ'zɜ:t/（名）甜点

destroy /dɪ'strɔɪ/（动）破坏，毁坏

determination /dɪˌtɜ:mɪ'neɪʃən/（名）决心

determine /dɪ'tɜ:mɪn/（动）决定；决心

develop /dɪ'veləp/（动）（使）发展

development /dɪ'veləpmənt/（名）发展

devote /dɪ'vəʊt/（动）把…奉献给

devotion /dɪ'vəʊʃən/（名）奉献

diagram /'daɪəgræm/（名）图表，图样

dial /'daɪəl/（动）拨（电话号码）

diamond /'daɪəmənd/（名）钻石，金刚石；纸牌中的方块

dictation /dɪk'teɪʃən/（名）听写

diet /'daɪət/（名）饮食

differ /'dɪfə/（动）相异，有区别

difference /'dɪfrəns/（名）不同

different /'dɪfrənt/（形）不同的，有差异的

difficulty /'dɪfɪkəlti/（名）困难，费力

digest /daɪ'dʒest/（动）消化

digital /'dɪdʒɪtəl/（形）数字的

dim /dɪm/（名）昏暗的

dine /daɪn/（动）吃饭；（尤指正式地）进餐

dip /dɪp/（动）浸

diploma /dɪ'pləʊmə/（名）毕业文凭；学位证书

direct /daɪ'rekt/ 1.（形）直接的 2.（动）指挥

direction /daɪ'rekʃən/（名）方向

director /daɪ'rektə/（名）主任

directory /daɪ'rektərɪ/（名）姓名地址录

dirt /dɜːt/（名）污物，脏物

disability /ˌdɪsə'bɪlɪti/（名）残疾；无能

disabled /dɪ'seɪbəld/（形）残废的，残疾的

disadvantage /ˌdɪsəd'vɑːntɪdʒ/（名）不利条件；弱点

disagree /ˌdɪsə'griː/（动）意见不一致，持不同意见

disagreement /ˌdɪsə'griːmənt/（名）意见不一致；相违；争论

disappear /ˌdɪsə'pɪə/（动）消失

disappoint /ˌdɪsə'pɔɪnt/（动）使失望

disappointment /ˌdɪsə'pɔɪntmənt/（名）失望，沮丧

disaster /dɪ'zɑːstə/（名）灾难，祸患

discount /'dɪskaʊnt/（名）折扣

discourage /dɪs'kʌrɪdʒ/（动）（使）气馁；打消（做…的念头）

discovery /dɪs'kʌvərɪ/（名）发现

discrimination /dɪsˌkrɪmɪ'neɪʃən/（名）歧视

discussion /dɪs'kʌʃən/（名）讨论，辩论

disease /dɪ'ziːz/（名）病，疾病

dislike /ˌdɪs'laɪk/（动）不喜爱，厌恶

dismiss /ˌdɪs'mɪs/（动）让…离开；遣散；解散；解雇

Disneyland /'dɪznɪlænd/（名）迪斯尼乐园

disobey /ˌdɪsə'beɪ/（动）不服从

distance /'dɪstəns/（名）距离

distant /'dɪstənt/（形）远的，遥远的

district /'dɪstrɪkt/（名）区；地区；区域

disturb /dɪ'stɜːb/（动）扰乱；打扰

dive /daɪv/（动）跳水

divide /dɪ'vaɪd/（动）分，划分；除

division /dɪ'vɪʒən/（名）除（算术用语）

dizzy /'dɪzɪ/（形）头眩目晕的

document /'dɒkjəmənt/（名）文件；文献

dot /dɒt/（名）点，小点，圆点

double /'dʌbəl/ 1.（形）两倍的；双的 2.（名）两个；双

double-decker /ˌdʌbəl'dekə/（名）双层公共汽车

doubt /daʊt/（名，动）怀疑，疑惑

download /'daʊnləʊd/（名，动）下载（计算机用语）

downstairs /ˌdaʊn'steəz/（副）在楼下；到楼下

downtown /ˌdaʊntaʊn/ 1.（副）往（或在）城市的商业区（或中心区、闹市区）2.（名）城市的商业区，中心区，闹市区 3.（形）城市商业区的，中心区的，闹市区的

downward /'daʊnwəd/（副）向下

dozen /'dʌzən/（名）十二个，打

Dr. /'dɒktə/（缩)（名）医生，大夫；博士

drag /dræg/（动）拖，拽

drawer /'drɔːə/（名）抽屉

dream-talking /driːm'tɔːkɪŋ/（名）梦话

drier /draɪə/（名）烘干机；吹风机

drill /drɪl/（动）重复训练

drop /drɒp/ 1.（动）掉落 2.（名）水滴

drown /draʊn/（动）溺死；淹没

drug /drʌg/（名）药，药物；毒品

drunk /drʌŋk/（形）醉的

dryer /draɪə/（名）吹风机

due /djuː/（形）预期的，约定的

dull /dʌl/（形）阴暗的；单调无味的

dumpling /'dʌmplɪŋ/（名）饺子

dusk /dʌsk/（名）黄昏

dusty /'dʌstɪ/（形）尘土多的

DVD /ˌdiː viː 'diː/（名）数码影碟 (digital versatile disk 的缩写)

earn /ɜːn/（动）挣得，赚得

earthquake /'ɜːθkweɪk/（名）地震

ease /iːz/（动）减轻

easily /'iːzɪlɪ/（副）容易地

Easter /'iːstə/（名）复活节

eastward /'iːstwəd/（副）向东

easygoing /ˌiːzɪgʌɪŋ/（形）随和的

edge /edʒ/（名）边缘

400

edition /ɪˈdɪʃən/（名）版（本）

editor /ˈedɪtə/（名）编辑

educate /ˈedʒʊkeɪt/（动）教育，培养

educator /ˈedʒʊkeɪtə/（名）教育家

effect /ɪˈfekt/（名）效果；作用

effort /ˈefət/（名）努力，艰难的尝试

eggplant /ˈegplɑːnt/（名）（美）茄子

Egyptian /ɪˈdʒɪpʃən/ 1.（形）埃及的；埃及人的；埃及语的 2.（名）埃及人

eighth /eɪθ/（数）第八

elect /ɪˈlekt/（动）（投票）选举

electric /ɪˈlektrɪk/（形）电的

electrical /ɪˈlektrɪkəl/（形）电的；电器的

electricity /ɪlekˈtrɪsɪti/（名）电；电流

electronic /ɪlekˈtrɒnɪk/（形）电子的

else /els/（副）另外，其他

embassy /ˈembəsi/（名）大使馆

emergency /ɪˈmɜːdʒənsi/（名）紧急情况（或状态）

empire /ˈempaɪə/（名）帝国

employ /ɪmˈplɔɪ/（动）雇佣

empress /ˈemprɪs/（名）女皇，皇后

encourage /ɪnˈkʌrɪdʒ/（动）鼓励

encouragement /ɪnˈkʌrɪdʒmənt/（名）鼓励

end /end/ 1.（名）末尾；终点；结束 2.（动）结束，终止

ending /ˈendɪŋ/（名）结尾

endless /ˈendləs/（形）无止境的；没完没了的

energetic /ˌenəˈdʒetɪk/（形）精力旺盛的

energy /ˈenədʒi/（名）精力，能量

engine /ˈendʒɪn/（名）发动机，引擎

engineer /ˌendʒɪˈnɪə/（名）工程师；技师

English-speaking /ˈɪŋglɪʃ spiːkɪŋ/（形）说英语的

enjoyable /ɪnˈdʒɔɪəbəl/（形）愉快的；有趣的

enlarge /ɪnˈlɑːdʒ/（动）扩大

enquiry /ɪnˈkwaɪəri/（名）询问

enter /ˈentə/（动）进入

enterprise /ˈentəpraɪz/（名）企业

entertainment /ˌentəˈteɪnmənt/（名）娱乐

entire /ɪnˈtaɪə/（形）整个的，全部的

entrance /ˈentrəns/（名）入口

entry /ˈentri/（名）进入

envy /ˈenvi/（动，名）忌妒；羡慕

equal /ˈiːkwəl/ 1.（动）等于 2.（形）平等的

equality /ɪˈkwɒlɪti/（名）平等

equip /ɪˈkwɪp/（动）装备

equipment /ɪˈkwɪpmənt/（名）装备，设备

eraser /ɪˈreɪzə/（名）橡皮擦；黑板擦

error /ˈerə/（名）错误，差错

escape /ɪˈskeɪp/（名，动）逃跑；逃脱

especially /ɪˈspeʃəli/（副）特别，尤其

essay /ˈeseɪ/（名）散文

ethnic /ˈeθnɪk/（形）民族的

euro /ˈjʊərəʊ/（名）欧元

European /ˌjʊərəˈpiːən/ 1.（形）欧洲的；欧洲人的 2.（名）欧洲人

eve /iːv/（名）前夜，前一天

even /ˈiːvən/（副）甚至

event /ɪˈvent/（名）事件，大事

eventually /ɪˈventʃʊəli/（副）最终地

ever /ˈevə/（副）曾经

everywhere /ˈevriweə/（副）到处

exact /ɪgˈzækt/（形）精确的；确切的

exactly /ɪgˈzæktli/（副）精确地；确切地

examine /ɪgˈzæmɪn/（动）检查；诊察

excellent /ˈeksələnt/（形）极好的，优秀的

except /ɪkˈsept/（介）除…之外

exchange /ɪksˈtʃeɪndʒ/（动，名）交换

excite /ɪkˈsaɪt/（动）使兴奋，使激动

exhibition /ˌeksɪˈbɪʃən/（名）展览；展览会

exist /ɪgˈzɪst/（动）存在

existence /ɪgˈzɪstəns/（名）生存

exit /ˈegzɪt/（名）出口，太平门

expect /ɪkˈspekt/（动）盼望

expectation /ˌekspek'teɪʃən/（名）预料；期望

expedition /ˌekspɪ'dɪʃən/（名）远征（队）；探险（队）

expense /ɪk'spens/（名）消费；支出

experience /ɪk'spɪərɪəns/（名）经验；经历

experiment /ɪk'sperɪmənt/（名）实验

expert /'ekspɜːt/（名）专家，能手

explanation /ˌekspləˈneɪʃən/（名）解释，说明

explode /ɪk'spləʊd/（动）（使）爆炸

exploit /ɪk'splɔɪt/（动）开采

explorer /ɪk'splɔːrə/（名）探险者

expose /ɪk'spəʊz/（动）揭露

express /ɪk'spres/（动）表达

expression /ɪk'spreʃən/（名）表达

extinct /ɪk'stɪŋkt/（形）灭绝的

extra /'ekstrə/（形）额外的，外加的

extraordinary /ɪk'strɔːdnri/（形）使人惊奇的

extremely /ɪk'striːmli/（副）极其，非常

eyesight /'aɪsaɪt/（名）视力；视觉

eyewitness /'aɪwɪtnəs/（名）目击证人

facial /'feɪʃəl/（形）面部用的

fade /feɪd/（动）褪色

failure /'feɪljə/（名）失败

fair¹ /feə/（形）公平的，合理的

fair² /feə/（名）集市；庙会；展览会

fairly /'feəli/（副）公正地

fairness /'feənəs/（名）公平；公正

fairy /'feəri/（名）小仙子，小精灵

faith /feɪθ/（名）信仰，信念

fall /fɔːl/（名）（美）秋季

false /fɔːls/（形）不正确的，假的

familiar /fə'mɪlɪə/（形）熟悉的

fancy /'fænsi/（形）花式的；装饰的；奇特的

fantasy /'fæntəzi/（名）幻想，梦想

fare /feə/（名）票（价）

farmland /'fɑːmlænd/（名）农田

fasten /'fɑːsən/（动）扎牢；扣住

favor /'feɪvə/（名）帮助

fax /fæks/（名）传真

federal /'fedərəl/（形）联邦的

fee /fiː/（名）费，费用

feeler /'fiːlə/（名）触角

feeling /'fiːlɪŋ/（名）感情；感觉

fell /fel/（动）伐木

fellow /'feləʊ/（名）同伴，伙伴

ferry /'feri/（名）渡船

fiber /'faɪbə/（名）纤维

fifth /fɪfθ/（数）第五

fight /faɪt/（名）打仗；争论

fighter /'faɪtə/（名）战士；战斗机

file /faɪl/（名）（计算机）文档

fingernail /'fɪŋɡəneɪl/（名）指甲

finish /'fɪnɪʃ/（动）结束，做完

firefighter /'faɪəfaɪtə/（名）消防员

fireplace /'faɪəpleɪs/（名）壁炉

firewood /'faɪəwʊd/（名）木柴

fireworks /'faɪəwɜːks/（名）焰火

firm¹ /fɜːm/（名）公司，企业

firm² /fɜːm/（形）坚固的，坚定的

firmly /'fɜːmli/（副）牢牢地

fisherman /'fɪʃəmən/（名）渔民；钓鱼者

fist /fɪst/（名）拳（头）

fit /fɪt/ 1.（形）健康的，适合的 2.（动）（使）适合；安装

fitting room /fiː'tɪŋ ruːm/ 试衣间

fix /fɪks/（动）修理；安装；确定，决定

flame /fleɪm/（名）火焰；光辉

flaming /'fleɪmɪŋ/（形）火红的；火焰般的

flash /flæʃ/（名）闪光

flashlight /'flæʃlaɪt/（名）手电

flee (fled, fled) /fliː/（动）逃走；逃跑

flesh /fleʃ/（名）肉

flight¹ /flaɪt/（名）航班

flight² /flaɪt/（名）楼梯的一段

402

float /fləʊt/（动）漂浮；飘浮

flock /flɒk/（动）群集；簇拥

floppy /'flɒpi/（形）松软的

flow /fləʊ/（动）流动

flu /fluː/（名）流行性感冒

fluent /'fluːənt/（形）流利的

foggy /'fɒgi/（形）多雾的

fold /fəʊld/（动）折叠；合拢

folk /fəʊk/（形）民间的

following /'fɒləʊɪŋ/（形）接着的；以下的

fond /fɒnd/（形）喜爱的，爱好的

footstep /'fʊtstep/（名）脚步

forbid (forbade, forbidden) /fə'bɪd/（动）禁止，不许

force /fɔːs/（动）强迫，迫使

forecast /'fɔːkɑːst/（名，动）预告

forehead /'fɒrɪd/（名）前额

foresee (-saw, -seen) /fɔː'siː/（动）预见，预知

forgetful /fə'getfʊl/（形）健忘的

forgive (forgave, forgiven) /fə'gɪv/（动）原谅，宽恕

forgiveness /fə'gɪvnɪs/（名）原谅，宽恕

form /fɔːm/ 1.（名）表格 2.（动）形成

former /'fɔːmə/（形）以前的

fortnight /'fɔːtnaɪt/（名）两星期

fortunate /'fɔːtʃʊnɪt/（形）幸运的；侥幸的

fortune /'fɔːtʃuːn/（名）财富；运气

forward /'fɔːwəd/（副）将来，今后

found /faʊnd/（动）成立，建立

founding /'faʊndɪŋ/（名）成立，建立

fountain /'faʊntɪn/（名）喷泉

fourth /fɔːθ/（数）第四

franc /fræŋk/（名）法郎

freedom /'friːdəm/（名）自由

freeway /'friːweɪ/（名）高速公路

freeze (froze, frozen) /friːz/（动）结冰；突然停止；不动

freezing /'friːzɪŋ/（形）冻结的；极冷的

Frenchman (复 Frenchmen) /'frentʃmən/（名）法国人

frequent /'friːkwənt/（形）经常的，频繁的

fried /fraɪd/（形）油煎的

friendship /'frendʃɪp/（名）友谊，友情

fright /fraɪt/（名）惊恐；恐吓

frighten /'fraɪtən/（动）使惊恐，吓唬

frontier /'frʌntɪə/（名）前沿，边界；前线

frost /frɒst/（名）霜

fry /fraɪ/（动）用油煎，用油炸

fuel /'fjuːəl/（名）燃料

funeral /'fjuːnərəl/（名）葬礼

fur /fɜː/（名）毛皮，皮子

furnished /'fɜːnɪʃt/（形）配备了家具的

furniture /'fɜːnɪtʃə/（名）家具（总称）

gain /geɪn/（动）赢得；挣得

gale /geɪl/（名）强风（约每小时60英里）

gallery /'gæləri/（名）画廊

gallon /'gælən/（名）加仑

gardening /'gɑːdənɪŋ/（名）园艺学

gay /geɪ/（形）欢快的，愉快的

gaze /geɪz/（动）凝视

general /'dʒenərəl/（形）普通的

generation /ˌdʒenə'reɪʃən/（名）代，一代

gentle /'dʒentəl/（形）温柔的，轻轻的

gently /'dʒentli/（副）温柔地，轻轻地

geometry /dʒi'ɒmɪtri/（名）几何学

German /'dʒɜːmən/（名）德国人；德语

gesture /'dʒestʃə/（名）姿势；手势

get-together /'gettəgeðə/（名）聚会

gifted /'gɪftɪd/（形）有天赋的；有才华的

giraffe /dʒɪ'rɑːf/（名）长颈鹿

glance /glɑːns/（动）匆匆一看；瞥

glare /gleə/（动）怒目而视

global /'gləʊbəl/（形）全球的

glory /'glɔːri/（名）荣誉

goodness /'ɡʊdnəs/（名）善良，美德

govern /'ɡʌvən/（动）统治，管理

government /'ɡʌvənmənt/（名）政府

gown /ɡaʊn/（名）睡衣

gradually /'ɡrædʒʊəli/（副）逐渐地

graduate /'ɡrædʒʊeɪt/（动）毕业

graduation /ˌɡrædʒʊ'eɪʃən/（名）毕业；毕业典礼

gram /ɡræm/（名）克（重量单位）

grand /ɡrænd/（形）宏伟的

grandparents /'ɡrænpeərənts/（名）祖父母，外祖父母

grasp /ɡrɑːsp/（动）抓住，紧握

grateful /'ɡreɪtfʊl/（形）感激的，感谢的

Greece /ɡriːs/（名）希腊

Greek /ɡriːk/ 1.（形）希腊的；希腊人的；希腊语的 2.（名）希腊人；希腊语

greengrocer /'ɡriːnɡrəʊsə/（名）（英）蔬菜水果商

greenhouse /'ɡriːnhaʊs/（名）温室，暖房

greet /ɡriːt/（动）问候；向…致敬；迎接

greeting /'ɡriːtɪŋ/（名）祝贺

grill /ɡrɪl/（名）（烧食物的）烤架

grocer /'ɡrəʊsə/（名）零售商人；食品店

growth /ɡrəʊθ/（名）生长；增长

gruel /ɡruːəl/（名）稀粥

guidance /'ɡaɪdəns/（名）引导，指导

guilty /'ɡɪlti/（形）有罪的，犯法的；做错事的

gymnastics /dʒɪm'næstɪks/（名）体操

ha /hɑː/（叹）哈（笑声）

hacker /'hækə/（名）（计算机）黑客

haircut /'heəkʌt/（名）（男子）理发

hammer /'hæmə/（名）锤子；锣锤

handbag /'hændbæɡ/（名）女用皮包，手提包

handful /'hændfʊl/（名）（一）把；少数，少量

handkerchief /'hæŋkətʃɪf/（名）手帕

handtruck /'hændtrʌk/（名）手推运货车

happily /'hæpɪli/（副）幸福地，快乐地

happiness /'hæpɪnɪs/（名）幸福，愉快

harbor /'hɑːbə/（名）港口

hardly /'hɑːdli/（副）几乎不

hardship /'hɑːdʃɪp/（名）困难

hardware /'hɑːdweə/（名）硬件

hardworking /ˌhɑːd'wɜːkɪŋ/（形）努力工作的

harm /hɑːm/（名，动）伤害，损伤

harmful /'hɑːmfʊl/（形）有害的；致伤的

harmless /'hɑːmləs/（形）无害的；不致伤的

hatch /hætʃ/（动）（鸟、鸡）孵蛋

hay /heɪ/（名）作饲料用的干草

headline /'hedlaɪn/（名）（报刊的）大字标题

headmistress /ˌhed'mɪstrɪs/（名）女校长

headphones /'hedfəʊnz/（名）耳机

head teacher（名）中小学班主任

heap /hiːp/ 1.（名）堆 2.（动）堆起来

hearing /'hɪərɪŋ/（名）听力

heavily /'hevɪli/（副）沉重地

heel /hiːl/（名）脚后跟

helmet /'helmɪt/（名）头盔

herb /hɜːb/（名）草药

heroine /'herəʊɪn/（名）女英雄；女主角

hey /heɪ/（叹）嘿

hibernate /'haɪbəneɪt/（动）冬眠

hibernation /ˌhaɪbə'neɪʃən/（名）冬眠

hide-and-seek（名）捉迷藏

hillside /'hɪlsaɪd/（名）（小山的）山腰，山坡

hilly /'hɪli/（形）丘陵的；多小山的

hippo /'hɪpəʊ/（名）河马

hire /haɪə/（动）租用

hive /haɪv/（名）蜂房，蜂箱

holy /'həʊli/（形）神圣的

homeland /'həʊmlænd/（名）祖国

honeydew /'hʌnidju:/（名）蜜汁

honeymoon /'hʌnimu:n/（名）蜜月

Hong Kong /,hɒŋ'kɒŋ/（名）香港

honor /'ɒnə/（名）荣誉，光荣

hook /hʊk/ 1.（名）钩子 2.（动）把…钩住

hooray /hʊ'reɪ/（叹）好哇（欢呼声）

hopeful /'həʊpfʊl/（形）有希望的

hopeless /'həʊpləs/（形）没有希望的；不可救药的

hostess /'həʊstɪs/（名）女主人

housewife /'haʊswaɪf/（名）家庭主妇

housework /'haʊswɜ:k/（名）家务劳动

however /haʊ'evə/ 1.（副）可是 2.（连）然而，可是，尽管如此

howl /haʊl/（动）嚎叫，嚎哭

human being /,hju:mən 'bi:ɪŋ/（名）人，人类

hunger /'hʌŋgə/（名）饥饿

hunt /hʌnt/（动）寻找；狩猎

hurricane /'hʌrɪkən/（名）飓风

hydrogen /'haɪdrədʒən/（名）氢

iceberg /'aɪsbɜ:g/（名）冰山

Iceland /'aɪslənd/（名）冰岛

idiom /'ɪdiəm/（名）习语，成语

immediate /ɪ'mi:diət/（形）立即的，马上

immigration /,ɪmɪ'greɪʃən/（名）移民

impolite /,ɪmpə'laɪt/（形）不礼貌的

import /ɪm'pɔ:t/（动）进口，输入

importance /ɪm'pɔ:təns/（名）重要性

impress /ɪm'pres/（动）给…留下极深的印象

impression /ɪm'preʃən/（名）印象，感觉

improve /ɪm'pru:v/（动）改进，更新

inch /ɪntʃ/（名）英寸

incident /'ɪnsɪdənt/（名）事件

income /'ɪnkʌm/（名）收入，所得

incorrect /,ɪnkə'rekt/（形）不正确的，错误的

independence /,ɪndɪ'pendəns/（名）独立

independent /,ɪndɪ'pendənt/（形）独立的；有主见的

India /'ɪndɪə/（名）印度

Indian /'ɪndɪən/（名）印地安人；印度人

industry /'ɪndəstri/（名）工业，产业

influence /'ɪnflʊəns/（名，动）影响

inform /ɪn'fɔ:m/（动）告诉，通知

information /,ɪnfə'meɪʃən/（名）信息

information desk（名）问讯处

initial /ɪ'nɪʃəl/（形）开始的，最初的

injure /'ɪndʒə/（动）损害，伤害

injury /'ɪndʒəri/（名）受伤处

inland /'ɪnlænd/（形）内陆的；内地的

inn /ɪn/（名）小旅店；小饭店

insert /ɪn'sɜ:t/（动）插入

insist /ɪn'sɪst/（动）坚持，坚决认为

inspect /ɪn'spekt/（动）检查

inspire /ɪn'spaɪə/（动）鼓舞，激励

instance /'ɪnstəns/（名）例子，实例

instant /'ɪnstənt/（形）瞬间的，刹那的

institute /'ɪnstɪtju:t/（名）（研究）所，院，学院

institution /,ɪnstɪ'tju:ʃən/（名）机构，团体

instruct /ɪn'strʌkt/（动）通知；指示；教

instruction /ɪn'strʌkʃən/（名）说明，须知；教导

instrument /'ɪnstrəmənt/（名）乐器；工具，器械

insurance /ɪn'ʃʊərəns/（名）保险

insure /ɪn'ʃʊə/（动）给…上保险

intend /ɪn'tend/（动）想要，打算

international /,ɪntə'næʃənəl/（形）国际的

interpreter /ɪn'tɜ:prɪtə/（名）翻译，译员

interval /'ɪntəvəl/（名）间歇，间隔

interview /'ɪntəvju:/（名，动）采访，会见，面试

introduction /,ɪntrə'dʌkʃən/（名）引进；介绍

inventor /ɪn'ventə/（名）发明者，创造者

invitation /ˌɪnvɪ'teɪʃn/（名）邀请；请帖

Ireland /'aɪələnd/（名）爱尔兰

Irish /'aɪərɪʃ/（形）爱尔兰的；爱尔兰人的

iron /aɪən/ 1.（名）铁；熨斗 2.（动）熨烫

irrigate /'ɪrɪgeɪt/（动）灌溉

irrigation /ˌɪrɪ'geɪʃn/（名）灌溉

Italian /ɪ'tæljən/ 1.（形）意大利的；意大利人的；意大利语的 2.（名）意大利人；意大利语

Italy /'ɪtəlɪ/（名）意大利

Japanese /dʒæpə'niːz/ 1.（形）日本的；日本人的；日语的 2.（名）日本人；日语

jazz /dʒæz/（名）爵士乐，爵士舞曲

jeep /dʒiːp/（名）吉普车

jet /dʒet/（名）喷气式飞机；喷射（器）

jewelry /'dʒuːəlrɪ/（名）珠宝（总称）

jog /dʒɒg/（动）慢跑

journalist /'dʒɜːnəlɪst/（名）记者，新闻工作者

journey /'dʒɜːnɪ/（名）旅行，旅程

judgment /'dʒʌdʒmənt/（名）裁判

judo /'dʒuːdəu/（名）柔道

juicy /'dʒuːsɪ/（形）多汁的；水分多的

jungle /'dʒʌŋgəl/（名）丛林，密林

junior /'dʒuːnɪə/（形）初级的；年少的

junk /dʒʌŋk/（名）（口语）废品，破烂

junk mail（名）垃圾邮件

just /dʒʌst/（形）公正的

justice /'dʒʌstɪs/（名）正义；公正；司法

karaoke /ˌkærɪ'əuki/（名）卡拉OK

keeper /'kiːpə/（名）（动物园的）饲养员

kettle /'ketəl/（名）（烧水用的）水壶

kilogram /'kɪləgræm/（名）千克

kindhearted /ˌkaɪnd'hɑːtɪd/（形）好心的

kindness /'kaɪndnəs/（名）仁慈；善良

kingdom /'kɪŋdəm/（名）王国

kitty /'kɪti/（名）小猫

knee /niː/（名）膝盖

laboratory /lə'bɒrətri/（名）实验室

laborer /'leɪbərə/（名）体力劳动者

lack /læk/（名，动）缺乏，缺少

lame /leɪm/（形）跛的

lap /læp/（名）（跑道的）一圈

laptop /'læptɒp/（名）笔记本电脑

laser /'leɪzə/（名）激光

last /lɑːst/（动）持续

lately /'leɪtli/（副）最近，不久前

latest /'leɪtɪst/（形）最近的

latter /'lætə/（名）（两者之中的）后者

laughter /'lɑːftə/（名）笑；笑声

laundry /'lɔːndrɪ/（名）洗衣店

lavatory /'lævətri/（名）厕所

lawyer /'lɔɪə/（名）律师

layer /'leɪə/（名）层

lazybones /'leɪzibəunz/（名）懒鬼，懒骨头

lead /liːd/（名）铅

leader /'liːdə/（名）领袖，领导人

leading /'liːdɪŋ/（形）第一位的

league /liːg/（名）联盟，社团

leak /liːk/（动）漏，渗

learned /'lɜːnɪd/（形）有才华的；博学的

lecture /'lektʃə/（名）讲课，演讲

left-handed /ˌleft'hændɪd/（形）惯用左手的

leftover /'leftəuvə/ 1.（形）剩余的，剩下的 2.（名）剩饭菜

left wing /ˌleft'wɪŋ/（形）左翼的

leisure /'leʒə/（名）空闲

lemonade /ˌlemə'neɪd/（名）柠檬水

level /'levəl/（名）水平线；水平

liberate /'lɪbəreɪt/（动）解放，使获自由

liberation /ˌlɪbə'reɪʃn/（名）解放

librarian /laɪ'breərɪən/（名）图书管理员

license /'laɪsəns/（名）执照，许可证

lid /lɪd/（名）盖子

lifetime /'laɪftaɪm/（名）一生，终生

likely /'laɪkli/（形）很可能的

limit /'lɪmɪt/（动）限制；减少

link /lɪŋk/（动）连接；联系

literary /'lɪtərəri/（形）文学的

literature /'lɪtrətʃə/（名）文学

liter /'liːtə/（名）升，公升（容积单位）

litter /'lɪtə/（动）乱丢（杂物）

live /laɪv/（形）活的，活着的；实况的，现场（直播）的

living /'lɪvɪŋ/ 1.（形）活着的 2.（名）生计

load /ləʊd/（名）担子，货物

loaf /ləʊf/（名）一个面包

local /'ləʊkəl/（形）当地的；地方的

locust /'ləʊkəst/（名）蝗虫

log on /'lɒɡ ɒn/ 登陆（计算机系统）

loss /lɒs/（名）丧失；损耗

Lost & Found（名）失物招领处

lot /lɒt/（名）许多，好些

loudly /'laʊdli/（副）大声地

loudspeaker /laʊd'spiːkə/（名）扬声器，喇叭

lounge /laʊndʒ/（名）休息厅；休息室

lovable /'lʌvəbəl/（形）可爱的

lower /'ləʊə/（动）降低

luggage /'lʌɡɪdʒ/（名）行李（总称）

lung /lʌŋ/（名）肺，肺脏

lute /luːt/（名）鲁特琴

m（缩）= male /meɪl/（名）雄性的，男性的

Macao /mə'kaʊ/（名）澳门

magic /'mædʒɪk/（形）有魔力的

magician /mə'dʒɪʃən/（名）魔术师

maid /meɪd/（名）女仆，侍女

mailbox /'meɪlbɒks/（名）邮筒，邮箱

mainland /'meɪnlænd/（名）大陆

major /'meɪdʒə/（形）较大的；主要的

majority /mə'dʒɒrɪti/（名）大多数

make /meɪk/（名）样式；制造

mammal /'mæməl/（名）哺乳动物

manage /'mænɪdʒ/（动）管理；设法对付

man-made /ˌmæn'meɪd/（形）人造的，人工的

manner /'mænə/（名）方式；态度；举止

    table manners（名）餐桌礼节，用餐的规矩

maple /'meɪpəl/（名）枫树

maple leaves（名）枫叶

marathon /'mærəθən/（名）马拉松

marble /'mɑːbəl/（名）大理石；玻璃弹子

march /mɑːtʃ/（名）游行，行进

marketplace /'mɑːkɪtpleɪs/（名）市场，集市

marriage /'mærɪdʒ/（名）结婚，婚姻

married /'mærid/（形）已婚的

mask /mɑːsk/（名）面罩，面具

mass /mæs/（名）群众

master /'mɑːstə/ 1.（动）精通，掌握 2.（名）大师

mat /mæt/（名）垫子

match /mætʃ/（动）使相配，使成对

material /mə'tɪərɪəl/（名）材料，原料

math /mæθ/（美口语）数学

maximum /'mæksɪməm/ 1.（形）最大量的；最大限度的 2.（名）最大量；最大限度

maze /meɪz/（名）迷宫

means /miːnz/（名）方法

meanwhile /'miːnwaɪl/（副）同时

measure /'meʒə/（动）测量

medal /'medəl/（名）奖牌

    gold medal 金牌

medical /'medɪkəl/（形）医学的，医疗的

medium /'miːdiəm/（名）媒体

melt /melt/（动）融化

memorial /mɪ'mɔːrɪəl/（名）纪念馆

memory /'meməri/（名）回忆，记忆

mental /'mentəl/（形）精神的，脑力的

mentally /'mentəli/（副）精神上，智力上

mention /'menʃən/ 1.（名）提及 2.（动）提到

merchant /'mɜːtʃənt/ 1.（形）商业的；商人的 2.（名）商人，生意人

merciful /'mɜːsiful/（形）仁慈的，宽大的

mercy /'mɜːsi/（名）怜悯

merely /'miəli/（副）仅仅，只不过

merry /'meri/（形）高兴的，愉快的

messy /'mesi/（形）乱七八糟的

meteor /'miːtiə/（名）流星

method /'meθəd/（名）方法，办法

mew /mjuː/（名）咪，喵

Mexican /'meksikən/（形）墨西哥的

Mexico /'meksikəu/（名）墨西哥

microcomputer /ˌmaikrəukəm'pjuːtə/（名）微机

microphone /'maikrəfəun/（名）麦克风

microscope /'maikrəskəup/（名）显微镜

microwave /'maikrəuweiv/（名）微波

mid-autumn /ˌmid'ɔːtəm/（名）中秋

midday /ˌmid'dei/（名）中午，正午

Middle East（名）中东

midnight /'midnait/（名）午夜

midterm /'midˌtəm/（名）期中

might /mait/（情态动）（may的过去式）可能，也许，或许

mike /maik/（名）麦克风

mild /maild/（形）温和的，暖和的

millionaire /ˌmiliə'neə/（名）百万富翁

mineral /'minərəl/（名）矿物质，矿物

minibus /'minibʌs/（名）小型公共汽车

minimum /'miniməm/（形）最小的

miniskirt /'miniskɜːt/（名）超短裙

minister /'ministə/（名）部长；牧师

minority /mi'nɒriti/（名）少数；少数民族

minus /'mainəs/ 1.（介）减（去）2.（形）零下，负的

miracle /'mirəkəl/（名）奇迹

missile /'misail/（名）导弹

mist /mist/（名）雾

mistaken /mi'steikən/（形）错误的

misunderstand (-stood) /ˌmisʌndə'stænd/（动）误会，不理解

mixture /'mikstʃə/（名）混合物

mm（缩）=millimeter /'miliˌmiːtə/（名）毫米

mobile /'məubail/（形）活动的，可移动的

modest /'mɒdist/（形）谦虚的

Mom /mɒm/（名）（美）妈妈

mommy /'mɒmi/（名）（美）妈妈

monument /'mɒnjumənt/（名）纪念碑

moon cake /'muːn ˌkeik/（名）月饼

moral /'mɒrəl/ 1.（名）寓意 2.（形）道德的

Moscow /'mɒskəu/（名）莫斯科

Moslem /'mɒzləm/（名）伊斯兰教徒，回教徒

mosquito /mɒ'skiːtəu/（名）蚊子

motherland /'mʌðələænd/（名）祖国

motor /'məutə/（名）发动机，马达

motorcycle /'məutəsaikəl/（名）摩托车

motto /'mɒtəu/（名）格言

mountainous /'mauntinəs/（形）多山的

mourn /mɔːn/（动）哀悼

moustache /mə'stɑːʃ/（名）小胡子

mouthful /'mauθful/（名）满口，一口
from mouth to mouth 口口相传；人传人地

movement /'muːvmənt/（名）运动

movie /'muːvi/（名）（口语）电影

multiply /'mʌltiplai/（动）乘

murder /'mɜːdə/（动）谋杀

muscle /'mʌsəl/（名）肌肉

musical /'mjuːzikəl/（形）音乐的

musician /mjuː'ziʃən/（名）音乐家，乐师

mustard /ˈmʌstəd/（名）芥末

nanny /ˈnæni/（名）保姆

napkin /ˈnæpkɪn/（名）餐巾

nationality /ˌnæʃəˈnæliti/（名）国籍

nationwide /ˌneɪʃənˈwaɪd/（副）全国范围地

native /ˈneɪtɪv/（形）本土的，本国的

natural /ˈnætʃərəl/（形）自然的；天生的

navy /ˈneɪvi/（名）海军

nearby /ˌnɪəˈbaɪ/（形）附近的

nearly /ˈnɪəli/（副）将近，几乎

neat /niːt/（形）整洁的

necessary /ˈnesɪsəri/（形）必需的，必要的

neckerchief /ˈnekətʃɪf/（名）围巾，领巾

necktie /ˈnektaɪ/（名）领带

neighborhood /ˈneɪbəhʊd/（名）四邻；邻近地区

network /ˈnetwɜːk/（名）网络，网状系统

New York /ˌnjuː ˈjɔːk/（名）纽约

New Zealand /ˌnjuː ˈziːlənd/（名）新西兰

New Zealander /ˌnjuː ˈziːləndə/（名）新西兰人

nightclub /ˈnaɪtklʌb/（名）夜总会

ninth /naɪnθ/（数）第九

No.（缩）= number /ˈnʌmbə/（名）数字，号码

noble /ˈnəʊbəl/（形）贵族的

noisily /ˈnɔɪzili/（副）喧闹地

nonsense /ˈnɒnsəns/（名）胡说，废话

nonstop /ˌnʌnˈstɒp/（副）不停地

nonviolent /ˌnʌnˈvaɪələnt/（形）非暴力的

normal /ˈnɔːməl/ 1.（名）正常状态 2.（形）正常的

northeast /ˌnɔːˈθiːst/（名）东北（部）

northern /ˈnɔːðən/（形）北方的，北部的

northward /ˈnɔːθwəd/（副）向北

northwest /ˌnɔːˈθwest/（名）西北

notebook /ˈnəʊtbʊk/（名）笔记簿；笔记本电脑

novel /ˈnɒvəl/（名）（长篇）小说

novelist /ˈnɒvəlɪst/（名）小说家

nowadays /ˈnaʊədeɪz/（副）当今，现在

nowhere /ˈnəʊweə/（副）任何地方都不，无处

nuclear /ˈnjuːkliə/（形）原子核的，原子能的

nursery /ˈnɜːsəri/（名）托儿所

nursing /ˈnɜːsɪŋ/（名）（职业性的）保育，护理

nylon /ˈnaɪlɒn/（名）尼龙

obey /əʊˈbeɪ/（动）服从

observe /əbˈzɜːv/（动）观察

obtain /ɒbˈteɪn/（动）获得，得到

obvious /ˈɒbvɪəs/（形）显然的

occupation /ˌɒkjʊˈpeɪʃən/（名）职业，工作

occur /əˈkɜː/（动）发生

Oceania /ˌəʊʃɪˈeɪnɪə/（名）大洋洲

offer /ˈɒfə/（名，动）提供

official /əˈfɪʃəl/（名）（公司、团体或政府的）官员，高级职员

offshore /ˌɒfˈʃɔː/（形）近海的

oilfield /ˈɔɪlfiːld/（名）油田

Olympic /əˈlɪmpɪk/（形）奥运会的

Olympics /əˈlɪmpɪks/（名）奥林匹克运动会

omelette /ˈɒmlət/（名）煎蛋卷，煎蛋饼

oneself /wʌnˈself/（代）自己，自身

onto /ˈɒntuː/（介）到…的上面

opener /ˈəʊpənə/（名）启子

opening /ˈəʊpənɪŋ/（名）口子

opera /ˈɒpərə/（名）歌剧

opera house（名）歌剧院

operate /ˈɒpəreɪt/（动）做手术

operator /ˈɒpəreɪtə/（名）接线员

opinion /əˈpɪnjən/（名）看法，见解

opportunity /ˌɒpəˈtjuːnɪti/（名）机会

oppose /ə'pəʊz/（动）反对，反抗

opposite /'ɒpəzɪt/ 1.（名）相反，对面 2.（形）相反的，对面的

oral /'ɔːrəl/（形）口头上的

orbit /'ɔːbɪt/（名）（天体等的）运行轨道

ordinary /'ɔːdɪnri/（形）普通的，平常的

organic /ɔː'gænɪk/（形）不使用化肥的

organize /'ɔːgənaɪz/（动）组织

organizer /'ɔːgənaɪzə/（名）组织者

organization /ˌɔːgənaɪ'zeɪʃən/（名）组织，机构

origin /'ɒrɪdʒɪn/（名）起源，由来

otherwise /'ʌðəwaɪz/（副）要不然，否则

Ottawa /'ɒtəwə/（名）渥太华

ouch /aʊtʃ/（叹）（突然受痛时的叫声）哎哟

ought /ɔːt/（情态动）应该，应当

outdoors /ˌaʊt'dɔːz/（副）在户外；在野外

outer /'aʊtə/（形）外面的

outing /'aʊtɪŋ/（名）郊游，远足

outward /'aʊtwəd/（副）向外地

oval /'əʊvəl/ 1.（名）椭圆 2.（形）椭圆形的

overcoat /'əʊvəkəʊt/（名）大衣

overhead /'əʊvəhed/（形）在头顶上的

overseas /ˌəʊvə'siːz/（形）来自海外的

owe /əʊ/（动）欠（债等）

owl /aʊl/（名）猫头鹰

ownership /'əʊnəʃɪp/（名）所有制

oxygen /'ɒksɪdʒən/（名）氧，氧气

pace /peɪs/（名）步子

Pacific /pə'sɪfɪk/（形）太平洋的

pack /pæk/（名）包，捆

package /'pækɪdʒ/（名）（尤指包装好或密封的容器）一包，一袋，一盒

packet /'pækɪt/（名）小包裹，袋

paddle /'pædəl/（名）桨状物，蹼

painful /'peɪnful/（形）疼痛的

painter /'peɪntə/（名）（油）画家

pal /pæl/（名）好友

pan /pæn/（名）平底锅

pancake /'pænkeɪk/（名）薄煎饼

pant /pænt/（名）裤子

paperwork /'peɪpəwɜːk/（名）日常文书工作

paragraph /'pærəgrɑːf/（名）（文章的）段落

parcel /'pɑːsəl/（名）包裹

Paris /'pærɪs/（名）巴黎

parking /'pɑːkɪŋ/（名）停车

parking lot（名）（美）停车场

particular /pə'tɪkjʊlə/（形）特殊的，个别的

partly /'pɑːtli/（副）部分地

partner /'pɑːtnə/（名）搭档

part-time /ˌpɑːt'taɪm/（形，副）兼职的（地）；部分时间的（地）

passage /'pæsɪdʒ/（名）（文章等的）一节，一段

passenger /'pæsɪndʒə/（名）乘客，旅客

passerby /ˌpɑːsə'baɪ/（名）过路人

passive /'pæsɪv/（形）被动的

passport /'pɑːspɔːt/（名）护照

password /'pɑːswɜːd/（名）密码

pastry /'peɪstri/（名）油酥糕点

patience /'peɪʃəns/（名）耐心

pattern /'pætən/（名）式样

pause /pɔːz/（名，动）暂停

peaceful /'piːsful/（形）和平的，安宁的

pearl /pɜːl/（名）珍珠

peasant /'pezənt/（名）农民

pedestrian /pɪ'destriən/（名）行人

penpal /'penpəl/（名）笔友

penguin /'peŋgwɪn/（名）企鹅

penny (英复 pence，美复 pennies) /'peni/（名）（英）便士；（美）美分

pension /'penʃən/（名）养老金

pepper /'pepə/（名）胡椒粉

per /pɜː/（介）每，每一

percent /pə'sent/（名）百分之…

percentage /pə'sentɪdʒ/（名）百分率

perfect /'pɜːfɪkt/（形）完美的，极好的

perform /pə'fɔːm/（动）表演

performance /pə'fɔːməns/（名）演出，
表演

performer /pə'fɔːmə/（名）表演者

perfume /'pɜːfjuːm/（名）香水

period /'pɪəriəd/（名）时期，时代

permission /pə'mɪʃən/（名）允许

permit /pə'mɪt/（动）许可，允许

personal /'pɜːsənəl/（形）个人的

personally /'pɜːsənəli/（副）就自己而言

persuade /pə'sweɪd/（动）说服，劝说

pest /pest/（名）害虫

phone booth /'fəʊn buːð/（名）公用电
话间

photograph /'fəʊtəgrɑːf/（名）照片

photographer /fə'tɒgrəfə/（名）摄影师

phrase /freɪz/（名）短语

physical /'fɪzɪkəl/（形）身体的；物理的

physician /fɪ'zɪʃən/（名）（有行医执照的）
医生

physicist /'fɪzɪsɪst/（名）物理学家

pickle /'pɪkəl/（名）腌菜，泡菜

pile /paɪl/（名）堆

pill /pɪl/（名）药丸，药片

pillow /'pɪləʊ/（名）枕头

pin /pɪn/ 1.（名）别针 2.（动）别住，
钉住

pine /paɪn/（名）松树

pint /paɪnt/（名）（液量单位）品脱

pipe /paɪp/（名）管子，输送管

pity /'pɪti/（名）同情

plain /pleɪn/（形）家常的；普通的

planet /'plænɪt/（名）行星

platform /'plætfɔːm/（名）讲台

player /'pleɪə/（名）比赛者，选手

playground /'pleɪgraʊnd/（名）操场，运
动场

playmate /'pleɪmeɪt/（名）玩伴

playroom /'pleɪruːm/（名）游戏室

pleasant /'plezənt/（形）令人愉快的，
舒适的

plug /plʌg/（名）塞子

poetry /'pəʊɪtri/（名）诗歌

point /pɔɪnt/ 1.（动）指，指向 2.（名）
点；分数

pointed /'pɔɪntɪd/（形）尖的

poison /'pɔɪzən/（名）毒药

poisonous /'pɔɪzənəs/（形）有毒的

poker /'pəʊkə/（名）扑克

pole /pəʊl/（名）（地球的）极，极地

policeman (复-men) /pə'liːsmən/（名）
警察，巡警

policewoman /pə'liːswʊmən/（复-women）
女警察

political /pə'lɪtɪkəl/（形）政治的

politician /ˌpɒlɪ'tɪʃən/（名）政治家

politics /'pɒlɪtɪks/（名）政治

pollute /pə'luːt/（动）污染

pollution /pə'luːʃən/（名）污染

porridge /'pɒrɪdʒ/（名）粥

port /pɔːt/（名）港口，码头

porter /'pɔːtə/（名）（火车站或旅馆处的）
搬运工

position /pə'zɪʃən/（名）位置

possess /pə'zes/（动）占有；拥有

possession /pə'zeʃən/（名）所有，拥有

possibility /ˌpɒsɪ'bɪlɪti/（名）可能，可
能性

possibly /'pɒsɪbli/（副）可能地，也许

postage /'pəʊstɪdʒ/（名）邮费

postbox /'pəʊstbɒks/（名）邮箱

postcode /'pəʊstkəʊd/（名）（英）邮政
编码

poster /'pəʊstə/（名）（贴在公共场所的
大型）招贴

postpone /pəʊs'pəʊn/（动）推迟，延期

pour /pɔː/（动）倾泻

411

powder /'paʊdə/（名）粉，粉末

power /paʊə/（名）力；电力；强国

powerful /'paʊəful/（形）强有力的

practical /'præktɪkəl/（形）实际的，适用的

prairie /'preəri/（名）大草原

pray /preɪ/（动）祈祷，祈求

prayer /preə/（名）祈祷

precious /'preʃəs/（形）宝贵的，珍贵的

prefer /prɪ'fɜː/（动）宁愿（选择），更喜欢

preference /'prefərəns/（名）选择，趋向

preparation /ˌprepə'reɪʃən/（名）准备

preposition /ˌprepə'zɪʃən/（名）介词

prescription /prɪ'skrɪpʃən/（名）处方

presentation /ˌprezən'teɪʃən/（名）演示

press /pres/（动）压，按

pressure /'preʃə/（名）压力

pretend /prɪ'tend/（动）假装，装作

prevent /prɪ'vent/（动）防止，预防

preview /'priːvjuː/（动）预习

primary /'praɪməri/（形）初等的，初级的

print /prɪnt/（动）印刷

printer /'prɪntə/（名）打印机

printing /'prɪntɪŋ/（名）印刷；印刷术

prison /'prɪzən/（名）监狱

prisoner /'prɪzənə/（名）囚犯

private /'praɪvɪt/（形）私人的

probable /'prɒbəbəl/（形）很可能的

probably /'prɒbəbli/（副）很可能，大概

production /prə'dʌkʃən/（名）生产；制造

profession /prə'feʃən/（名）（需要有高等教育学位的）职业（如医生或律师）

professor /prə'fesə/（名）教授

project /'prɒdʒekt/（名）工程

pronoun /'prəʊnaʊn/（名）代词

pronounce /prə'naʊns/（动）发音

pronunciation /prəˌnʌnsi'eɪʃən/（名）发音；语音

proper /'prɒpə/（形）恰当的，合适的

properly /'prɒpəli/（副）适当地

protection /prə'tekʃən/（名）保护

prove /pruːv/（动）证明

provide /prə'vaɪd/（动）提供

pub /pʌb/（名）酒吧

publicly /'pʌblɪkli/（副）公开地

publish /'pʌblɪʃ/（动）出版，发行

pulse /pʌls/（名）脉搏

pump /pʌmp/（动）用泵抽水

pumpkin /'pʌmpkɪn/（名）南瓜

punctual /'pʌŋktʃʊəl/（形）准时的

punctuate /'pʌŋktʃʊeɪt/（动）加标点

punctuation /ˌpʌŋktʃʊ'eɪʃən/（名）标点符号

punishment /'pʌnɪʃmənt/（名）惩罚

puppet /'pʌpɪt/（名）木偶

puppy /'pʌpi/（名）小狗

pure /pjʊə/（形）纯的

purpose /'pɜːpəs/（名）目的

purse /pɜːs/（名）钱包

puzzled /'pʌzəld/（形）迷惑的

pyramid /'pɪrəmɪd/（名）金字塔

quake /kweɪk/（名，动）震动

quality /'kwɒlɪti/（名）质量

quantity /'kwɒntɪti/（名）数量

queue /kjuː/（名）行列，长队

race /reɪs/（名）种族，民族

racial /'reɪʃəl/（形）种族的

radar /'reɪdɑː/（名）雷达

radiation /ˌreɪdi'eɪʃən/（名）放射；放射物

radioactive /ˌreɪdiəʊ'æktɪv/（形）放射性的

radish /'rædɪʃ/（名）萝卜

radium /'reɪdiəm/（名）镭

rag /ræg/（名）破布，抹布

rail /reɪl/（名）铁路

rainbow /'reɪnbəʊ/（名）虹，彩虹

raincoat /'reɪnkəʊt/（名）雨衣

rainfall /'reɪnfɔːl/（名）一场雨；降雨量

rainforest /'reɪnfɒrɪst/（名）雨林

raise /reɪz/（动）使升高；饲养

rank /ræŋk/（名）职衔，军衔

rapid /'ræpɪd/（形）快的，迅速的

rare /reə/（形）罕见的

rather /'rɑːðə/（副）相当，宁可

raw /rɔː/（形）生的

ray /reɪ/（名）光线

razor /'reɪzə/（名）剃须刀

reading /'riːdɪŋ/（名）阅读

reality /rɪ'ælɪti/（名）现实

realize /'riːəlaɪz/（动）认识到，实现

reasonable /'riːzənəbəl/（形）合乎情理的

rebuild /ˌriː'bɪld/（动）重建

receipt /rɪ'siːt/（名）收据

receiver /rɪ'siːvə/（名）电话听筒

recent /'riːsənt/（形）近来的，最近的

reception /rɪ'sepʃən/（名）接待

receptionist /rɪ'sepʃənɪst/（名）接待员

recite /rɪ'saɪt/（动）背诵

recognize /'rekəgnaɪz/（动）认出

recommend /ˌrekə'mend/（动）推荐

record /'rekɔːd/ 1.（名）记录；唱片 2.（动）录制

recorder /rɪ'kɔːdə/（名）录音机

recover /rɪ'kʌvə/（动）痊愈

rectangle /'rektæŋgəl/ 1.（名）长方形 2.（形）长方形的

recycle /ˌriː'saɪkəl/（动）回收；再循环

redirect /ˌriːdɪ'rekt/（动）使改变，使转移

reduce /rɪ'djuːs/（动）减少，缩减

refer /rɪ'fɜː/（动）涉及

refreshments /rɪ'freʃmənts/（名）点心，便餐

refrigerator /rɪ'frɪdʒəreɪtə/（名）冰箱

refusal /rɪ'fjuːzəl/（名）拒绝

regard /rɪ'gɑːd/（动）把…看作

regards /rɪ'gɑːdz/（名）问候，致意

register /'redʒɪstə/（动）登记，注册

regret /rɪ'gret/（名，动）遗憾

regular /'regjulə/（形）规则的

regulation /ˌregjʊ'leɪʃən/（名）规则，规章

reject /rɪ'dʒekt/（动）拒绝

relate /rɪ'leɪt/（动）有关；涉及

relation /rɪ'leɪʃən/（名）关系

relationship /rɪ'leɪʃənʃɪp/（名）关系

relative /'relətɪv/（名）亲属，亲戚

relax /rɪ'læks/（动）（使）放松

relay /'riːleɪ/（名）接力

religion /rɪ'lɪdʒən/（名）宗教

religious /rɪ'lɪdʒəs/（形）宗教的

remain /rɪ'meɪn/（动）余下，留下

remark /rɪ'mɑːk/（名）话

remind /rɪ'maɪnd/（动）提醒

remove /rɪ'muːv/（动）移动，拿走；脱掉（衣服等）

rent /rent/ 1.（名）租金 2.（动）出租

replace /rɪ'pleɪs/（动）取代

report /rɪ'pɔːt/（名，动）报道

reporter /rɪ'pɔːtə/（名）记者

represent /ˌreprɪ'zent/（动）代表

republic /rɪ'pʌblɪk/（名）共和国

request /rɪ'kwest/（名）请求

require /rɪ'kwaɪə/（动）需求，要求

requirement /rɪ'kwaɪəmənt/（名）需要

rescue /'reskjuː/（动）营救

research /rɪ'sɜːtʃ/（名）研究

reservation /ˌrezə'veɪʃən/（名）预订

reserve /rɪ'zɜːv/（名，动）储备；预订

resist /rɪ'zɪst/（动）抵抗

respect /rɪ'spekt/（动，名）尊敬，尊重

restrict /rɪ'strɪkt/（动）限制

retell /ˌriː'tel/（动）重讲，复述

retire /rɪ'taɪə/（动）退休

reuse /ˌriː'juːz/（动）重新使用；循环使用

reviewer /rɪ'vjuːə/（名）评论者，书评家

revision /rɪ'vɪʒən/（名）复习，温习

revolution /ˌrevə'luːʃən/（名）革命，变革

reward /rɪ'wɔːd/（名）奖赏

rewind /ˌriːˈwaɪnd/（动）回转（磁带等）

rewrite /ˌriːˈraɪt/（动）重写

rid /rɪd/（动）使摆脱

right-handed /ˌraɪtˈhændɪd/（形）惯用右手的

right wing /ˌraɪtˈwɪŋ/（形）右翼的

ring road /ˈrɪŋ rəʊd/（名）环形公路

ripe /raɪp/（形）成熟的，熟的

ripen /ˈraɪpən/（动）成熟

roast /rəʊst/（动）烤（肉）

rock /rɒk/（动）摇，摇晃

role /rəʊl/（名）角色

roller /ˈrəʊlə/（名）滚筒

roller coaster /ˈrəʊlə ˌkəʊstə/（名）过山车

Rome /rəʊm/（名）罗马

rot /rɒt/（动）烂，腐败

rough /rʌf/（形）粗糙的

roundabout /ˈraʊndəbaʊt/ 1.（形）绕道的 2.（名）环岛，环形交叉路口

rugby /ˈrʌgbi/（名）（英）橄榄球

ruin /ˈruːɪn/（动）（使）毁坏

runner /ˈrʌnə/（名）赛跑者；操作者；滑行装置

running /ˈrʌnɪŋ/（名）跑步

rush /rʌʃ/（动）冲，奔跑

Russian /ˈrʌʃən/ 1.（形）俄国人的，俄语的 2.（名）俄国人，俄语

sacrifice /ˈsækrɪfaɪs/（动）牺牲

sadness /ˈsædnɪs/（名）悲哀，忧伤

sailing /ˈseɪlɪŋ/（名）航海

salary /ˈsæləri/（名）薪水

salesgirl /ˈseɪlzgɜːl/（名）女售货员

salesman /ˈseɪlzmən/（名）男售货员

saleswoman /ˈseɪlzwʊmən/（名）女售货员

salute /səˈluːt/（动，名）敬礼

satellite /ˈsætəlaɪt/（名）卫星

satisfaction /ˌsætɪsˈfækʃən/（名）满意

satisfied /ˈsætɪsfaɪd/（形）满意的

saucer /ˈsɔːsə/（名）茶碟

savage /ˈsævɪdʒ/（名）野蛮人

saying /ˈseɪɪŋ/（名）谚语

scarf /skɑːf/（名）领巾，围巾

scarlet /ˈskɑːlət/（名）鲜红色

scene /siːn/（名）场景

scenery /ˈsiːnəri/（名）风景

scholar /ˈskɒlə/（名）学者

scholarship /ˈskɒləʃɪp/（名）奖学金

schoolbag /ˈskuːlbæg/（名）书包

schoolmate /ˈskuːlmeɪt/（名）同校同学

scientific /ˌsaɪənˈtɪfɪk/（形）科学的

scold /skəʊld/（动）责骂

scores /skɔːz/（名）许多，很多

Scotland /ˈskɒtlənd/（名）苏格兰

Scottish /ˈskɒtɪʃ/ 1.（形）苏格兰的；苏格兰人的 2.（名）苏格兰人

scream /skriːm/（名）尖叫

screen /skriːn/（名）幕，荧光屏

sculpture /ˈskʌlptʃə/（名）雕塑（术），雕刻（术）

seagull /ˈsiːgʌl/（名）海鸥

seal /siːl/（名）海豹

seaman /ˈsiːmən/（名）水手，海员

seashell /ˈsiːʃel/（名）海贝

seaside /ˈsiːsaɪd/（名）海滨

seaweed /ˈsiːwiːd/（名）海草，海藻

secondhand /ˌsekəndˈhænd/（名）二手货；旧货

secretary /ˈsekrətri/（名）秘书

section /ˈsekʃən/（名）部分

seek /siːk/（动）探寻

seesaw /ˈsiːsɔː/（名）跷跷板（游戏）

seize /siːz/（动）抓住（时机等）

seldom /ˈseldəm/（副）很少，不常

self /self/（名）自己

self-service /ˌselfˈsɜːvɪs/（形）自助的

semicircle /ˈsemɪsɜːkəl/（名）半圆

senior /ˈsiːnjə/（形）高年级的

separately /ˈsepərətli/（副）单独地，各自地

414

separation /ˌsepə'reɪʃən/（名）分离，隔离

serious /'sɪərɪəs/（形）严肃的；严重的

servant /'sɜ:vənt/（名）仆人，用人

serve /sɜ:v/（动）服务

service /'sɜ:vɪs/（名）服务

settle /'setəl/（动）安家，定居

settlement /'setəlmənt/（名）新拓居地

settler /'setələ/（名）移居者；开拓者

seventh /'sevənθ/（数）第七

sew (sewed, sewn 或 sewing) /səu/（动）缝制；缝补

shabby /'ʃæbi/（形）破旧的；衣衫褴褛的

shade /ʃeɪd/（名）阴凉处，树阴处

shadow /'ʃædəu/（名）影子，阴影

shallow /'ʃæləu/（形）浅的

shame /ʃeɪm/（名）羞愧

shampoo /ʃæm'pu:/（名）香波

shark /ʃɑ:k/（名）鲨鱼

sharp /ʃɑ:p/（形）锋利的，尖的

sharpen /'ʃɑ:pən/（动）（使）变锐利，削尖

sharpener /'ʃɑ:pənə/（名）削尖用的器具

shave (shaved, shaved 或 shaven) /ʃeɪv/（动）刮（脸、胡子）

shaver /'ʃeɪvə/（名）电动剃须刀

sheet /ʃi:t/（名）薄板，薄片

shelter /'ʃeltə/ 1.（名）隐蔽处 2.（动）躲藏

shepherd /'ʃepəd/（名）牧羊人

shiver /'ʃɪvə/（动）（因寒冷或害怕而）颤抖，哆嗦

shock /ʃɒk/（动）使震惊

shoelace /'ʃu:leɪs/（名）鞋带

shoot[1] /ʃu:t/（名）嫩枝，苗，芽

shoot[2] (shot, shot) /ʃu:t/（动）射击

shooting /'ʃu:tɪŋ/（名）射击

shop assistant（名）（英）售货员

shopkeeper /'ʃɒpki:pə/（名）店主；零售商人

shopping /'ʃɒpɪŋ/（名）买东西

shore /ʃɔ:/（名）滨，岸

shortcoming /'ʃɔ:tkʌmɪŋ/（名）缺点，短处

shortly /'ʃɔ:tli/（副）不久

shortwave（名）短波

shot /ʃɒt/（名）射击

shower /'ʃauə/（名）淋浴

shrimp /ʃrɪmp/（名）虾

shuttle /'ʃʌtəl/（名）（往返与两个定点之间的）班车，班机

shuttlecock /'ʃʌtəlkɒk/（名）毽子

sickness /'sɪknəs/（名）疾病

side /saɪd/（名）边，旁边，面，侧面

sidewalk /'saɪdwɔ:k/（英 pavement）（名）（美）人行道

sideway /'saɪdweɪ/（名）岔路，旁路

sideways /'saɪdweɪz/（副）斜向一边

sigh /saɪ/（动）叹息

sight /saɪt/（名）风景；视力

sightseeing /'saɪtsi:ɪŋ/（名）浏览；观光

signal /'sɪgnəl/（名）信号

signature /'sɪgnətʃə/（名）签名

silver /'sɪlvə/（名）银

similar /'sɪmɪlə/（形）相似的

simpleminded /ˌsɪmpəl'maɪndɪd/（形）头脑简单的

simply /'sɪmpli/（副）简单地

sincerely /sɪn'sɪəli/（副）真诚地

single /'sɪŋgəl/（形）单一的，单个的

sink /sɪŋk/ 1.（名）洗涤槽；污水槽 2.（动）下沉

sister-in-law /'sɪstər ɪnlɔ:/（名）嫂，弟媳

situation /ˌsɪtʃu'eɪʃən/（名）形势，情况

sixth /sɪksθ/（数）第六

sixteenth /ˌsɪks'ti:nθ/（数）第十六

skateboard /'skeɪtbɔ:d/（名）冰鞋；滑板

skill /skɪl/（名）技能，技巧

skilled /skɪld/（形）熟练的

415

skillful /'skɪlful/（形）熟练的，精湛的

skillfully /'skɪfuli/（副）精湛地，巧妙地

skip /skɪp/（动）蹦蹦跳跳；跳绳

skyscraper /'skaɪskreɪpə/（名）摩天大楼

slave /sleɪv/（名）奴隶

slavery /'sleɪvəri/（名）奴隶制度

sleeve /sliːv/（名）袖子

slice /slaɪs/（名）片

slide /slaɪd/（名）幻灯片

slight /slaɪt/（形）轻微的，细小的

slim /slɪm/（形）苗条的

slip /slɪp/（名）片，条

smelly /'smeli/（形）有臭味的

smog /smɒg/（名）烟雾

smoke-free /sməuk'friː/（形）无烟的

smoker /'sməukə/（名）吸烟者

smoking /'sməukɪŋ/（名）吸烟

smokeless /'sməukləs/（形）无烟的

smooth /smuːð/（形）光滑的

snatch /snætʃ/（动）夺

sneaker /'sniːkə/（名）（美）轻便运动鞋

sneeze /sniːz/（动）打喷嚏

snowball /'snəubɔːl/（名）雪球

snowflake /'snəufleɪk/（名）雪花

snowman /'snəumæn/（名）雪人

snowy /'snəui/（形）雪（白）的；下雪的

sob /sɒb/（名，动）抽泣，啜泣

social /'səuʃəl/（形）社会的；社交的

socialism /'səuʃəlɪzəm/（名）社会主义

socialist /'səuʃəlɪst/（形）社会主义的

society /sə'saɪɪti/（名）社会

soda /'səudə/（名）汽水

soft drink /sɒft drɪŋk/（名）（不含酒精的）软饮料

softball /'sɒftbɔːl/（名）垒球

soil /sɔɪl/（名）土壤

sorrow /'sɒrəu/（名）悲伤，悲痛

so-so /ˌsəu'səu/（形）一般的；不怎么样的

soul /səul/（名）灵魂

southern /'sʌðən/（形）南部的，南方的

southerner /'sʌðənə/（名）南方人

south pole /ˌsauθ 'pəul/（名）南极

southwest /ˌsauθ'west/（名）西南

souvenir /ˌsuːvə'nɪə/（名）（旅游）纪念品，纪念物

sow (sowed, sown或-ed) /səu/（动）播种

spaceship /'speɪsʃɪp/（名）宇宙飞船

spade /speɪd/（名）铲子

spaghetti /spə'geti/（名）意大利式面条

Spain /speɪn/（名）西班牙

Spanish /'spænɪʃ/ 1.（形）西班牙的；西班牙人的；西班牙语的 2.（名）西班牙语

sparrow /'spærəu/（名）麻雀

speaker /'spiːkə/（名）演讲人，演说家

spear /spɪə/（名）矛，梭镖

specialist /'speʃəlɪst/（名）（医学）专家，专业人员

spin /spɪn/（动，名）纺；旋转

spinach /'spɪnɪdʒ/（名）菠菜

spirit /'spɪrɪt/（名）精神

spirits /'spɪrɪts/（名）烈性酒

spiritual /'spɪrɪtʃuəl/（形）精神的；心灵的

spit /spɪt/（动）吐唾沫；吐痰

splendid /'splendɪd/（形）辉煌的；（口语）极好的

split /splɪt/（动）撕开；切开

spoil /spɔɪl/（动）破坏

spoken /'spəukən/（形）口语的

spoonful /'spuːnful/（名）一匙（的量）

sportsman /'spɔːtsmən/（名）运动员

sportswoman /'spɔːtswumən/（名）女运动员

spot /spɒt/（名）斑点，污点

spray /spreɪ/ 1.（动）喷，向…喷射 2.（名）喷雾

spread /spred/（动）延伸；展开

spring /sprɪŋ/（名）泉水；泉

spy /spaɪ/（名）间谍

squeeze /skwi:z/（动）挤

squid /skwɪd/（名）鱿鱼

stadium /'steɪdiəm/（名）(露天)体育场

stage /steɪdʒ/（名）舞台；阶段

standard /'stændəd/ 1.（名）标准 2.（形）标准的

stare /steə/（动）盯，凝视

starvation /stɑ:'veɪʃən/（名）饥饿；饿死

starve /stɑ:v/（动）饿死

steady /'stedi/（形）稳固的；平稳的

steam /sti:m/ 1.（名）水蒸气 2.（动）蒸

steel /sti:l/（名）钢，钢铁

steep /sti:p/（形）险峻的；陡峭的

step /step/ 1.（名）脚步；台阶 2.（动）踩

stepmother /'stepmʌðə/（名）继母

steward /'stjuːəd/（名）(火车、飞机、轮船等的)男服务员，男乘务员

stewardess /ˌstjuːə'des/（名）女乘务员，空中小姐

stick /stɪk/（名）木棒，木棍

stocking /'stɒkɪŋ/（名）长统袜

stomachache /'stʌmək eɪk/（名）胃疼

stool /stu:l/（名）凳子

stopwatch /'stɒpwɒtʃ/（名）秒表，跑表

storage /'stɔːrɪdʒ/（名）贮藏；储存

story /'stɔːri/（名）楼层

stove /stəuv/（名）(供烹饪用的)火炉

strait /streɪt/（名）海峡

strength /streŋθ/（名）力量，力气

strengthen /'streŋθən/（动）加强，增强

stress /stres/（动）强调

strike[1] /straɪk/（动）罢工

strike[2] (struck, struck 或 stricken) /straɪk/（动）打火；侵袭

string /strɪŋ/（名）细绳，线

struggle /'strʌgəl/（动）斗争

stuck /stʌk/（形）卡住的

studio /'stjuːdiəu/（名）工作室；演播室

stuff /stʌf/（动）填馅于

subject /'sʌbdʒɪkt/（形）隶属的；受支配的

subtraction /səb'trækʃən/（名）(算数中的)减

suburb /'sʌbɜ:b/（名）(城镇的)郊区

successful /sək'sesful/（形）成功的，有成就的

suck /sʌk/（动）吸吮

sudden /'sʌdən/（形）突然的

suffer /'sʌfə/（动）受苦，遭受

suffering /'sʌfərɪŋ/（名）痛苦，苦难

suggest /sə'dʒest/（动）建议，提议

suggestion /sə'dʒestʃən/（名）建议

suit /su:t/ 1.（动）适合 2.（名）一套(衣服)

suitable /'su:təbəl/（形）合适的，适宜的

suitcase /'su:tkeɪs/（名）(旅行用)小提箱，衣箱

suite /swi:t/（名）套间

summary /'sʌməri/（名）摘要，概要

sunburned /'sʌnbɜ:nd/（形）晒黑的

sunglasses /'sʌnglɑ:sɪz/（名）太阳眼镜，墨镜

sunlight /'sʌnlaɪt/（名）日光，阳光

sunrise /'sʌnraɪz/（名）黎明，拂晓

sunset /'sʌnset/（名）日落(时分)

sunshine /'sʌnʃaɪn/（名）阳光

superhighway /ˌsu:pə'haɪweɪ/（名）高速公路

superman /'su:pəmæn/（名）超人

superpower /'su:pəpauə/（名）超级大国

superstar /'su:pəstɑ:/（名）超级明星

supply /sə'plaɪ/（动，名）供给，供应

support /sə'pɔ:t/（动，名）支持，赞助

suppose /sə'pəuz/（动）猜想，假定

surface /'sɜ:fɪs/（名）表面

surgeon /'sɜ:dʒən/（名）外科医生

surround /sə'raund/（动）围绕

surrounding /sə'raʊndɪŋ/（形）周围的

suspect /'sʌspekt/（名）犯罪嫌疑人

swallow /'swɒləʊ/（动）吞下，咽下

sweat /swet/（名）汗，汗水

swift /swɪft/（形）快的，迅速的

swimming /'swɪmɪŋ/（名）游泳

swimming pool（名）游泳池

swirl /swɜːl/（动）旋动，打旋

Swiss /swɪs/ 1.（形）瑞士的；瑞士人的 2.（名）瑞士人

Switzerland /'swɪtsələnd/（名）瑞士

sword /sɔːd/（名）剑

symbol /'sɪmbəl/（名）符号；象征

system /'sɪstəm/（名）体系；系统

tablet /'tæblət/（名）药片

tailor /'teɪlə/（名）裁缝

tank /tæŋk/（名）坦克

tanker /'tæŋkə/（名）油船

tap /tæp/（名）（自来水、煤气等的）龙头

task /tɑːsk/（名）任务，工作

taste /teɪst/ 1.（动）品尝 2.（名）味觉

tasteless /'teɪstləs/（形）无味的

tasty /'teɪsti/（形）味道好的

tax /tæks/（名）税，税款

tax free /tæks'friː/（形）免税的

teamwork /'tiːmwɜːk/（名）合作，协同工作

teapot /'tiːpɒt/（名）茶壶

technical /'teknɪkəl/（形）技术的

technique /tek'niːk/（名）技术

teen /tiːn/（名）（13—19岁的）青少年

teenage /'tiːneɪdʒ/（形）十几岁的，少年的

teenager /'tiːneɪdʒə/（名）（13—19岁的）青少年，十几岁的少年

telegram /'telɪgræm/（名）电报

telegraph /'telɪgrɑːf/（动）拍（电报）

temper /'tempə/（名）脾气

temperature /'temprətʃə/（名）温度

temple /'tempəl/（名）庙宇，寺院

temptation /temp'teɪʃən/（名）引诱，诱惑

tense /tens/（形）心烦意乱的，紧张的

terminal /'tɜːmɪnəl/（形）（火车、汽车、飞机的）终点站

terrific /tə'rɪfɪk/（形）极好的

terrify /'terɪfaɪ/（动）使感到恐怖

textbook /'tekstbʊk/（名）课本，教科书

thankful /'θæŋkfʊl/（形）感谢的，感激的

theft /θeft/（名）盗窃（案）

theme /θiːm/（名）主题

theoretical /ˌθiːə'retɪkəl/（形）理论的

theory /'θɪəri/（名）理论

therefore /'ðeəfɔː/（副）因此，所以

thermos /'θɜːmɒs/（名）热水瓶

thinking /'θɪŋkɪŋ/（名）见解；想法

thirst /θɜːst/（名）渴；口渴

thirteen /ˌθɜː'tiːn/（数）十三

thorough /'θʌrə/（形）彻底的

though /ðəʊ/（连）虽然，可是

thought /θɔːt/（名）思想，念头

thoughtful /'θɔːtfʊl/（形）体贴的，周到的

throat /θrəʊt/（名）喉咙

throughout /θruː'aʊt/（介）遍及

thunderstorm /'θʌndəstɔːm/（名）雷电交加的暴风雨

thus /ðʌs/（副）这样；因而

Tibet /tɪ'bet/（名）西藏

Tibetan /tɪ'betən/（名）西藏人；西藏语

tick /tɪk/ 1.（动）给…标记号 2.（名）对号

tight /taɪt/（形）紧的

till /tɪl/（连）直到…为止

timetable /'taɪmteɪbəl/（名）（火车、公共汽车等的）时间表；（学校的）课表

tin /tɪn/（名）（英）罐头

tiny /'taɪni/（形）极小的，微小的

tip /tɪp/（名）提示

tire /taɪə/（动）使疲劳

418

tiresome /'taɪəsəm/（形）令人厌倦的

title /'taɪtəl/（名）标题，题目

toad /təʊd/（名）蟾蜍，蛤蟆

toast /təʊst/（名）烤面包（片），吐司

tobacco /tə'bækəʊ/（名）烟草，烟叶

tofu /'təʊfuː/（名）豆腐

Tokyo /'təʊkjəʊ/（名）东京

tomb /tuːm/（名）坟墓

ton /tʌn/（名）（重量单位）吨

toothbrush /'tuːθbrʌʃ/（名）牙刷

toothpaste /'tuːθpeɪst/（名）牙膏

torn /tɔːn/（形）破了的

totally /'təʊtəli/（副）完全地

tough /tʌf/（形）坚硬的；结实的

tour /tʊə/（名）旅行

tourism /'tʊərɪzəm/（名） 观光

tourist /'tʊərɪst/（名）旅行者，观光者

track /træk/（名）轨道；田径

tractor /'træktə/（名）拖拉机

trade /treɪd/ 1.（名）贸易 2.（动）用…进行交换

traditional /trə'dɪʃənəl/（形）传统的

trainer /'treɪnə/（名）训练人，教练；运动鞋

training /'treɪnɪŋ/（名）培训

tram /træm/（名）有轨电车

translate /trænz'leɪt/（动）翻译

translation /trænz'leɪʃən/（名）翻译

translator /'trænz'leɪtə/（名）翻译家，译者

transport 1. /træns'pɔːt/（动）运输

2. /'trænspɔːt/（名）运输

trap /træp/（名）陷阱

traveler /'trævələ/（名）旅行者

treat /triːt/（动）对待，看待

treatment /'triːtmənt/（名）治疗

tremble /'trembəl/（动）颤抖

trial /'traɪəl/（名）审判

trolley /'trɒli/（名）无轨电车

troop /truːp/（动）成群结队地走

troops /truːps/（名）部队

troublesome /'trʌbəlsəm/（形）令人烦恼的；讨厌的

truant /'truːənt/（名）逃学者，旷课生

truly /'truːli/（副）真正地，真实地

trunk /trʌŋk/（名）树干；象鼻

tunnel /'tʌnəl/（名）隧道

turning /'tɜːnɪŋ/（名）拐弯处，拐角处

turtle /'tɜːtəl/（名）海龟

twelfth /twelfθ/（数）第十二

twentieth /'twentiəθ/（数）第二十

twenty-first /,twenti'fɜːst/（数）第二十一

twenty-one /,twenti'wʌn/（数）二十一

type /taɪp/（动）打字

typewriter /'taɪpraɪtə/（名）打字机

typhoon /taɪ'fuːn/（名）台风

typical /'tɪpɪkəl/（形）典型的

typist /'taɪpɪst/（名）打字员

U.K. /UK（缩）/ˌjuː 'keɪ/=United Kingdom（名）英国，联合王国

um /ʌm/（叹）嗯

U.N. /UN（缩）/ˌjuː 'en/= the United Nations（名）联合国

unable /ʌn'eɪbəl/（形）不能的，不能胜任的

uncertain /ʌn'sɜːtən/（形）不确定的

uncomfortable /ʌn'kʌmftəbəl/（形）不舒服的

understanding /ˌʌndə'stændɪŋ/（名）领会；理解

underwear /'ʌndəweə/（名）内衣

undivided /ˌʌndɪ'vaɪdɪd/（形）没分开的

undo /ʌn'duː/（动）解开，松开

uneasy /ʌn'iːzi/（形）不安的，不自在的

unemployment /ˌʌnɪm'plɔɪmənt/（名）失业

unfair /ʌn'feə/（形）不公平的，不公正的

unfit /ʌn'fɪt/（形）不合宜的，不相宜的

unfold /ʌn'fəʊld/（动）展开，打开

unfortunate /ʌn'fɔːtʃʊnət/（形）不幸的

unfortunately /ʌn'fɔːtʃunətli/（副）不幸地

unhappy /ʌn'hæpi/（形）不高兴的，伤心的

unhealthy /ʌn'helθi/（形）不健康的

unimportant /ˌʌnɪm'pɔːtənt/（形）不重要的，无意义的

union /'juːnjən/（名）联合，联盟；工会

unit /'juːnɪt/（名）单元，单位

unite /juː'naɪt/（动）联合，团结

united /juː'naɪtɪd/（形）联合的

universe /'juːnɪvɜːs/（名）宇宙

unknown /ˌʌn'nəun/（形）不知道的

unless /ʌn'les/（连）如果不，除非

unlike /ˌʌn'laɪk/（介）不像，和…不同

unmarried /ˌʌn'mærid/（形）未婚的，独身的

unpleasant /ʌn'plezənt/（形）使人不愉快的

unrest /ˌʌn'rest/（名）不安，骚动

unsafe /ˌʌn'seɪf/（形）不安全的；危险的

unsuccessful /ˌʌnsək'sesful/（形）不成功的，失败的

untrue /ˌʌn'truː/（形）不真实的，假的

unusual /ʌn'juːʒuəl/（形）不平常的，异常的

upon /ə'pɒn/（介）在…上面

upper /'ʌpə/（形）较高的，较上的

upset /ʌp'set/（形）心烦的，苦恼的

upstairs /ʌp'steəz/（副）在楼上，到楼上

upward /'ʌpwəd/（副）向上，往上

U.S.A. /ˌjuːnaɪtɪd 'steɪts/ 美国

used /juːzd/（形）用过的；旧的

useless /'juːsləs/（形）无用的

user /'juːzə/（名）使用者，用户

vacation /və'keɪʃən/（名）假期

vain /veɪn/（名）自负的，徒劳的

valley /'væli/（名）山谷

valuable /'væljuəbəl/（形）值钱的，贵重的

value /'væljuː/ 1.（名）价值，益处 2.（动）爱惜

vanilla /və'nɪlə/（名）香草

variety /və'raɪɪti/（名）种种，种类

various /'veəriəs/（形）各种各样的，不同的

vase /vɑːz/（名）（花）瓶

vast /vɑːst/（形）巨大的，广阔的

VCD /ˌviː siː 'diː/（名）影碟光盘

veal /viːl/（名）（食用）小牛肉

vest /vest/（名）背心

victory /'vɪktəri/（名）胜利

videophone /'vɪdiəufəun/（名）可视电话

viewer /'vjuːə/（名）观看者

villager /'vɪlɪdʒə/（名）村民

vinegar /'vɪnɪgə/（名）醋

violence /'vaɪələns/（名）暴力行为

violent /'vaɪələnt/（形）暴力的

violinist /ˌvaɪə'lɪnɪst/（名）提琴家，提琴手

virtue /'vɜːtʃuː/（名）美德

virus /'vaɪərəs/（名）病毒

visa /'viːzə/（名）签证

vocabulary /vəu'kæbjuləri/（名）词汇（量）；词汇表

vote /vəut/（动）选举

voyage /'vɔɪɪdʒ/（名）航行，旅行

wag /wæg/（动）摇动，摆动

wage /weɪdʒ/（名）工资

wail /weɪl/（名）嚎啕大哭声

waist /weɪst/（名）腰

waitress /'weɪtrəs/（名）女服务员

Wales /weɪlz/（名）威尔士

Walkman /'wɔːkmən/（名）随身听

wallet /'wɒlɪt/（名）（放钱、证件等的）皮夹子

wander /'wɒndə/（动）漫游，流浪

ward /wɔːd/（名）病房；收容所

warmhearted /ˌwɔːm'hɑːtɪd/（形）热心的

warn /wɔːn/（动）警告

warning /'wɔːnɪŋ/（名）警报

washroom /'wɒʃruːm/（名）盥洗室

waterfall /'wɔːtəfɔːl/（名）瀑布

watermelon /'wɔːtəmelən/（名）西瓜

wayside /'weɪsaɪd/（形）路边的

weakness /'wiːknəs/（名）软弱；缺点

wealthy /'welθi/（形）富有的

weatherman /'weðəmæn/（名）气象员，预报天气的人

web /web/（名）蜘蛛网

weed /wiːd/（名）杂草，野草

weekday /'wiːkdeɪ/（名）平日，工作日

weekly /'wiːkli/（形）每周的

weep /wiːp/（动）哭泣，流泪

weigh /weɪ/（动）称…的重量，重（若干）

weight /weɪt/（名）重，重量

well-known /ˌwel'nəʊn/（形）出名的，众所周知的

westerner /'westənə/（名）西方人

westward /'westwəd/（副）向西

whatever /wɒt'evə/（连，代）无论什么，不管什么

whenever /wen'evə/（连）每当，无论何时

wherever /weər'evə/（连）无论在哪里

whichever /wɪtʃ'evə/（代）无论哪个；无论哪些

whiskey /'wɪski/（名）威士忌

whisper /'wɪspə/（动）低语

whistle /'wɪsəl/（名）口哨，口哨声

widespread /'waɪdspred/（形）分布广的；普遍的

wildlife /'waɪldlaɪf/（名）野生生物

will /wɪl/（名）意志；遗嘱

willing /'wɪlɪŋ/（形）乐意的

willingly /'wɪlɪŋli/（副）乐意地

willingness /'wɪlɪŋnəs/（名）意愿

wind (wound, wound) /waɪnd/（动）蜿蜒

windbreaker /'wɪndbreɪkə/（名）风衣，防风（皮）夹克

winner /'wɪnə/（名）获胜者

wipe /waɪp/（动）擦

wire /waɪə/（名）电线

wisdom /'wɪzdəm/（名）智慧

within /wɪ'ðɪn/（介）在…里面

without /wɪ'ðaʊt/（介）没有

wonton /ˌwɒn'tɒn/（名）馄饨

wooden /'wʊdən/（形）木制的

wool /wʊl/（名）羊毛，羊绒

woollen /'wʊlən/（形）羊毛的，羊毛制的

workday /'wɜːkdeɪ/（名）工作日

workforce /'wɜːkfɔːs/（名）劳动力

workmate /'wɜːkmeɪt/（名）同事；工友

workplace /'wɜːkpleɪs/（名）工作场所，车间

works /wɜːks/（名）著作，作品

world famous /ˌwɜːld'feɪməs/（形）世界闻名的

worldwide /ˌwɜːld'waɪd/（形）遍及全球的，世界范围的

worse /wɜːs/（形）（bad的比较级）更坏的

worst /wɜːst/（形）（bad的最高级）最坏的

worthless /'wɜːθləs/（形）没有价值的，没有用的

worthwhile /ˌwɜːθ'waɪl/（形）值得做的

wound /wuːnd/ 1.（动）使受伤 2.（名）伤口

wounded /'wuːndɪd/（形）受伤的

writing /'raɪtɪŋ/（名）书写，写

yolk /jəʊk/（名）蛋黄

yours /jɔːz/（代）你的；你们的（名词性物主代词）

youth / juːθ/（名）青春；青年

youthful /ˈjuːθfʊl/（形）青年人特有的，朝气蓬勃的

youthfulness /ˈjuːθfʊlnɪs/（名）朝气蓬勃

zebra crossing （名）人行横道线，斑马线

zip /zɪp/（名）拉链

zip code （英 postcode）（名）（美）邮政编码

zipper /ˈzɪpə/（名）拉链

zone /zəʊn/（名）区域

注：补充词汇表中的词性标注 "（名）、（动）、（形）、（情态动）、（副）、（介）、（连）、（数）、（叹）" 分别表示 "（名词）、（动词）、（形容词）、（情态动词）、（副词）、（介词）、（连词）、（数词）、（叹词）"。

422

FIND OUT ABOUT CHINA
Zheng Qing

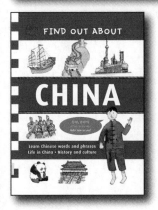

Barron's *Find Out About* China takes young readers on a delightful tour through this fascinating country with vivid descriptions of the land, its history, and its people. A simplified but geographically accurate map of China opens up on a gatefold page flap, showing major cities and geographical features. Accompanying the map are facts about the country's area, population, important rivers, and its location on the globe. The book's four separate sections have different color page tabs to mark the divisions. The four sections are as follows:

Part One: Introduction—Takes readers on a journey across China, pointing out major cities, places of special interest, and favorite sports and pastimes.

Part Two: Everyday Life—Kids attend school and enjoy after-school activities, while the grown-ups pursue their professions, occupations, and trades.

Part Three: History and Culture—Readers learn about China's political leaders and cultural figures, and visit distinctive landmarks and monuments.

Part Four: The Language—Readers learn fundamentals of Mandarin Chinese including phrases for meeting people, finding their way around cities and towns, counting, telling time, and more.

China is described from a child's point of view, and pages are filled with child-friendly color illustrations. This book is as entertaining as it is informative, and makes a fine supplement to textbooks in elementary social studies classes. (Ages 8 and older)

Hardcover with hidden spiral binding, 64 pp., ISBN 978-0-7641-5952-7

More Find
Out About
*titles available
from Barron's*

ISBN 978-0-7641-5953-4

ISBN 978-0-7641-5954-1

ISBN 978-0-7641-6169-8

ISBN 978-0-7641-5955-8

ISBN 978-0-7641-6168-1

Please visit
www.barronseduc.com
to view current prices and
to order books.

Barron's Educational Series, Inc.
250 Wireless Boulevard
Hauppauge, New York 11788
In Canada:
Georgetown Book Warehouse
34 Armstrong Avenue
Georgetown, Ontario L7G 4R9

(#175) R1/09